Sails of the Maritimes

D1028536

This book tells the story of the large cargo schooners which were built in Atlantic Canada during the eighty-odd years of their existence. These vessels were built until the early 1920s and the last of them disappeared just after World War 2. They were a familiar sight in the ports of the North and South Atlantic until ending their days as marine casualties in the open sea or slowly disintegrating on a deserted shore. They will remain in the minds of the people who knew them as graceful ships of the days that are gone.

In its hardcover edition this book quickly became one of the classics of Maritime history. This paperback edition contains the complete text and pictures of the hardcover edition.

JOHN P. PARKER has been interested in sailing vessels for the greater part of his life. As a young man, he owned and operated one of the tern schooners described in this book. The author spent many years afloat in cargo and passenger ships before coming ashore to be Superintendent of Pilots for Sydney Harbour and the Bras D'Or Lakes in Nova Scotia. Captain Parker now resides in North Sydney, Nova Scotia, devoting his spare time to his favourite hobbies—writing and sailing.

CUTTY SARK, *609 tons*
built 1919, Saint John, N.B.
courtesy of the
Mariners Museum

see page 159

Sails
of the
Maritimes

John P. Parker, M.B.E.,
Master Mariner

*The story of the three-and four-masted
cargo schooners of Atlantic Canada,
1859-1929*

de Vuun HiRbG
Eagle Head U5

McGraw-Hill Ryerson Limited
Toronto   Montreal   New York   London   Sydney   Auckland
Johannesburg   Mexico   Panama   Düsseldorf   Singapore
São Paulo   Kuala Lumpur   New Delhi

DEDICATED TO MY WIFE **MARY**

Sails of the Maritimes
© Copyright John P. Parker, 1960
First paperback edition published 1976

ISBN 0-07-082424-x

1 2 3 4 5 6 7 8 9 10 D5 4 3 2 1 0 9 8 7 6

Printed and bound in Canada

ACKNOWLEDGMENTS

The material used in this book has come from many sources. The list of schooners was compiled from the Registers of Lloyds, the American Bureau of Shipping, the Registry of Nova Scotia Shipping, the Record of the Shipping of Yarmouth, N.S., The New-foundland Shipping Registry and the Dominion Archives at Ottawa. The New Brunswick Museum, the Fort Anne Museum and the Mariners Museum at Newport News, Virginia, supplied much information.

It was the late Frederick William Wallace who proposed that I undertake this project and he provided me with a wealth of material from his marine library. His knowledge as an editor and his untiring interest have been of invaluable assistance.

While it is impossible for me to give due credit by naming all of the many ship-masters, schooner seamen, shipbuilders, vessel owners, etc., whom I have interviewed personally, or who have forwarded information by correspondence, for the list would be a lengthy one, I wish to thank especially the following for their assistance and kindness: Captain V. O. Peardon, Captain Joseph Cutten, Captain Malcolm Wilkie, Captain J. J. Whalen, Captain Martin Frampton, Captain G. E. Hartling, Captain R. A. Lohnes, Miss Louise Manny, Miss Laura Hardy, Mr. J. T. Moulton, Mr. P. Kendrick, Mr. J. L. Lockhead, Dr. C. B. Fergusson, Mr. Albert Barnes, Dr. George MacBeath, Mr. W. W. Archibald, Mr. G. W. Hogg, Mr. W. D. McLean, Mr. W. W. Buffett, Mr. T. G. Tibbo, Mr. R. T. LeFeuvre, Mr. Michael Harrington, Mr. F. F. Hill, Col. H. I. Chapelle, Rear-Admiral H. F. Pullen, o.b.e., c.d., r.c.n., Commander C. H. Little, r.c.n. (Ret.), Commander P. G. Chance, c.d. r.c.n.

To the many people who furnished me with pictures of Canadian schooners, I am deeply grateful for the privilege of reproducing them in this record. They will be rewarded by the fact that these pictures will be viewed by a more numerous audience.

JOHN P. PARKER

FOREWORD

On many occasions the well-known marine historian, the late Frederick William Wallace, and I discussed the large cargo schooners of Atlantic Canada and lamented the fact that no one had as yet compiled the record and story of these vessels. He suggested that I undertake this task and with his great help and encouragement this volume has been completed. The Foreword was to have been written by him, but his untimely death in July, 1958, precluded this.

A popular legend attributes the invention of the schooner to a Captain Andrew Robinson of Gloucester, Massachusetts, who designed and built a two-masted vessel of strictly fore-and-aft rig in 1713. It was, we understand, a modification of a then existing type of fore-and-after known as a "ketch"—still quite popular today in the yachting field. The story goes that when Robinson's new vessel was launched, a spectator cried: "See how she schoons!" And the Captain replied: "Then a schooner let her be!" But the name would be more reasonably applied to the hull design and the manner in which it entered the water, rather than to her novel rig.

It is not my purpose to attempt a dissertation upon the origin of the schooner, for others have studied the subject intensively. But two-masted vessels, with fore-and-aft sails only, are to be seen in Dutch engravings of 1650. And while seamen of the windship days were presumed to be ultra-conservative and opposed to change, it is nevertheless a fact that practically all innovations in hull design, rigging, deck gear and sail plans have been dictated by seamen. For theirs was the task of handling and sailing ships, and through lengthy experience they have suggested ideas that have been adopted. Therefore I am inclined to believe that the usefulness of the fore-and-aft rig in a two-masted vessel, for certain trades, was recognized and employed long before Captain Robinson's time.

The subsequent development of the schooner, as distinct from the type using square-sails in combination with fore-and-aft, is peculiarly American both in the fishing and cargo-carrying fleets of the North Atlantic coasts. At the close of the eighteenth century United States schooners were numbered in the hundreds, for it was found they were eminently suited to the class of trade, the weather and geographical conditions existing from Labrador to the Caribbean.

A century or more of two-masted schooner operation in cargo trades along the North Atlantic coasts, and to the West Indies countries of the Spanish Main (in which British North America also participated), suggested to some enterprising American the construction of a three-masted schooner which could be managed by fewer men in proportion to their cargo-carrying capacity than either a two-master or square-rigged vessel. It was a move dictated by the necessity for reducing operating costs.

According to a statement in Bulletin 127 of the U.S. Marine Museum, it was said that the first three-masted schooner built in the United States was the *Magnolia* of 100 tons, built at Blue Hill, Maine, for Captain Daniel Clough, about 1850. Another authority claims that the *Zachary Taylor*, 250 tons, built in Philadelphia in 1849 was the pioneer three-master. Both these statements appear to be refuted by a quotation in the catalogue of the Peabody Museum, Salem, Mass., which ascribes to a Captain Andrew Ward the honour of having made the first entry at Zanzibar in the three-masted schooner *Spy* in 1827. That she was an actual three-master remains open to question. In a book compiled by Arthur H. Gardner, entitled *Wrecks around Nantucket, 1664-1915*, he gives an account of a mishap to the American three-masted schooner *Richmond* of Salem, in the year 1844. That also remains to be proved as to rig.

Be all that as it may, the three-mast fore-and-after became so popular with ship-owners after 1850 that something like fifteen hundred of them were built on the U.S. Atlantic coast from that date until the decline of sailing-ship construction in the 1920's. And this does not take into account the numerous four-masters (over two hundred since 1881), the less numerous five- and six-masters (with one huge seven-master) launched along the eastern U.S. coast within that period. In this account we are not dealing with the Great Lakes or Pacific Coast of the United States and Canada, in which areas many large schooners were built and employed.

In Atlantic Canada, comprising the provinces of Nova Scotia, New Brunswick, Prince Edward Island, Quebec and the later Canadian province of Newfoundland, the construction and operation of wooden sailing vessels have been an important industry, parelleling that of the United States in date of establishment and duration. In the year 1878, Canada ranked fourth among the ship-owning nations with a fleet of 7,196 vessels aggregating 1,333,000 tons. For much the same reasons that inspired the adoption of a more economical type of cargo sailing vessel, as compared with the square-rigged craft expensive to maintain and operate, the Canadians followed the lead of their American cousins and embarked on the building and running of three- and four-masted schooners for the coasting trade between Canada and the United States, the West Indies, South America and trans-Atlantic voyages to Europe and West Africa. While the American fleet of these particular types of fore-and-afters greatly exceeded that of the Canadian in number, *nevertheless we built and operated between seven and eight hundred of them*. When one considers the great disparity in population, national wealth and trade, in comparing the two countries, the figure is quite an imposing one. In this business, as in the case of our wooden square-riggers, we followed the New England fashion in schooner design and rig, more or less. For in Nova Scotia and New Brunswick, in particular, there has long existed a close affinity with the New England states.

Many American three-masters of large tonnage but shoal draft were fitted with center-boards, permitting them to navigate in shoal waters such as the Chesapeake estuary. I do not know if any Canadian-built schooners were thus equipped, other than on our Great Lakes. For the Canadian schooner was more or less a deepwater craft, plying in and out of deepwater ports and built stout enough to rest high and dry alongside the wharves in places having an abnormal tidal range such as exists in the Bay of Fundy.

Like the old square-riggers, the three- and four-masted schooners have finished and their places in the familiar trades have been usurped by the cargo liner, tramp steamer, and the smaller diesel-engined coaster. The majority of the Canadian fleet had passed out of the picture by 1939. A few survived to give useful service during the years of World War Two, but by 1945 their era was finished. This work, compiled in 1953-58, attempts to tell the story of this particular type of schooner during the eighty-odd years of their existence.

North Sydney, N.S., August, 1959   JOHN P. PARKER

CONTENTS

Part Six

Part Seven

Alphabetical List

Ballads

Index

ILLUSTRATIONS

P A R T O N E

January, 1939

A small group of dispirited men stood on the boat-deck of a large British freighter in the eastern North Atlantic as she staggered in the high swell of the moderate gale which followed the full storm of the preceding week. The men gazed at the smoke billowing from a three-masted schooner, out of which they had been rescued, as she lifted on the wavecrests half a mile away. Suddenly a large sheet of flame accompanied by black smoke shot up from the abandoned vessel and small fires ran up the halyards as the big fuel tank in her stern exploded. Then slowly she sank beneath the waves.

The men turned unhappily away. A chapter of their lives had passed and they consoled themselves in the fact they were lucky to be alive. For days they had battled against the disintegration of their schooner, and they had failed. The vessel was a Nova Scotiaman, the *St. Clair Theriault*, and she came to an end that wild afternoon off Ushant as she burned to the water's edge and disappeared into the depths. With her went my seaborne home for three years, and my aspirations to become a shipowner.

The year 1919 saw the largest number of big wooden schooners launched in Atlantic Canada. The world's shipping had been decimated by war action. Ocean freights were sky-high and the shipbuilding programs of the big nations had not been able to replace the enormous losses in steel steamship tonnage. One hundred and fourteen wooden schooners, three- and four-masters, slid down the ways in the Maritime Provinces that year. Many of them were hastily built for quick profit and did not last long. But others were put together of the best materials and workmanship by builders who took a pride in their jobs. One of these three-masted cargo schooners was the *St. Clair Theriault*.

Along what is called the "French Shore", between Yarmouth and Weymouth, Bay of Fundy coast of Nova Scotia, lived the descendants of generations of French-Canadian shipbuilders. Back from the sea were great stands of virgin timber that could be hauled out cheaply to the building yards. The Theriault family, of Acadian ancestry, were long interested in building and operating sailing vessels, both square-rigged and fore-and-aft. In 1919, at Belliveau Cove, they built and launched two staunch terns that were destined to be prominent in shipping news for the full life of a softwood vessel. They

17

were the *E. P. Theriault* and her slightly smaller sistership, the *St. Clair Theriault*. The story of the *E. P. Theriault* is told elsewhere and there is a yarn for every year of her life until she ended her career in Cuba about 1951. This part will deal with the *St. Clair*.

For the first few years of her existence she was engaged in the trades for which she had been built—fish or lumber to the West Indies or Brazil, with bulk salt or barreled molasses back to Nova Scotia; wood products to United States ports and cargoes of hard coal in return. She was built with the carriage of dry or pickled fish in mind, having what was called a "Brazilian poop". This was an additional deck above the main-deck running from just abaft the mainmast to aft. It was about four feet in height and provided additional underdeck stowage for wooden drums or casks of dried salt fish cargoes. Access was by means of a hatch in the poop-deck, which, of course, also served for the main-hold. In the forward bulkhead of this upper deck there were removable ports fitted to allow lumber to be passed in and out. The poop-deck ran right aft and was built around the cabin trunk, which started from the main-deck, so the cabin projected about three feet above the poop-deck. In practically all other respects, rigging, sails, gear, accommodations, etc., she was equipped similarly to other schooners of her era. The *St. Clair Theriault* was built of spruce, birch and oak to the highest standard of the American Bureau of Shipping and was fastened with galvanized iron.

Her registered measurements were 135.5 feet in length, measured from the aft side of the stem to the sternpost along the main deck-line, her beam was 31.6 feet and her depth 11.3 feet. The gross tonnage was 347 and the net register tons 284. She could lift about 550 tons of coal or 350 thousand board feet of lumber. Her master builder was Siffroy Deveau and she was built from a model carved for this one vessel. I have not been able to locate this model although Mrs. Margaret LeBlanc, daughter of the registered owner-builder, P. A. Theriault, assisted me in searching through a number of models stowed in a loft at their establishment at Belliveau Cove, none of which fitted the dimensions. The cost of the schooner has been given variously as 62,000 to 70,000 dollars, but it seems the former figure is the more likely. She paid only a part of this sum back to her owners and was the last tern schooner built by the Theriaults.

As mentioned before, the *Theriault* was kept busy on voyages south with occasional runs to United States ports, and did very well in her freightings. Eventually, however, in the early 1920's, the world's steel shipbuilding yards were beginning to overtake wartime losses in shipping, and with the appearance of new tonnage, high-paying freights fell off sharply and peacetime cargo rates were established. This caused hardship among the schooner owners who had new expensively built vessels on their hands and not enough remunerative work to pay back their cost. Many of these vessels were lost as the more experienced seamen went into the new postwar steamships. In Canada, a Crown Company, the Canadian Government Merchant Marine, Ltd., built and operated under Canadian registry a large fleet of some sixty-five steamships in the West Indies and offshore trades and these vessels siphoned off many, perhaps hundreds, of the able men formerly in sail. Ocean freights became depressed and it was difficult to operate the schooners and make a profit on the investment.

When new, the *Theriault* was commanded by Captain Rangdale but later under

Captain Leander Pottier she sailed for Madeira with a cargo of lumber. From there she proceeded to the West Coast of Africa to load for home. During the passage out to Africa the freight rates dropped and on her arrival a legal fight began as to the amount of her freight. After waiting for some months with the rates still dropping steadily the vessel received orders to proceed to Turks Island, Bahamas, for a salt cargo. Her bad luck hung on and she was fifty days from Turks Island when she was towed into Shelburne, N.S., battered and with her crew sick.

In the dawn of the 1920's, however, a new trade developed which brought a measure of relief to some of the schooner owners. Prohibition in the United States, and later in Canada, created a thirsty population ready to pay any amount of money for "real hard liquor". As the domestic sources dried up and import restrictions were brought into effect, a new commercial enterprise in supplying ardent spirits, the "rum runners", came into being. Two supply bases of spirits and wines of all sorts existed near the Atlantic coasts of the United States. St. Pierre et Miquelon, a French possession off the south coast of Newfoundland, and the various islands of the British and foreign West Indies were well stocked with the contraband liquor and export to "the High Seas" was legal. This carried on for several years.

At this time a new kind of ship charter was also created. It was to carry the contraband from the legal port of export to the offshore limits of United States territorial waters. From thence it was transported by swift motor launches to the shore. Many Canadian schooners were chartered to the liquor interests for carrying the cargoes and among them was the *St. Clair Theriault*. In this trade there were many risks and pitfalls and while the owners emphasized their orders upon skippers and supercargoes to keep strictly within the law and on no account to hazard their investments in the vessel, nevertheless some of the schooners ran foul of the Revenue Preventative Services of either the U.S. or Canada, and were captured when they accidentally or deliberately, invaded territorial waters. Many of the vessels were sold outright to the rum runners during prohibition and so passed out of Canadian registry. The *Theriault* came under seizure in 1927 as being illegally employed and was towed into Halifax as a prize.

She was taken to Eastern Passage near the entrance of Halifax Harbour and left at anchor with other laid-up vessels and in due course was put up for sale at public auction by the Canadian Exchequer Court. During her period in the "game", as it was called, she had been let "run down". Her bowsprit had been sprung at the time she had been towed in, and she had been unceremoniously left with her sails and gear "let go" as when they had been lowered to the deck. She was bid in at the auction by Captain V. O. Peardon, a Nova Scotian, who took her to the Marine Railway at Dartmouth, opposite Halifax, and had her completely overhauled. She was given all new standing rigging, caulked all over, fitted with new sails, scraped and brightly painted. Late in 1927 she was ready for sea and Captain Peardon took charge of her and proceeded to Shelburne, N.S., to load a cargo of lumber for Barbados. This first voyage under new ownership turned out to be a heart-breaker.

The vessel sailed the morning of Christmas Eve from Shelburne with a fair wind and a hold and deck load of lumber, and later that day the wind freshened until it reached gale-force in the evening. The sea made up until the swell was high and the *Theriault* had the misfortune to encounter a "strayed sea". This is part of an old swell from another disturbance and is sometimes met with running at a different angle to the waves caused by the wind then blowing. This great "old sea" struck the *Theriault* just aft of amidships and engulfed her forward, carrying all with it. When the water ran off, it was seen that a good part of the deck load was gone, the forecastle house was smashed in, and the reefed mainsail and forestaysail—the only sails the ship was carrying at the time—had been torn away by the impact of the sea that charged down on the schooner. The vessel began to make water immediately and it was some hours later before it was discovered that most of it was coming into her through the main-hatch where the tarpaulin had been torn away when the deck-load went overside. After many hours of work, the vessel was pumped out and made fit again, but the beating she took, and the seas she shipped, got at the food stores and it resulted in a hungry passage. When she finally got to Barbados, there was another big repair job.

On another voyage in the *Theriault*, Captain Peardon picked up a dory and two fishermen adrift from the schooner *Madeleine Hebb*, one of the Lunenburg, N.S., bankers. The *Theriault* was heading offshore from Nova Scotia at the time, bound for Madeira, and when she picked up the fishermen they had been adrift for three days and were exhausted by cold and exposure. The two men remained in the schooner for the round trip, which was to Madeira, thence to Barbados and back to Nova Scotia.

Captain Peardon made a good many voyages in the *Theriault* and then had a stake to go into steamships. He left the schooner in charge of his mate, but his interest in her dwindled and she became shabby, took longer on voyages, and was in trouble on several occasions. Her last episode of this particular era was to strike the abutment of the swingbridge at Grand Narrows in Cape Breton, Nova Scotia. Her bow was stove-in and she was kept afloat only by the frantic efforts of her crew. With temporary repairs she was able to complete her voyage in tow and was sent to Port Hawkesbury, N.S.—a small port in the Straits of Canso—to have the damage made good. At some time in the preceding year or so she had been in other trouble and her fore- and mizzen-topmasts were down.

I entered her story in the summer of 1936 as she lay at anchor at Port Hawkesbury with one of her old crew aboard as watchman. She was then in her seventeenth year of seafaring service and a lot of the water of the North Atlantic had run beneath her keel. Her bows had plowed courses across the Western Ocean and stirred up the flying-fish of the tropics. But she was still a handsome schooner, stoutly built, and she had a good hull on her. I fell in love with her right away and made up my mind to possess, operate and sail her. In spite of the fact that her physical appearance looked anything but attractive, I was enough of a sailor to know that appearance in a ship means but little. With new topmasts, new manilla running rigging rove off, sails replaced or repaired, some scrubbing, scraping, painting, and a general overhaul of blocks, shackles and otherwise sound gear which had deteriorated for want of care, the *Theriault* could be put into good shape without any great expenditure of hard cash.

I could visualize the white-hulled *Theriault* with her three topsails aloft over three lowers, her long jib-boom pointing at the far horizon, her sheets straining at the wind-filled canvas, her forefoot cleaving the seas and a white wake streaming astern, with myself as master and owner of her and exercising all my seamanly knowledge and skill to deliver a cargo for which I would acquire a modest profit on the freight thereof. It was an intriguing and delightful fancy which ended in my buying the tern schooner *St. Clair Theriault* in the summer of 1936.

My adventure in schooner ownership and sailing, and writing a history of the three- and four-masters built in Atlantic Canada, may well call for some explanation. I will be very frank about the circumstances that inspired me to go seafaring, while the subsequent events that influenced my career will possibly account for my role as a recorder of the era of the cargo-carrying fore-and-after.

I was born in Sydney, Cape Breton, Nova Scotia, the eldest of four brothers. My father was a prominent dentist in that city, and two of my brothers followed in his footsteps. Another brother graduated in accountancy. Many members of the Parker family in Nova Scotia were interested in shipbuilding and seafaring. My mother's people were among the pioneer Scots who emigrated to Nova Scotia in the early 1800's and my grandfather on her side was a surgeon and the Port Doctor for many years.

During my school days in Sydney I was what they called "a looker out of windows". In other words, I found it difficult to concentrate on my books and what the teacher was expounding, for my gaze was constantly straying to the vista of clouds blowing across a blue sky, or the rain or snow beating down in a storm. After window-gazing in school, I found surcease from the task of acquiring an education by loafing around the Sydney wharves looking over the numerous coasting schooners which used to frequent the port. As a consequence my school marks were depressingly low.

In an effort, no doubt, to correct this mental attitude toward absorbing necessary knowledge, and none too pleased with the low grades on my school reports, my father sent me to Rothesay Collegiate School, a Church of England establishment for boys near Saint John, New Brunswick. There, in that boarding school and far from home, where the discipline was strict and I was too remote from the Saint John docks to stimulate my sea-fever, I did manage to get a matriculation. However, during the vacation periods when I was in Sydney, Mr. W. N. MacDonald, a local shipowner, gave me a chance to make short voyages in some of the ships which he operated. These brief periods of seafaring provided a great interest for me.

Having no definite aim in life, and thwarted from a seafaring career, since opportunities in Canada at that period were more or less non-existent unless I wanted to go on the Lakes or aboard coasting vessels, or to the U.K., or the U.S., my very tolerant father enrolled me at the Royal Military College, Kingston, Ontario. I was quite agreeable and thought that I might find an indication as to my future in that institution which in educational ranking is on a par with West Point in the United States and Sandhurst in England.

Discipline at R.M.C. was necessarily strict and there was no nonsense tolerated in classrooms, dormitories, parade square or anywhere else within its precincts. I was quite good in athletics and played on one or more of the teams at all times, and while my marks in the military and practical spheres were high, my rating in the other branches of the educational curriculum was low. Nevertheless, I struggled along until the fourth and final year at R.M.C. and while I did not pass the academic standard, it did not prevent me from obtaining a commission in the Permanent Force of the Canadian Army.

As a Lieutenant, I joined The Royal Canadian Regiment (Infantry) at London, Ontario, in 1929. For four years I served as an officer in the Canadian Army at several stations of the force, including Toronto and St. Johns (St. Jean), Quebec. I think I made a fair officer-soldier during that period, though my heart was definitely not in the work. I still wanted to be a sailor and when one is not satisfied with his position he should quit. But during the depression era in Canada, which then existed, one did not quit a job too quickly, so I drifted along.

My frustration, my aimlessness in life, my lack of interest in a shore profession, the apparent futility of my efforts to get to sea and make a career in that sphere—unless I was content to live in England or the United States—together with my advancing age and detours into fields that were remote from seafaring, all combined to siphon me into a condition of "live for today and to hell with tomorrow".

The Permanent Army was no place for an officer who has no enthusiasm in his job. He does his work, puts in his time at drills and parade and orderly room duties, etc., but after that he is through and has much spare time to kill, especially if he is a bachelor with no permanent feminine attachments. I was one of the unattached and none too enthusiastic about my profession. As a consequence, I gravitated into the company of a number of young officers whose feelings were inhibited similar to myself. Had it been wartime, all of us would have been on our toes and working double-tides. After parades and duty jobs we spent a lot of time in the officers' mess and in private rooms, often "bending the elbow" a bit recklessly.

In my own case I had the unhappy faculty of getting "plastered" at the wrong time and inopportunely, usually in full view of visiting Generals. These *contretemps* failed to disturb me very much, for I had acquired a keen dislike of army life. My commanding officers hailed me on the carpet several times, but their lectures didn't seem to penetrate. After several warnings to amend my behaviour—particularly over the Christmas and New Year holidays of 1933-34—the higher command decided that a parting was necessary.

I thereupon resigned my commission, which was accepted, and when it took effect I went to New York and visited an uncle of mine who at that time was Marine Superintendent for the Sinclair Oil and Refining Company. This concern operated a number of oil-tank steamers transporting oil from the south. At my request he shipped me out as an Ordinary Seaman aboard one of their oil-tankers. This was something better and though the work was frequently degrading and harsh—washing down decks and paintwork, chipping rust and painting, handling mooring lines, etc., and bunking in with some good fellows and some morons—I soon felt right at home. I was in the environment that I wanted, though I would have liked it better under sail than under steam. Nevertheless, I was at sea, aboard a ship, listening to the bell strike the half-hours, and turning out for my watch whenever I was called. I felt really happy in my work. Why hadn't I insisted on going to sea when I left high school? Had I done so I could possibly have been a certificated officer by the time I was mucking around decks as an insignificant Ordinary Seaman. But a fellow never knows.

In 1936 I had passed my examination for my first certificate—Mate, Home Trade—and with this in my pocket I was looking for a job out of the forecastle. But in the depressed mid-thirties there were more sailors than ships and jobs were not hanging on the trees for one to pick. So when Mr. W. N. MacDonald of Sydney, N.S., part-owner of the *St. Clair Theriault*, suggested to me that I might buy the schooner at a reasonable price and make a success of operating her, I jumped at the chance. My father and a brother produced some money and I became the proud owner of the *St. Clair Theriault* with a down payment—the remainder on mortgage, and a few hundred dollars left to get started out on the first voyage.

All the foregoing is preliminary to how I happened to acquire the *St. Clair Theriault* after I looked her over at Port Hawkesbury in the summer of 1936. I was taking a desperate chance, but one born of a love of ships and the hope and feeling of making good. The shipping business was at a low ebb. I had no experience in the schooner-freighting trade and no experience in handling a sailing vessel, for my seafaring career up to that date had been as Ordinary and Able Seaman in steam-driven oil-tankers. Nevertheless, I had sailed small yachts and knew the technique of sailing. In my tanker voyaging I had learned about knots, splicing, how to reeve off tackles, and to stitch a good seam on canvas, for we did have to do this sort of work on awnings, boat covers, bridge-dodgers, covers for different instruments and hatch tarpaulins. So with palm, needle, marlinspike, fid and sail-hook, I was no amateur. And I was well versed in coastal and deep-sea navigation. When I took the *Theriault* over in Port Hawkesbury I could see her restored to her original beauty and earning a fortune at the same time. On such romantic fancies do the thoughts of young men run!

I took an experienced schooner man, Sam Farrell of North Sydney, N.S., with me when I joined the vessel in Port Hawkesbury. It was necessary to have her hauled out on the Marine Railway, there to complete her seaworthiness inspection and obtain the required certificate. This Marine Slip was operated at that time, and still is, by A. J. Langley and has been in existence for many years. The inspector was not too hard on me, for I promised to renew much of the gear with the money I hoped to make. The vessel's hull was in good condition, but her sails and running gear were poor. But it was summertime and I hoped for a few quick trips and to have lots of money for new equipment. Before leaving home at Sydney I had entered into a charter party to carry a cargo of baled pulp from Bridgewater, N.S., to New Haven, Conn., and had it all worked out in my mind how long it would take. Every time I figured out one of these voyages I frequently underestimated the time required by several hundred percent.

We mended the old sails, rove off new halyards and sheets, put some stores aboard and were ready to go. But the wind was southwest—the prevailing quarter during the summer months. I was told there was no use trying to beat one of these vessels along the coast with no light sails and in ballast. So we waited a week, during which period I became acquainted with the ship. The donkey-engine was old and had been abused for years. It wouldn't start at times, but one was never sure. On occasion it would start easily but wouldn't stop, even after the ignition was shut off. This engine turned out to be one of my particular devils all the time I had the schooner. There was a wrecking pump run off this engine, also two bilge pumps along aft by the mizzen. At the time of the accident at Grand Narrows, a new engine had been installed to run these two pumps. It was similar to, but smaller than, the donkey-engine and was very efficient—always easy to start and would run a spell after the gas tank had drained dry. With this equipment, pumping out the vessel was easily accomplished. In the olden days, when pumping had to be done by hand, it was often a long and arduous task. These softwood vessels all leaked more or less after they were a few years old, especially in a seaway when they were heavily laden. In many craft under such conditions they had to be pumped almost continuously.

Along with the experienced schoonerman I had brought up from Sydney and the watchman who was game for another hitch, I took on two young fellows to make up a crew. There was no cook available at this stage, so all hands took a turn at cooking and the results were frankly terrible.

After about a week lying to an anchor windbound, I became impatient, as we were eating up all the scanty stores I had put on board, the wages were going on and we were getting nowhere. It is well to remember I had never been in a sailing vessel before, other than small craft. The previous few years I had spent in a full-powered American tanker under the best sort of living and working conditions afloat. Able seamen in that ship were being paid $47.50 a month, and supplied with good food, clean linen and an eight-hour day with three watches. In the schooner the pay was $25 a month for the sailors with two watches, four hours on and four off, with the watch below on call in case it was necessary to set or shorten sail. I did not realize that waiting for wind was one of the hazards of the schooner business.

Waiting for a fair wind finally became too irksome, so we started off to beat the vessel through the Strait of Canso with a favourable tide. After a long time and many tacks we ultimately got clear of the land and commenced a lengthy beat along the Nova Scotia coast toward Bridgewater. After several days we had sailed as far as Halifax when a summer storm blew up and we had to take in our weak old sails and let her go offshore. When it moderated we put back and arrived off Halifax about the time the wind dropped out completely, leaving a heavy swell. She began to drift ashore and we set all the sails in the hope that a draft of wind would come off the land. But no such luck!

In the windless swell, she began slatting very hard, which in a fore-and-aft vessel is exceedingly rough on the gear. The long gaffs swing over a lengthy arc with the motion of the ship and no wind to keep them steady. As the gaffs fly inboard and outboard the shock is passed down the sails to the booms. These heavy spars are held in place by the sheets and boom-tackles, but when the strain comes down from aloft they fetch up with a jerk and everything comes taut. This thundering and crashing has to be experienced to realize the heavy strain put on the gear, and only the best material will hold up for any length of time. After a period of rolling and banging about, the boom-tackle on the spanker let go and the long heavy boom started swinging free. Before we could get it under control, the boom broke at the bail-iron, but the sail held the broken end up and this heavy piece of spar began to smash the rails and steering gear each time it swung across the deck. Someone let go the halyards and down came the sail and all. This was a sorry mess. Not even to the loading port and already the vessel was in trouble—boom broken, sail torn, wheel damaged, running short of food and drifting ashore. Shortly after this the worn-out foresail slatted itself to pieces.

A little while later a draft of wind came from the east and we fetched the *Theriault* into Lunenburg and anchored in the harbour. In this port I arranged for a tow around to Bridgewater and also bought a main-boom off one of the Banks fishermen and cut it down to fit our spanker. The fitted boom was fifty-six feet long. I also bought a second-hand foresail and cap-jib that I had altered to fit. To pay for this gear and alterations I managed to fix up matters with the charterers to advance enough money to pay the bills. With these expenses and the fact that the passage took so much longer than I had expected, there was very little left of the cash advance by the time the schooner was loaded. In the schooners it was customary for the crew to work cargo. At the loading port a stevedore was often engaged to supervise the loading in order to get as much cargo as possible into the ship.

While in Bridgewater I had another setback. The Canadian Government had been tightening down on clearing ships from Canadian ports unless they had certificated masters. The *St. Clair Theriault*, like many Canadian-owned schooners, was registered in Bridge-town, Barbados, and previously entering and clearing by an unlicensed master was within the law. But now I was advised by the Customs that it was necessary to have a certificated master to clear the ship. I had not counted on this. Another man to run the vessel was not within my plans, but I was unable to do anything but try to find the right man. This I did and engaged Captain John S. Smith, an elderly man from La Have, N.S., who had been in fishing and freighting vessels all his life. He was nearly eighty at the time and he finished out the season with me. Later he died off the coast of Haiti early in World War Two while acting as mate in a Nova Scotia motor-vessel.

One of the young fellows I had taken on at Port Hawkesbury decided he had had enough of seafaring by this time and he departed to go apple picking in the Annapolis Valley. In his place I signed on a character who had hung around the vessel since our arrival in Bridgewater. He claimed to be a good cook, or a mate, or an A.B. He was a good handy fellow and was made cook. But as sailors say: "God sends food, but the Devil sends cooks!" For this man was one of his graduates and his efforts at cooking were awful.

After ten days loading baled pulp in Bridgewater, we towed down the La Have River, set sail outside and had a good slant across until we picked up Thatcher's Light on Cape Ann, Massachusetts. Coming along toward Cape Cod, the weather looked threatening and we put into Provincetown—remaining at anchor there for several days while the wind held southeast with rain. After it cleared, we entered Pollock Rip and proceeded over the Shoals and down the Long Island Sound to New Haven, Connecticut, where we towed in and discharged the cargo. The passage took seventeen days. There was nothing offering in the way of a return cargo, although I contacted several agents in Boston and New York, and the only alternative was to return to Nova Scotia. We came back light to Yarmouth, N.S., to load a cargo of lumber for Lynn, Mass. This passage back, and loading the schooner in Yarmouth, was carried through without incident. I settled the crew wages and put some stores aboard with the cash advance I received in Yarmouth. So I was still holding my own.

On the passage to Lynn the first major calamity in my ownership of the *Theriault* occurred. It was into October by this time and late one Fall evening we were off the approaches to Boston. Captain Johnny Smith was sure he knew all the lights and the lay of the land. The wind was fresh easterly and breezing up. The vessel's head was set into what we thought was the entrance to Lynn Harbour, but it turned out to be a stretch of low land over which we could see lights, and in particular a red light which Captain Johnny recognized and claimed should be there. He insisted that he was right. The vessel was on the correct course for entering Lynn and the wind was fair aft and blowing hard—making the *Theriault* foam along with all her lowers drawing full and running at the best speed she had done since I had been in her. The night was dark and overcast and it was coming on to midnight.

Unfortunately it was not Lynn we were entering, but toward the land around Swampscott, several miles east. The land here was low lying with high lights behind, and offshore were rocks known as Dread Ledges. I was forward and quickly realized something was wrong when the lights began to disappear. Suddenly one of the boys on the forecastlehead shouted: "Breakers ahead!" and he came running aft. With the helm and the sheets we tried frantically to bring her around, but she had a roaring bone in her teeth and the shore was too close.

The *Theriault* fetched up all-standing with a mighty crunch. How the masts and all that old gear held on was a miracle beyond comprehension. Halyards were cast off instantly and the sails came thundering down to crash about the deck as they pleased. The schooner hung by her forefoot, having slid up a ledge, with her after-end afloat. She rolled heavily in the swell with a tremendous grinding and groaning of timbers.

Within a few miles of our destination, this was a fine mess. We dropped an anchor, looked to the lifeboat and grabbed our belongings ready to abandon ship when she started to break up. None of us ever thought that a wooden ship of the *Theriault's* age could possibly survive that crash. But the schooner was tougher than we thought. We burned some flares, sounded the foghorn, but apparently we failed to attract the attention of anyone ashore. We were sure that we must have been in sight of the U.S. Coastguard Station in the vicinity, but later found that they could not see us in the position we happened to be in.

Hung up, as she was, by her forefoot, the schooner wallowed in the swell, but nothing in her hull or spars had started to give way. I took a lantern and went down into the chain locker. While I could hear the sound of water running into her, I was surprised to see no sign of damage. These vessels were built so solid in the bows with great natural

ST. CLAIR THERIAULT. 284 tons. Built 1919 at Belliveau Cove, N.S.

Deck view of
ST. CLAIR THERIAULT.

ST. CLAIR THERIAULT.
Ted Parker at wheel of schooner
Note binnacle set into
after part of cabin.

Author by after cabin of
ST. CLAIR THERIAULT.

Deck load of laths aboard
ST. CLAIR THERIAULT

ST. CLAIR THERIAULT. Loading salt from lighters at Turks Island.

knees, a deep keelson and solid deadwood that one couldn't get too far down to ascertain damage. In the meantime, we had the pumps going and were able to get a suck—which showed that she wasn't taking in more water than we could clear. Nevertheless, from the manner in which she was banging and grinding on the ledge with every timber, plank and bolt complaining audibly with the shock and strain, I was amazed that she hadn't knocked the bottom out of her. Since the schooner appeared to be in no immediate danger after investigation, we talked the situation over. The shore was handy and we had a boat if the worst came to the worst. I looked up in the Tide Tables and found the tide was flooding. The anchor cable was slacked off and the watch below turned in, as nothing could be done until she lifted up from the ledge in the rising tide. Fortunately as the tide made in the early morning hours the wind came off the land and the vessel rolled much easier. Soon the cable tightened and we gave her more chain. The pumps were kept running until the ship was dry. Then, with half an hour's respite, they were started up again. It took about two hours pumping each time to free the hold of water that had leaked in.

When daylight came I rowed ashore and eventually met an early riser who directed me to a telephone. I called the company in Boston with whom we had done business, told them of our predicament, and they promised to send a towboat when I told them that the schooner was insured.

After I left the vessel, Captain Johnny decided to slack away more cable and get the *Theriault* as far away from the reef as possible. As she lifted off the ledge and the wind blew her clear, he let go the port anchor. Sometime after daylight the wind came easterly again and the swell was getting up, but the offshore anchor held and the schooner rolled easily and safely to her hook.

The towboat finally arrived alongside and passed her hawser. We had the donkey-engine going and got the offshore anchor up, but when we tried to recover the anchor on the reef, with all its many fathoms of cable out, the wretched machine quit cold. It simply stopped and refused to start—just as if it had enough intelligence to know it was absolutely futile to try to heave in that lengthy cable. The skipper of the towboat, straining against the schooner to keep her clear, burst into a volley of curses and threats at our attempt to recover the cable, so we knocked out the shackle and away went the best part of the starboard chain and a good anchor. By this time I was too tired to care.

We towed up to T wharf in Boston and made fast. The insurance people and our agents in Boston decided that the best thing to do was for the schooner to proceed to Lynn and discharge the timber cargo and then return to Boston for dry-docking and survey. Oddly enough, by this time the *Theriault* had become much tighter and the pumping gradually declined until she leaked but a little more than normal.

In respect to the insurance on the *Theriault*, I had only a policy covering "Constructive Total Loss" on the vessel. Reduced to its simplest terms, that meant that the ship had to be completely lost, such as by fire or foundering or by damage to her hull so extensive that it would cost more to repair than the value that was placed on the vessel. I had to carry this insurance on account of the mortgage held on her and it was costly.

We towed to Lynn and discharged the cargo. We unloaded these cargoes ourselves and the cargo on this occasion amounted to about 300,000 board feet. Captain Johnny didn't work cargo, nor did the so-called cook, and that left three sailors and myself to pass the lumber out and stack it on the dock. For the heavier stuff we used the donkey-engine with a whip rove through a gin-block on the gaff. The hauling part was taken to the winch head and the load was slowly hoisted out. I had to leave for Boston quite often and the work didn't go too fast when I was away. In due course we got the lumber out of her and towed to East Boston for dry-docking.

In the graving-dock we saw that the damage to the *Theriault* was quite severe. So much so that it was difficult to understand why the ocean didn't pour into her. The stem and cut-water were gone to about seven feet above where the fore-foot had been. The garboard and five strakes of planking each side were sprung off and brushed out, and about sixty feet of the keel was ground off up to the garboard and all split along the greater part of her length. But these schooners, of the *Theriault* class, were so solidly and soundly built that she had come back to shape and sealed the leaks off.

The surveyors looked her over and decided that she was a constructive total loss, but if she could be got to a repair yard in Nova Scotia, where costs were far less than in the United States, it would be an economic proposition to repair her. Temporary repairs were made and a seaworthy certificate granted with the proviso that the vessel proceeded to Nova Scotia in tow.

All this took time and the vessel wasn't making any money. The temporary repairs were soon completed and the schooner was floated out and secured to the fitting-out dock. Christmas and New Year came and went before the money from the insurance company came through and I worried my head off during what was normally a care-free and festive season, for the crew were still standing by the ship with their wages going on and their meals to be provided for. Several times I considered paying them off and sending them home, but I had not nearly enough cash in hand and no source of credit. By the time the cheque came I was deeply in debt. I had to buy an anchor and many fathoms of chain cable to replace the gear we had lost on the ledges.

The next phase in this gloomy episode was to arrange for a tow to Yarmouth, Nova Scotia, 240 miles from Boston. It would have been too costly to have engaged a Boston tug for this haul, so I scouted around for a deal with one of the small wooden motor-coasters that plied between Yarmouth and Boston carrying fish, lobsters, produce, etc. In this effort I was fortunate to contract for a tow with the motorship *Accuracy*, a Yarmouth, N.S., freighter, to pull the *Theriault* across to Meteghan, N.S., not far from Yarmouth, and only a few miles from where the schooner had been built. At Meteghan there was a marine railway and a repair yard for wooden vessels which had been in operation for many years.

On a chilly day in January, 1937, the *Accuracy* took our hawser and we started off for Meteghan on our 240-mile tow. Everything went along well until the following night, when we were off the entrance to St. Mary's Bay, Bay of Fundy. It was blowing hard with the wind northwest and bitterly cold when the *Accuracy* ran into engine trouble and cast off our hawser. This hawser belonged to me, as part of my deal with the *Accuracy* was that I would provide the towing hawser. I therefore bought a good second-hand seven-inch manilla line of 1000 feet in Boston. When the *Accuracy* cast us off, most of this rope was out. I didn't want to have that length of rope dragging on the bottom all night, and to work the schooner under sail with all the hawser over the bows wasn't practicable. So we had to get it aboard.

The hawser was too large to lead to the donkey-engine winch-head we usually used for this purpose. Besides, the January night was particularly frigid with the wind fresh and northwest, and the hawser froze solid as soon as it left the water. It was next to impossible to handle by hand. The only alternative was to heave it in by bights. We unhooked the throat-halyard tackle of the foresail, passed a strop around the hawser, and hooked in the tackle—leading the fall to the donkey-engine winch-head. The temperamental engine, as usual when its services were urgently required, refused to work. So we had to take it in by hand.

We were about exhausted by the time we had managed to haul up the hawser fleet by fleet to the masthead, stopping it off, lowering down and fleeting again. To keep the schooner from going out to sea, it was necessary to set the mainsail and forestaysail. To hoist the former piece of canvas, I took the halyards to the winch-head of the donkey-engine, and quite prepared to have it baulk at the job, but to my surprise it worked right away and walked the mainsail up in a jiffy, then banged away for about two minutes after I cut the ignition.

It blew hard early in the morning and under short sail we managed to keep the schooner clear of Trinity Ledge and the numerous shoals in the vicinity of Cape St. Mary while still hanging on to the spot where the *Accuracy* let us go. Late in the morning the *Accuracy* showed up, took our line again, and so the *Theriault* came to Meteghan. Here I paid off all hands and remained by the schooner alone to superintend the repairs necessary to fit her out for the 1937 season.

The Meteghan shipyard, when I took the *Theriault* there to be repaired, was an old and somewhat primitive outfit. Everything was done the hard way. Its chief assets were a plentiful supply of suitable timber for shipbuilding, drawn from the adjacent forests, and any number of local men skilled in the work of building and repairing wooden ships. The yard also benefited from the abnormal rise and fall of the Fundy tides. The tracks of their marine railway were left high and dry at low water and could easily be repaired, maintained and adjusted for whatever type of ship was to be hauled out. In the *Theriault's* case, the cradle was run out on the tracks at high tide and the schooner warped into her place. The hauling-out part of the cradle purchase was taken to a capstan and teams of oxen provided the power. Two teams of these animals were employed for the *Theriault*. One pair at a time hooked onto the capstan bar, and these patient and sturdy oxen walked in a circle—stepping over the rope at every circuit. When they got tired and slacked up in their efforts, another pair of oxen took over. The *Theriault* was put on the railway in the morning. In the late afternoon she was up and high and dry above high tide.

The yard was quite busy at the time. They were building a scallop-dragger for Digby interests, and also the training schooner H.M.C.S. *Venture* for the Royal Canadian Navy. This latter vessel was built as an auxiliary tern schooner supposedly on the lines of the famous *Bluenose*, but from what I have heard she was not a success. During World War Two she was used as a depot ship in Halifax and later was sold to become a motor-driven coaster.

But to return to the *Theriault*. A deal was made with the manager of the yard and work was started on repairing the vessel. The split and broken garboards and planks were cut away and the damaged forward end of the keel was removed. This was actually a big job and had to be seen before it could be realized how strongly the *Theriault* was put together. Every plank was fastened to the timbers with bolts, spikes and treenails (or trunnels). To remove a plank, it was necessary for a man to go at it with a hammer and large chisel and cut it out in small pieces. The work went forward slowly but thoroughly in the leisurely Acadian fashion, but before long the damage was repaired and the *Theriault* was as good as she had ever been. While this work was being carried out, I employed the fine days in painting the topsides and deck-houses, and in innumerable small jobs aboard the schooner. Other times I rambled around the yard and watched the men at their work of building ships and repairing them. A fascinating and useful pastime for me.

While my ship was being repaired, I came to know some of the people living nearby and ended by having a fine time with these hospitable Acadians of the French Shore. I lived aboard the schooner, but I must admit my domestic arrangements were sketchy. From the local stores I purchased eggs and bacon and bread, but a lot of my meals came out of cans. I used up all the clean pots and dishes aboard the vessel and they piled up on me to such an extent that I was glad to enrol the assistance of my local girl-friends to help in a weekly clean-up.

Once more afloat, the *Theriault* was moored alongside an adjacent wharf where it was necessary that she be "tide tended". This meant that I had to be on hand to see that she was listed against the dock when the tide fell twice a day. At Meteghan the tidal rise varied from seventeen to twenty-two feet and at low water the vessel rested on the bottom. To ensure that she wouldn't fall over, the booms were swung across the deck toward the wharf, but their weight was not enough to list her when the wind was off. At times I had to take a throat-halyard across the dock and then heave on it with the engine to make sure she wouldn't list the wrong way. There was another alternative, which was to bore holes in the hull and let the tide run into her hold to keep her aground all the time, but I was unwilling to do that although the method was frequently employed.

During this period I had the yard mechanic overhaul the deck-engine. This grease-stained character was a mechanical genius. Most of the power employed in the shipyard was taken off a huge old-type kerosene engine and he could keep this ancient contraption running sweetly as long as he had an ample supply of wire and string. All my donkey-engine needed to show signs of life was for him to look in at the door. The mechanic said it was a lovely engine. Certainly it would perform perfectly in the presence of genius, but was spitefully contrary with those of us less qualified.

Thus passed the winter days and the *Theriault* was in shape to do business again. I secured another lumber freight for Lynn, Massachusetts, loading same at Yarmouth,

N.S. As I did not have enough money to square up the bills for fitting out, the advance freight, was "hocked" again before we left Meteghan for the loading port. This time I started out with a new gang. Fidele Boudreau was engaged as master and the others of the crew were picked up along the shore. These men were more experienced and handier than my former crew, and I was able to sign on a man who was an infinitely better cook than the food-spoilers I had to endure previously. After all the troubles we had gone through, I looked forward to better days.

All the season of 1937, the *Theriault* was employed running between ports in the Bay of Fundy and Boston and vicinity. Gradually the appearance of the schooner changed for the better as during the waiting for a fair wind the men worked about the ship on one job or another. But much of her gear was old and needed replacing, and I couldn't afford it until she made some money.

She could hardly pay her way. In the first place, freights were low. Secondly, losses in operation were caused through delays in waiting for wind, or for the wood cargoes to be brought to the dock, while the lack of return cargoes contributed to the poor returns on the round voyage. At times there were coal cargoes offering, but they were shipped from farther south on the U.S. coast and it seemed unwise to sail too far until the *Theriault* had better gear. There were other possible trades, but they were all off-shore and our equipment was not good enough for such voyaging. I kept hoping for two or three quick voyages and to put the profits into new sails and gear, but the chance never came. The towing bills were a steady drain and the insurance, wages and victualling of the ship came out about even with the freight money.

To get away from towing bills and delays caused by wind conditions, I concluded that an auxiliary engine was an absolute necessity. If I could raise the money, I planned to bring the schooner back to Port Hawkesbury and have an engine installed. As the winter came on, it was no longer safe to run the *Theriault* with her weak old sails and poor gear. So in January, 1938, we left Boston for Port Hawkesbury in ballast, but off Halifax the weather turned bad and we went into the harbour and anchored. I had barely enough cash to settle up with the crew and decided to pay them off there and have a go at raising money to buy and install an auxiliary.

In Sydney I was able to talk my backer into making a further investment. The schooner had a good sound hull, was a good carrier, but took too long on passages and too much money was spent on necessary towing. As we could not afford a new one, I managed to locate a secondhand engine in Halifax suitable for the purpose. One of the Halifax pilot-boats had been recently re-engined and I was able to buy the old one. It was a three-cylinder semi-diesel made by Bergeson of Sweden, and developed 105 h.p. at 300 r.p.m. We secured it at a bargain price and all the gear went with it. The *Theriault* was towed to the Marine Railway at Dartmouth, N.S., hauled out and the job was started.

Fitting the engine into the vessel turned out to be a very difficult job. When she was built, a shaft-log was installed, bored out to $2\frac{1}{2}$ inches and left with a plug driven in. In the earlier days it was considered that a gasolene engine might be fitted at a later date. But the power we had purchased called for an opening of 5½ or 6 inches for the shaft and lead sleeve. When the shipyard men started to ream out the hole, the auger came into contact with the long vertical bolts used to fasten the keelson, deadwood and keel. In the end a bar had to be set up in the shaft-hole and a cutting tool used with an air-motor to turn it. Also, the schooner had been built with a sternpost and rudderpost with deadwood between and this had to be cut out. Ultimately, the job was completed and the sleeve, shaft, bearings and propeller fitted, then the *Theriault* was lowered back into the water again.

The shipyard left us on our own after this and I engaged a mechanic to overhaul the engine and set it up. Previously I had picked up a Newfoundland sailor to keep me company on the vessel and lend a hand when required, and he and I went to work and installed the tanks and built a bulkhead in the after hold. It was found the engine did not take up much space. It was right aft and the ship was fine at this part in any case.

At this time I was able to squeeze in a new spanker along with the other expenses. It was made by Murphy of Halifax and was an excellent fit. I felt a glow of pleasure to see it come aboard. As the better weather came on, the schooner was often visited by men looking for a job. Conditions in the shipping business were still depressed and the Canadian Government Merchant Steamships were being sold off, thereby leaving many Canadian and Newfoundland seamen "on the beach". Thus I was able to line up some good sailors. Some of the men I took on began to work before their pay started so long as they could eat and live aboard. They scraped down the spars, booms and gaffs and gave her a coat of paint while we were waiting to complete the machinery job. On trial runs in the harbour, the engine drove the *Theriault* along at about seven knots, which was quite sufficient.

We were now in shape for the 1938 season. Captain E. O. Fudge was engaged as master, myself as mate, and Eric Caines as second mate and bosun. A young fellow with some experience around diesels was taken on with the understanding that he would turn to for other work when the engine was idle. Peter Rose was signed as cook, and with two sailors we were seven hands in all.

Our first charter was to load laths at Gagetown, N.B., up the Saint John River, for New York. I planned to keep looking for return cargoes back to Nova Scotia, but if one did not materialize the vessel would carry on to Turks Island in the Caicos group in the British West Indies, where salt cargoes for Canada could always be obtained. While the Caicos are geographically a southeast continuation of the Bahamas chain, they are part of the Jamaica dependency.

Leaving Halifax, I felt happy and optimistic as to the future. Although the *Theriault* was $6000 further in debt, she was now a going concern. The newly installed diesel was chugging along. We had electric lights run off a set of batteries charged by a Delco engine, which also served to pump up the air tanks for the diesel. As soon as we were clear of the harbour, the wind came fair; up went the sails and the engine was stopped. The *Theriault*, clean and shining in fresh paint, with her new spanker drawing full, went surging through the water and it seemed she had entered a new life. The sight of her, and her actions, suggested that she felt young again, lively and swift. And for the first time I nursed the feeling that now, after I had learned all the hard lessons, the schooner would be made to pay and I would have a grand time doing it.

In due course we made around into the Bay of Fundy and up the Saint John Harbour toward the Reversing Falls of the Saint John River. Here it was necessary to engage a towboat to get us through the tidal falls, but once past the swift water we proceeded under our own auxiliary power and arrived at Gagetown, N.B.

Loading the cargo of one million three hundred thousand laths in bundles was soon completed, and we dropped down the River to Saint John. My young brother Ted had just completed his term at university for the summer and was to make the voyage with us. Off to New York we sailed—child's play, it seemed—with the engine to hook up every time the wind dropped out. In no time the *Theriault* passed through Long Island Sound, came to City Island, then down the East River to Newtown Creek, Brooklyn, to discharge the load.

Up to now everything had gone well. The laths were nearly out and plans were being made to proceed to Turks Island on completion. One hot June day the donkey-engine began acting up. The young engineer went to the forward house to look it over and somehow caused the engine to back-fire. The flash ignited some gasolene in a can placed under the carburetor to catch the drip. He lost his head and in attempting to rectify matters made things much worse. He grabbed the gasolene tank from its rack and tried to tear it clear of the engine, to which it was attached by the copper fuel pipe. He probably thought that by doing this he would avert a serious explosion in the engine compartment. But what happened was that the highly inflammable oil pouring out from the broken pipe sprayed him with gasolene, which instantly caught fire and he dropped the tank and came running out with his clothing all in flames. I was on deck at the time and heard the tank explode, saw the flame and smoke bursting out of the engine-room, and the young fellow running out with his clothing afire. Somebody shouted to him: "Go over the side!" In a panic, he obeyed the order and ran to the outboard rail and jumped over. But his luck was out. For that morning a boom of logs had been floated alongside the *Theriault* and the engineer landed on top of them and lay there with his clothing burning until in his painful struggles he rolled over and fell into the water. This all happened as quick as the telling of it. But when he rolled off the logs I went over the rail, jumped into the water and grabbed him. The men on deck passed me a line and we hauled the poor fellow aboard.

Although only a few minutes had elapsed from the time of the outbreak until I got back on deck, the Brooklyn Fire Department was already there. A lumber yard with a large oil-distribution station just across the creek and in the centre of Brooklyn was a danger spot that was well watched. Captain Fudge took charge of the injured man and I went forward to see what was happening in the engine-room. But the firemen were aboard the schooner and promptly extinguished the blaze with portable cylinders of foam-type chemicals. Within a few minutes it was black out. Except for the engine-room being completely charred, the wiring of the engine gone, and everything in a mess, the damage was not serious. In very quick time an ambulance sped down the dock to the schooner and the young man was rushed to hospital. The gasolene had sprayed over his neck, shoulders and back and caught fire. As we loaded him into the ambulance, I promised to see him that evening.

We spent the rest of the afternoon cleaning up the engine-room and getting the engine in operation again. In the evening I went to the hospital to see the engineer, to learn the extent of his injuries and whether he would be able to sail with us after treatment. The medical interne attending him told me that it would not be possible for him to resume work for quite a while and that, after a period of treatment, he should be sent home to Nova Scotia. Although his burns were of a third-degree character and he was in great pain, he was very keen on continuing the voyage to the south. He insisted that he would be alright, and could he come back to the ship? Reluctantly, I had to tell him that he must remain in hospital until such time as the doctor considered that he could be discharged.

However, about two days later, on a Saturday afternoon, he arrived back to the vessel in a taxi, having signed himself out of the hospital. He was in terrible shape, all swathed up in bandages, but he pleaded not to be sent back to the hospital, as he wished to remain with us. The condition he was in simply forbade any idea of his making the voyage. We looked after him until Monday morning, then took him up to the British Consul's office for advice. The *Theriault* was all ready to sail and as soon as we disposed of the engineer's case we would depart. We wrapped him up in cotton wool well smeared with Unguentine and I interviewed the Consul. After talking the situation over, it was decided to put him on the train for Halifax. It seemed a hard thing to do, but he was so dead set against the hospital and while on the train he was at least headed for home. He was given a big bottle of aspirin and escorted aboard the train. Later, he told me that he had a very trying ride back but made a good recovery in his own home. As this situation made a change in our organization, Eric Caines and I looked after the auxiliary engine in our own watches, a system that worked well until we got home.

Following this, we sailed for Turks Island that evening, got clear of New York and under sail stretched away to the south'ard. The course is a little east of south and about 1200 miles in direct distance, but it was necessary for the schooner to proceed much farther east so as to pick up the Northeast Trade Wind and avoid getting to leeward. Though I had made many trips in southern waters before, it was my first under sail and the passage was warm and pleasant with the old *Theriault* rolling along over the blue seas with the "steady Trade Wind blowing". The sight of the floating streaks of Gulf Weed, and the flying-fish skittering up out of the water from under our foaming bows, the warm sunshine and the white clouds aloft—all combined to make a delightful contrast to my previous voyaging in the *Theriault*. The only fly in the ointment was that we were sailing a long way in ballast to secure a cargo, and the vessel was making no money on the passage. However, the crowd of us had a chance to overhaul the sails and gear and we got her into pretty good shape considering the old stuff we had to work on.

Turks Island is the most southeasterly of the numerous and widely scattered Bahamas group and is located in 21° 30′ N., 71° 10′ W., just north of the island of Haiti. There is more than one island in the low-lying coral group of the Turks, and their chief industry was the production of sea-salt used primarily in the fisheries up north. The salt is derived from the evaporation of sea-water—the hot sun and the fresh Trade Wind being the drying agents. The process is a primitive one and has been in use for a century or more. Sea-water was pumped into shallow artificial ponds by the power derived from windmills. Evaporation of the water takes place quickly and when a sufficient quantity of salt has been deposited, the pond is allowed to dry up and the salt shovelled out by the negro labourers.

After a good run down, we arrived off the main island, proceeded in slowly and anchored on the outlying reef. Contact was made with the local agent and we proceeded immediately to load cargo. The salt was loaded aboard the ships from lighters carrying five or six tons each. The coloured stevedores lashed hatch covers over the side to make platforms and passed the salt up in half-bushel bags which were filled ashore. The draw-string which secured the mouth of the bag was opened with a quick movement by the last man to throw it, and the bag was then emptied into the vessel's hold, in bulk. At first appearance, this seemed a very slow way to load, but the stevedores kept the salt moving in a steady stream and it soon began to mount up. The *Theriault* loaded 12,000 bushels in about ten hours' working time and we were able to sail for home the day after arrival. My brother's opportunities to ramble around a tropic island and observe the flora and fauna were necessarily brief, but we were not a cruise ship and getting back in quick time with our cargo was imperative if it was to make a profit. Besides, there wasn't much to see on Turks Island anyway.

Our salt was consigned to Riverport, Nova Scotia, and we had a good passage home in fine weather and without incident. This voyage showed what a little auxiliary power could do for a schooner. We had left Saint John on May 21st, and arrived back at River-port on July 16th, having discharged a cargo at New York and loaded one at Turks Island. There was a profit this time and the money was placed against the main debt on the vessel. Thus in two months we had sailed the *Theriault* over 3000 miles and loaded and delivered two cargoes. The previous summer, without auxiliary power, it had taken *over a month* from the time the schooner was loaded at the head of the Bay of Fundy, before we arrived at Boston, a distance of about 400 miles.

While discharging the salt cargo at Riverport, the vessel was offered a similar charter and she could have been made to pay quite well on this type of voyage, barring accidents. The drawback now was the West Indian hurricane season prevailing from August to October. Most of these violent storms cross north of Haiti and the waters in which we would have to travel for the whole voyage would come under the influence of possible hurricanes at one stage or another. To combat a storm of this character called for a well-geared ship in rigging and sails, and the *Theriault* hardly ranked in that category.

When offered the salt charter I had the option of another to carry a load of lumber across to Ireland at a good figure. I thought this would be better. We would have a pre-vailing westerly wind in the North Atlantic summertime to get her across. After discharging, we could head south for the Northeast Trade Winds that make up off the coast of Spain to push us out to the West Indies again, where we could load salt for home. The hurricane season would then be over. It seemed logical and good business, so I closed the proposition to carry a load of deals from Pictou, Nova Scotia, to Ballina, Northwest coast of Ireland, and we sailed around to the former port in short order.

Before leaving Pictou another trouble developed to plague me. This voyage would be foreign-going in the true sense of the word, and the Shipping Master advised me that we would have to change our Articles from Coasting to Foreign. This meant my Home Trade mate's ticket in steam did not qualify me to serve as mate in a foreign-going sailing ship and a certificated man had to be obtained ere we could be granted clearance. This became an added expense. Here I was, the owner and actually in charge of the vessel, but through the lack of necessary certificates required by law, I was forced to hire a master, and now a mate, and this added to the expense of operating the schooner. But one has to learn the hard way.

After about two weeks in Pictou, we got our cargo of lumber aboard and the vessel sailed from Nova Scotia for Ireland across the Western Ocean. There was a fair wind nearly every day and when it fell light we gave her the engine. On the thirteenth day out from Pictou we raised the Irish coast. An excellent passage but the complete end of my good luck.

We sailed into Killala Bay, an indentation flanked by grassy hills so intensely green in colour as to uphold Ireland's claim to be the "Emerald Isle". We had the pilot flag flying and came to an anchor. Before long a boat came off with the harbour master and a pilot from Ballina. This port was located on the River Moy about five miles from where it entered the bay. The pilot checked up on our draft of water and debated the chances of taking the schooner up to the port on the existing range of tides. None of us was in a position to discuss the question with him, for he was supposed to have the local knowledge of the channel depths and suchlike. On his sayso, we hove up the anchor, and with the pilot in charge and the schooner under power, we proceeded up the river just before high water.

About half-way up to Ballina the *Theriault* grounded on a sandbank and stuck fast, despite our efforts to free her. The pilot remained aboard for a spell, seemingly flabbergasted at the mishap and shouting futile orders. The schooner was obviously out of the channel, but the pilot evidently considered that discretion was the better part of valour and retired from the scene. While we were all busy trying to get the schooner off the bank, he slipped quietly overside into his boat and deserted us, Although I was in the vicinity for several months afterwards, I never set eyes on him again.

When the tide began to fall, our predicament became really serious. The schooner had a hold full of spruce deals, with a deck load of the wood and the Brazilian poop stowed to the beams. With this heavy cargo aboard, and the vessel stranded across a sandbank, she became seriously injured when the tide fell. As she settled with her keel imbedded in the sand, she hogged badly. The main rigging let go and the deck opened. Then she filled with water.

Ballina was a small town in the county of Mayo, northwest Eire. It was the center of a farming area and on market days it was a busy place. It had a quay flanking the River Moy where cargoes of lumber and building materials were landed, produce and livestock shipped to Scotland and England. The quay was a short distance from the town of about five or six thousand people and had little else on it other than a warehouse and a "pub".

Our shipment of timber was consigned to Beckett and Company, the leading builders of the area, and was an experimental cargo, as previously all their timber had been imported from the Baltic. Our consignee was represented by Mr. Frank Beckett, a well-built jovial fellow, who was the manager of the company and the nephew of the absentee owner. All our subsequent business was done with him and I became very attached to Mr. Beckett before our troubles were all over. He did everything in his power to help me out.

The mishap occurred in the afternoon and that evening in Ballina I had some very bitter thoughts. Here we were, only a stone's throw from our destination, having made a swift passage across the Atlantic to get there and to run into disaster at journey's end was heartbreaking. Frank Beckett, like the good fellow he was, took me to the local hotel and we had a few drinks before he left, promising to call the local Lloyd's agent early in the morning. Then the agent, Mr. Beckett and myself would travel down-river to the *Theriault*.

We did so, and the schooner was a sad sight when she came into our view. I could see by the angle of the spring-stay that she had hogged very badly, and by that time she had listed about ten degrees. With the situation the *Theriault* was in, the first step was to lighten her and deliver some cargo as soon as possible. This was done in the following three days. The deck load was discharged first and made into rafts which were towed up the River Moy to the quay. By the time the deck load was off, the tides were coming better and the old schooner seemed to stir in her unwanted berth. My Canadian crew, skipper, mates and all, did everything in their power to relieve the predicament the vessel was in. The pumps were started and fortunately we were able to clear her of water. The engine was put to work and with the propeller whirling away and a good full tide lifting her off the bank, we steamed the *Theriault* the rest of the distance to the quay—with no pilot this time and no mishaps. In spite of the strains she had been subjected to, the leaking gradually decreased and by the time the cargo was out, the ship was tight again.

With our cargo of deals delivered, the next part of the story was to find out what we could do with our damaged schooner and what the marine insurance people had to say. This entailed lengthy negotiations with the underwriters of the vessel and cargo. I felt that the *Theriault* was finished and I wanted to abandon the vessel to the underwriters and get home with the crew. However, it was necessary to hold on for a while and await the outcome of the underwriter's survey. This time the values concerned were much higher than formerly. The amount of money originally tied up in the schooner, plus the sums spent in installing the auxiliary engine and fittings, amounted to about $10,000 and she was insured for this sum on the basis of a constructive total loss. In addition the cargo underwriters were liable for some of the damage and expenses in the delivery thereof.

A survey was called and the underwriters sent their representative. For the ship's interest I obtained the services of the Belfast surveyor of the American Bureau of Shipping. The two men examined the schooner and assessed the damage. Once again the *Theriault* was declared a constructive total loss. However, as in her previous mishap, they decided that if the vessel could be got back to Nova Scotia she could be permanently repaired there and put in shape again. The surveyor who represented the ship said that if I would have certain temporary repairs made in Ballina he would give me a seaworthy certificate—provided they passed his inspection. At this point the underwriters agreed to pay on the basis of a constructive loss. At the same time they intimated that they would consider an offer for the *Theriault* as she lay damaged at Ballina. After cabling back and forth with Mr. MacDonald in Canada, a price was offered to the underwriters which they accepted. The balance of the $10,000 insurance was forwarded to Canada and I received sums from time to time to maintain myself and the crew and make the temporary repairs. The proposition seemed to be a good one, for the price we had paid for the vessel as she lay damaged at Ballina was small, and, as before, repairs could be completed in Nova Scotia quite reasonably. Optimistically, I began to feel that the disastrous voyage might yet show a profit.

When the *Theriault* hogged across the sand-bar, she strained herself severely. The main damage done to the ship was to the longitudinal strength about amidships. The water-ways had fractured and the clamp and shelf had probably failed—although they seemed to have come back into shape. The main-rigging, both sides, had parted, also the mizzen wire on the starboard side. The surveyor said he would require new rigging at these places, and the largest strengthening timbers we could locate. He said he would settle for 8 × 8-inch hardwood for stiffening the fore-and-aft strength by bolting to the keelson and under the deck beams, securely bolted to every beam. When this was done the surveyor would return to Ballina and "sight" the vessel on the beach at low tide, at which time the caulking and the rudder could also be examined for sea-fitness.

By the time these negotiations had been carried out, it was late in the Fall of 1938. In that part of Ireland it was difficult to secure materials to repair ships. Wire rigging was in short supply, for England had awakened to the war threat of Hitler Germany and was rearming, but in the end we got our wire. The problem of the hardwood timbers gave me a headache, but was ultimately solved by driving around the country, buying the trees, having them cut down and taken to the mill to be sawn to the required dimensions. All the work aboard the ship was done by the crew—renewing and setting up the rigging; boring and bolting the strengthening timbers into their places. And while waiting for the rigging, I bought sufficient heavy duck to make a new mainsail. Under the direction of Captain Fudge, the crew made a fine new sail. As was the case with the old-time Nova Scotiamen, we employed no shore labour if the hands aboard were capable of doing the work.

During our time in Ballina, the engineer overhauled the main engine but was unable to do anything with the Delco auxiliary. This little engine, located below deck, had become thoroughly soaked with salt water when the ship filled, and though we removed it as soon as possible after arriving and dried it out, it could never be properly repaired. We could get along without electric lights, but it was essential to have an engine to operate the air-compressor to fill the air-starting tanks for the main diesel engine. In the end I bought an ancient Morris car of the smallest size, dismantled it on the dock and took the engine aboard. If my memory is correct I paid four English pounds for it. The car had acetylene lamps and must have been about thirty years old, but the engine ran like a charm so long as we kept the magneto behind the cabin stove when not in use to be sure it was dry. We hooked a wooden pulley to the shaft, after removing the transmission and that problem was finally finished.

Christmas and New Year came and went and then we were ready for inspection. The surveyor from Belfast arrived back, approved repairs, and gave the schooner a seaworthy certificate to return to Canada in ballast to effect permanent repairs.

During the lengthy period we had passed in Ballina all of us had plenty of time to kill while waiting for this or that—particularly in the evenings. Frank Beckett became my daily companion and almost every evening he drove Captain Fudge and me all around the country in different directions. In the course of these excursions we became acquainted with every "pub" within a fifty-mile radius and got to know that part of Ireland pretty well. Frank was good-looking, well off and extremely eligible for marriage in a country where such males are scarce. At any rate, he had every girl in the county after him, so when we went out we always had lots of company. His friendship and hospitality proved a godsend to me, as they took my mind off our troubles. The crew also enjoyed a full measure of Irish hospitality, and on sailing day, January 5th, 1939, there was a group of sorrowing girls at the quay to say goodbye. Amid tears and cheers we cast off our lines and proceeded down the River Moy.

For the first few days after clearing the Irish coast the outlook was very good. The wind was easterly and fresh and the *Theriault* made good time to the westward, using the engine when the wind was light. We planned on making as far to the west as possible before the prevailing westerlies set in. When that happened, we proposed to put the vessel on the starboard tack and let her go south to pick up the Northeast Trades and head for Turks Island. My plan was to try to "square up" the voyage by picking up a part salt cargo for Nova Scotia and use the freight-money to pay the crew off. They had considerable money coming to them by the time we left Ireland, although I had been doling out advances at regular intervals since arriving at Ballina. Before leaving, I advised Mr. MacDonald to insure the vessel for the amount she was in debt plus some money over for crew wages, but by some unfortunate mischance or other he was unable to do so. Unquestionably, insurance on this particular passage would command a high premium, especially since a vessel in our condition, and in ballast, crossing to the westward in January would hardly be accounted a good risk.

For over a week the *Theriault* went along very well—the wind was mostly fair and the weather good. Then, on the ninth day out, the wind came ahead and we put the schooner on the starboard tack and started to jog down to the latitude of the Northeast Trade. The vessel was in good order, engine working away when required, and we had hopes of a good passage. However, the westerly wind freshened, the barometer fell and on the second day of the west wind we had to take in the jibs, foresail and mizzen—leaving the schooner nearly hove-to under the forestaysail and mainsail. The wind continued to breeze up and the swell to increase. Soon the *Theriault* was climbing over long grey rollers, but everything was going according to schedule. The motor was chugging along and under the shortened sail the schooner was making headway toward the better weather and the Trades. But it was not to be. The wind increased to a moderate gale and a reef was put in the mainsail. Then the trouble began.

The Bergeson engine had functioned perfectly since it had been installed and had worked away without complaint, but now it developed a hard knock. Investigation showed that number one bottom-end-bearing had run hot and the babbit was about done. At first this did not seem too bad, as we had a spare. When we had overhauled this engine in Halifax the former operators told me that it had a habit of burning out this particular bearing. We had the bearing fixed up at that time and carried a spare for emergencies.

The engineer and I removed the burned-out bottom-end and found the pin scored. There was doubt if it would do or not, but finally we fitted the new bearing with plenty of clearance. It was awkward toilsome work in the confined quarters, yet in due course we managed to get the engine going again, only to find that it would not run faster than half-speed before heating up. We took the bearing out once more and rigged a device to smooth off the scored pin. This turned out to be a hard job and was not successful. Running at half-speed was alright for the bearing, but the propeller effect on the ship at that speed, under reigning conditions, was very feeble. We kept trying to smooth off the pin.

In the meantime the weather had become steadily worse. It was now approaching a full storm and the *Theriault* was heeled over but still head-to and riding like a duck. Then one of the men on deck reported that he thought he saw the foremast wobble. On examination it was found that the mast had fractured just above where it came through the foreward house. Extra stays were quickly rigged to prevent the mast from going over the side, but it was unfit for heavy work until we could contrive a way to "fish it". Talking it over afterwards, it was assumed that the foremast had been under a heavy strain when the vessel grounded in the River Moy and the severe head pitching she was now undergoing had finished it off.

On about the fifth day after the engine breakdown we were getting tired. Some of the other men had come down below to give a hand at grinding down the pin. This was a laborious job, as it had to be accomplished with one arm thrust into the opening in the lower part of the engine while lying on one's side. The schooner was rolling and pitching continuously in the high sea and fatigue was beginning to creep over us. But in spite of all our efforts we could not get the engine to run cool. Since those days I have talked to many of the Western Ocean sailors and they have the same story. Oftentimes it was not a single incident that led to the ships being lost, but to a succession of damages sustained in the kind of weather that saps all the strength out of a man. Long periods without a good sleep in bad weather, irregular meals and frequently only cold snacks—even though the cook, poor fellow, was doing his best and tired too—and lengthy spells of hard backbreaking labour while chilled and soaking wet.

About the eighth night the third item of damage occurred in the accumulated list of mishaps to plague the *Theriault*. It was nearly midnight and the wind was screaming through the rigging. The master decided to take in the forestaysail and during a lull it was furled. The vessel was then lying under the double-reefed mainsail with her head still up, but for several days now going to leeward at what rate we did not know. The seas had reached the great length and height only to be found in an Atlantic storm of long duration. The air was full of flying water and it was impossible to face into the wind and see and breathe.

Shortly after the lull during which we stowed the forestaysail, and all hands had gone below except the watch on deck, a terrific squall struck the schooner and we could feel her quiver under the impact. With an explosive sound, audible in the darkness amidst the roar and howl of the squall, the mainsail blew out of the boltropes and wrapped itself around the lee shrouds, where it was whipped by the gale and shredded itself to pieces. This was the new sail, made by the crew in Ireland of nought (0) duck and so stout in fibre that it would hardly roll up.

In the intense darkness of the winter night, and under the reigning conditions, and with her stormsail gone, the *Theriault* was unable to head up and fell off into the trough of the sea. The relieving gear was taken off the rudder and we tried to run her under bare poles. But she was boarded by great seas which quickly took their toll. First to go was the dory lashed bottom-up on the main hatch, and it was smashed into kindling wood and swept overside. Soon after, another boarding sea pooped the schooner and carried off the lifeboat slung on the stern davits and we never even saw it go. The same sea smashed in the aft cabin door and windows and flooded the cabin. This could not go on, so we let her broach-to and lie in the trough of the waves, swinging wildly, listing to leeward heavily each time she rose to the foaming crests by the pressure of the fierce gale on her spars and rigging. The rudder was slamming and straining against the steering gear and we rigged chains and tackles to ease it.

The final blow in this disastrous chain of events followed quickly. After several successive violent swings, the tackles relieving the rudder let go and put all the strain on the steering gear. It was already strained and broke almost immediately. The rudder was now free to swing and we tried desperately to recapture it. But after another heavy spell of swinging and banging it broke out the pintle-block, which caused the rudder to rise a few inches. Then in a particularly vicious rampage it unshipped itself from the gudgeons and dropped down free until the iron band on the head of the rudder-post fetched up against the deck-collar.

Now the predicament. Here was the rudder and stock swinging almost free and exerting a tremendous leverage force on the rudder case and the whole stern of the schooner. The stock, eighteen feet long and twelve inches in diameter, of good seasoned oak and nearly as strong as steel, with the rudder blade attached, levered away violently as the vessel wallowed in the trough of the seas. Unless we could get it free, it would tear the whole stern of the schooner apart.

The iron band on the top end of the rudder-post was a divided one with the two parts held together by bolts. Frantically we tried to ease up the rusted bolts to get the band off. All this time the wind was howling through the rigging, the big seas charging down on us and drenching everything in sprays. As she rolled and jerked, we pulled and cursed at the nuts that held the band and finally got them loosened up. The band pulled off, and the rudder-stock dropped down through the casing out of sight and the vessel was rudderless.

All that night we knew the ship was doomed. Shortly after daybreak a big sea struck her amidships and shattered the starboard bulwarks. A long plank in the sheerstrake was sprung, and when she took a heavy roll, the water gushed into the hold. One great boarding comber made a desolate wreck of the forecastle, already soggy with repeated washouts.

And now the misfortunes of the *Theriault* were coming to an end. Almost any of the failures in the ship could have been dealt with singly. Added together, the schooner had become an unmanageable derelict. To review the situation: the engine was out of commission and could not be run at a speed at which the vessel would respond. This type of engine required a comparatively large volume of air for starting, thus necessitating the running of the separate air-compressor for lengthy periods. In the extraordinary circumstances, where we were trying everything to make the engine run smoothly, we had used a lot of gasolene running the small engine operating the compressor. As we ran short of gasolene we took the compressor up on deck and operated it from the aft pumping engine. We found enough pipe to connect up with the air-tanks. All this work was extra for the hands on the wildly plunging vessel. After discovering the condition of the fractured foremast, some spare wire was hauled out and preventer stays rigged leading aft to the bulwarks on both sides. A year or so previously I had put two preventer stays from the foremasthead to the catheads on each bow. The foremast was now securely stayed in an upright position, but a transverse strain on the mast would cause it to part quite easily at the fracture just above the galley overhead. In fore-and-aft vessels all the strain is passed down the foremast when under sail. The main and mizzen are held in place by the springstay to the foremast, which mast, in turn, is heavily stayed to the knightheads. In short, when the foremast is weak the main support is removed. In our case, the only thing that would remedy the situation was to "fish" the mast in the vicinity of the fracture. For this we had no opportunity, as any work of this nature would have to await better weather. After our new mainsail blew away, we hauled out the old one and bent it on, but the continuous gale did not permit of any sail being hoisted, and certainly not an old one.

During the last days aboard the *Theriault*, a great weariness came over the crew which I would ascribe mainly to lack of sleep. Although the ship was run on four-hour watches with four below, unless sails had to be handled, and all hands were used to this routine over the period of their seagoing time, the conditions were different on this occasion. By now, everything was well soaked. The seas she had shipped had broken in the cabin windows and water had been sloshing about and drowning everything below. We had bored holes in the deck to let the water run to the bilges. The forward house had been washed out several times, saturating the bedding and ruining the food stored there. The cook had done his best to provide hot meals, but much of his stores had become spoiled by salt water and there was no chance to dry anything out. Under these conditions, combined with long periods of hard labour, physical exhaustion gradually overcame the crowd of us and we lived in frigid discomfort and a feeling of hopelessness.

The vessel actually leaked very little during this period, but we knew we would have to leave her at the first opportunity. For twelve wretchedly cold and stormy days we had been drifting steadily to leeward, and in that direction stood the rocky cliffs of the Spanish peninsula and the Bay of Biscay. Having lost both boats, the rudder and vital sails, and with a weak foremast, we decided to hail the first ship and get aboard her. We knew that no steamer would take an old schooner in tow. So the daytime distress signal flags "N-C" were run up. For a night signal we knocked the head out of an oil drum and filled it with oil-soaked rags all ready to be ignited.

And thus we drifted helplessly across the steamship lane between Cape Finisterre and the English Channel. For days we had seen no ship. Then one morning we sighted three on the horizon. Later, one of them, the *Hertford*, a large steamer belonging to the New Zealand Shipping Company, bound home, came up close, having seen our Distress Signal, and made preparations to send a boat over to take us off.

At this time the gale was still howling. The sea was running very high and the wave crests were being torn off and blown away in wind-driven spume. The *Hertford* worked her way to windward, her hull dropping from view as we and she plunged into the troughs. She made a lee and we watched them getting ready to send a boat over. As they lowered the boat we could see them frapping the falls to minimize the swing of the little craft against the ship's side. Later, to our intense dismay, we saw them hoisting the boat up again as they abandoned the rescue attempt for the time being. But the steamer remained in the vicinity. Toward evening they tried again. This time the *Hertford* headed more into the waves and in the gloom we could see the boat drop astern. But there did not appear to be any men in it and presently the boat passed us a few hundred yards off, unmanned and full of water. We lit our fire in the barrel and waited throughout another night.

All night long the gallant *Hertford* lay hove-to and drifted slowly to leeward. The tardy daylight came at length and we could see her steaming up again. For the first time in many days the weather showed improvement. The wind was down to a moderate gale and the sea was not so savage. Another attempt to lower a boat was successful and they eased down toward our helpless schooner. We were all ready to go. The mate in the sternsheets of the lifeboat shouted as he came alongside: "No baggage!", but a couple of the men threw in their seabags anyway. The schooner had been prepared for setting afire and the last thing done was to ignite the oil-soaked blankets in the forward house and cabin. We then jumped down into the lifeboat, which dropped down to leeward where the *Hertford* had circled around. Getting the boat back aboard the steamer was a tricky business, but she was skilfully handled and it was finally accomplished. As soon as it was hoisted up, the *Hertford* resumed her course for the English Channel and Dunkirk, France.

The steamer was on a routine voyage from the East and on the night before coming up to the schooner had dipped the port wing of the bridge into a giant sea which carried away the cab and smashed the engine-room telegraph on that side. She was a large steamship of 6889 tons net, and even in the high sea she seemed very steady to us after the wild tossing we had endured aboard the schooner. On the chart, her Master showed us where our vessel had got to. It was eighty miles due west of Ushant. Our last sight of the *Theriault* was a big flash of flame as her fuel tank exploded and belched a great column of black smoke into the air.

The people aboard the *Hertford* were very good to us and we had a refreshing rest before arriving at Dunkirk, her first port of call. Here it was decided best for us to stay with the ship until her arrival in the United Kingdom, as we were now rated as "D.B.S." (Distressed British Seamen), and arrangements could then be made in England to repatriate the crew to Canada. On arrival at the next port, Hull, England, the steamer was met by our good friend Frank Beckett from Ballina. He had read of the *Theriault's* ordeal in the press and had rushed across Ireland and England to see if he could be of any help.

After a day in Hull we went to London to arrange with Canada House about returning home. We were billeted in a Sailors' Institute during this time, and Mr. Beckett escorted us about, seeing the sights. A week later the Canadian Government officials made arrangements to send us home and we went on to Liverpool and boarded the Canadian Pacific liner *Montclare* for Halifax. In cases like ours, where a shipwrecked crew have to get home, a British ship is required to take the men and the owners of the lost vessel are obliged to pay a shilling a man a day for such time as they stay in the transporting vessel.

On arrival in Halifax arrangements were made to pay off the crew. Here I found there was no insurance placed on the *Theriault* for her last passage, therefore I had no assets and the schooner was still in debt to some extent. The Canada Shipping Act, which regulates all matters dealing with Canadian ships and crews, states that if a crew is shipwrecked they are entitled to two months' extra wages in such a case. Fortunately, our crew were not too far back in their current wages, and after a hearing in court, during which I had to establish that I had no other assets, the crew were willing to settle for part of the account owing to them and which I was able to borrow.

And thus another Canadian schooner was scratched off the list. By this year of 1939 there were only a few left and they were mostly sold in the West Indies for trading, where they would encounter only moderate weather. I came into the game rather late in the day for the cargo schooner to survive and make money, and perhaps would have shown better judgment had I kept out of it and continued a seafaring career in steamships. But the sailing vessel had a fascination which intrigued me and I had to learn my lesson "the hard way". Nevertheless, the charm inherent in sail, in spite of the somewhat rugged manner of life aboard square-rigger or schooner, still commands my interest.

After a rest at home, I went off to sea again in steamships and while away was sent for to rejoin the army. That was in 1939, but I had committed myself to a seafaring career and did not intend to interrupt it with a military one. During World War Two I spent the whole period of the conflict in various parts of the Atlantic and Mediterranean as a ship's officer—ending up my wartime service as Chief Officer of the *Lady Rodney*, a Canadian troopship. By then I had acquired my Master's Certificate and was employed in cargo and passenger liners until 1950, when I gave up seagoing to assume a shore position in connexion with pilotage. Here, in my home area, I have been able to indulge my fondness for sailing craft by designing and building a twenty-four-foot cabin sloop in my backyard and cruising around in her during the summer months with my family and friends. Also to compile and set forth the present record of Canada's cargo-carrying fore-and-afters before their story is forgotten.

PART TWO

When the first white men came ashore in North America the forests extended to the water's edge. These included all varieties of the native virgin timber—spruce, pine and juniper, or hackmatack, as it was often called, and the hardwoods, including oak, birch, maple and beech. It was only natural that the first sailors saw the possibilities of shipbuilding at almost any place on the Canadian Atlantic coast.

". . . and so Pontgreve, whom Demonts had left at Annapolis, N.S., on the Bay of Fundy, when the promised supply ships did not arrive in time, set to work in 1606 to build the first vessels ever constructed on the North American continent. They were a barque and a shallop and were launched to carry the settlers east to Canseau or Port Royal (Cape Breton) where they might fall in with ships bound home."

From this small start thousands of ships of all sizes were built. During the latter part of the nineteenth century the Nova Scotia foreign-going merchant fleet was among the greatest in the world. From small pinks to the great *W. D. Lawrence*, 2450 tons register, the largest wooden square-rigged sailing ship ever built in Canada, thousands of schooners, brigs, barques, barquentines and full-rigged ships—almost all of them built completely of native wood—were sent afloat. The main structural parts, the stem, sternpost and keel, were usually of oak or birch, and the timbers, beams and planking of spruce and other coniferous woods. They were built in hundreds of coves over the hundreds of miles of coastline, from the big shipyards where all the workers were skilled, to an inlet on a man's farm where the farmer and his friends built a boat in the off-season to use for fishing or for taking produce to market.

Nearby, in the northern part of the United States, the seamen and builders had brought the small schooners to a high degree of perfection. Schooners with their fore-and-aft sails were generally handier for coastal work than square-rigged brigs or brigantines, as they required a smaller crew and were more easily handled. But a limit was reached in the size of a two-masted schooner. As they got larger and larger they developed faults, the worst one being the size of the mainsail. This class of vessel, when fully developed, evolved into fast, tough and efficient sailing ships as used on the Grand Banks by the fishermen of Nova Scotia and the New England States and reached perfection in the 1920's as represented by the *Bluenose, Columbia, Gertrude Thebauld* and others in international fishing schooner racing contests. But in the fishing vessels there was a crew of twenty-odd and it was nothing for this number of hands to take in or reef the huge mainsail, with a main boom up to eighty-five feet in length, on the approach of a blow. In the cargo coaster this sort of crew was out of the question, so the limit was reached in the two-master by the ratio of the size of her mainsail to the economical number of her crew. In the end, a vessel was built with a third mast and sail. This made all sails smaller and easier to handle. The first authentic tern was launched in the United States in 1849, and the first Canadian tern, *Lady Mulgrave,* was built in 1858 at Arichat, N.S. The terns, as the three-masters were usually called, and the four-masters were produced steadily throughout the next sixty years, with the peak output occurring at the end of World War One. Owing to different trades and conditions, no schooners with more than four masts were built in Canada. In comparison the United States schooner owners used five, six, and one huge seven-master, all designed especially for their coastal coal trade. The soundness of the schooner rig and their economical superiority was proved in that very few square-rigged vessels were built during the twentieth century, and the surviving terns have persisted until a very recent date.

When the three-masted schooner attained popularity among the shipping fraternity in the United States, someone got the idea that they should be given a specific name to distinguish them from the two-masted fore-and-afters, two- and three-mast topsail schooners and other variations. The name "tern schooner" was invented and applied to the three-masted fore-and-after, later simplified to the word "tern". It was a name never adopted by the British, but it was commonly used by Americans to identify the rig, and the designation "tern" is to be found in their Registries and official documents as far back as 1873.

It most certainly was not a term invented by sailors. Some college-educated shipowner or naval architect, or perhaps the schoolteacher wife or daughter of a pioneer builder, delved into the problem of devising a name for the new type. They probably discovered that the Latin word *terni*, meaning "three each", a "set of three", "a trio", "a triplet", or in poker-playing parlance "three of a kind", appropriately filled the bill. The English words "ternal", "ternary", "ternately" have a similar meaning. The name, unquestionably, was derived from the Latin term and had no connexion with the seabird of the same name.

Three-masted schooners carrying two or more square-sails on their foremasts were designated as "topsail terns" in U.S. Registries. Through our proximity to the United States, and from the fact that a large number of three-masted schooners built in Atlantic Canada were surveyed and classified by the American Bureau of Shipping, the name "tern" was understood and accepted by our shipping and seafaring fraternity, even though in Canadian Registries they were usually described as "three-masted schooners".

In the four Atlantic Provinces, Nova Scotia, New Brunswick, Prince Edward Island and Newfoundland, the vessels were built in many places. The materials were at hand and it only required skilled leadership and some ordinary hired labour to start a shipyard. In the days before 1900 there was little machinery employed. Mr. Winslow McKay, a well-known builder in Shelburne, N.S., told me that while they had circular saws, there were no bandsaws in any of the south shore yards before that date. The work was all done by hand with the assistance of a few teams of oxen to drag the heavy timbers into position for working.

The Small Shipyards

The majority of the terns constructed in Atlantic Canada were launched from numerous small shipyards adjacent to villages or minor towns, though quite a number were built in the old-established yards within, or nearby, the city of Saint John, New Brunswick. In the small shipyards scattered around the coast the prime requisites were a sheltered beach with an ample depth of water at high tide to float a sizable vessel, together with a sufficient supply of suitable timber within easy hauling distance from the yard. In the early days such timber could be cut in dense forests immediately in the rear of the building site. This fact inspired the old sailors' epithet—"Built in the woods up some Nova Scotia creek!"

The timber for a ship was cut and hauled out to a field or cleared space adjacent to the building site. Our people have always been handy with wood tools and all they needed was expert direction. A steam plant was required to run the big saw, the planers and for heat in the steam-box where planks could be "softened up" for bending. Apart from the steam plant, a few teams of horses or oxen, a blacksmith's forge and a covered floor for laying off lines, there was little else required than individual carpenter tools. It can be understood that there was not much capital tied up in equipment. In the early days it was even less. The logs were squared by broad-axe and placed over a saw pit, where two men, one on top and one below, worked a long hand-saw up and down and ripped the great square baulks into planks. The man underneath in the pit worked all day in a shower of sawdust—usually with a veil over his hat to shield his eyes. The work was hard and slow and has not been seen for the past two or three generations.

In this age of machines it is hard to remember that the old ships were literally hacked out of the forest by hand. As time went on, some of the hardest work, such as sawing, planing and boring, was taken over by mechanical power, but even so, many parts were hand made up to the last. The skills of working wood and joining it together to make a stout vessel were not easily come by and many years of hard apprenticeship were necessary before a man could qualify as a master shipwright.

In general, the men were sent to the woods in winter to cut down suitable timber for a projected vessel. It was hauled out while the snow lay deep over the woodland roads by teams of horses or oxen. Many farmers employed themselves in producing ship timber out of their wood lots in the winter months and earned many a welcome dollar by cutting out curved branches and roots—especially those of hackmatack, also known as juniper—for use as ship's knees, for which purpose this material was unexcelled. There was a steady demand for hackmatack knees, not only in Canada, but also from the building yards in the United States.

When freights were high and money could be made in ship operation, many schooners were built by small outfits of a temporary character. They would construct one or more vessels while times were good and abandon the business when a slump set in. But there were a number of shipyards permanently established which continued to build vessels year after year. These plants were well equipped, employed skilled labour, and maintained large stocks of seasoned ship timber on hand.

Building from Earliest Times

Around the shores of the Atlantic since earliest times every community had a shipyard. In most places only small vessels and boats were constructed to supply the needs of the community, for in our earlier days the sea was the main highway.

The building of the railways and the later improvement of roads and motor transport has almost completely changed the transportation system. Up to the turn of the century, travel and the carriage of goods were primarily waterborne. Even after the railroads came, much of the commerce was transported more quickly and cheaply by water, until the day of the paved road and efficient motor transport.

Down through the generations a tradition of fine shipbuilding was established as a vast number of large sailing ships went out from the small yards to engage in commerce all over the world. After the large wooden foreign-going sailing ships went into decline they were followed by the handier cargo schooners, and these vessels fought off other forms of transport and were still plying the old trades until World War Two.

The story of the evolution of the schooner, and in particular the tern, or three-masted schooner, is an involved subject and a controversial one. Sufficient to say that our first vessel of this class, a three-masted vessel with three masts of the same height topped with three topmasts of equal length, and fitted with sails of the fore-and-aft type only, appeared first in the *Lady Mulgrave*, built at Arichat, N.S. In the years that followed until the last one was launched they were slowly improved as discussion and argument preceded and followed each vessel as she was designed, built and launched in respect to her carrying capacity, her speed and her handiness.

Except for one or two large vessels built during World War One, all the schooners were designed by the shipbuilders themselves. There were no blueprints, hull lines or calculated sail plans used. The procedure was always the same in the case of a new vessel. A half-model of the hull made up of horizontally laminated wood, with the layers parallel to the waterplanes, was carved to a shape that suited the particular requirements of the projected vessel.

The carving of a half-hull model was a task not undertaken by an amateur. Many owners and masters were experienced in the employment of the schooners in various trades, and it was to their specifications that the carver worked out the dimensions of the proposed vessel. Such details as the capacity in thousands of board feet of lumber, or thousands of casks of fish; the draft, sailing qualities or any of the many other items were discussed at great length. Most of the models were made to the scale of three-eighths of an inch to the foot, but it varied. It often happened that when a new ship turned out to be successful, the same model was used again for other vessels, making alterations when necessary.

As long as ships have been built, men have argued about their qualities. The result of these discussions led to the elimination of weak points and a gradual improvement in design. When the discussions had been carried out for generations, only the best was retained.

This work does not pretend to be a manual on shipbuilding, so no great detail will be gone into regarding construction. Briefly, the half-model of a vessel was fashioned out of a block of wood made up of horizontal layers in such a way that it could be dismantled and the off-sets measured at the different waterplanes. From these measurements full-scale sections were laid off on a loft floor and full-sized moulds of the sections were put together.

During the generations of shipbuilding the proficiency and instinct acquired by the master shipbuilders were such that their personal characteristics showed up in their completed ships. A keen observer of vessels could spot details at a distance which could tell him where the ship was built and the name of her builder.

The first step for a prospective owner was to make all arrangements with a yard to build a schooner and approve a hull model. In those days there were no scale models made and tank-tested for the variable factors, such as seaworthiness, stability or resistance. Unless the design was extreme, the performance of the projected ship could be quite accurately estimated by experience.

With the exception of iron for some of the fastenings, chain plates, anchor gear, etc., everything was made of wood. Only the better later schooners had iron beam knees. All the iron work for the older vessels was completed in the yard forge. These items included anchors and chains, the bands for the masts, booms, rudder, etc., and the fastenings. In the later vessels it was more economical to obtain some of the larger items, such as anchors and windlasses, from a manufacturer, but up until the turn of the century they were made by hand in many places. The simpler windlasses were made of oak and had metal half-bearings to hold them in place.

Getting on with the Job

While the material was being accumulated, the building ways were set up, or if in an established yard, the ways were overhauled. It was most important to have a secure base on which the great weight of the completed vessel would rest and be strong enough to hold fast under the stresses of the sliding bulk at launching time. In isolated cases the failure of the ways caused damage and delays.

The keel was laid, the stem and sternpost erected. From the laying-off loft came the moulds from which the frames (or ribs) were shaped. These frames were made in sections fastened together by treenails and bolts. After being made, they were erected on top of the keel in their proper places and bolted.

It should be mentioned here that the old vessels used wood extensively in their fastenings. These wooden bolts were called "trunnels" or treenails and were made of selected juniper. Many of the integral parts of the ship and planking were held together by trunnels, the use of which was governed by the building and classification societies.

By the time the tern and four-masted schooners were being built, the details of the various parts of a vessel had been well defined by the Rules of Lloyd's, Bureau Veritas

Bow of a schooner in frame.

Courtesy of Mr. F. W. Wallace

Large schooners being framed.

Construction crew alongside MINAS QUEEN. 456 tons. Built 1915 at Parrsboro, N.S.

and the American Bureau of Shipping. The purpose of the Rules was to set a standard to which ships were constructed and thus pass reliable information to underwriters for insurance purposes. The three societies noted above issue an annual volume listing all ships, with the names of the masters and owners, the principal measurements, date and place of building and other details of her construction and class.

Many of the schooners were built to standards below that required by the societies. This meant that for insurance purposes they were not an automatic risk but had to be assessed for each voyage when insurance was involved.

A few of the better vessels had copper fastenings, but iron was considered durable enough to last out this type of ship, and galvanized iron was used in the later vessels. The higher-class schooners had bronze pintles and gudgeons for the rudder gear. Copper sheathing was commonly used by ships intended to be used in tropical waters, but for the ordinary coaster it was exceptional.

It was in the best interest of the owner if his vessel was built under the supervision of a surveyor designated by one of the classification societies. His duties were to pass on all materials for soundness and size, and to inspect the vessel at progressive stages of construction in order to report completely as to her "character". For the surveyor's services a fee of so much per ton was charged.

The rules laid down by the classification societies were evolved over a long period and completed from information provided by seamen who reported failures in design, material or fastening. Ships built from rules which were very exact in specifying accurately such particulars as the size of the keel, the timbers, deck beams, thickness of planking and deck, the number of fastenings and a thousand other details tended to standardization of ships, no matter where they were built.

A ship acquired "character" depending on the quality of her building materials and workmanship. The best wooden ships and those with the longest life expectation were constructed almost entirely of hardwoods. This tended to make them expensive and introduced other difficulties. Except for certain key parts practically all the later Canadian schooners were built of mixed woods, with spruce predominating.

Classification

Most of the better schooners were built under the supervision of the surveyors of the American Bureau of Shipping and a smaller number under the Bureau Veritas. Lloyd's had the smallest representation of all, as they did not appear to be interested in this class of ship at the time.

The ships built under supervision were given classification for a fixed number of years, depending on the materials used and the method of construction. The highest standard which the best schooners reached was 14 years A1. There were only a few of these and they were built early. In later years when they were constructed of mixed native woods, a class of 12 years A1 was considered good for these schooners. Cheaper schooners were given lower ratings.

To retain these standards it was necessary to dry-dock the vessel at regular periods and undergo an examination by a surveyor of the society concerned. He would make recommendations for repairs or renewals, which when carried out would enable the vessel to retain her class.

The General Design of the Schooners

The great majority of the schooners were built along the same general design with small alterations. Sailing ships were of two types; flush decked, which meant that the weather, or upper, deck ran unbroken from the bow to the stern, and those which had the ends of the vessel raised to make a forecastlehead deck or a poop deck aft, or both. In the United States the flush deck, often called the hurricane deck, was generally used, especially in the larger vessels. Among the Canadian schooners there were few of these, the *Sirdar* built in 1902, and the *Frieda E*, one of the last of the large schooners, are the only ones I can identify. It was found handiest to have a raised forecastlehead and a raised poop, but many of the smaller schooners employed in the salt-fish trade had a flush deck forward and a monkey poop aft. It was usual to build the cabin on the main deck and extend it vertically through the poop deck, above which it projected about three feet. The main deck was sealed off on top to prevent the entry of water. With the exception of the chain cable openings to the locker and the cargo hatches, the deck was continuous for the length and breadth of the vessel. The parts above this deck therefore were superficial to the watertight integrity of the vessel.

In the larger vessels it was necessary to put in a 'tween deck for strengthening purposes. In most cases this deck was not complete, in that it was formed of beams not planked over. Very few of the schooners were deep draft and it was only when the depth of the hold became great that it was necessary to fit the 'tween deck. The schooners were built without any watertight bulkheads. It was customary to strengthen the bows with beams and knees a short distance from the stem and fit some planking to make a partial bulkhead which formed the after section of the chain locker. As the larger vessels customarily used the bow-ports for loading timber, a permanent bulkhead was not practical.

Although oil engines had been installed in foreign sailing vessels for auxiliary purposes as early as 1908, only a few Canadian schooners were built with auxiliary power. However, some of them, including the *St. Clair Theriault* of 1919, were constructed with the possibility that an engine might be installed later. In these vessels both a stern and rudderpost were fitted, the planking butting into the sternpost and the space between the stern and rudderposts being filled with deadwood. A conventional shaft log was built into the deadwood at the stern. On conversion to auxiliary power as in the *St. Clair Theriault* it was only necessary to build an engine bed, install suitable bearings and knock out the deadwood that filled the propeller aperture.

A Vessel is Built

In the spring, with the approach of fine weather, the work proceeded and a shipbuilding site was a hive of industry. Early in the morning the men turned to their tasks. Soon would be heard the sounds of the various tools—the click of the maul, the steady clang from the forge, the ring of the caulker's mallet, the thumping beat of the adze and the working chorus of sawing, planing and cutting. There were to be seen the various gangs of men intent on their particular job, one group carrying a hot plank from the steam-box to be clamped and wedged into place, another gang overhauling chains—sheerlegs being raised—buckets of rock salt carried to be laid in the deck beam recesses. At a little distance from the hull the spars were being broad-axed from round tree to square timber, from that to tapered octagons and latterly to their final long slim form—the curls dripping from the old wood block planes—and above, through and everywhere came the smell of freshly cut and planed lumber.

The Launching

As the time neared, the launching ways were made ready. The piles had been fairly driven to carry the great weight of the sliding ship. The tides had to be watched for the Springs, when the height of water would be greatest. The work went on quickly as the rigging was completed and the sails bent, for many of these vessels were launched virtually ready for sea. It was usually planned to start the vessel in the Spring and take advantage of the good weather, but this was not always the case. The time taken to build, outfit and launch a moderate-sized vessel varied greatly. In the case of the *Peaceland*, of 262 tons net, one of the last vessels built at Annapolis Royal, in the year 1919, the time taken was 146 days, and this was considered very good.

The date was set for the launching and the last days before this were always exciting and bustling. To have everything ready on time was the aim of all hands and nobody could delay the ship, lose a high tide or let the yard down thereby.

Launching day was a great event and a memorable occasion for many people. The master and mate of the new vessel were there to take over. Often the master had a share in the ship and he was very careful to check over all the details of her construction and gear. The owners were glad to see the result of their effort so near completion and hoped for a quick return on their investment. The relatives of the workmen, who for months had heard little else from the breadwinner except talk of the building schooner, were all ready to come. In the small localities, where those living near had an interest in the ship, it was the custom to suspend business, including school, if it was the season. It was just as well to declare a holiday, as all the boys would be there in any case.

The schooner would be gay with flags. From her main truck flew the large pennant with her name in big letters. The gang aboard who would go down the ways with her were all ready, the stages removed from the sides and the grease spread on the ways to keep her sliding along. The tense moment was approaching. The shores were knocked out. A large gang on both sides of the keel were striking away steadily to raise her up. At last she was ready and the foreman took a final look around, then gave the order to knock out the dog-shores. At this moment she was hurriedly christened, as majestically she quivered and slowly moved away. Those watching stood up and a great cheer burst forth as her stern took the water, plowed down as she rushed along, then rose happily as her bow floated and she was fully waterborne. Everybody smiled at his neighbour and exclaimed how handsome she looked.

It was not always so. Sometimes the worst fears of the men in charge would come true and she would stick on the ways. Even worse, the ways would spread and there would be a terrible moment while the vessel trembled before either falling over or just remaining there with her keel dug into the ground.

Fortunately these happenings were rare. So much was at stake that nothing was left to chance and the most expert advice was always obtained before the launch was attempted. In addition, there was the insurance to consider. While lying on the stocks under construction the vessel was insured against land hazards, and when waterborne her marine insurance was in effect. But for the interval between—the actual time of the launching—there was no insurance.

As a vessel was launched nearly ready for sea, she was soon off on her first voyage and the great gamble started as to whether or not she would soon be lost, or earn back the money that had gone into her and continue to pay dividends until the end of her days.

How the Life of a Schooner Terminated

The majority of the schooners met with what may be described as a "violent end" and very few "died in bed of old age". Stranding on rocks and shoals wrecked many; destruction by fire accounted for quite a few. But heavy weather at sea, with the loss of sails, rudders and spars, the opening of hulls or staving in of hatches, and many disablements that officers and crew were unable to overcome, was responsible for the loss of innumerable Canadian schooners. Many of them vanished utterly under such mishaps, but a considerable number of our schooner losses were classified under the heading of "Abandoned at Sea". It was some consolation to learn that under such a classification was often appended, "crew saved by a passing ship". The crew might have been saved, but an epic story could be written of nearly all such episodes which led to the abandonment of the vessel. For very few vessels were abandoned without a serious cause.

Many were sold to colonial and foreign buyers and passed from our knowledge. But only a few lived to a good old age to end their careers as derelict hulls on a Canadian beach.

Small Crews

The crews of the schooners were kept to a minimum. As a small crew bill was one of the main reasons why they survived, six or seven men manned the three-masters and often only five. In winter time especially, the crew were kept on the jump pumping ship, making repairs, taking in and setting sail as necessary to ensure a safe speedy passage. The four hours on and four hours off with a dog-watch, was universal. Field days, as we termed them, especially on the homeward voyages, were usual, and this arrangement called for work on deck throughout the day with no time out for the watch below, for the vessel was expected to arrive home clean and sparkling. Good masters strove to make the sail-handling work coincide with eight bells, the time of the change of the watch, when all hands were out.

To enlarge on this subject, the crew were divided into two watches, one for the master, and one for the mate. In the master's watch was an extra man, called the bosun, or second mate, who was capable of taking charge of the deck while the master was below. The mate, of course, took charge of the deck during his own watch. At midnight one watch took the deck until 4 a.m. At this time they were relieved by the other until 8 a.m.—and so on throughout the day. The monotony was broken by the dogwatch, which from 4 p.m. to 6 p.m. was taken by the watch on turn and from 6 p.m. to 8 p.m. by the other. This arrangement created a break in that the watches took turns in having one four-hour watch out one night and two four-hour watches out the following night.

Decline of the Big Ships in Foreign Trade

In the great days of Maritime Provinces' shipping, our vessels went all over the globe. Yarmouth, Nova Scotia, as a registry port, was able to claim fourth place among the large shipping ports of the world. From the Bay of Fundy went a procession of stately square-riggers carrying away our timber cargoes and thence to tramp all the oceans and trade lanes until the end of their days. In the 1860's, '70's and '80's, great square-rigged ships and barques were modelled, built, sailed and owned by men of the locality. Thousands of tons were added yearly to Canada's merchant marine.

The business of building ships on speculation for sale abroad, such as was carried out along the St. Lawrence River and Gulf, where thousands of square-rigged ships were launched, loaded with timber and sent to the United Kingdom to be sold complete with cargo at the best price obtainable, was not undertaken as a general practice in Atlantic Canada. Many of our builders kept their staffs busy during slack times building vessels which they operated themselves until a suitable buyer came along.

From time to time, however, vessels were built on order from firms abroad and in World War One many such vessels, but fore-and-afters then, were built and delivered.

During the great period mentioned above freighting was very remunerative for the vessels in foreign trade. In this period it has been estimated that in one of the counties bordering the Bay of Fundy, one million dollars was sent home as crew pay and profit in a single year: surely a very large sum in those days.

The reasons for the decline of this great industry are many. Steam vessels were being developed and as they became more dependable and regular in their passages they took the cream of the freights. Coaling stations being established at convenient places and the opening of the Suez Canal were contributing factors. Perhaps the greatest blow was the use of iron for the construction of sailing ships in other countries, a lead which we did not follow in Canada. The iron sailing ships were greatly superior to those constructed of wood. They were vastly stronger, had no leaky seams or worm-eaten wood to contend with and, due to their construction, could stow a much larger cargo than a wooden ship of comparable size. While they were better than the wooden ships, many were lost through faults and peculiarities which developed in this type of craft.

Our foreign-going sailing ships disappeared, but there was still a big opportunity for the smaller sailing vessels. Our country had a small foreign trade of its own. We had three main items of export in Atlantic Canada—gypsum, lumber products and processed fish. At periods coal was exported. These exports are still among our most important. The gypsum industry developed the largest type of schooner, and the first one, the *Uruguay*, a four-master of 726 tons net, was built at Windsor, N.S., in 1889 and was followed by a fleet of these schooners.

Our coastal trade with the United States has been carried on for a long time. Lumber has always been exported to the New England States. Hard coal was brought back from New York and other ports and at times coal from the Cape Breton mines was sold there.

Timber and salt fish went to the West Indies and South America. It was found convenient to deliver these cargoes in small ships, as a whole shipment for one of them could be collected in one outport, and the buyers down south did not want large bulk cargoes in one shipment for various reasons. On return voyages the ships carried salt from the West Indies Caicos group for curing fish back home, or molasses from Barbados for domestic consumption.

Owing to restrictions placed on foreign shipping by the United States government from earliest times, our ships have never been permitted to carry cargoes from one port to another in that country. However, they could and did engage in trade, either bringing cargoes into the United States or taking them out. A trade that kept many of our vessels busy over a long period was the hard-pine transport from the Southern States to the West Indies and other countries. This item will be gone into later in this work.

Up until the time of the motor truck and the system of improved highways was developed, these provinces depended almost entirely on waterborne trade. Around our coasts were thousands of all types of small sailing craft engaged in transporting all types of cargoes. These small coasters were not affected by the decline of the great foreign-going fleet.

Comparisons of Rig

Our older merchants and sailors preferred the square rig. For small vessels trading off-shore the brig was the best. These two-masted vessels, square-rigged on both masts, were handy and efficient, but as competition developed it was found that the crew required was too large and the brigantine was evolved. The brigantine, which carried square sails on the foremast only, and fore-and-aft sails on the main, could be sailed with fewer men, and it gradually displaced the brig. Larger ships of this type, having three or four masts, with square-rig on the foremast only, and fore-and-aft sails on the other masts, were called barquentines. Over a long period of time both types were displaced by the larger schooners which carried all sails rigged fore-and-aft and which could get along with a still smaller crew.

Around the coast the cargoes were carried in the smaller classes of vessels. In the offshore trades the brig, brigantine and barquentine held on until displaced by the schooner. While our seamen clung to the square-rig for offshore voyages, the Americans were developing the fore-and-aft rig to a high degree.

The reasons for preferring the square-rig for offshore passages may briefly be given as follows. For running off before the wind the square sails were much superior, as the resolving forces of the wind on the sail were directly transmitted to the hull through the masts and the ship was easy to steer. In a fore-and-aft vessel the sails had to swing outboard and were held in place by the sheets. To prevent them from swinging inboard the booms were held in place by boom-tackles. Under these conditions the forces propelling the vessel were not as direct or efficient as in square-rig and, running before the wind, the steering was more difficult. In bad weather the difference was more marked. In the square-rig vessels the first sails taken off on the approach of bad weather were the light upper sails, followed by the lower courses. The upper and lower topsails were the sails left on for the longest time and were reefed as the weather got worse. This left the ship with a high center of effort and the effect of the sails being blanketed by the vessel dropping into a trough was small. On the other hand, in a schooner, the sequence was to take off the topsails, jibs and spanker as the wind increased. As conditions deteriorated, the remaining sails were reefed and this brought the center of effort near the deck. In the troughs these sails became slack as they were blanketed from the wind. On rising to the crest, the wind filled them suddenly and placed a heavy strain on the gear.

However, the square-rigged vessels could not sail as close to the wind as a schooner. In other words, when the wind was right ahead, the schooner could make better progress against it than the square-rigger, for the reason that her sails could be trimmed in flat, in a fore-and-aft line.

In the last days of the big United States coastal coal schooners, after they had reached their largest size, some of them attempted to compete in foreign trade. They were developed for the domestic coal trade and their gear was exceptionally strong. It was thought they might do well in offshore trade after they had been displaced in their own trade by steam colliers. The vessels could handle large bulk cargoes and because all their heavy gear was managed by machinery, only a small crew was required. But it was proved that the beating given the ships by heavy gales, and by slatting in calms, was too great to be economical.

Alternative Designs for Different Trades

Nearly all the larger vessels intended for the lumber trade were fitted with bow ports to facilitate loading long pieces of timber. These ports, situated just below the hawse pipes, were about three feet square and were provided with clamp fastenings so they could easily be taken out and replaced as required. On being put back into place the boundary seam was caulked over with oakum. For the schooners intended for lumber and coal cargoes it was usual to have a short poop-deck, generally extending from the mizzen to right aft in order to leave the main deck as clear as possible for the stowage of lumber or other wood cargoes. But in many of the craft, the poop-deck was extended forward to nearly the mainmast in order to accommodate under-deck cargo, such as processed fish or molasses. This latter class had movable ports fitted in the forward bulkhead for stowing long pieces of lumber in the poop-deck space. It was known as a "Brazilian poop".

These ports were quite small, about six inches by eighteen. One was fitted on each side near the top of the bulkhead and the long planks were pushed in.

Man-power and Deck Engines

In the earlier days the sailors had few mechanical aids outside of the simple capstan, windlass and the ordinary block and tackle. Man-power was cheap and all hauling such as heaving in the anchor, hoisting sails and pumping the ship were done in the age-old ways. The Americans first introduced steam-power in the large-class schooners and this enabled the small crew to handle the heavy anchors and sail gear with ease. It also enabled the designers to use heavier equipment. The large class of gypsum schooners built in Canada in the 1890's followed this lead, but it was many years later that it became practical to install power in the smaller vessels. Time had to pass before the "one-lung" gasolene donkey-engine could be made reliable and produced at an economical price. Right up to the last days of sail many of the smaller vessels had no power of any kind.

Handling cargo was another use that deck engines were later put to. Lumber carriers passed the cargo in and out by hand, but they were equipped with small hand winches, usually fitted on top of the forward house, for heavier classes of cargo, such as molasses, salt or coal. As most of the ports used by the schooners were operated on a small scale, hardly any of the places were fitted with cranes or grabs and the cargoes were handled with the ship's gear. Where a cargo was to be discharged from a vessel without a deck engine, a horse was frequently employed as the hauling power and was harnessed to a burten or tackles to lift the puncheons or tubs from the hold to the dock.

Times change quickly, more so than we realize. Some of the tern schooners produced during the last days of building had no power put aboard. It is forgotten how simple the economy was, and how it was cheaper to hire a man than buy an engine. In later years, when the use of a donkey-engine became more economical, it was customary to add the engine to help out with the sail gear, the anchors and cargo work.

Hand Pullers

As time went on and more of the vessels became equipped with donkey-engines, the poorer schooners became known as "hand pullers" and were shunned by all sailors except the down-and-out. These unfortunates, not being able to locate a soft berth on a modern vessel, were forced to go into the old ones. This did not apply to the Newfoundland schooners, aboard which deck engines were not fitted until long after the better type of Nova Scotia craft.

Steering Gear

Many types of steering gear were used to turn the rudder. The simplest were merely a wheel and drum over which a few turns of rope were led by fairleads to the tiller. Most of the later vessels were fitted with a simple rugged spindle which had a pair of opposing threads screwed through a double yoke made fast to the rudder head. This was an effective, positive and flexible system and seldom gave trouble.

Masters and Crews

During the era of the schooners, the master-crew relationship was old style. There was no Seamen's Union to contend with and the master's word was law. There were exceptions when the will of the master was overcome, but in general the master picked his own men and fired them when they did not come up to his expectations.

As in all the old ships, the treatment, victualling and accommodation varied greatly. Most of the schooners were happy ships with a master and mate who looked after the young crew members. The food was good, although monotonous, especially if compared with the days when refrigeration became commonplace. Accommodation was very simple, merely a forecastle containing a table, bunks and benches. The crew invariably had to supply their own mattresses and blankets. During cold weather a stove was kept going for warmth. In most of the schooners the galley was adjacent to the forecastle. The crew washed their own dishes and kept the forecastle clean.

There were a few hard-case masters through the years who became well known for their tough ways. The old tricks of making life so miserable for the seamen that they preferred to desert and leave their uncollected pay behind rather than serve out the time specified by the Articles were still practised. Scrimping on food was a favorite device for disheartening the crew, as was unnecessary sail drill. The pay left behind by these unfortunates found its way into the pocket of the master, and many, through these means, were able to accumulate sizable funds and thus retired early to spend their declining days in ease.

Living Arrangements

The great majority of the schooners had their galleys forward and the prepared meals were passed into the forecastle for the crew and carried aft to the cabin for the master and mates. The food was carried in a "dog box" or basket and in bad weather the cook had to scramble along the deck of the wildly pitching and rolling schooner as best he could. A deck load provided additional hazards. Many a meal was lost in transit, or at best arrived aft cold and liberally soaked in salt water. In addition to cooking, serving the meals and looking after the cabins aft, the cook was charged with the responsibility of lighting and placing the lanterns in the port and starboard side lights each evening. At daylight he took them out and cleaned them.

Some of the small terns, especially those in the fish trade, were laid out like the bank fishermen. Those vessels had a forecastle forward under the main deck. Access was by means of a companionway and the cooking was done in the after part with the bunks extending forward. The master and mates had bunks in the small quarters aft in the cabin and came forward for their meals. There were variations in the routine, depending on individual masters.

Many of the schooners had fine cabins fitted out with paneled hardwood and decorated in the style of fashionable quarters ashore. A large coal stove provided heat for the whole space, which consisted of the saloon for sitting around and for officers' meals, rooms for master, mates and cook, a bathroom of sorts, and a pantry containing the smaller items of the ship's stores and usually provided with a sink for cleaning up. In large vessels the masters often took their wives and families on voyages and the influence of the ladies was often seen in the decorations. These cabins were laid out very much like our small modern apartments and everything was kept spick and span.

This class of vessel which followed the large foreign-going square-rigged ships carried on the tradition for smartness which had been set by the great fleet. Spotless sail-covers, bright paint and varnish work, decorations on hatch covers, water breakers, etc., were done in a painstaking manner which identified these schooners in all the ports they visited.

Anchors and Windlasses

A few of the vessels turned out at the end of the period were fitted with patent stockless anchors, but the great majority had the wooden-stock type. The great difference between the two was the ease in stowing the patent anchor, which was hauled up into the hawse pipe until the flukes fetched up against metal pads placed there for that purpose. The old stock anchors had to be lifted from their hove-up position below the hawse pipe with a purchase, called the "anchor burten", to the cathead and secured there. The better classes of vessels had a full complement composed of two bower anchors, a spare, a stream anchor and a kedge.

There were two classes of windlass, those in the higher class which had the conventional wildcats (or gypsies) with engaging gear and brakes, and the old primitive type which was simply a horizontal hardwood shaft with two or three turns of the chain cable around it. The shaft was rotated by means of ratchets actuated by long bars. In the larger vessels, where the crew was small in proportion to the size of the ship, it was necessary to have mechanical power to handle the heavy ground tackle, but in the smaller schooners, where the anchors and chains were much lighter, it was practical to have a very simple device.

To go into too much detail on this item is not intended here, but the usual mechanical installation to handle the anchors, raise the sails, warp the vessel and work the cargo was carried out by connecting a large gasolene donkey-engine with a system of sprockets and chains to a central shaft which ran through the forward house athwartships and was fitted with a winch-head on each side. These winch-heads were used for warping and also for raising the sails when the throat halyards were taken to one side and the peak halyards to the other. The shaft was actuated by a clutch, which was controlled by a long rod which also ran from side to side and could be operated by the man using the winch-head. This same shaft had a sprocket and chain which could be engaged to operate the windlass. In addition, another sprocket and chain was often used to run a cargo winch generally set up on top of the forward house. Finally, the shaft was usually fitted with an eccentric and strap which operated a large bilge pump. This equipment was simple, rugged and efficient and performed all the tasks requiring power aboard the schooners.

All the larger vessels were also fitted with a mechanical capstan operated by man-power. This was generally a geared type turned by hand spikes and supplemented the equipment noted above. It was installed well forward. The best class of capstan had a double gear. For light hauls the capstan was turned in one direction; for heavy pulls it was turned in the opposite way in double gear.

The Sails

All the sails of a schooner were fitted in a fore-and-aft line. In the three-masted vessels the largest sails, starting at the foremast, were the fore, main and mizzen. In a four-master the aft sail was called the spanker. These sails were fastened to their respective masts with hoops and laced with rope to their booms and gaffs. As the masts were equidistant, the sails were interchangeable, except the after sail, which was the largest.

The first sail forward of the foremast was called the forestaysail, although in later years it was commonly known as the jumbo, a term borrowed from the same sail in a two-masted Bank fisherman. The forestaysail was always rigged on a boom. The next sail forward was the inner jib, the next, the outer jib, and finally the flying jib. Many vessels had an additional headsail, called the balloon jib, for fair weather only, secured to the outer stay with snap hooks and always taken off when the wind freshened.

Each of the large sails mentioned first was topped with a gaff topsail. These so-called light sails were made fast to the topmast with hoops, and set with halyards and sheets. Gaff topsails, except in the case of the aft sail, provided a problem in handling that was never completely overcome in that the foot of the sail and the sheets had to be passed over the spring-stay each time the vessel was tacked. There were different systems rigged for raising the foot of the sail over the stay so that it could be sheeted home without the crew going aloft.

Smaller sails, the mastheadstaysails, were fitted between the topmasts. As these sails did not customarily pass below the spring-stay there was no difficulty with the sheets. Many of the schooners were fitted with large mastheadstaysails which came half-way down to the deck. These were fair-weather sails only and were not set unless the vessel was on one tack for a considerable time. If the schooner was tacked it was necessary to lower them to the deck and later raise them on the other side.

Many of the smaller schooners were outfitted with a small storm trisail which was bent on when the mizzen was furled and helped to keep the ship's head to the sea during severe weather.

Variations of Rig

In earlier days many experiments were tried to improve the general sail plan of the schooners. Yards were fitted on the fore or main to carry a large square sail to assist when running off with a fair wind. Some of them had yards on the foretopmast as well and these were known as topsail schooners. In the end all such innovations were abandoned, as they were more trouble than they were worth.

The sails classed as light sails, which included the jibs, topsails and mizzen, were made of light-weight canvas. The remainder, the forestaysail, the fore, main and trisail were made from the strongest canvas available, as they were the sails the ships depended on when the wind was heavy.

Rigging and Gear

The rigging of a schooner was simple compared with the square-rigged ships. Heavy shrouds to the mastheads were fastened to the chain plates in earlier days by lanyard and dead-eyes and later by turnbuckles or shroud-screws; topmast stays and swifters, and the head and jibstays. The spring-stay ran from forward to aft at the mastheads and the jib-boom was held in place by the conventional chain stays, gammoning, martingale stays and braces. The jib-boom and the after end of the spanker boom were fitted with foot-ropes for handling the sails.

In the smaller vessels, particularly the Newfoundland fish traders, a spike bowsprit was used. This single spar was butted against the windlass pawl-post, made fast to the stem-head by the gammoning. This rigid spar did not require a martingale but was stayed directly to the stem by a chain or chains. It was braced similarly to a fishing schooner and was rigged with foot-ropes and ratlins.

The running gear was completed by halyards, sheets, downhauls, topping lifts, jigs and boom-tackles.

The principal sails of a schooner were fitted to the masts with hoops and to the booms and gaffs with rope. Setting these lower sails was accomplished by raising the gaffs with the throat and peak halyards. The size of these purchases depended on the weight of the sails and gear, but usually a set of double blocks on each was sufficient for the fore and main, and triples for the mizzen, in a moderately sized tern.

The booms and gaffs were fitted with jaws which spanned the masts. The heavy booms were kept in position by means of sheets and topping lifts, both made fast to a band and fitting called the bail-iron and secured to the after end of the booms. The topping lift was doubled, one to a side, the lee lift being slacked off when under way. The sheets were very heavy, usually a double or triple purchase, terminating in the traveller, which was very strongly secured to the ship's structure. In the larger vessels a device—a sheet jiber—was used to lessen the shock of jibing over or easing the strain when slatting. To prevent the booms from swinging inboard during periods of calms and slatting, a boom-tackle was used.

The large sails had the hauling parts of the throat and peak halyards led through fixed lead blocks set in the deck. A messenger was hooked into the end of the halyard and taken to the winch-head at the forward house, one to a side. The engine hoisted the gaff and sail into position when the halyards were stopped-off and secured to the pin rail. The other end of the halyard, the standing part, was made fast to a jig which was a small purchase made fast to the rail. When the sails slacked down, a couple of men could go around and sway them up again with the jigs. The sheets were usually hauled by hand, easing the ship up if necessary, but on occasion they were taken to the winch-head.

The lighter sails were set by hand, as it was no great chore and they were only used in moderate or light weather in any case.

Lifeboats

Because the swinging booms and sails of the schooner required a clear deck, the lifeboat was generally carried on a set of davits rigged across the stern. This was not a perfect arrangement, as the rolling of the vessel made it difficult to secure the boat. The davits were braced against these strains by iron stays and the boat was frapped securely against the taff-rail. Many of these boats were equipped with gasolene engines and, being heavier, required extra attention. Usually a smaller boat was carried as well, but the second boat was stowed in a variety of places, often bottom-up across a hatch or in any convenient place.

SAIL PLAN OF A TERN SCHOONER

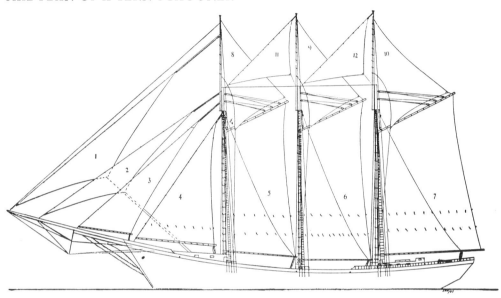

1. Flying jib.	5. Foresail.	9. Main gaff topsail.
2. Outer Jib.	6. Mainsail.	10. Mizzen gaff topsail.
3. Inner jib.	7. Mizzen or spanker.	11. Main masthead staysail.
4. Fore staysail (jumbo).	8. Fore gaff topsail.	12. Mizzen Masthead staysail.

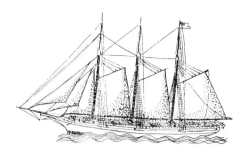

PART THREE

The Early Schooners

The first Canadian-recorded tern schooner I have been able to locate was the *Bonito* of 95 tons, owned in Yarmouth, N.S., in 1857, by Nelson Hammond. There is no clue as to her dimensions or builder. The next three-master was the *Lady Mulgrave* of 108 tons net built at Arichat, Cape Breton, for Hypolite Marmaud in 1858. This vessel is the only tern I have determined as having a figurehead. In 1867 she was sold to T. N. Mallory of St. John's, Nfld., but no St. John's entry could be found so she passes out of the record. The next three-master is well documented. The *Zebra* of 143 tons net was built at La Have, N.S., in 1859 and was owned by Henry Smith and others. In the 1870's she passed to S. Rothenhizer and was engaged in trading to the United States, the West Indies and Newfoundland. Later she was sold to Newfoundland owners and was in the coal trade out of North Sydney. In May, 1889, she was posted as lost while owned by J. Bartlett.

A number of vessels were built in the next sixty years with different rigs and were subsequently altered to tern schooners. Also some were first launched as terns and later altered. At times it has been confusing to keep the record straight, but where possible I have included these details.

After the *Zebra*, the next tern was built at Canning, Queen's County, New Brunswick, in 1865. She was the *A. F. Randolph* of 155 tons net and was owned by W. C. Warren of Digby, N.S. In February, 1880, this small vessel was wrecked on the Fingers, on the coast of North Carolina.

The next three-master was the *McPherson* of 271 tons net, built by McPherson of Halifax in 1868. This vessel soon passed to Danish owners and had the following renames, *Alfhild* and *Bothnia*. Her dimensions are noteworthy, as they resemble very closely those of vessels built in the last era of these craft, viz. the early 1920's. These details can be seen in the appendix.

During the next decade, from 1870 to 1880, the rate of building was accelerated. Seamen have always been very conservative in regard to change in design and in adopting this new rig our old sailors and merchants took their time.

In Prince Edward Island during this decade six tern schooners were built and sold

64

abroad. Three of these were built to the account of S. Hoskins & Co. of Swansea Wales. The vessels were the *Bride* of 443 tons net, built in 1873 and abandoned off Cape Horn on May 1st, 1882, while on a voyage from Swansea to Valparaiso with coal, the crew being taken off. The *Bridegroom* of 498 tons net, built in 1874, was abandoned on fire at sea when three months out on a voyage from Garston, England, to Valparaiso, on September 3rd, 1884. The third was the *Bridesmaid* of 484 tons net launched the same year. Hoskins & Co. sold her in Norway after converting the schooner to a barquentine. She was renamed *Flora* and was posted missing since November, 1902. Judging from the passages on which the first two of these vessels were engaged when lost, it is assumed that they were employed in the coal and copper-ore trade between Wales and Chile. The little vessels which made up this particular fleet were very strongly built and specially fitted to transport the heavy ore cargoes around the stormy Horn. Lubbock, in his book *Last of the Windjammers*, mentions the fact that several of the "Swansea copper-ore-men" were built in Prince Edward Island. In the same year, 1874, the *Albert T. Young* of 271 tons net was built by Young, but soon after was sold to Norwegian owners and renamed *Heistad*. At Georgetown, on the eastern end of the island, the *Devenport* of 291 tons net was launched in 1878 and was sold to owners in New Zealand. About 1890 this schooner was rerigged as a barque. In the same year the *Gordon* of 350 tons net was built at Bideford and sold to Swansea, where this type of vessel was popular. She was later sold to the Norwegians and had the following renames: *Push*, *Efeu* and *Potengy*. The vessels produced in Prince Edward Island during this era were well built and strong and gave long service.

During the same decade, 1870–80, more three-masted schooners were built in New Brunswick. In 1870 John Whelpley, builder and merchant of Saint John, built the *Annie Bayard* of 205 tons gross. This small schooner was lost on Bilbao Bar, Spain, in February, 1873, while on a passage from New York with a cargo of case oil.

Scammel Bros

Scammel Bros. built three terns at Saint John during this period. The firm was well known as an operator of large sailing ships. Their first schooner was the *Fred E. Scammel* of 234 tons net, launched in 1871 for E. D. Jewett and others. She became a total loss at Beaver Harbour, N.B., on January 3rd, 1876. The *Lothair* was their second tern; she was smaller, being of 195 tons net, and was destined to have a short life, as on September 4th, 1873, she was lost on a passage from Maracaibo, Venezuela, to New York. The third vessel, *Charles E. Scammel* of 254 tons net, suffered a similar fate and was lost near Tenedo, Brazil, on April 14th, 1883.

Other Terns Built in New Brunswick, 1870–80

The *Lizzie R* of 210 tons net was built at Hopewell Cape for John R. Russel & Co. in 1872. She was in the coal trade between Cape Breton ports and New York, and while on a passage from the latter, in ballast, disappeared with all hands, and has not been heard from since August 9th, 1873. The *Moss Glen* of 198 tons net, built at Saint John in 1873 for E. D. Jewett and others, was abandoned at sea on October 16th, 1878, about forty-five miles southeast of Cape Cod and three of her crew were lost. In the same year, 1873, the *Morning Dew* of 279 tons net was also built at Saint John for her owner-master. Three other terns were built in 1873, the *Herbert J. Olive* of 315 tons net at Saint John for G. F. Harding & Co., T. B. Jones, master. Later she was registered as a brigantine in the name of H. J. Olive and the master's name was Stewart. The *Aldytha* of 231 tons net was built at Kingston, N.B., for D. V. Roberts, later owned by W. G. Beagle, and was wrecked in October, 1885, but I do not have the locality. The *Freddie C. Ebbett* of 259 tons net was built at Black River, N.B., for J. W. Penny; Captain Wm. Veal, master. The final vessel noted for this era is the *Christina*, 365 tons net, built at St. Andrews, N.B., in 1874, for G. F. Stickney and others. Two or three years later this schooner was rerigged as a barquentine and considerable alterations were made in her structure. At that time she was owned by John Watson.

The preceding schooners were built to the high standard set up by the New Brunswick shipbuilders and lived out the full life of the wooden ships of the era.

Nova Scotian Schooners

In Nova Scotia the new rig was being adopted. At Shelburne, Captain B. P. King had two terns built, the *B. P. King* of 133 tons net and the *Spring* of 150 tons net, both launched in 1870. In 1872 the *Experiment* of 228 tons net was built for C. Spenser with Captain J. Tucker as master. Even the nature of the name given the latter vessel gives an idea of the risk these builders and owners imagined that they took with the new rig.

Along the coast at Yarmouth, the home of hundreds of large square-rigged vessels, the large fore-and-aft schooner was breaking in, although they never became a popular type with the shipowners of this port. The *Austin* of 320 tons net was launched for Churchill and Davis in 1873 and first commanded by Captain D. A. Saunders. However, she did not come up to expectations and about 1875 was altered extensively and rerigged as a barquentine. After these alterations she was commanded by Captain James M. Davis and apparently did well until she sailed on a voyage from Laguna, Mexico, for Le Havre, France, on August 10th, 1879, with a cargo of mahogany logs. She put into Key West, Florida, on September 29th, leaking and with three feet of water in the hold and the foremast sprung as a result of being ashore on the Mexican coast. She was subsequently condemned and sold. Owned by the master, she was insured for a total of $11,000 in Yarmouth and Halifax.

The only other tern schooner built in Nova Scotia during this decade was the *J. E. Pettis* of 150 tons net, launched in 1879 at Parrsboro and named after the well-known builder. She was the first of several hundred large fore-and-afters constructed in the locality and was sold to foreigners at New York in 1888, renamed *Christina* and later registered at Vera Cruz, Mexico.

Increased Rate of Building in the Decade 1880-90

After 1880 the number of terns built increased annually. It should be remembered that many vessels of other rigs were being produced in many places at the same time. All our transportation at this period depended on shipping and there were hundreds of vessels

WALTER HOLLY. 273 tons. Built 1888 at Gardiner's Creek, N.B.   *Courtesy of the New Brunswick Museum*

GYPSUM EMPEROR. 695 tons. Built 1892 at Parrsboro, N.S.   *Courtesy of the Mariners Museum*

GYPSUM EMPEROR. 695 tons. Under repair while engaged as a sailing barge.
Courtesy of the Mariners Museum

PREFERENCE. 243 tons. Built 1893 at Canning, N.S.

Courtesy of the Nova Scotia Archives

operating or under construction around the shores of the Atlantic. But the growing importance of rig was being realized as more shipowners converted to fore-and-aft sail. There was a saving in building costs alone where a fore-and-aft rigged mast cost only half as much as a conventional square-rigged mast. Mentioned elsewhere was the great economy in man-power. A general rule for manning a fore-and-aft schooner was roughly gauged by the number of masts. For the vessel, two men for each mast, plus one or two, as compared with twice as many in a comparable square-rigged vessel.

In this decade of 1880–90, Prince Edward Island produced very few vessels and almost disappeared as a builder of tern schooners, while New Brunswick was surpassed as a builder by Nova Scotia for the first time. Newfoundland was not to build any for many years to come.

Many Nova Scotians had been to sea in the square-rigged ships that were being slowly driven from the oceans from the early seventies onward. A great labour pool was created and shipowners took advantage of the situation to build up fleets of smaller cheaper vessels with smaller crews required and thus were able to compete in the coastal trades all along the American coast, the West Indies and South America. The basic exports of lumber, coal, cured fish and gypsum were well adapted to this class of transport and new ships were built to carry them. In this decade of 1880–90 a total of fifty-six three- and four-masted schooners were launched.

Prince Edward Island Schooners, 1880–90

Prince Edward Island contributed only two tern schooners in the above period. The *Harry*, a large tern of 525 tons net, was launched in 1881. She later went under the French flag. The other vessel was the *Severn* of 398 tons net and was built at Egmont Bay in 1884. After sale to Norway she was renamed *Severa*.

Schooners built in New Brunswick between 1880 and 1890

Twenty-three tern schooners were launched in New Brunswick in this decade. Most of them were built in the old-established yards around Saint John. Farther up the Bay others were built and they will be considered first. At Dorchester, in 1881, the *P. J. Palmer*, a large tern of 415 tons net, was launched for her namesake. After sale to English owners her rig was altered to a barque, her name was changed to *J. S. Sterry* and she was registered at Lowestoft. She was a sturdy vessel and remained in operation until after World War One. The *Clara J. Wilbur* of 197 tons net was also built here in 1883 by T. B. Wilbur and was later owned by Driscoll Bros. She was condemned as unfit in 1894. Three terns were built at nearby Hopewell, N.B., the first being the *Carlotta* of 244 tons net, launched in 1882. She had several owners, including G. F. Baird, J. Cook and H. R. McLean. This vessel was lost under the following circumstances. During the night of December 30th, 1897, the *Carlotta*, of Saint John, N.B., Captain Gale, was anchored near the Horseshoe Shoal on Nantucket Shoals while on a passage from Saint John to New York with a lumber cargo. In the heavy wind and swell the *Carlotta* parted her anchor cables and drove on Tuckernuck Shoal. Next day the Tuckernuck life-saving crew attempted to reach her, but owing to the severity of the gale were unable to get alongside, so went to Maddaket and sent word to the town to have a tug notified. The U.S. Revenue Cutter *Dexter* came from Edgartown the following morning(January 1st), but was unable to get within one half-mile of the stranded schooner on account of her greater draft. However, she sent in her surfboat and took off the crew. Owing to the shallow water none of the wrecking tugs could reach the vessel, but a crew was later put aboard and they jettisoned the cargo and after several attempts succeeded in hauling her off on January 3rd, 1898, and towed the schooner to Vineyard Haven. She must have been abandoned and sold at this time, as she does not appear again in the records.

In the same year, 1882, the *Magellan* of 226 tons net was built at Hopewell by Dowling and was in the usual trades until December 20th, 1892, when she was wrecked at Cape Charles, Va., while on a voyage from Newport News to Halifax with coal. The third vessel built at Hopewell was the *Harry W. Lewis* of 279 tons net, launched in 1889 for Wm. McLaughlin. She had several later owners, including F. W. Sumner and H. Elderkin & Co. The schooner was wrecked on Little Inagua Island in the Bahamas on February 11th, 1919, while on a voyage from Gulfport to Haiti with lumber.

Another tern built in 1889 was the *Beatrice McLean* of 249 tons net, launched at Chipman, N.B., by Hugh McLean for G. F. Baird. On a voyage from Mobile, Ala., to Santo Domingo City, she ran ashore at S.W. Reef, Tortugas, Fla., and was a total loss, being condemned after a survey held in December, 1895.

The Saint John Vessels of the Period

A vessel built near Saint John at this time was the *St. John* of 248 tons net and known as an unlucky ship. From the *Standard* of Saint John of December 9th, 1916, the following is quoted: "This City was accorded the honour of having a namesake in the schooner fleet, when in 1881 the *St. John* was put over the ways at the yard of Richard Titus in Rothesay. Charles A. Palmer and others of Saint John were the owners and Captain G. G. Haley her commander. She came to an untimely end thirteen years later when she was lost, the mate and a seaman perishing. The *St. John* sailed from this port August 20th, 1894, for St. George's, Grenada, with a cargo of boards, planks and shingles. When in latitude 32 North and longitude 61 West she was hit by a furious cyclone (hurricane) on September 6th, of that year. The sea ran to a tremendous height and swept the decks, the crew lashing themselves in the rigging. The mate and a seaman were carried away by a huge wave and drowned. The survivors were able to hold on to the waterlogged hulk until September 29th, when the British steamer *Greenwood* providently hove in sight and saw the plight of the unfortunate mariners, who were taken from their doomed craft. This was the end of Saint John's namesake." In the same paper, same date, it is noted that the *Syanara* of 318 tons net, built and owned by J. A. Likely and his associates of Saint John in 1884, was abandoned at Barbados in December, 1903.

The other ships built at Saint John in the 1880's were the *M. A. Nutter* of 291 tons net, launched by Hilyard Bros., owned by the R. C. Elkin Co., and lost at sea on September 6th, 1892; the *Orinoco* of 298 tons net, built in 1883 by J. Ruddock & Sons at Portland, near Saint John, Sylvas T. McLellan, master, and wrecked on July 16th

1896. The *Adelene* of 193 tons net was built by R. Titus at Rothesay in 1885 for G. F. Baird & Co; Charles W. Starkey, master. This vessel was abandoned at sea on March 6th, 1906, being at that time owned by F. N. Chalmers. F. L. Bonnell built the *C. E. White* of 227 tons net at Saint John in 1886; F. S. Bonnell, managing owner and A. L. Bonnell, master. She later loaded a lumber cargo at Digby, N.S., for Cienfuegos, Cuba, sailed on August 1st, 1889, and was never heard of again.

In 1887 the McGuiggan yard in Saint John launched the *Gazelle* of 263 tons net for G. F. Baird & Co. With C. W. Starkey as master she was wrecked and abandoned off the port of Arecibo, Puerto Rico, on March 5th, 1896.

The first of a fleet of terns built by the Parkers of Tynemouth, N.B., was launched for the R. C. Elkin Co. of Saint John in 1887. The *Jennie Parker* of 211 tons net had an average life until she was abandoned at sea while on a passage from Kingsport, N.S., to Havana, on December 28th, 1895. The R. C. Elkin Co. entered the schooner business in this era and continued as owners and agents for many vessels up to the last days.

In 1888 the *Walter Holly* of 273 tons net was built for F. E. Sayre at Gardiner's Creek, N.B., by W. & R. Wallace. Her life was short, as she was wrecked on June 30th, 1892. An attractive water-colour of this schooner shows her to be a graceful craft with all sails set, including the masthead staysails.

The *H. B. Homan* of 299 tons net was launched by E. McGuiggan at Courtney Bay in 1888 to join the R. C. Elkin fleet. Many years later, while proceeding up the river to Jacksonville, Florida, on February 3rd, 1905, she stranded and became a total loss. Other terns built for the R. C. Elkin Co. during this period were the *Frances* of 293 tons net, from the yard of E. McGuiggan in 1889, and the *Bessie Parker* of 227 tons net, launched by R. L. Parker at Tynemouth, N.B., the same year. The *Frances* was abandoned on October 25th, 1895, and the *Bessie* was wrecked at Quoddy Head, Maine, on October 7th, 1906.

The *M. L. Bonnell* of 297 tons net was built by and for the Bonnells at Saint John in 1889. She was later owned by F. Ritchie and was destroyed by fire on January 5th, 1897. The *La Plata* of 350 tons net was launched by the McGuiggan yard at Saint John for Troop & Son in 1889. This schooner was sold to Brazilian owners in 1897.

It is noted that 1889 was a very active year for the shipbuilders in Saint John. I will remind the reader that the great fleet of large wooden sailing ships was passing rapidly out of existence. These smaller vessels were the reply of the owners and builders to keep in business.

Another Saint John schooner launched in 1889 was the *Valkyrie* of 323 tons net by F. E. Sayre. The schooner has been reported missing since September, 1893.

The last vessel launched in this period at Saint John was the *Waterside* of 161 tons net, built at Waterside, N.B., in 1889 by W. S. Starrett and owned by Wm. McLaughlin. She was abandoned on January 9th, 1897.

The Nova Scotia Schooners built between 1880 and 1890

In the same decade Nova Scotia built thirty terns and a four-master. This latter was the *Uruguay*, built in 1889 at Windsor, N.S., by Shubael Dimock, a longtime builder of big ships. Her net tonnage was 726, by far the largest of this rig built so far in Canada. On October 24th, 1891, on a passage from Windsor, N.S., to New York with gypsum, this large schooner struck a shoal at the mouth of the Bay of Fundy. She was subsequently sighted bottom-up with her crew missing. In this connexion it is interesting to note the first American four-master was built at Bath in 1880, nine years before the *Uruguay*, as by this time the American three-masters had reached a practical limit in size. As the coal trade increased in the New England States the terns had become larger and larger and the first four-master, the *William L. White* of 995 tons gross, was the forerunner of the big multi-masted schooners of the United States coal fleet. The *William L. White* has been described by Henry Hall in *Shipbuilding Industry* as follows:

"The hull of the vessel was large enough for a Californian. She was 205 feet long on deck, 40 feet in beam, and 17 feet deep in the hold, being 309 feet overall from the end of her jib-boom to the end of the spanker boom. She registered 996 tons and was able to carry 1450 tons of anthracite coal. To have her fitted with three masts would have required such large lower sails that the strains on the lower masts would have been destructive, and she was therefore fitted with four, the after spar being called the spanker mast. This divided her 5017 yards of canvas into smaller sails, and made her a good schooner, sailing well, easily handled, and requiring a crew of only five men before the mast, besides her two mates and Captain."

To return to the Canadian tern schooners: at Maitland, N.S., famed for the building of the great full-rigged sailing ship, *W. D. Lawrence*, the largest wooden ship ever built in Canada, the *Eva Maud* of 267 tons net was launched here in 1880 for J. F. Watson. This schooner left North Sydney, N.S., about October 13th, 1895, for St. John's, Nfld., and has not been heard from since.

Parrsboro and Port Greville, Nova Scotia, emerged about this time as the most prolific builders of large schooners. In 1881 the *Davida* of 377 tons net and the *Calabria* of 530 tons net were launched at Parrsboro. The *Davida* was owned and sailed by Captain D. S. Howard, who sold her after some years to George W. Newcomb, and he operated her as owner-master until she ran ashore at Grand Manan, N.B., on September 26th, 1892, and became a total wreck. The *Calabria* had a varied career and a somewhat confusing one. There is no doubt that she was a speedy vessel. In a newspaper of the time, the *Calabria* was reported as having arrived at Parrsboro about January 1st, 1883, after a passage of sixty-three hours from New York. Her first owner is given as E. W. Dimock of Windsor, N.S. On May 1st, 1885, she was stranded on the north coast of Cuba. The same year she is shown as being registered at Nassau, Bahamas, but was transferred to Windsor in 1898. After the first casualty she was shown as being owned by the Gypsum Packet Company. On December 2nd, 1908, she was ashore at Margaretsville, N.S., but was salvaged and on May 10th, 1910, she was sold to Christopher Splane of St. John's, Nfld.

In 1882 the *E. Merriam* was built at Port Greville for her namesake. She was a moderate-sized tern of 331 tons net and at a later date was sold to L. Hatfield. After thirty years' service she was lost on a passage from Saint John, N.B., to New York when she went ashore on Green Island Ledge, Maine, and became a total loss on November 18th, 1912.

Skillful Seamanship by Masters

There are many accounts of the skillful seamanship displayed by some of the masters of the old schooners. To be able to manoeuvre a sailing ship in constricted quarters without hired assistance was money in hand and required nerve, a quick grasp of the ability of the ship to respond and the will to carry out a daring manoeuvre. The *E. Merriam* was returning from a voyage to New York about 1909 after discharging a cargo of piling. In the evening she was outside Port Greville with the wind fresh to strong. Captain Pettis was in command of the vessel at the time and my relative, Yorke Barrington, and some others were watching from the cliff at the entrance to the port. Captain Pettis came up to Port Greville and appeared to be in doubt as to the wisdom of attempting to dock under the wind conditions and then evidently made up his mind to try. He stood off and set all sail, then came about and headed for the dock. She came in with all canvas drawing and a great bone in her teeth as she soared along. At the right moment Captain Pettis shouted and all halyards were cast off while he hove the wheel hard up. The sails came fluttering down and the ship ranged to the dock with just enough way for the crew to pass the lines.

The *Wandrian* of 311 tons net was built at Parrsboro in 1883 by L. Hatfield for B. L. Tucker. This vessel, like the one preceding, had a long life and was lost on a voyage from Havana toward Mobile, Ala., in ballast, when she ran ashore on the Cuban coast on February 27th, 1916, and became a total loss after thirty-three years' service afloat.

The *Phoenix* and the *A. B. Crosby* were also launched at Parrsboro in 1883. The *Phoenix* of 396 tons net was built by J. E. Pettis for her first owner, G. W. Newcomb. She had a long life and was managed at different times by R. S. Kerr and G. E. Bentley. This fine vessel was stranded on the northeast end of Big Libby Island, Maine, on June 24th, 1909, and afterward towed to Saint John, N.B., condemned and sold. The *A. B. Crosby* of 174 tons net was built by John Durant and lost on a passage from Cow Bay, Cape Breton, to a United States port with a coal cargo. She stranded on Half Moon Ledge, near Barrington, N.S., when only a year old. The crew were saved by the Shelburne Life Saving Station. The vessel was insured in Halifax for $7500.00.

After these vessels were launched there was a lapse in building up the Bay until 1889, when J. E. Pettis built the *James Wotherspoon* of 268 tons net at Port Greville for Thos. P. Ball & Co. of New York. This vessel was lost on December 4th, 1892, on a reef in the Caribbean Sea. The *Wentworth* of 328 tons net was built for the Gypsum Packet Co. in the same year at Port Greville by H. Elderkin & Co. She was a total loss on Chatham Bar, Mass., on October 14th, 1904. The next year, 1889, another small tern was launched at Port Greville for H. Gillespie & Co. This schooner, the *Keewadin* of 189 tons net, was in a lot of difficulty. A later owner was Captain E. Brown. On October 7th, 1906, while on a voyage from New York to Wolfville, N.S., she became a constructive total loss by running ashore at Horton's Point, on Long Island. She was repaired and put back into operation until November 16th, 1907, when she was again a total loss at Sydney, N.S. She was taken to Liverpool, N.S., and rebuilt by D. C. Mulhall. In 1908 her name was changed to *Myrtle V. Hopkins* and her owner was I. A. Hopkins. This did not change her luck and on December 6th, 1909, she became a total loss for the third time and thus passes from the record.

Total Loss

I have noted before that when a vessel is a total loss it does not necessarily mean that she has ceased to exist as a ship. When a vessel has been damaged to the extent that her repairs exceed the value set on her for insurance purposes, she is known as a constructive total loss. However, if she can be bought from the underwriters at a reasonable price and repaired to comply with the rules of the classification societies, she may resume operations for many more years.

Schooners launched from other Yards, 1880–90

During the years of the decade 1880–90 other yards took up building the schooners. In 1882 a small tern, the *Leo* of 123 tons net, was launched by Langille of Mahone Bay. This vessel had many owners during her long forty years' career and latterly was registered at Charlottetown, P.E.I. M. McLeod was a later owner, also J. M. Chapman. Late in her life she was selected to take part in a pageant at Pictou, N.S., in the early 1920's. This celebration was to commemorate the arrival of the ship *Hector* at Pictou with Scottish settlers a century before. The *Leo* was fitted with yards to resemble an old-time ship and was manned by a crew of volunteers under Colin Fraser. She was supposed to appear at the entrance of the harbour at the height of the festivities, but by mischance she got ashore on the way in. A small ferry went to her assistance and hauled the *Leo* off, so although late, she was greeted with great cheers by the descendants of the original settlers. The little schooner was completely worn out a few years later and was abandoned on the beach at Murray River, P.E.I., about 1928.

In 1882, at Meteghan, N.S., another small tern, the *F. Richard* of 74 tons net, was launched by A. Therriau. This vessel, having a registered length of 81.5 feet and a beam of 23, was one of the smallest of the three-masted schooners. At Sherbrooke, N.S., the *Minnie Louise* of 223 tons net was built in 1883 by Chas. McIntosh. One of her owners was Sylvester Boudrot of Arichat, C.B. While loaded with phosphate for Barbados and lying at anchor at Fernandina, Florida, on January 14th, 1891, she broke away from her mooring during a storm, went ashore and was a total loss. In Cape Breton at Great Bras D'Or, the *Ocean Lily* of 136 tons was built in 1885 by Kenneth MacDonald of Baddeck. The venture of this vessel is interesting, as it is an example of a small group placing their skills, assets and labour to their credit in a completed ship. The builder owned twenty shares; Allen MacLean and Norman Morrison, farmers, owned fourteen and ten respectively, and it is safe to assume they provided the timber and some of the labour. John A. MacDonald of Boularderie, carpenter, had ten shares and Thomas A. Young, shipwright, had two shares. The labour and materials supplied by these men could produce almost everything required but the ironwork, sails and rigging. This ship lasted for ten years until she was lost on Hogsty Reef in the Bahamas on October 14th, 1895.

The other ships built in this decade came from the old-established yards. In 1883 the *Galena* of 381 tons net was built at Hantsport, N.S., for Alan Haley. She was wrecked at Moose River, Maine, on May 4th, 1892, while on a passage from Hillsboro, N.B., with a cargo of gypsum for New York. The same year Mr. Haley had the *Iolanthe* built at Avondale. Her size was similar to the previous vessel, being 393 tons net, and she was abandoned at sea in 1902. The *Rio* of 317 tons net was built by Churchill at Hantsport in 1881 but was soon sold to New Zealand owners.

It will be noted that the schooners built in this locality, in Minas Basin, were all quite large for three-masters. From these places had come a vast number of square-rigged ships, barques and smaller vessels. In the old registers it is noted that their rig was often changed and it was not unusual to rerig a three-masted schooner into a barquentine or vice versa. It has been stated before that some men liked square-rig best for sailing qualities when on voyages off the land, especially where the trade winds were encountered and the square sails provided a great advantage. On the other hand, the economies that could be effected with fore-and-aft rig influenced owners and masters of some square-rigged vessels to make a change.

Wm. Dimock, a former builder of large ships, built the *Clifton* of 473 tons net at Windsor, N.S., in 1883. This vessel was dismasted while on a passage off New York in 1901 during a gale. A native of Nova Scotia, Captain H. S. Hilton of Yarmouth, N.S., while acting as mate of the Bristol City liner *City of Exeter*, was in charge of the lifeboat sent to take off the crew when the steamer had come upon the schooner after the gale. Captain Hilton was presented with a gold watch by the Canadian Government for his part in the rescue. In 1953 he was living in British Columbia and about eighty years of age.

The *Grenada* of 635 tons net was one of the largest schooners rigged as a three-master. At first she was rigged as a barquentine, but was altered to a tern schooner. She was built at Horton, N.S., in 1888, for David E. North and J. Terry North. On a passage from Campbellton, N.B., to Vineyard Haven, she was abandoned in October, 1908, at 40° N. and 61° W. Wm. F. Watt, master, and her crew were taken off by the s.s. *Manchester Spinner* and landed at Rotterdam.

The *Emma R. Smith* of 387 tons net was built at Hantsport in 1883 for R. G. Faulkner. She was later rerigged as a barquentine and sold foreign.

Another big schooner built in the locality was the *Severn* of 446 tons net, launched at Avondale in 1884 by W. H. Mosher for Rufus Curry. This vessel passed to New York owners and on the outbreak of the war in 1914 was sold to the Norwegians.

Three tern schooners were launched in the Windsor vicinity in 1888. Shubael Dimock built the *Newburgh* of 481 tons net for the gypsum trade. The schooner was wrecked at Nantucket, Mass., on November 28th, 1898, and the wreck was sold by the underwriters to J. F. Whitney & Co. of New York. Many years later she was still at work under the French flag, being registered at Rouen and renamed *Nievre*. The next vessel was the *Alberta* of 610 tons net, one of the largest terns and launched the same year by Thos. A. Mosher for Rufus Curry. On one of her first voyages this vessel made a remarkable passage from Rio to Hantsport, being only twenty-eight days on the trip and only eighteen days from the Equator. This passage is recorded in a contemporary newspaper of 1889 and she was commanded by Captain L. E. Parker. She was later sold to Reynard and McBride and like several of the other large vessels produced in this vicinity was rerigged into a barquentine. The *Alberta* was condemned at a survey held in July, 1900, but was sold and reappeared as the *A. Elida*, registered at Buenos Ayres and owned by A. Johanson. She was wrecked at Cape Corrientes, Cuba, on December 14th, 1901, while on a passage from Jamaica to New York with logwood. The final vessel for this vicinity is the *Bianca* of 180 tons net, built at Windsor in 1888. The facts regarding this schooner are obscure, but she was in the usual trades until August 1st, 1899, when she sailed from San Pedro de Macoris for New York with a cargo of sugar and was never reported again. Many years after another *Bianca* was built, but she will be dealt with later.

The First Annapolis Schooners

In Annapolis, N.S., several companies began to use the large schooners. H. C. Longmire built the *Granville* of 300 tons net at Parker's Cove in 1889. She was owned by C. D. Pickels and Captain Samuel Groves. While under the command of Captain Charles Starrett of Digby, N.S., she was abandoned and sank in the North Atlantic on February 12th, 1895, while on a passage from Annapolis to Cardenas, Cuba, with lumber.

Another vessel of this period owned in Annapolis County was the *Ida M. Shafner* of 184 tons net, built in 1888 at Bridgetown, N.S., for L. D. Shafner. The schooner was named after his wife and is reported to have been a lucky ship. In later years she was sold to Colwell Bros. of Halifax and was lost on December 9th, 1905, on South East Ledge near Country Harbour, Nova Scotia.

Farther along the Bay of Fundy, the *Alert* of 248 tons net was built at Port Gilbert in 1889 by E. N. Everett for B. G. Morse. On June 23rd, 1901, this vessel arrived at New York from Lagos, West Coast of Africa, after a passage of ninety-two days. Three men, including Captain Foote, a native of Yarmouth County, were ill with beri-beri and two of the others, including the mate, died on the voyage and were buried at sea. This vessel was broken up at Barbados in February, 1904.

Captain Richard Marshall

A small tern was built at Weymouth, N.S., in St. Mary's Bay, during this era. The *Grace Rice* of 145 tons net was launched by LeBlanc for Thomas G. Rice in 1888. Captain Richard Marshall commanded this vessel for eleven and a half years. His sea career started when he sailed as cook at the age of fourteen in the brig *John Oliver*. He sailed in many of the larger ships out of Weymouth for years before joining the *Grace Rice*, went to sea for forty-two years, was in command for thirty-two and had his ninety-first birthday in 1932. In all that time he never lost a deckload, lost only one man overboard and had one die of fever. He made fifteen trips across the Atlantic and one hundred and ten to the West Indies, and although he was there every month of the year, never experienced a hurricane. He sailed the *Grace Rice* over the West Indies route for the eleven and a half years he was in her. Soon after he left to join another *Rice* vessel the *Grace* was lost with all hands in a hurricane. He notes that the only time he came close to being shipwrecked was coming up the Bay of Fundy in the *Grace Rice*. Off Briar Island a thick southeast snowstorm came up and it was impossible to keep her off the land. "I was at the wheel myself," he relates, "when I saw we must go ashore and shouted to look out for any opening ahead we could run into, when I spied a small inlet called Hogyard Cove. I had just time to heave the wheel hard up when she stuck her nose in the bank, swung broadside and listed shoreward. We crawled out on the jib-boom and lowered ourselves down on the bank." The ship was later hauled off and taken to Meteghan for repairs. This took place in 1895. The vessel was later sold to John H. Killam of Yarmouth and came to a tragic end as, on July 14th, 1899, she sailed from Halifax for Ponce, Puerto Rico, with a fish cargo, and was not afterwards heard from.

Another small tern built in St. Mary's Bay in 1883 was the *Sainte Marie* of 167 tons net, built for L. A. Melanson, and her builder was J. H. Munroe. After some years she was sold to H. C. Outerbridge of Bermuda.

The last vessel mentioned for this era is the *Molega* of 148 tons net, built in 1888 by J. N. Rafuse of Conquerall Bank, N.S., a locality below Bridgewater on the La Have River. She was owned by H. Davidson and was the forerunner of many tern schooners built there by the Rafuse interests. She was posted as wrecked in January, 1897, but I do not have the locality.

Life and Trades in the Schooners, 1890–1900

The large schooners had increased in number and size, starting with the *Lady Mulgrave*, and by the decade 1890-1900 the fore-and-aft rig had reached its greatest development and effectiveness. They displaced the square-rigged ships and except for the speculative building at the end of World War One were never to be as popular as during this period. A great class of seamen had grown up with the terns and a new spirit of adventure emerged, both for owners and crews, as the ships sailed away on long and short charters. There was money coming home from abroad to pay the ships' cost, profit and crews' wages. The schooners went all over the Atlantic, with hard pine from the southern United States to South America, the West Indies and Africa, case and barrel oil to Europe and Africa and back home with the fragrant products of the tropics. The spirit of the times is well illustrated by the rollicking tone of "Corbitt's Barquentine" and while the rig is not exact, the description of a voyage from Nova Scotia to Demerara, then to Boston and return home, is typical of the schooner runs. This ballad will be found in the appendix.

Life at sea, especially in winter, was hard, as it always was hard in the old sailing ships. There were good times too, with the vessel driving along in fine weather with all sails drawing full, cleaving through the waves and the wake bubbling astern—outward bound, looking forward to days in a foreign port, with a cash advance, lots of drinks and fun with the native girls. The days in the tropic ports flew past as the crew discharged the cargo in the sweltering heat. At knockoff time, a wash-up, supper aboard, then off ashore in the gathering darkness of the tropical nights that seemed too good to be true. This sort of life caught many a young fellow on his first voyage. It was wonderful to leave home with ice and snow over all, with hard days running down to the moderate weather, to cross the Gulf Stream and find the air fine and warm, the sea a new colour. To a young fellow, the first time in the tropics struck him so forcibly he never got over it—the light-green sea fringing the white sand beaches, waving palms, exotic blooms, and the pungent aromatic spicy smell that pervades almost every tropic port. The young man might be in a ship that was a living hell before he got home. He might spend back-breaking hours at the pumps, be drenched time after time by icy seas, sleep in a wet bunk, risk his life a dozen times clawing in canvas, and eating coarse poor food. But after he got home he always remembered the good times and as a consequence ships never wanted for crews. Naturally there were the drones as well. Men who were no good ashore were no good on a ship either—last of the watch to turn out, last to tail onto a rope, quarrelling, and the first one in after the four-hour hitch. Some of these fellows made a first trip and were so glad to get back that they never left home again.

But the spirit was there. The men who loved the ship they were in regarded her as something alive, to be helped along and they suffered every time there was a damage. There will always be men like that who will give their lives to a succession of ships, although the cold steel machines of today will never command the same respect as the carefully constructed wooden vessels of days gone by. The modern steam and motor ships are too much of an assembly-line product to inspire affection and times and conditions change.

Some of the Trades

The schooners were built primarily to carry away our exports. At times they were used extensively for other purposes, but they differed from the big square-rigged vessels which were built solely as foreign-going ocean traders. This is the reason the schooners survived the passing of the square-rigged sailing ship.

The growing efficiency of the ocean-going steam tramp and the iron-built sailing ships from the 1870's onward drove the bigger wooden sailing vessels from the sea. However, this did not affect the big schooners until comparatively recent times. The terns built before World War One were designed for definite trades and the steamer did not compete.

Many of these vessels were built with capital provided by the three main exporters. These three interests were the lumber, fish and gypsum industries. It is easy to see a lumber merchant supplying the timber for building a schooner that was later intended to carry his own product to market. In the same way a fish exporter often put up some or all of the money for a vessel intended for his later use in freighting his product abroad and returning with salt used in processing his fish. The gypsum trade was a little different. In the earlier days the movement of gypsum from the Bay of Fundy to the United States was carried out during the good weather months only and the owners often made their last trip up the Bay of Fundy to load lumber for a southern port and planned to keep the vessel at work during the winter in a milder climate.

The main reason that these schooners persisted and fought the steamers to a standstill until after World War One was because they offered such cheap means of transporting local products to market. In addition, these vessels carried a cargo of from 300 to 700 tons usually loaded at one port. Often the cargo was some days being collected and this was to their advantage as "lay days" were not as costly as in the steamships with their larger crews and fuel bills.

These large freighting schooners had other advantages. As they were mostly owned in the vicinity of operation they could be laid up under the eye of the master or owner and the crew dispersed to their homes nearby, where they were available when a cargo offered. Many of the men who manned these vessels were small farm owners who went to sea to supplement their incomes.

Toward the middle of the nineteenth century the Maritime salt-fish trade became very brisk. Salt dried fish was an ideal cheap item of diet for the people of the warm countries where food spoilage was great. In particular the areas demanding this product were the Mediterranean countries, South America and the West Indies. I do not mention the fresh-fish trade or fishing in general, as terns were not employed in this sort of work, although many of our vessels were sold to France, Spain and Portugal to be used as salt-fish bankers. From very early times large amounts of fish were caught on the Banks off our coasts and were taken ashore for curing to the coves and harbours of Nova Scotia and Newfoundland. Certain European countries were the first customers for dried fish, but soon the market extended to South America, so that in 1870 there were seventy-five cargoes totalling 216,160 drums of salt fish exported from St. John's, Nfld., to Pernambuco, Brazil, alone. The Newfoundland merchants at this time were content to charter English schooners to send their fish abroad and a fine type of vessel was developed by the English firms. These schooners became known as the "Western Ocean Yachts" on account of their fine lines, trim rig and general seamanlike appearance. At the same time much of the fish was carried away by their own small two-masted schooners. In Nova Scotia, the fish was carried abroad in the terns and also by brigs, brigantines and barquentines, but as in the other trades the tern schooner outlived the square-riggers. In Newfoundland, as the fisheries prospered, the merchants eventually took on an added interest in getting their product to market and began to charter or buy Nova Scotian schooners and late in the game to build their own.

Many of the two-masted Bank fishermen made a trip to Europe or South America after the fishing season, but there were not many of this class engaged all the year around in the export trade. In Newfoundland the first tern schooner built for the trade was the *Duchess of Cornwall*, launched at Burgeo in 1901. This vessel will be mentioned later.

Shipbuilding in the Decade 1890–1900

In this decade the large schooners reached their peak. They were cheap to build, operated with a small crew and could get around quickly and in their trades the steamers could not compete.

Life in the three- and four-masters was far from being easy for the crews. Though they carried no yards and square sails aloft as in the barques, barquentines, brigs and brigantines of the old days, nevertheless they were built with hulls and carrying capacity up to 1500 tons deadweight and were as large as many of the old square-riggers.

But they sailed with crews of half the number of men required to sail a square-rigged ship of similar dimensions and tonnage. A schooner of 500 tons register on a deep-water voyage to ports in the eastern and western North and South Atlantic would be handled by a crew of no more than seven or eight men. In a square-rigged craft of the same tonnage the number of crew members would be three or four men more. Thus to ship operators, in the declining days of sail, the schooner became a very popular type of sailing vessel to load, move and discharge cargoes of all kinds—even general cargoes of a valuable character.

Prince Edward Island Schooners

As in the previous decade, Prince Edward Island contributed to the schooner fleet. In this period they built only two small vessels, the *Delight* of 109 tons net, built in 1894 at Souris, William MacDonald, master. She was abandoned in May, 1900. The other was the *Arclight* of 103 tons net, built 1898 at Souris by T. Kirkham for J. Poole. She was sunk in New York Harbour on July 12th, 1912, and was a total loss.

The New Brunswick Schooners, 1890–1900

In this decade New Brunswick produced seventeen terns, nearly all of which were completed in the early 1890's. The *Arthur M. Gibson* of 296 tons net was built at Gibson, N.B., in 1890, and owned by A. M. Gibson. She had various owners, including J. W. Smith of Saint John, N.B., who later owned many of the schooners. She was transferred to Barbados registry in 1906 and during or after World War One she was sold foreign and appeared briefly under the Portuguese flag. This vessel and the one which follows lasted for many years. The *Beaver* was built by J. H. Murphy at Perry's Point, N.B., in 1890 with a net tonnage of 192. She had many owners in her long career, including R. C. Elkin & Co., S. F. Hatfield, Edward Pettipas, W. McFatridge, A. Rattenbury and C. H. Benoit. Her final resting place is not known, but she was off the register in 1936 as being out of existence. This old vessel was known all over the Maritimes for many years in the coasting trade.

The *Moskwa* was built at Saint John by F. E. Sayre in 1890. She was a very large tern of 593 tons net and was owned by J. W. Smith, but unfortunately soon came to grief and was wrecked at Bahia, Brazil, on April 21st, 1894. The same builder, F. E. Sayre, was active during this period and the following year he completed two more terns. The *Vamoose* of 349 tons net was owned by the builder and was wrecked on December 4th, 1898, on a voyage from Sydney, N.S., to Saint John, N.B., with a cargo of coal. The *Coniston* of 360 tons net was also owned by the builder and others; Reuben T. Morehouse, master. This latter vessel was lost on April 11th, 1895.

At Tynemouth, N.B., Leonard Parker built two terns. In 1891 the *John S. Parker* of 239 tons net was launched for the R. C. Elkin Co., W. B. Millbury, master. She was wrecked on November 7th, 1901. The other tern was named after himself, *Leonard Parker*, of 246 tons net and built in 1897. This vessel was also owned by the R. C. Elkin Co. and was wrecked on September 17th, 1913, while on a voyage from Gulfport, Miss., to Louisburg, N.S., with a cargo of hard pine; C. I. McNeill, master.

At Black River, N.B., John McLeod built the *Helen E. Kenny* of 294 tons net in 1891. This vessel was owned by Geo. S. Parker and later by Troop & Son of Saint John. She was wrecked on March 3rd, 1908. The next year J. R. McLeod built the *Moama* of 384 tons net and her first owner was H. B. Smith. She had various owners through the years, including P. McIntyre and J. W. Smith. She ended her days when she became waterlogged at the Delaware Breakwater in February, 1917. Another tern launched at Black River, N.B., in 1892 was the *Mola* of 351 tons net, built by W. Wallace and owned by J. W. Smith. She is reported as being first rigged as a topsail tern. This vessel was sold to Mexican owners about 1905 and was renamed *Minerva*.

A large tern was launched at Hopewell Cape by Warren Dixon in 1892. She was the *Gladys McLauchlin* of 420 tons net and was owned by the builder. She was lost in her first year, in December, 1892, but I do not know the details.

Other vessels launched in various places in New Brunswick were the *Deerhill* of 332 tons net, launched by G. Merritt in 1891 at Moss Glen for W. H. Merritt. She was abandoned on December 12th, 1898. The *Sirocco* of 298 tons net was built the same year by R. Carson at St. Martin's for Troop & Son. This vessel was designed expressly for the West Indian and South American trade. The *Sirocco* sustained great damage in a gale on September 27th, 1906, reached Nassau and was condemned and sold.

The *Allen A. McIntyre* of 199 tons net was owned by Peter McIntyre and built by J. H. Murphy at Perry's Point, N.B., in 1891. She was lost at sea on January 23rd, 1900.

In 1894 the large tern *Fred. H. Gibson* of 418 tons net was launched at St. Mary's, N.B., for John H. Gibson. There is little information on this vessel until she was abandoned at sea on September 15th, 1904.

The last schooner launched in New Brunswick during this era was the *Melba* of 388 tons net. She was built by W. & R. Wallace at Gardiner's Creek in 1899. Her first owner was F. C. Lockhart and she was registered at Windsor, N.S. Later she was purchased by J. W. Smith and then by R. C. Elkin & Co. In early registers she is noted as being a topsail tern. During World War One she was sold to English owners and was registered at Newcastle, England.

Difficulties with Canadian Registered Schooners

About this time many of the shipowners began to register their vessels outside of Canada. This unfortunate practice, which has persisted to present postwar days when more than one hundred large steamships of the World War Two fleet were transferred to English register, was brought on by several conditions. The Canadian Government, through legislation and the local ownership taxes, made economical operation of the shipping fleet very difficult. From time to time the Government brought in regulations affecting the building, manning and inspection of ships to the extent that increased costs led the owners to transfer their vessels to other parts of the Commonwealth. Since the early days many of the legal loopholes have been plugged and the fact remains that, to keep operating, Canadian shipowners have always had to evade or fight regulations in order to compete.

I do not pretend to know what has been the trouble with Canadian shipping since the 1870's. During the periods the fleet was built up, either through the aggressive action of the merchants and seamen, or by reason of the two large-scale wars, the Government has made no constructive steps to assist the Maritime shipowners. Ten years after World War Two there was only a handful of foreign-going steam and motor merchant ships on the Canadian Register and this after building a wartime fleet of several hundred ships of all types. So it was, back in 1890, when the owners were forced to transfer their ships to Barbados or St. John's, Nfld., in order to remain in business. It should be noted that from this time on, whole fleets of our sailing vessels were transferred in ever-growing numbers. It is true that the Government makes the laws for the good of all concerned, but it seems the shipping industry in Atlantic Canada suffered, as here the life of the community is truly maritime.

Larger Schooners were built in Nova Scotia during the 1890's

The first few years of this decade, 1890-1900, were very active as far as the large schooners were concerned. Excepting the boom building years of World War One the yards were kept busy. To work toward the main center of construction in Nova Scotia at the head of the Bay of Fundy, the *Lena Pickup* of 292 tons net was built by Jos. Hall at Granville Ferry, N.S., in 1890, for S. W. W. Pickup. Her master was Norman Roop and she was lost when she went ashore at Black River, N.B., on November 21st, 1900, and became a total wreck. The *Tyree* of 326 tons net was built for T. A. Wilson at Bridgewater the same year. In later years this schooner was sold to the Quebec Salvage and Wrecking Co., and for many years was used as a barge. The *John E. Shatford* of 154 tons net was built by Winslow McKay in 1890 at Shelburne. This vessel was bought by owners from the Cape Verde Islands and was renamed *Vera Cruz II*.

A large vessel was built at Cheverie on the Minas Basin by Roderick Rose in 1890. The *Glenrosa* of 504 tons gross was launched as a barquentine and later rerigged as a tern. She was owned by E. M. Bill and was lost on the coast of Maine about October, 1902.

In the same year at Hantsport the schooner *L. W. Norton* of 464 tons net was launched by G. B. North. She is first described as a barquentine and later rerigged as a tern and her owners were G. B. Lockhart & Co. This vessel had the misfortune to be at anchor in the Roads at Martinique when the great volcanic eruption of Mount Pelee took place on May 8th, 1902. The ships at anchor were destroyed in the great heat of the explosion and their crews perished, along with thousands of the native inhabitants.

The *Hattie May* of 149 tons net was built in 1890 at Clifton, N.S., at the head of Minas Basin, for James Crowe and others. She was abandoned at sea on October 3rd, 1898. At the other end of the Basin the *Nettie Shaw* of 250 tons net was launched in 1890 by A. Knowleton at Advocate for Mark Bailey and others. She ran ashore at Apple River, N.S., on a voyage from Liverpool, N.S., to Hillsboro, N.B., and became a total loss on October 15th, 1893.

During this busy year of 1890 three terns were built at Port Greville. The *Trojan* of 557 tons net, a large schooner, was not at all lucky and lasted only a year. She was built by J. E. Pettis and others and was sunk at Southwest Harbour, Maine, on December 5th, 1891. He also launched the *Tacoma* of 209 tons net the same year. Later she was sold to Captain Jos. Hatch and was wrecked on Fortune Island in the Bahamas on October 31st, 1899. H. Elderkin & Co. built the *Laconia* of 485 tons net in the same year; John Card, master. Later she was sold to P. S. Blake and her registry was transferred to Barbados in 1898. She was abandoned at sea on November 8th, 1908, while on a passage from Ingramport, N.S., to New York with lumber.

Captain W. F. Durant built the *J. W. Durant* of 124 tons net at Parrsboro in 1890. The vessel was in trouble almost immediately, as she drove ashore at Shulie, N.S., on November 1st, 1890. The wreck was sold and eventually went under Mexican register.

Loss of the 'H. P. Kirkham'

Eight terns were built in Nova Scotia during 1891. At Liverpool, Robie McLeod, later to become known as a master at making hull models and a great shipbuilder, built the *H. P. Kirkham* of 186 tons net for W. S. McLeod. This vessel was lost the following year under the hardest conditions of human endurance. Under Captain W. S. McLeod the schooner was on a passage from Halifax to New York with a cargo of dry and pickled fish. On the evening of January 20th, 1892, she struck on the Rose and Crown Shoal off Nantucket, Mass., and filled with water. The seas broke over her immediately, compelling the crew to take to the rigging. At daybreak she was sighted from Sankaty Lighthouse by the keeper, who telephoned the life-saving station. The life-saving crew started immediately with their small lifeboat on wheels, hauling her across the beach and launching on the outside of Great Point. They reached the vessel about 11 a.m. and with great difficulty took off the crew of seven men from the rigging, where they had been exposed for fifteen hours, suffering intensely from cold and frequently being drenched by the breaking seas. Then commenced a long hard struggle for life. The little lifeboat, overcrowded with the double crew, took in water frequently, necessitating constant bailing to keep her afloat. Siasconset, the nearest land, was ten miles to windward. The wind and sea increased and the dashing spray froze on the men as they struggled at the oars. Hour after hour they rowed without perceptibly nearing the shore. In less than an hour after leaving the vessel, the schooner had gone to pieces. Three hours later, and again during the night, they were obliged to anchor to prevent their being carried to sea. Darkness settled upon them and all through the night they toiled on, guided by the flash from Sankaty's beacon.

Meanwhile they had been given up by anxious friends ashore, but when the day dawned the little boat was descried in the offing, still buffeted by the fierce gale and sea, and at ten o'clock in the forenoon they landed on Siasconset Beach. For twenty-six hours since leaving their station they had battled with wind and wave without nourishment and under conditions of extreme peril. In recognition of their efforts the United States Government awarded to Keeper Chase a gold medal and to each of the surfmen a silver medal. Before the medals were presented, one of the surfmen died as a result of the severe exposure.

To continue on with the schooners built in 1891, Alfred Knowlton launched the

R. L. Dewis of 324 tons net at Parrsboro for A. W. Atkinson & Co. While on a voyage from a United States port to Halifax she was in a collision on May 21st, 1897, and sank at Vineyard Haven, Mass.

Thomas Mosher built the *Arona*, a large schooner of 532 tons net, at Avonport in this busy year of 1891. She had many changes of ownership through the years, being first built for Mark Curry with Percy Parker as master. A later owner was C. R. Burridge and in 1905 her owner-master was John B. Spurr. She was abandoned off the United States coast on January 18th, 1908, her owner at that time being John Ditmars.

The *Blomidon* of 271 tons net was built for Alfred Potter by J. E. Biglow at Canning, N.S., in 1891. She was lost in the summer of 1901 on the Grand Cayman Bank in the Caribbean. In this same year J. A. Balcom, an owner-builder who was in the shipping business for many years, launched the *Shenandoah* of 198 tons net at Margaretsville, in the Bay of Fundy. This vessel was destroyed by fire in Chesapeake Bay on the night of January 14th, 1898.

Three vessels were built in 1891 for the Annapolis interests. The *Moneta* of 199 tons net was launched by John Wagstaff at Annapolis for Pickels and Mills. The *Moneta* foundered after being dismasted in a gale in September, 1893. The *Rita* of 197 tons net was built by J. E. Shafner at Bridgetown for L. D. Shafner and others. The *Rita* was abandoned at sea on January 1st, 1893, and her crew were landed at Philadelphia. The *Bartholdi* was the third vessel. She was 298 tons net and was built by Israel L. Delap at Black Point and owned by J. E. Shafner. This schooner, along with many of the others, often went on long charters out of Mobile, Ala., and they were managed by Horace Turner of that place. On one of her voyages, Captain Walter Amberman died, and the schooner was taken into a West Indian port by the mate. Other masters in this vessel were Norman Berry and J. W. Scott. On January 14th, 1913, the *Bartholdi* sailed from Mobile with hard pine for San Pedro de Macoris, Hispaniola, and after a long battle against head winds to get out of the Gulf of Mexico she put into Key West, Florida, for repairs on the 13th of March—two months to get a distance of 550 miles. A few days later she put out to continue the voyage. About daylight on March 22nd, she began to leak seriously and the crew were obliged to leave in a hurry. They were picked up by the *Margaret B. Rouss*, an American three-master, with only the clothes they stood in. This loss was the result of continual head winds with the resultant head-pitching that loosened the hull and masts and wore out the gear.

The Fleet of Large Gypsum Schooners

A fleet of schooners of the largest size now came into being and were built for the gypsum export trade. This mineral is very plentiful in many parts of the Maritimes and vast quantities have been shipped to United States ports.

These vessels were doubtless inspired by the success of the big schooners built in the United States for their coastal coal trade. During the 1880's over a hundred large four-masters and one five-master had been built and put into the coal trade between Virginia and New England. In addition there was a great fleet of smaller vessels including a considerable number of tern schooners.

EARL OF ABERDEEN. 416 tons. Built 1894 at Parrsboro, N.S.
(Stemhead broken off.) *Courtesy of Mr. Albert Barnes*

Crew of the EARL OF ABERDEEN.   *Courtesy of Commander W. J. L. Parker*

SIRDAR.   498 tons.   Built 1899 at River John, N.S.   *Courtesy of Mrs. Dorothy Haliburton*

The big schooners built in Canada for the gypsum trade were either owned or chartered by the Gypsum Packet Co., a subsidiary of the U.S. Gypsum Co. These vessels were built in two places during 1890-92 and Parrsboro will be considered first. Captain D. S. Howard was the builder and he launched four of them, the first being the *Gypsum King* of 640 tons net and rigged as a tern. Her first owners were the J. B. King Co., but later she was sold to E. W. Dimock of Windsor, N.S., and her name was changed to *Millie*. She was lost on a voyage from Saint John, N.B., to New York, on Cross Ledge, Machias, Me., on March 4th, 1906. In 1891 the *Gypsum Queen*, another large tern of 609 tons net, went down the ways. E. W. Dimock was an early owner, but later disposed of his interest. During World War One she was on a passage to the United Kingdom with a cargo of deals from the Bay of Fundy when she was abandoned at sea at 48° 16′ N. and 23° 16′ W., her crew being taken off by a lifeboat from the White Star liner s.s. *Cymric* on July 31st, 1915. Subsequently the master and owners claimed compensation, as it was alleged the vessel had been attacked by a German submarine and enemy damage led to her abandonment. The claim was settled by the Government as a war casualty, but many years later the case was reopened on the production of new evidence and the master and owners were charged with fraud. The case ended disastrously for the defence.

The next large schooner for this trade built by D. S. Howard was the *Gypsum Princess*, also a tern and of 664 tons net. She was owned by the J. B. King & Co. shipping interests and came to a tragic ending on a voyage from Parrsboro to New York when she was run down by the German s.s. *Ems*. The master, David Merriam, his wife Annie, his two children Vera and Elvin, also his son Edgar Merriam the first mate, and Murray Langford the cook, were lost. The survivors were landed at New York and the Consul's report was dated June 27th, 1898.

The last of this class of schooners built by Captain Howard was the *Gypsum Emperor* of 695 tons net, rigged as a four-master, and owned by the Gypsum Co. After some years she was sold to F. C. Lockhart and while under the command of Captain Thomas L. Martin was dismasted and abandoned in November, 1913.

The other two vessels of this fleet were built by J. B. North at Hantsport and Horton, N.S. The *Gypsum Prince*, a four-master of 723 tons net, was a close rival in size to the four-masted schooner *Uruguay* of 726 tons net built nearby in 1889 at Windsor, N.S., by Shubael Dimock for the same trade. The *Gypsum Prince* was launched at Hantsport in 1892 for the Gypsum Packet Co. and had a comparatively short life, as she was lost on Old Proprietor Ledge, Grand Manan, N.B., on July 16th, 1895.

J. B. North's other large schooner, also a four-master, was the *Gypsum Empress* of 723 tons net and launched at Horton, N.S., in 1892. It is noted that she had nearly the same dimensions as the *Gypsum Prince*. The *Empress* was later sold to the Cowles Ship Supply Co., of Mobile, Ala., and was abandoned in June, 1917.

Winter Trades for the Gypsum Schooners

As previously mentioned, owing to the rigorous climate and the exposed route between the loading and discharge ports, it was the custom, where possible, to send the big gypsum or "plaster rock" schooners south in the winter months. A winter charter was considered desirable, as the schooner could be earning money instead of laying-up. In the late Fall a lumber charter for West Indian ports was sought and the vessels often proceeded from the port of discharge to one of the hard-pine loading ports in the southern states. It is noted that the *Gypsum Empress* became involved in trouble on her way home from one of these charters. While on a passage from Bahia, Brazil, to New York, under Captain Jeremiah Gayton, she encountered doldrums and head winds and was finally towed into Bermuda on April 6th, 1901, with her stores very short and her crew ill.

Construction and Equipment in the Big Vessels

These six schooners were constructed to the highest standard with the best materials and workmanship. The work for which they were built was the hardest imaginable for any ship. Gypsum is a rock material and is a heavy dead cargo. The schooners were loaded at Windsor, N.S., and also at several smaller places, ports with the greatest range of tide found anywhere in the world. The ships were brought to the dock at high tide and placed over a bed made of timbers fastened down to the bed-rock. When the tide left, the ships were high and dry while loading was carried on. The strains thus placed on the wooden hulls were very destructive and no vessel was expected to last very long in this trade. As the vessels became weaker and leaking started, they were sold and used in other trades where the strains set up were not so great. All our large schooners were built to be loaded while lying aground and all the loading ports at the head of the Bay of Fundy and at other places in the vicinity with extreme ranges of tide were provided with loading berths which furnished a firm level bed to support the stranded vessel.

The six gypsum vessels were equipped with all the most modern equipment of the time. Steam donkey-boilers were fitted to perform the heavy work of handling the big sails, pumps and anchors. This power meant that the equipment could be made very heavy and strong, the stoutest grade of canvas duck for sails could be fitted without regard to the weight of hoisting. One of the dreariest tasks of the old sailors was cut out as the steam pump took over the job of keeping the vessels clear of water. An engineer was added to the ship's crew and his job was looking after the machinery and maintaining a head of steam. He stood no regular watch, but was on call at all times to assist the crew setting sail as required.

This equipment was placed on board only the large schooners. It was too expensive for the smaller vessels and many years were to pass before the gasolene donkey-engine was developed to the point where it was considered reliable enough for this type of installation.

Other Schooners built at the Head of the Bay in the Decade

For the remainder of the decade, 1890-1900, schooners were launched regularly at the head of the Bay of Fundy. At Port Greville in 1892 the *G. E. Bentley* of 250 tons net was built and operated by her namesake. She was later sold to John S. Woods and after a gale on March 2nd, 1904, was towed into Matanzas, Cuba, a total wreck. The firm of H. Elderkin & Co. built three terns here during the decade. In 1892 the *Walleda* of 249 tons net was launched for Captain J. H. Newcomb. Later she was sold to McIntosh, Terrio & Co. and in November, 1899, she was abandoned and broken up. The *Lewanika* of 298 tons net was built in 1894 and later sold to Jos. Manchester of Saint John. She was wrecked on October 25th, 1909. The third schooner was the *Wanola* of 272 tons net, launched in 1899. She was purchased by J. W. Smith and was last listed in 1917.

At Port Greville, G. W. Cochrane launched the *Cheslie* of 330 tons net in 1896 for his own account; Freeman Hatfield, master. This vessel was in the hard-pine trade and on a passage from Pascagoula, Miss., to Havana went ashore on the coast of Cuba in 1914 and was a total loss.

James E. Pettis built four vessels at Port Greville during the decade 1890-1900. The *B. C. Borden* of 385 tons net was launched in 1894. She was abandoned and sunk off La Have, N.S., on January 2nd, 1901, on a voyage from Cadiz to Halifax. The *St. Maurice* of 272 tons net was built for S. T. Salter in 1896. After a long career this vessel was a total loss by fire twenty-five miles southeast of Cape Cruz, Cuba, and her register was closed in January, 1920. The last tern of the decade launched by Mr. Pettis was the *Charlevoix* of 427 tons net. The schooner had a succession of owners, including J. B. Westaway, C. F. Taylor and M. Roberts. She was abandoned at sea on February 4th, 1919, while on a voyage from St. Andrews, N.B., to Macoris, Hispaniola, with a lumber cargo. Before building the above vessel Mr. Pettis had launched the *Harry* of 421 tons net at Parrsboro in 1892. She was later owned by the C. T. White interests of New Brunswick and was abandoned at sea on May 28th, 1915, off Seal Island, N.S.

The *A. T. Davison* of 361 tons net was launched by A. T. Davison at Parrsboro in 1892 for his own account. She was not a fortunate ship, as the following year, on October 9th, she was lost on Long Key Reef in the Bahamas while on a voyage from Barbados. Captain D. S. Howard, who was the most active builder of this period in Parrsboro, launched the *Florence R. Hewson* of 289 tons net for the Pickels & Mills interests of Annapolis in 1893. She was named after the only daughter of Doctor C. W. Hewson, a prominent citizen of Amherst, N.S., and a member of the Shulee Lumber Co., by whom she was largely owned. John T. King, whom I met as an old retired gentleman at Jordan, N.S., told me he was mate of this vessel for some years in the hard-pine trade. Her career was ended on October 12th, 1909, when she was caught in a hurricane in the Florida Straits. Mr. King related the ordeal of having the vessel smashed beyond repair by the great seas piled up in the storm. She was on a voyage from Mobile, Ala., to Demerara at the time and after the storm subsided a steamer came along and towed the water-filled schooner to Matanzas in Cuba, where she was condemned. John King's brother Archie was master and they returned to Canada with the crew and took over another schooner for the same firm.

Captain Howard's last vessel of the decade was the *Earl of Aberdeen* of 416 tons net. He later sold her to the Portuguese, who sailed her for many years under the following re-names—*Minho, Maria Helene* and finally the *Maria Ferreira.*

Another schooner built along the head of the Bay of Fundy between 1890 and 1900 was the *Exception* of 380 tons net launched at Spencer's Island for W. H. Baxter in 1892. This vessel was originally fitted out as a "topsail tern" and this expression may be confusing. The conventional three- and four-masted schooners had masts and topmasts all the same length and were rigged with fore-and-aft sails only. However, the influence of square-rig was still felt and many seamen liked a few square sails to set when running off the wind. This arrangement was usually carried out by fitting a yard on the foremast directly below the masthead and one or more smaller yards on the topmast. In some cases this rig was applied to the mainmast only and I have yet to find anyone who can tell me what the latter rig was called except a "jack-ass" rig. A picture of the *Preference* of this period shows these yards on the main and maintopmast only. In days to follow these odd rigs gradually disappeared as not being worth the bother and all sails carried were fore-and-aft. To return to the *Exception*, like many of the others she was in the hard-pine trade and on a passage from Pascagoula, Miss., to Havana, never arrived at her destination and is supposed to have foundered with all hands in the hurricane of September 24th, 1906.

Two vessels were built at Advocate, N.S. The *Robert Ewing* of 399 tons net was launched by the A. W. Atkinson Co. in 1892. She was originally fitted out as a barquentine, but was rerigged as a tern. This vessel was wrecked on June 16th, 1907, in the Orinoco River while on a voyage from New York to Cuidad Bolivar with a general cargo. The other vessel, the *Athlete* of 197 tons net, was built in 1893 by A. C. and C. W. Elderkin. She passed to the French flag in 1902 and was then renamed the *Cousins-Reunis*.

At Apple River, N.S., the C. T. White interests of New Brunswick built the *Ulrica* of 298 tons net in 1892. She was lost on a passage from Hillsboro, N.B., to Hoboken, N.J., when she went ashore at Nantasket Beach, Mass., on December 16th, 1896. This rescue was carried out by the famous Captain Joshua James. He had an amazingly long life devoted to life-saving. It is said that in 1842, at the age of fifteen, he was in the crew of a lifeboat belonging to the Massachusetts Humane Society. From that time on until he died on the beach in 1902 at the age of seventy-five immediately after exercising his boat crew in rough weather, his main occupation was life-saving.

At the time of the wreck of the *Ulrica* there were several life-saving organizations set up in this area and both the Humane Society Volunteers and Captain James' life-saving crew arrived at the same time. While one crew set up the beach apparatus Captain James launched his boat. In the heavy surf the first two attempts failed and the boat was filled with water. On the third try the boat got away, but halfway to the wreck a great sea up-ended the craft and the Captain and crew were thrown into the water and driven back to the beach. At this date Captain James was seventy years of age. The Captain and crew were dragged out of the water and proceeded to get a line aboard the stranded *Ulrica*. After several attempts a hawser fell across the wreck, but the schooner crew were too exhausted to help themselves, so Captain James again took to the boat and hauled out to the wreck with the aid of the fouled hawser.

Alongside the wreck the life-saving crew had to board to assist the frozen and exhausted crew, after which the surfboat was hauled ashore quickly by the hawser.

Of this quality were the men who manned the life-saving stations along this part of the coast where every year many ships were cast ashore and many men died.

Across the Basin the old yards around Windsor were still turning out ships. Roderick Rose built two schooners at Cheverie for Rodman Pratt. The *Delta* of 286 tons net was launched in 1892 and after many years of trading down south was sold to foreigners at Gulfport, Miss. The *Omega* was a smaller vessel of 199 tons net and was built in 1896. Rodman Pratt, the owner of these vessels and several others, had a preference for Greek letter names. The *Omega* was wrecked on the coast of Cuba on October 16th, 1910. The builder of these two vessels, Roderick Rose, had many fine ships to his credit. Three of his sons became well-known shipmasters in the United States. Captain Reginald Rose became master of the s.s. *City of New York*, Captain William Rose the marine superintendent for the United Fruit Co., and Captain J. F. Rose commanded several of the large Grace Line steamers.

At Canning, N.S., the *Bahama* of 321 tons net was built by John E. Biglow for Alfred Potter in 1892. This vessel had a confusing life, as she started as a tern schooner and was altered to a topsail tern. She was wrecked in 1902 on the Nova Scotia coast and again at Brunswick, Georgia, in 1903. Shortly after this her name was altered to *Rescue*. Again rerigged, she appeared as a barquentine and as such was wrecked a third time off Nuevitas, Cuba, on December 27th, 1913, while on a passage from Barbados toward Pensacola in ballast.

The next year at Canning, in 1893, the *Preference* of 243 tons net was launched for W. H. Baxter. This vessel is described in the registers of the day as a barquentine, but her picture, taken at launching time, shows yards on her mainmast, although in all other respects the schooner is a typical tern. Her first master, Harvey Mitchener, doubtless had his own ideas of how a schooner should be rigged. At any rate these freak rigs never caught on to any extent and soon disappeared. The *Preference* sailed until December 18th, 1910, on which date she was abandoned 125 miles east of Thatcher's Island Light, Mass., George E. Gale, master and owner at the time.

One of the smallest three-masted vessels was built near Windsor in 1893. The *Gertie* of 45 tons net was launched for Hugh Gillespie and she was engaged in trading until December 12th, 1910, when she sank on a trip from Joggins, N.S., to Digby.

At Maitland in 1894 the *Lillie* of 311 tons net was built by H. Roy for H. M. Davis. This vessel went into the hard-pine trade and was sold to foreign owners at Gulfport, Miss.

On the Bay of Fundy at Margaretsville, N.S., the *Elma* of 299 tons net was built for Captain M. C. Miller by S. Harris in 1892. She was later owned by J. F. Whitney & Co. of New York and was lost off Brewster, Me., on May 6th, 1915, while proceeding from Perth Amboy, N.J., toward Halifax with a cargo of coal. In 1893 the *Canaria* of 242 tons net was launched by G. Purdy of Saint John and was sold to C. W. Brown. In August, 1889, the vessel was sold to Boston owners.

This completes the list of tern schooners built around the Bay of Fundy during the era 1890-1900.

Schooners built in other parts of Nova Scotia, 1890-1900

Along the Northumberland Strait and on the south coast of Nova Scotia other tern schooners were built for various trades. At River John the *Sir Hibbert* of 246 tons net was built by M. L. Kitchin for C. H. McLennan in 1893. During the time he owned her she was engaged in the West Indies trade and one of her passages from Demerara to Halifax was a hard one. In those days there was little that could be done for sick men at sea but watch them get well or die. Except for a little practical knowledge of medical matters, a standard supply of laxatives and disinfectants, the master and mate were unable to do much. The winds and tides determined when a vessel reached port. On this passage, which was a long one, yellow fever broke out aboard and all appear to have contracted the disease. The mate died and eventually the schooner arrived at Halifax in a desperate condition with all hands very weak. The *Sir Hibbert* was sold to French owners in 1899 and was registered at St. Pierre et Miquelon. In the same place, and presumably to replace the *Sir Hibbert*, Mr. McLennan built the *Sirdar* in 1899. This fine schooner of 498 tons net was built with a flush deck, which was unusual in our schooners. Nearly all of them were designed with a raised forecastlehead and a poop deck. The forward house was built against the forecastlehead and this arrangement provided shelter for the windlass as well as breaking the force of the seas against the deck cargo, which in the case of lumber was always stowed to a considerable height. In a vessel with a cargo of sawn boards, deals, laths or shingles, it was the custom to stow about one-third of the cargo on deck. The length and height of the poop deck varied for different trades and this subject was covered in Part II. A painting of this vessel shows her under reefed lowers off the port of Le Havre, France. It is reported that soon after launching this vessel was chartered for service on the west coast of Africa and remained abroad for some years. She was later altered to a barquentine and ended up in the hard-pine trade, being abandoned in the Gulf of Mexico on December 27th, 1913, on a voyage from Mobile to Port of Spain, Trinidad, with lumber.

At Pugwash, N.S., the *Cavalier* of 243 tons net was built in 1893 by David Redmond. She was later owned by W. H. Dean and on January 28th, 1902, was a total loss in Central America while loaded with mahogany and lignum vitae.

The tern schooners were never very popular in Lunenburg, as this place was primarily a fishing port and while an occasional tern was built in the various yards of Lunenburg the two-masted fishing vessel reigned supreme. For many years the Lunenburg and Gloucester fisheries developed their fishing schooners to a very high degree of efficiency. What they required was a fast, tough, able vessel in which to make a quick passage to and from the Banks, carrying a fishing crew and all their equipment, including dories, trawls, bait, etc., and still be able to handle the vilest weather with ease. The Grand Banks and the offshore fishing grounds are no place for a vessel that is not one hundred percent efficient. The saga of these fishing vessels and the men who sailed them is another story. These fishermen developed the type of vessel that led to the famous *Bluenose*, the undefeated racing champion of the Atlantic Fishing Fleet and considered by many to be the finest two-masted commercial schooner built anywhere in the world. The *Bluenose* came from the drawing board of W. J. Roue, Halifax, and was built in the shipyard of Smith & Rhuland, Lunenburg, in 1920. Her exploits are too well known to be repeated in this work. After her fishing and racing days were over, as a cargo motor vessel she was lost in the Caribbean after sale to foreigners.

While many of the fishing schooners carried away cured-fish cargoes to distant ports in the off-fishing seasons, and did it successfully, they were not full-time cargo vessels and will not be dealt with in this work.

The merchants of Lunenburg and elsewhere used many three-masted schooners to carry their salt fish to the distant markets and for bringing salt from Spain and the West Indies to their curing sheds. The *Moss Rose* was built at Pleasantville, N.S., in 1892 by Albert McKean for S. Shankle. She was a small tern of 149 tons net and in 1902 was sold to French owners, registered at St. Pierre et Miquelon and renamed *Helene*. The *Bravo* of 147 tons net was built at Lunenburg for Zwicker & Co. in 1895 and used for the export of fish. She was sold to G. A. Cruikshank of Sydney, N.S., and was lost on a voyage from United States ports at Vineyard Haven in 1915. E. N. Zwicker also had the *Narka* of 154 tons net in this trade. The *Narka* was built by E. P. Young at Lunenburg in 1896 and she may have been outfitted first as a two-master. An old photo in the office of Zwicker & Co. of Lunenburg definitely places her as a tern. Henry Burke, a longtime seaman and master in the tern schooners, was mate in this vessel for six years and sometime after he left, the *Narka* foundered on a passage from Puerto Rico to Halifax, but her crew were rescued.

The *Morales* of 168 tons net was built at Lunenburg in 1896 by John Smith for Captain Howard Hebb. After some years she was sold to French owners and registered at Bayonne. All these schooners were small compared to the fine large schooners up the Bay of Fundy and were built to supplement the fishing industry. At this time many of the Lunenburg merchants used larger ships to transport most of their cargoes and they favoured square-rigged vessels of various types, as most of their voyages were offshore, where this type of vessel was preferred.

Farther along the coast the *Kildare*, first called the *A. J. McKean* after her owner-builder, of 58 tons net, a very small tern schooner, was built at La Have, N.S. She was sold to Alex J. McFadden as a coaster. Following along the shore, the *Windermere* of 299 tons net was built by John Hutt in 1892 at Port Medway for J. G. Hall & Co. of Boston. She had a short life, as she was lost in September, 1893. At Liverpool, the *Juanita* of 147 tons net was built by Robie McLeod in 1897 for French owners and was registered at St. Pierre et Miquelon.

The *Mary Hendry* of 249 tons net was the first of a large fleet of schooners built for A. W. Hendry. She was launched at Liverpool, N.S., and was originally fitted as a topsail tern. St. Clair Geldert, to be prominent in the later schooners, was a master in this vessel. She was lost at Burgeo, Nfld., on August 12th, 1916, while proceeding from Lunenburg to Ramea, Nfld., in ballast.

The last vessel listed for the era 1890-1900 is the *Evelyn* of 167 tons net, built and owned by John A. McGowan in 1899 at Shelburne, N.S. She was in the usual trades until January 9th, 1913, when she was wrecked at Isle au Bois, twenty miles from Cape Race, Nfld., while proceeding toward St. John's Nfld., from Pernambuco.

PART FOUR

The Period between 1900 and the Outbreak of World War One

At ports all around the Atlantic Ocean the yachtlike white-painted schooners were to be seen. The crews of the vessels had carried on the tradition of the earlier sailors of the square-rigged ships of the great days when the Maritime craft were distinguished by their fine well-kept appearance. As soon as the cargo work was finished the decks were scrubbed until they were snow white, the paintwork washed, the hardwood trim and bitts sanded and varnished. An art quite gone now was the painting of designs on water-breaker heads and hatches, and intricate rope-work with Turk's heads and rose konts by the dozen. Woe betide the mate arriving home with the schooner not spotless and shining.

The number of ocean-going three- and four-masted schooners launched in Atlantic Canada increased steadily until a year or so before World War One. At that period the schooners had begun to lose out in some of the trades as other forms of transportation replaced them. Roads were getting better. Small steamers became more available and, while they were more costly to build, were able to last so much longer and with less risk of loss that they had a lower insurance rate. The big schooners were well built and had good gear, but they were constructed principally of softwood, and bad luck, either through a stranding or a hard passage, often strained them to the extent they were always leaky afterward. Some owners held to the principle that after seven years of service it was time to sell and replace a softwood vessel, as repairs from that time on cut deeply into profits.

Many of the schooners were lost. Certainly, it is more difficult to navigate around the coast in a sailing ship than in a steamer. No canvas-driven vessel could sail directly against the wind or tide and many were caught on a lee shore. In those days there were no weather reports broadcast every few hours and it is now considered that oldtime weather prophets, as a rule, were at the best only guessers. They did have barometers which indicated the approach of a depression—but gave no clue as to its course or intensity until the storm arrived. The laws concerning circular storms were well known and a smart navigator could at times get out of the worst part of a storm, but he had little advance warning. In later years, when hurricanes were better understood and their expected track and intensity were predicted for a considerable time ahead, shipping was able to avoid them by a change of course, or by seeking shelter. But until the radio became a standard piece of equipment there was no way for a master to ascertain in advance what he was up against.

In the North Atlantic it was impossible to avoid the big storms. A sailing vessel just had to ride out a gale as best she could. Often the schooners had too great a weight of cargo and became strained, which started excessive leaking. A great many of them were left after a hard blow, leaking badly and with gear damaged. Far from shore, there was no hope of an economical tow to port and the only practical way out was to keep afloat until a passing ship could take the crew off and abandon the vessel.

The schooners had two big advantages. They were built without a great capital investment and there was a pool of able experienced men to operate them. There was a demand for a limited number of vessels in the trades and they were kept busy. In Newfoundland, where for a long time cured and dry fish was carried abroad in small English schooners, a change was made when the shippers began to invest in Canadian cargo vessels to carry their fish product to market. In this period, 1900-14, seven tern schooners were built in Newfoundland to carry their own exports. In the same period New Brunswick almost ceased building and produced only three moderately sized schooners and one very small one. Shipbuilding in that province would probably have come to an end about 1914 if the demand for shipping in the latter part of World War One had not been so urgent. It will be seen that great results were obtained there when ships were required in a hurry.

Early Twentieth-century Schooners built in New Brunswick

In New Brunswick, interest in building tern schooners was becoming less and owners who desired vessels bought them in Nova Scotia, where construction was spasmodically carried on until the outbreak of World War One. However, three moderately sized terns were produced early in the century. The *Ethyl B. Sumner* of 353 tons net was launched in 1901 at Harvey, N.B., for F. W. Sumner. This schooner was lost in 1912 when she was stranded in the Petitcodiac River and became a total wreck. The *Annie M. Parker* of 398 tons net was the last of the series of six terns launched by the Parkers of Tynemouth, N.B. She worked out most of her life in the hard-pine trade out of Mobile, Ala., but her final days are obscure and there is no information on her after striking a bar near Cape Bauld, N.B., on November 13th, 1915, and losing her deck load. The third vessel was the *Harry Miller* of 243 tons net built in 1904 by J. E. Miller at Water-borough, N.B. Some years later she was sold to J. W. Smith and as an old vessel she went under the French flag and was renamed *Donaumont*.

Occasionally very small vessels were built as three-masted schooners. The very small ones were never fully rigged and mostly they were pole-masted and had a spike bowsprit, if any, and they really do not come under the scope of this study, as they were too small to engage in anything but local trade. The *Mapleleaf* of 21.29 tons net was built by S. T. Girvan in 1902 at Welsford, N.B., and was later owned by L. H. Herring of Murray River, P.E.I. This little schooner was latterly engaged in carrying produce from

Prince Edward Island to the mainland and Cape Breton and returned to her home ports with coal. She was dismantled and put on the beach at Murray Harbour about 1928. During this period there were two tern schooners and one two-masted schooner with the name *Mapleleaf*. There seems to be no explanation for three vessels in the same area having the same name.

Early Part of the Century Schooners built in P.E.I

Shipbuilding declined in Prince Edward Island to the point where only three terns were built in the period 1900 to the start of World War One. G. W. Wightman launched the *Empress* of 335 tons net at Montague in 1901. She was bought by C. Anderson of the lumber interests in Guysborough, N.S., and was destroyed by fire in November, 1915. The *Corona* of 179 tons net was built at Cardigan in 1904 by Georgina MacDonald. She soon passed to Newfoundland registry and was owned by Robert Moulton. On March 31st, 1912, she was abandoned in the Atlantic. The third was the *Limelight* of 126 tons net launched at Souris, P.E.I., by T. Kirkham in 1908. She was abandoned on the beach at Wine Harbour, N.S., on November 19th, 1914, and lay there for some years. When the war demand for schooners became acute she was brought to Port Hawkesbury, C.B., and rebuilt under the direction of A. V. Forbes. She was renamed *Riseover II* and sold to J. T. Moulton of Newfoundland for the salt-fish trade. According to him she was not satisfactory and after a passage from Burnt Islands and Burgeo, Nfld., to Oporto and return, which turned out to be a very lengthy voyage, she was sold to Venezuelan owners in May of 1921.

Newfoundland commenced to build Tern Schooners after 1900

The Newfoundland fish exporters had depended up to this time on chartering outside vessels for their export trade. They had built some small square-rigged vessels for this work, but the bulk of the salt dried fish was moved in small English and Scandinavian vessels especially built for the business. They also sent much of the fish abroad in their own two-masted fishing schooners at the end of the fishing season when the schooners would have otherwise been idle. Some of these small schooners made excellent passages to Spain and the Mediterranean, but we are not concerned with them here.

The Newfoundland shippers had acquired several of the large outside-built schooners up to this time and found them satisfactory. In 1900 the first Newfoundland-built tern was launched by T. French at Burnt Bay, Nfld. She was the *Nellie M* of 231 tons net and her first owner was R. K. Bishop and later W. S. Munroe. Tom Runsey was master for most of her life which was spent in the Brazilian trade. She was abandoned at sea many years later. In 1900 also, M. Nash built the *Duchess of Cornwall* of 129 tons net at Burgeo for Robert Moulton of that place. This little vessel was destroyed by a German raider on December 8th, 1916, and her crew were taken prisoner and carried to Germany.

The *Nina L* of 95 tons net, a very small tern, was built by J. Mannuel at Notre Dame Bay in 1907 for J. C. Crosbie. She was lost at sea on December 12th, 1911. A picture of this small tern shows her to be a very neat schooner with a hull very much like the fishing vessels of the period with a long overhang to the stern, no forward deck-house and flush-decked except for the break amidships. In 1908 J. Davidge built the *Chrissie C. Thomey* of 123 tons net. This schooner was later owned by the Government of Canada and was used on voyages to Hudson's Bay. Many years later this little vessel was lost in far northern waters of Canada at the mouth of Rupert River in James Bay.

Another of the very small three-masted schooners, and presumably only used for coasting, was the *Dorothy Lake* of 23.8 tons net built in 1911 by John E. Lake at Fortune, Nfld. She was later equipped with an auxiliary and was lost on St. Pierre Bank in 1923. The Lake interests were later to be prominent in the employment of tern schooners. In 1913 John E. Lake built the *George Ewart* at Fortune. This vessel was employed in the salt-fish trade to Spain and the Mediterranean until she was sunk in a collision in the Straits of Gibraltar on September 12th, 1917.

The *John Harvey* was built at Belleoram, Nfld., in 1912. The data on this vessel is scanty, but she became well known as the topic of a ballad. In 1917 George Kearly was master when this vessel went ashore during the winter months at Gabarus, C.B. The lives of the crew were saved by the heroism of a young seaman, Foote by name, who swam ashore with a line and later died of injuries and exhaustion. The wreck of this vessel is immortalized in Newfoundland by the famous song, "Loss of the *John Harvey*", which is set forth in the Appendix to this work.

The shortage of shipping following the war period after 1914 provided a stimulus for accelerated building in Newfoundland. With the schooners they built themselves and others they bought in Nova Scotia, they had a fleet of about 150 sail of vessels by 1920, all engaged in carrying salt fish to Europe, South America and the West Indies.

The Nova Scotia Schooners 1900-14

In this fifteen-year period 158 tern schooners were put in commission around the Nova Scotia coast. By 1912 the number of new vessels under construction had dropped and it appeared that the employment of large cargo schooners was on the way out. The war changed this trend and inspired the greatest shipbuilding era for the Maritime Provinces in fore-and-aft vessels.

At the head of the Bay of Fundy two terns were built in 1900. H. Elderkin & Co. built the *Benefit* of 229 tons net at Parrsboro for Alfred Potter. She operated until December 9th, 1913, when she was abandoned in the North Atlantic while on a voyage from Kingsport, N.S., to Havana. Across the Bay at Noel, N.S., the *Britannia* of 264 tons net was launched by Osmond O'Brien. After a short life she was lost on the Galera Zamba coast, near Cartagena, South America, on February 18th, 1904.

John Wagstaff, the well-known builder at Annapolis, N.S., launched the *Margaret May Riley* of 241 tons net in 1900 for S. W. W. Pickup. This vessel is reported to have been exceptionally fast for this class. In later years she was sold to Alex Wilson and later still came under the French flag renamed *Roclincourt*.

Two terns were launched at Liverpool, N.S., in this year of 1900. The *J. K. Dawson*, renamed the *Ariel*, of 249 tons net, was built by John Millard and bought by E. R. Bowring of St. John's Nfld. One night, about 1907, this vessel struck Petrie's Ledge at the entrance to Sydney Harbour, N.S., and went hard aground. As the vessel seemed to be in a bad place, and in danger of breaking up, the crew left and found shelter ashore for the night. Before morning a rising tide refloated the vessel, which then drifted across the harbour, struck on Cranberry Head and the swell worked her in close under the cliffs. The local men boarded her and found the ship deserted except for a dog. The vessel broke up quickly, but the dog was adopted by a local family and carried the vessel's name, *Ariel*, as long as he lived.

The other launching at Liverpool in 1900 was the *Success* of 199 tons net built for Paspebiac, Que., owners. Captain E. J. Inness was her first master and had an interest in the vessel. She was transferred to Barbados in 1907 and later sold to James Baird & Co. of St. John's, Nfld. In 1918 Captain P. D. Rafuse was in charge of this vessel while on a voyage to Oporto with salt fish. After a stormy passage the schooner arrived off the coast of Portugal and became becalmed in the heavy onshore swell. The vessel worked in close to the land and when she reached soundings the Captain let go both anchors in an effort to save her. But in the heavy swell the chains parted and there was nothing the crew could do but take to the boat and see the *Success* strike the beach and be smashed to pieces. This occurred in early December just after the end of World War One.

The Captain's Wife

When the Captain took his wife along in the vessel she immediately became known as "the old woman" no matter what her age or appearance. Mrs. Jennie Inness, wife of Captain E. J. Inness, who was noted in the previous paragraph as being master and part owner of the *Success*, was one of the wives who sailed with her husband in various vessels prior to and during World War One.

Mrs. Inness recently told me of those days. She was married in 1909 and shortly after sailed in the *Success* on a honeymoon voyage south. Captain Inness laid down some rules for her which included instructions not to interfere with the cook, to keep absolutely clear of the galley and to give no orders of any kind to the crew. She carried out this routine and greatly enjoyed the years she sailed in the vessels. After her first child was born she shipped again and took the baby with her. There was always one or more of the crew fond of children, so it was never necessary to hire a baby-sitter. As the children grew and required space to move about, chicken wire was stretched around the pin rail on the poop to cover the openings and to block the passages forward.

Captain Inness took his wife in other vessels in which he went master, including the *W. N. Zwicker* and the *Lavengro*. These schooners were active in the trades of the times: lumber and fish to the West Indies, Madeira and Brazil. Tropical cargoes north included molasses and sugar from Barbados, coconuts from the San Blas coast and salt from the Turks Island group.

Mrs. Inness' memories today are of a pleasant time spent in foreign ports where they met new and old friends afloat and ashore. She looked forward to seeing ships from home and especially those in which she knew the Captain had his wife along. She was a young person and loved the parties and courtesies which came the way of the Captain's wife in the far-off ports.

She recalls the food aboard the schooners as being ample and of good quality. Good vessels had good cooks and good stores. She missed having fresh butter more than anything else and always looked forward to having fresh vegetables and fruit on arrival in port. The days at sea passed pleasantly with chores around the cabin and there was always embroidery or needlework to do.

On one occasion, bound south in the spring, the schooner was trapped in drift ice. Part of the deck cargo of lumber was used for temporary sheathing as the ice jammed against the helpless vessel. Mrs. Inness still remembers the grinding and grating sound of the ice against the ship's stern. After a while the schooner worked clear and proceeded without damage.

The first Christmas Mrs. Inness spent at sea was very gloomy. The schooner was on her way north laden with salt from Turks Island and encountered winter storms. The cook fell ill and died. On Christmas Day the ship was hove-to in a gale and labouring heavily. One great boarding sea carried away the water casks secured on deck and left them with only a small amount, which had to be rationed severely until the ship made port. The food prepared that day was cooked by the mate, but Mrs. Inness, alone in the cabin, said she had absolutely no appetite. The vessel was damaged, but survived the gale. A later Christmas was different. She had her small girls with her on this occasion and the sailors rigged themselves out in ridiculous clothes, including wigs made out of combed manilla rope, and came aft to entertain the children, bringing gifts they had made. Ships like these never wanted for the best of men to man them and were always the best kept and prepared for any emergency.

Mrs. Inness spent about five years in all aboard the schooners.

At Lunenburg the *Canada* of 199 tons net was built by J. C. Young in 1900. A. Geldert was one of her early masters and she appears to have remained in Lunenburg throughout her life under different owners, including A. Conrad, J. Joseph Rudolph and W. Lithgow. She was wrecked at Matanzas, Cuba, on April 30th, 1917. The *Evadne* of 361 tons net was built by C. H. McLennan at River John, N.S., in 1900. She was later owned by Charles Archibald and was abandoned in the Straits of Florida on February 10th, 1916. Nearby, the last tern for the year 1900, the *McClure* of 191 tons net, was built at Tatamagouche by A. Weatherbie and others, including T. Dinsmore of Pictou. A later owner was I. A. Hopkins. In February, 1917, she was purchased at Halifax by J. T. Moulton for the salt-fish trade. She loaded general cargo at Halifax for St. John's, Nfld., and on completion of this voyage loaded fish for a Mediterranean port. The *McClure* was torpedoed and sent to the bottom on this trip by a German submarine off the Spanish coast on May 22nd, 1917. Captain Augustus Taylor and his crew escaped and landed in their boat at a nearby port.

In 1901 the *St. Bernard*, a small tern of 124 tons net, was built by P. McLaughlin at Parrsboro, N.S., for A. O. Seaman. She was later owned by J. N. Pugsley. Her master was J. E. George when she had the bad luck to be loading cargo at Halifax on December 6th, 1917. This was the day the steamers *Imo* and *Mont Blanc* collided in the harbour. The *Mont Blanc* was loaded with munitions for the Allied Armies in Europe. The force of the collision started a fire and soon after the cargo detonated, with devastating effect on the whole area, destroying a large part of the city and killing hundreds of people. The small *St. Bernard* was smashed against the dock by the great wave raised in the explosion and was a total loss.

Messrs. Cochrane & Soley built the *Dara C* of 380 tons net in 1901 at Port Greville. She was operated by her builders and was lost at Grand Cayman in the Caribbean on July 13th, 1914. At the same place H. Elderkin built the *Prosperare* of 378 tons net the same year. She was operated by Homer & Puddington of New York and retained her Canadian registry. On October 30th, 1908, the vessel was stranded on the north coast of Cuba and became a total wreck.

In 1901 Spencer's Island became a site for building tern schooners. In former days many fine large square-rigged ships had been built there by members of the well-known Spicer family, the best-known ship probably being the *E. J. Spicer*, noted for her many speedy trans-Atlantic crossings. Johnson Spicer launched the first tern there, the *M. J. Taylor* of 377 tons net. She had various owners, including O. F. Taylor of Charlotte-town, P.E.I., J. G. P. Murphy of Quebec and latterly J. R. P. Pettis. After a long career the worn-out vessel was hauled out on the beach at Parrsboro in 1930 and the hulk was bought by Captain Joseph Cutten, the harbourmaster, for her gear. The second schooner was the *Ophir* of 249 tons net, launched the same year by Johnson Spicer for Bartram Bros. of New York. She was wrecked at Jeremie, Haiti, while loading for New York on November 22nd, 1904, and the wreck was sold in the Dutch West Indies.

Across the Basin at Hantsport, N.S., the *Lord of Avon* of 325 tons net was built in 1901 by G. N. Pearson for D. Faulkner. She was later owned by R. C. Elkin of Saint John, N.B. Her career ended on December 26th, 1913, while on a passage from Pen-secola, Fla., to Cienfuegos, Cuba, with lumber, when she was abandoned in the Gulf of Mexico. She was later towed into Tampa, Fla., a total loss. At Cheverie, Rodman Pratt had another Greek letter named tern built, the *Theta* of 420 tons net. As with the other vessels in his fleet, the builder was Roderick Rose. The *Theta* joined the long list of missing ships when she sailed from Hillsboro, N.B., with a lumber cargo on December 3rd, 1910, and was never reported again.

To move to the end of the Bay, the *W. N. Zwicker* of 398 tons net was built at Clyde River for A. H. Zwicker. J. L. Publicover was a part owner and master in this vessel. A more complete story of Captain Publicover's career is given elsewhere, but while he was master of this vessel, on December 20th, 1912, on a passage off the U.S. coast, he came across the American tern schooner *Henry R. Tilton* while in a full gale. On this same day F. W. Wallace, author of many books having to do with ships and fishing, told me he was in the fishing schooner *Effie M. Morrissey* and not far from the *Tilton* when the squalls struck. He saw her sails blowing away and the seas crashing over the deck load. The *Zwicker* was making fair weather of the storm, proceeding along under very short sail, when the *Tilton* was sighted in a derelict condition, her crew lashed in the rigging and the vessel in imminent danger of breaking up. With great risk and superb seamanship, Captain Publicover got a dory over the side and with one of his men rowed over to the *Tilton* and took off half her crew. He feared that the whole com-plement of the *Tilton* would overload the dory, so he took only half of them and landed them aboard his own vessel. Then with his dory-mate he made another trip to get the remainder, and after safely landing them aboard the *Zwicker* he recovered oars and the dory and proceeded on his voyage. For his heroism he was presented with a gold watch from Woodrow Wilson, then President of the United States. The *Zwicker* was sold during the war in New York at a poor price on account of a previous agreement. In the meantime the prices for ships had sky-rocketed as the German submarines decimated Allied shipping and the demand for seagoing bottoms was very great. She arrived in New York from Buenos Ayres with a cargo of linseed, the freight on which was $26,000. The vessel was sold under the earlier agreement for the sum of $22,000. On that voyage she discharged at Black Tom Dock at Hoboken, New Jersey, and the day after she was towed out the terrific enemy-organized munitions explosion took place. The *Zwicker* was sold to the Windrush Lumber Co. of Boston, Mass., and was lost soon after on a voyage to French Guiana.

The *Alexandra* of 173 tons net was built in 1901 at Weymouth, N.S., by F. C. Rice for his own account. She was in the West Indies trade until she was lost at East Harbour, Turks Island, on November 28th, 1913. The same year the Clarke Bros. of nearby Bear River built the *Castano* of 215 tons net. This schooner went in the hard-pine trade and did not last long. She has not been heard of since August, 1901, and is supposed to have foundered in the Gulf of Mexico while on a voyage from Cienfuegos, Cuba, to Appalachicola, Fla. None of her crew ever showed up.

The *Doris M. Pickup* of 372 tons net was owned by S. W.W . Pickup and was built at Annapolis, N.S., in 1901. She was in the hard-pine trade and Norman Roop was her master for a time. Many of the vessels were sent south in those days to be operated by a ship's husband in Mobile, and while there this vessel was sold to J. G. P. Murphy, lumber merchant of Lauzon, Que. While owned by the latter she was lost at Praia, Cape Verde Islands, in June, 1914.

L. D. Shafner built the *Havelock*, 212 tons net, in nearby Bridgetown the same year. She was later owned by Pickels & Mills of Annapolis, N.S., and much later by many other owners. In August of 1909 she went ashore on the north coast of Cuba and was abandoned. She was ultimately salved and had various owners and the following re-names—*Tres Amigos, Jose Luis Orive* and finally *San Jose*.

In this busy year of 1901 two schooners were launched at Shelburne. The first was the *Carib II* of 195 tons net by J. A. McGowan for Harry Comer. This vessel was later sold to Robert Wilcox, who operated a shipping business at Panama and New York. Captain John S. Smith was master of this ship for a considerable time and he often told me what a smart vessel she was. She was sold to foreigners at Colon, Panama, in 1911. The other vessel was the *Vera Cruz VI*, a small tern of 110 tons net, built for foreign account and transferred to St. Vincent in the Cape Verde Islands after being launched by A. Hood.

Liverpool, N.S., came to the forefront in this year of the tern schooners. Two of them came from the yard of Robie McLeod. The first was the *Harry Troop* of 199 tons net, built for Captain George Thorburn. She was wrecked on the Nova Scotia coast on December 16th, 1904. The other was the *Brooklyn* of 247 tons net, built for Captain E.

M. Dexter and Harvey McLeod and later owned by C. Edgar Whidden. Captain Marshall O'Hara told me he was in this vessel as a young fellow and on a voyage from Moss Point, Miss., to Cayenne, French Guiana, in 1908, when as a consequence of heavy weather the schooner leaked very badly and finally filled. Fearing she would roll over, they hailed a passing steamer and were towed into Surinam, Dutch Guiana, where the vessel was condemned and sold. Captain Marshall O'Hara was later known to thousands of ship officers in his capacity of Instructor at the Navigation School in Halifax, N.S.

The *Laura* of 299 tons net was built in 1901 by J. Gardiner at Liverpool for Harlow & Kempton. Late in World War One, while under the command of Captain Loomer of Advocate, she vanished with all her crew and is believed to have been destroyed by an enemy submarine.

John W. Hutt built two schooners at Liverpool in 1901. The first was named the *J. W. Hutt* of 349 tons net and was lost in the Bahamas on October 16th, 1907. The other, the *E. A. Sabean* of 267 tons net, was designed by Robie McLeod and was abandoned at sea on July 5th, 1921.

The final vessel for the year 1901 at Liverpool was the *W. S. Fielding* of 199 tons net built for A. W. Hendry. This schooner was abandoned near Cape Antonio, Jamaica, on October 12th, 1909.

Along the coast at La Have, the *Nellie Louise* of 243 tons net was built in 1901 by J. N. Rafuse. This vessel had various Newfoundland owners and was badly damaged by going ashore while leaving Barbados molasses-laden for St. John's, Nfld., in April, 1916. She was salvaged and passed to Barbados owners.

The last vessels noted for the year 1901 were from the smaller yards. At Lunenburg the *Palma* of 249 tons net was launched by Young & Morash for Jas. Shankle. At Mahone Bay the small *Cyril* of 74 tons net was built by D. E. Burgoyne and sold later to Emile Delisle of St. Kitts, B.W.I., and disappeared from the lists about 1922. At the same place the *Edyth* of 197 tons net was built by J. Ernst & Sons. She was lost on Salt Cay, Turks Island, on June 5th, 1915, while in ballast from Pernambuco. Nearby, at Chester Basin, the *Maple Leaf* of 196 tons net was built by I. Wagner for S. Watson. She had various owners, including A. Arenburg and A. S. Publicover, and later passed to Newfoundland owners. She was abandoned at sea in the North Atlantic prior to December 4th, 1917, while on a voyage from Newfoundland to Valencia, Spain, with fish. On the other side of the province, at Pugwash on the Northumberland Strait, C. W. Redmond built the *Marion Louise* of 196 tons net for W. H. Baraud, Prince Edward Island. The schooner was not fated to last very long and was wrecked on the north coast of Cuba on March 7th, 1904.

The Rate of Building was kept up during 1902

Twenty-five large schooners came off the stocks during 1902. Included among these was the four-masted *H. J. Logan* of 771 tons net, the largest fore-and-aft vessel built in Canada up to this time. Her owner and builder was Captain D. S. Howard, who was mentioned before as the builder of four of the large gypsum schooners. At Parrsboro this large vessel, named after Hance J. Logan, M.P. for Cumberland County, N.S., was

MARGARET M. RILEY. 241 tons. Built 1900 at Granville, N.S. *Courtesy of the St. Anne Museum*

DARA C. 380 tons. Built 1901 at Port Greville, N.S. (Loading piling through bow ports.)
Courtesy of Commander W. J. L. Parker

H. J. LOGAN. 772 tons. Built 1902 at Parrsboro, N.S.

ALBANI. 249 tons. Built 1902 at Liverpool, N.S.

christened by Mrs. H. A. Tucker, daughter of Captain Howard, who broke a bottle of champagne over her bows as she slid down the ways. The foreman shipwright during her construction was Captain Wm. Egan of Sackville, N.B., and she was fitted out with a steam donkey-engine from the shops of the Robb Engineering Co. of Amherst, N.S.

Captain D. S. Howard, owner and builder, was born at Port Greville and went to sea as a boy. At nineteen he was master of the schooner *Gilbert Bent*, at twenty-one he commanded the barquentine *Landora*. When he was twenty-eight he left the sea and went into shipbuilding. In 1881 at Parrsboro he built the beautiful *Davida*, named after his daughter, and went back to sea in her until he sold the schooner. He then came ashore and during the next few years built the three large gypsum terns and the *Gypsum Emperor*, a four-master and the largest schooner built in Canada up to that time. In 1893 he built the *Florence R. Hewson*, followed by the *Earl of Aberdeen*. He returned to sea in the latter vessel and for some years made money in her before coming ashore for a well-earned rest. But he was not ready to lay back and in 1901 prepared to build the *H. J. Logan*.

Captain Howard twice contested as a Liberal candidate for the County of Cumberland, but failed to win a seat. He was very well known in the locality and was always foremost in holding up his end in anything pertaining to the public welfare. He remained as master in the *H. J. Logan* until her abandonment in the North Atlantic.

Loss of the 'H. J. Logan'

This vessel was abandoned in 1910 while on a passage from Chatham, N.B., to New York with a cargo of lumber. From the mate's log the following account has been compiled.

On October 20th, 1910, the *H. J. Logan* was ready for sea and early in the morning the pilot boarded and the schooner sailed down the river to the harbour, where she anchored to await a chance out. On the 24th the wind came N.W., blowing strong, and the schooner was got under way with all the lower sails reefed. When the anchor was hove-up it was seen that the stock was missing, so the spare bower was shackled to the cable and secured to the cat-head. After a short run with fair weather the wind hauled ahead and it was necessary to beat down Northumberland Strait. After anchoring several times to await a better chance, the *Logan* arrived at Port Hawkesbury, in the Strait of Canso, on October 28th.

It was November 2nd before the new stock had been fitted to the anchor and the big schooner beat her way down the Strait to enter the Atlantic and start the long run along the coast to the westward.

From this time on until the 19th of December the schooner encountered strong winds and gales from the west, northwest and southwest. For days the sails were reefed, double-reefed, reduced, hove-to in gales, reefs shaken out and a dogged try was made to win to the westward. But the net result was that she made little westing but worked steadily offshore to the south. On November 25th the rudder head was broken off and from this time she was steered by a jury-rig, several schemes being tried, but none working successfully. On December 7th the rudder became unshipped and was towed astern at first, but later was brought aboard and lashed on deck.

Up forward, the crew lost heart as a result of the bitter weather, the incessant sail drill, and agitated to leave the ship. Mate Angus Publicover had quarrelled with Captain Howard, but they patched up their differences to show a united front against the crew. By the time the trouble started, the schooner had lost part of her deck load, the mainsail had been torn badly, the rudder was on deck, useless, and the weather was too severe to attempt shipping it again. The schooner was leaking some, but she had a steam pump.

At this later date it is difficult to judge whether the vessel was eventually abandoned and lost because the seamen were not top quality. Captain Howard and Mate Angus Publicover were men of great experience and ability and the difficulty of getting the crew to work seems to have been the key to their troubles. As the *Logan* was in the steamer lanes, they sighted ships frequently and every time one came in sight the crew came aft with the request that they leave the schooner. Captain Howard refused to abandon the vessel, but attempted to persuade several of the passing steamers to tow them to the nearest port. This was hardly an economical proposition and the steamers refused. However, they did ask for, and received, various stores, including a barrel of beef, tea, sugar and tobacco from one of the steamers.

One can imagine Captain Howard's feelings at this time. His schooner was stout and in good shape. She had received no crippling damage and her leaking was easily handled by the steam pump. He knew if he hung on long enough the weather would moderate, allowing opportunity to ship the rudder and proceed on his voyage. By this time the schooner had drifted to a position 40° N. and 50° W.

But the gales persisted and on the morning of the 19th of December, after forty-seven days of battering, the master acceded to the wishes of the crew, and after hearing his request for a tow turned down, Captain Howard agreed to abandon his vessel and they went aboard a passing steamer, bound for Bremerhaven, and left the *H. J. Logan* to her fate.

The 1902 Schooners

The other large schooner built at Parrsboro in 1902 was the *Advent* of 256 tons net, launched by D. A. Huntley for R. Earl Burgess. She was later owned by Moulton Bisset Ltd. and was abandoned at sea on March 16th, 1916, her crew being taken off by the s.s. *Cloutshaw* and carried to Cherbourg. Captain S. L. Whalley commanded the schooner during the war years.

Johnson Spicer launched the first of the three "Leaf" schooners at Spencer's Island in 1902. The *Coral Leaf*, 374 tons net, was operated by Mr. Spicer for many years and later by J. F. Whitney & Co. of New York. In the war years she was bought by Magistrate E. C. McDade of Parrsboro and was captured by a German submarine and sunk by gunfire off the Irish coast on July 7th, 1917; Ed. Spicer, master.

The year 1902 was quiet for the shipyards along this shore except for the vessel noted above and two schooners which were launched at Port Greville, N.S. G. E. Bentley built the *Margaret G* of 299 tons net for Hugh Gillespie. In later years she was owned by F. Henderson of Mobile, Ala., and registered at Barbados. She was towed into Key

West, Fla., a derelict after having been abandoned at sea on January 6th, 1924. The other schooner was the *Mineola* of 270 tons net, completed for J. Willard Smith by H. Elderkin & Co. Captain Ezra Forsyth, a well-known master mariner of the erea, was in charge of this schooner for many years. Her career ended when she drove ashore at Alligator Pond Bay, Jamaica, on August 15th, 1916, while waiting to load logwood for New York.

Across the Basin at Canning, N.S., the *Advance* of 294 tons net was launched in 1902 by John E. Biglow for R. E. Burgess and others of Wolfville, N.S., for the usual trades. In 1909, while under the command of Captain Burgess on a voyage from southern ports to Halifax with hard pine and cypress used for construction of railway cars, this vessel encountered heavy weather and was forced to enter Bermuda to carry out repairs. After resuming her voyage she was driven south by further gales and later lost her deck cargo. Four months after starting her voyage she reached Halifax and discharged the remainder of her cargo. She went on to Sydney, C.B., to load coal for Campbellton, then loaded lumber for New York.

The *Advance* was wrecked in the West Indies on June 30th, 1914.

At Noel, N.S., the *Hibernia* of 298 tons net was built by Osmond O'Brien for the O'Brien interests. In ending her career this vessel led her crew into one of those terrible experiences that befell seamen often enough.

The schooner sailed from Hantsport, N.S., lumber-laden for Barbados on December 8th, 1911. On account of head winds and bad weather the schooner did not get along well and put into several ports to await a better chance. Her last stop was at Beaver Harbour, N.B., and she left there on Christmas Day to resume her journey. Running off the coast four days later, she encountered a heavy gale and was severely damaged, dismasted, rudder-head broken and rails smashed. The unmanageable vessel, by now waterlogged and swept over by the icy seas, drifted aimlessly and unseen for twenty-nine days afterward. The food stores were destroyed by sea water and there was no chance to build a fire against the January weather. The crew managed to exist in great misery until a steamer came up and took them off.

The *Lady of Avon*, a large schooner of 417 tons net, was built at Hantsport, N.S., in 1902 by W. C. Balcom. She was engaged in the usual trades until October 21st, 1914, when, proceeding toward Cienfuegos, Cuba, from Annapolis, N.S., with lumber, she struck on Grand Turk and became a total loss. The *Marjorie J. Sumner* of 354 tons net was launched at Maitland by C. W. Redmond for F. W. Sumner of Moncton, N.B. This vessel had a hard career, as on July 30th, 1906, she went ashore at Three Sisters, N.S., and later, on February 23rd, 1908, she stranded at North Caicos Island in the Bahamas. She must have survived this, as she went on for some time after.

The *Zeta* of 335 tons net was the last of the fleet of terns with Greek letter names built by Rodman Pratt. This vessel was later owned by Robert Wilcox with Captain Fred Remby in charge. This Captain claimed the honour of taking the first British three-masted schooner, the *Zeta*, through the Panama Canal. Captain Remby sailed several of the schooners for Robert Wilcox, who operated extensively in the trade between Central American ports and New York. "Captain Fred", as he was known to several generations of seamen, was brought up in the big square-riggers and was master in them until they passed out of existence. He died at La Have, N.S., in 1942, at the age of eighty-eight. The *Zeta* was wrecked on the French coast in November of 1919.

The *Ladysmith* of 596 tons net was built by R. S. Soley at Lower Economy, N.S., in 1902. She was first fitted out as a barquentine, but was altered to fore-and-aft rig in 1907. Captain Richard A. Lohnes was master in this vessel at the time of her loss. She was abandoned at sea in 1914 about 150 miles south of Nova Scotia while on a passage from Ingramport, N.S., to New York, the crew being taken off by the s.s. *Chignecto* and carried to Bermuda. Captain Lohnes started to sea as a boy of thirteen from his home in Riverport in the cod-fishing schooner *Joseph McGill*, being employed as a throater at the wage of $12 per month. After fifteen years of working his way up in the fishing vessels he obtained his master's certificate and went into the cargo schooners. During his long years at sea he commanded the tern schooners *Caledonia*, *Ponhook*, *Robert J. Dale*, *Agnes P. Duff*, *G. H. Murray* and *Maria A. Howes*. In 1944 he retired from the sea having spent fifty-five years afloat and in 1956 celebrated his eightieth birthday at his home in Riverport, N.S., hale and hearty except for the loss of a leg. As I locate some of the older men who sailed the vessels it is often amazing to find them so vitally interested in bygone days and with what enthusiasm they relive the fast passages they made in the schooners they commanded so long ago. Surely some of Frederick William Wallace's "Iron men" are still around.

Three Terns built at Liverpool in 1902

The three terns to come out of Liverpool, N.S., in 1902 were the *Arrow* of 183 tons net belonging to A. W. Hendry until December 22nd, 1906, when she was lost at Palenque, Santo Domingo, while loading sugar for New York; the *Damaraland* of 198 tons net launched by John Millard for Reynolds Harrington of Sydney, N.S.; and the *Albani* of 249 tons net, built by Robie McLeod and John Hutt. The *Damaraland* was abandoned at sea on July 11th, 1911. The *Albani* was owned by Captain Clin McKay and A. F. Davison of Bridgewater, N.S., until she was sold to the Portuguese in October, 1913. Captain Everett Nickerson told me he relieved Captain McKay for a voyage in 1907. Captain McKay had not been well, so Captain Nickerson took the vessel with a load of lumber to Havana in the good time of fifteen days, then to Mobile to load hard pine for Port of Spain, Trinidad. The vessel was finally lost carrying a load of liquor from the West Indies to France. Her Portuguese re-name was *Santa Maria*.

A very small Tern

The *Effie Howard*, a tiny tern of 23.8 tons net, was built at Sheet Harbour, N.S., in 1902. This little vessel was rebuilt in 1911 at Pugwash and was then owned by E. R. Heather. She foundered in Placentia Harbour, Nfld., on October 14th, 1920.

Various other Schooners built in Nova Scotia during 1902

J. C. Young built the *J. L. Nelson* of 249 tons net at Lunenburg for W. C. Smith & Co., Fish Merchants, Lunenburg. She was later owned by F. K. Warren of Halifax, and later still by London owners, who renamed the schooner *Annettina*. Mr. Young also launched the *Virginia* of 133 tons net in this year. She was originally a two-masted schooner and was bought by Captain J. L. Publicover and rerigged as a tern. The *Virginia* was wrecked on Rose Head, Lunenburg County, on January 9th, 1912. At La Have Wm. Naugler built the *Laura C* of 249 tons net for John M. Getson. Lemuel Creaser was master in this vessel and on March 16th, 1915, when carrying a cargo of coconuts from Central America to Nova Scotia, was stranded on the Colardo Reefs off the west end of Cuba.

At Shelburne Arthur Hood built two terns for Zephaniah Nickerson. The *Golden Rule* of 163 tons net was operated by the Nickersons until August 19th, 1908, when she struck a rock in Barrington Bay, N.S., and became a total loss. Captain Everett Nickerson told me he took charge of this vessel when she was a year old, found her to be very fast but difficult to load, as she went down by the bow. This schooner had her main cabin set down until the top was flush with the deck, thus reducing the cargo space in the after part of the hold. For all this, Captain Nickerson told me that once, while on a passage from Sydney to Yarmouth with coal, he logged at thirteen knots for two hours. The other vessel launched at Shelburne for the Nickersons was the *Ophelia* of 120 tons net. They kept this vessel for about a year, then sold her to French interests for the fisheries.

Captain Zephaniah Nickerson was prominent in shipping along the south coast at this time. He started his sea career at the age of fourteen and spent forty-five years at sea, during which he sailed in twenty-four ships and was master in fourteen of them. He was very strict about the men sailing aboard his ships, and made it a point to have all the men who signed with him pledge themselves to total abstinence from all alcoholic beverages, and to refrain from bad language. His son, Captain Everett Nickerson, told me his father had continual crew trouble. Captain Everett, on the other hand, never bothered the crew and had no trouble at all with them. This latter Captain left the sea prior to World War One and established a hardware business in Yarmouth, N.S., but always retained an interest in sailing ships until his death in 1956.

A few other vessels were launched in 1902. The *Lillian Blauvelt* of 174 tons net was built by A. H. Comeau at Meteghan River for John R. Blauvelt. In later years this vessel was sold to French owners and renamed *Marylucy*. L. D. Shafner built the *F. W. Pickels* of 385 tons net at Bridgetown for the firm of Pickels & Mills. She was sold later to J. G. P. Murphy of Lauzon, Que., and was lost in the hurricane of October, 1910, in the West Indies.

At River John, N.S., in 1902, C. H. McLennan built the *Unique* of 95 tons net out of materials left over from the *Sirdar*, and this probably accounted for her name. She was a small bald-headed three-master with a spike bowsprit. Later, she was dismasted off Liscomb, N.S., and was bought by Captain O'Hara of Issac's Harbour, N.S. Morris O'Hara, later a master in the Canadian National Steamships, told me his father made a two-topmast schooner out of her. When the schooner was ready, the elder O'Hara decided that it was time for young Morris to go to sea. According to Captain O'Hara, his father told him to leave off milking the cows and sent him to the barn to fill a paillasse with hay, put it in a forecastle bunk and sleep on it when off duty. In this fashion he began his sea career. Many years later the vessel was wrecked on Tuckernuck Shoal off Nantucket, Mass., on July 9th, 1917.

From the foregoing, it is seen that the large cargo schooners were in much demand in the early years of the century. Twenty-five vessels were sent down the ways in 1902, all launched in Nova Scotia, and they went into the prosperous trades of the times and made money for their owners. This is in contrast to other parts of the world where sail was dying out and more steamers were appearing every year. The flurry of Canadian schooner building in these years was to carry on almost to the outbreak of the war.

The 1903 Schooners

Steady construction of the three-masted schooners was maintained in the year 1903. Twenty-two schooners were launched, and as in the previous year they were all built in Nova Scotia, the Bay of Fundy producing the largest number.

Only one of the schooners came from the Windsor area. She was the *Bluenose* of 166 tons net, built at Falmouth by T. W. McKinley. An early owner was P. Blake and later A. E. Hickman of St. John's, Nfld., until November 14th, 1919, when she foundered off Peniche, Spain, with a cargo of dried fish.

Across the Basin, eight tern schooners were built in 1903. At Port Greville, four were launched. The *E. M. Roberts* of 296 tons net was launched by J. W. Cochrane for Captain Fred. W. Roberts. She was later owned by R. C. Elkin & Co. and while under the command of Captain W. Kelso was lost on Nantucket Shoals about 1923. J. W. Cochrane also built the *Hartney W* of 271 tons net for Captain W. E. Wasson. This vessel had a long life and several owners, including C. C. Langill, J. G. Cochrane and J. E. George. For a period she appears to have had French owners but retained her Canadian registry. She was broken up on the beach at Parrsboro in 1930. H. W. Elderkin & Co. built the *Lavonia* of 226 tons net for J. W. Smith. She was later taken over by John W. McManus & Co. of Pictou, N.S., and was lost on the north coast of Cuba in January, 1920. The fourth vessel built at Port Greville in 1903 was the *Ronald* of 268 tons net. She had various owners, including J. E. Pettis, H. J. Jones, Mrs. A. W. Cochrane and latterly J. Splane & Co. She was burned at St. Andrews, N.B., on December 20th, 1920, while loaded with lumber.

A few miles away at Parrsboro, P. J. McLaughlin built the *St. Olaf* of 277 tons net for Harvey MacAloney. This schooner was one of the first to enter the lumber trade between the Bay of Fundy and the United Kingdom in World War One. The employment of these sailing vessels in this business was brought on by the war-stimulated demand for timber and the shortage of ocean shipping. On a return voyage from Wales to Parrsboro, the *St. Olaf* encountered a German submarine on August 19th, 1915, near Galley Head, Ireland, and was destroyed. Also at Parrsboro, D. A. Huntley built the *John G. Walter* of 209 tons net for her owner-master J. G. Walter. After several owners she passed to Homer & Puddington and was registered at New York. On March 24th, 1918, she was attacked and left a derelict by a German submarine in the English Channel.

Johnson Spicer built two terns in 1903 at Spencer's Island. The *Myrtle Leaf* of 336 tons net was for his own account and later was taken over by Charles T. White. E. K.

Merriam was a longtime master in this ship and she was wrecked at San Pedro de Macoris on June 12th, 1919. The *Silver Leaf* was also for his own account and S. T. Salter and W. W. Baldwin are noted as later owners. In September, 1918, the *Silver Leaf* sailed from Saint John, N.B., after being sold to New York parties. She was lumber-laden for South Africa, which included delivering the lumber cargo, then loading hides for New York. The master, Captain Joseph A. Reid, decided that before sailing, the vessel should be fitted with a new set of motor-driven pumps, as he did not like the way she was leaking. The new gear was installed and the vessel sailed. She leaked considerably in the heavy weather encountered and later spent a long period becalmed. The schooner's bottom became very foul and the master decided to put into Barbados for cleaning and repairs. Owing to the difficulty of working the vessel in her soggy condition, she was stranded when making Barbados and was a total loss, but the lumber cargo was salvaged. Captain Reid was said to be the oldest navigator sailing out of Canada in 1918, but I have not determined his age at that time.

Down the Nova Scotia side of the Bay of Fundy, N. V. Munroe had the *Adonis* of 316 tons net launched for his own interest in 1903 at Bridgetown. This schooner was kept in the hard-pine trade for many years until she was abandoned at sea on October 19th, 1920, off Jupiter Inlet, Fla., and later drifted ashore a total loss. Farther along the coast at Weymouth, the *Frances* of 259 tons net was built by T. C. Rice for himself. In later years she passed to F. K. Warren of Halifax. She was wrecked at San Pedro de Macoris, Santo Domingo, while in ballast from New York, on August 2nd, 1918.

The *Albert D. Mills* of 326 tons net was launched at Meteghan River in 1903 by A. H. Comeau for the Pickels, Mills & Shafner interests at Bridgetown. Her last owner was J. C. Scott and she was wrecked near Mobile, Ala., on July 16th, 1916. The same year at Meteghan River, J. Cosman built the *Catherine* of 96 tons net for Clark Bros. Ltd., and later owned by J. H. Benson. She was lost at Grand Turk on June 5th, 1917. The third vessel built here at the same time was the little *Souvenir* of 31 tons net. Her builder was J. A. Robichaud and her owner was L. Outhouse of Beaver Harbour, N.B. The *Souvenir* was built as a two-master, but in 1919 she was taken back to Meteghan River, where she was cut in two and lengthened by ten feet and rigged as a three-mast schooner. In the repair they left the ceiling as it was and fitted new timbers equalling the thickness of the old timbers plus the thickness of the old ceiling. Then they put in a complete new ceiling over the old one. After this repair was completed she was taken to Digby to be remeasured and at the same time the owners decided to rename her *Gwenmarina* after three girls in the family. Captain Oscar L. Outhouse reported she was a perfect little craft and they operated her in the coastal trade, mostly freighting fish, until about 1938, when she was sold to owners near Halifax. The new owners installed diesels, but shortly after she was lost by going ashore somewhere west of Halifax. Captain Outhouse, who was eighty-five in 1954, wrote to me that he often dreams of her, and the idea of selling her to strangers nearly broke his heart. When he delivered her to the new owners at Shelburne she attracted a lot of attention, as she had been kept so well, and commanded the admiration of the oldtime sailors who came down to see her. At this time she was thirty-five years old.

There were a few other small schooners rigged thus, but as a rule they were better off rigged as two-masters. The sails of a small vessel are not difficult to handle and the added expense of a third mast, with stays and rigging, was not practical.

Terns built in Other Parts of Nova Scotia in 1903

Two terns were built in Shelburne in this year. The first, by A. Hood, was the *Elsie* of 149 tons net for the account of J. Hutt. She was lost at the mouth of the Palenque River, Santo Domingo, on June 13th, 1907. The other was the *E. A. Post* of 198 tons net from the yard of G. A. Cox for his own account. This vessel was wrecked on Corn Island off the coast of Nicaragua on October 9th, 1906.

Liverpool provided four terns in 1903. John Millard had the *Mona* of 299 tons net built for his own account. She was lost at Baracoa, Cuba, on March 22nd, 1917. The same year he had the *Lolita A* of 176 tons net launched. She was later owned by S. Courtney of Newfoundland and is noted as being abandoned in the North Atlantic on December 31st, 1908, but she may have been towed in and put back in service. Robie McLeod launched the *Caledonia* of 188 tons net at Liverpool and D. C. Mulhall built the *Leah A. Whidden* of 199 tons net. The Liverpool builders seemed to favour a vessel of this size and many of this approximate tonnage were built here later. The *Caledonia* was built for A. W. Hendry and was abandoned in the North Atlantic on February 12th, 1912. The *Leah A. Whidden* was owned by C. Edgar Whidden and in 1906 was sold to J. B. Porter of St. Vincent, B.W.I. Her master was W. A. Inness and he remained in her for a time after her sale. This schooner was a fine example of a well-kept Nova Scotia sailing vessel. Her white-painted hull, shining varnished spars and spotless deck showed how proud her master, mate and crew were of their trim craft. She was designed for the fish and coconut trade and until her sale had been employed in voyages to the San Blas Coast.

In the winter of 1907-8, under the new owners, Captain Inness, accompanied by his wife, was proceeding toward St. John's, Nfld., in ballast, when through a series of mishaps the schooner was dismasted in a storm. The gear was cut away and lost, but the spanker boom and some odds and ends of canvas were available. The spanker, which had been furled at the time of the dismasting, was safe. Captain Inness and his crew, assisted by Mrs. Inness, who could steer while the men worked, set up a jury-rig and were able to return to the West Indies safely. The schooner was renamed *Isabel* and later went under a foreign flag and had the third name, *Dilia*.

J. C. Young launched the *Helen Stewart* of 180 tons net at Lunenburg this year for W. A. Miller. She was later owned by A. E. Hickman & Co. of St. John's, Nfld., and her rig may have been changed to a two-master. She foundered ten miles N.W. of the Island of Graciosa, Azores, on December 10th, 1918, while on a trans-Atlantic passage.

On the other side of the province at River John, the *Maritana* of 490 tons net, a fine big schooner, was launched by C. H. McLennan for his own account. After a foreign-going charter on the west coast of Africa which lasted for some years she went into the hard-pine trade and was abandoned off the coast of Havana on September 18th, 1909.

SOUVENIR. 31 tons. Built 1903 at Meteghan River, N.S. (One of the smallest three-masters.)
Courtesy of Mr. F. W. Wallace

E. M. ROBERTS. 296 tons. Built 1903 at Port Greville, N.S. *Courtesy of the Canadian Pacific Railway*

MYRTLE LEAF. 336 tons. Built 1903 at Spencer's Island, N.S. (Towing up the East River, New York.)
Courtesy of the Mariners Museum

ARTHUR H. WIGHT. 99 tons. Built 1904 at Liverpool, N.S. (Discharging lumber, French West Indies.)
Courtesy of the Mariners Museum

G. M. COCHRANE. 220 tons. Built 1905 at Port Greville, N.S. *Courtesy of Commander W. J. L. Parker*

JEAN. 190 tons. Built 1907 at Liverpool, N.S. Under jury-rig at Bridgetown, Barbados, B.W.I.
Courtesy of Mrs. Dave Robertson

LUCILLE. 164 tons.
Built 1906 at Parrsboro, N.S.
Courtesy of Mr. F. W. Wallace

JAMES WILLIAM. 440 tons.
Built 1908 at New Glasgow, N.S.
(First and only steel sailing vessel
built in Canada.)
Courtesy of the Mariners Museum

Schooners built in 1904

In the following year, 1904, there were no large schooners built along the north shore of the Bay of Fundy at Parrsboro, Port Greville or Spencer's Island. It would seem that the number of schooners in service was sufficient to meet the demand, although building went on in other places.

At Hantsport, N.S., Geo. M. Pearson built the *King of Avon* of 417 tons net. The history of this large tern is not clear and another register gives her builder as W. C. Balcom and the place as Horton. Early owners were H. E. Mosher and Minnie Blanche Cain of Amherst. Her name was changed in 1907 to *Hieronymous* and about this time her registry was changed to Pensacola, Florida. She was abandoned at sea in the Gulf of Mexico in July, 1911, and was later salvaged. She was re-registered at Port of Spain, Trinidad, on August 20th, 1913, and afterward was a total loss in Mobile Bay, Ala.

Liverpool, N.S. contributed three terns in 1904. The *Helen* of 198 tons net was built by J. S. Gardiner for Benjamin Davis; Josiah L. Saunders, master. This vessel had a short career, as she stranded on Molasses Reef, Florida, on March 19th, 1905, while on a voyage from San Andreas toward Philadelphia. The *Arthur W. Wight*, a small tern of 99 tons net, was built by John Millard and was later owned by the Horwood Lumber Co. of St. John's, Nfld. She was abandoned in the North Atlantic on November 27th, 1916. A very similar vessel built the same year by the same builder was the *Ivanhoe* of 99 tons net. She was built for Thos. Moulton of Burgeo, Nfld., and ended in disaster very quickly. She sailed from Halifax for the Bahamas on November 5th, 1904, and disappeared. A passing vessel saw what was supposed to be the *Ivanhoe* bottom-up about 600-700 miles southwest of Halifax.

At Shelburne the *Burleigh* of 121 tons net was built by J. A. McGowan in 1904. She had many owners after being built for Nathaniel Smith. The Canadian Government owned this ship for a time and in 1914 they sent her on a fishing exploration trip to Hudson's Bay. On this voyage, under Napoleon Comeau, she left Halifax in July and returned in September. F. W. Bisset was her owner afterward, then she was purchased by J. T. Moulton of Burgeo, Nfld. In August, 1919, she was abandoned at sea while on a passage from Cadiz to Burgeo with a cargo of salt and her crew were rescued by a passing ship.

The *Invictus* of 327 tons net was built at Salmon River, N.S., by A. Perry for N. V. Munroe in this year. She was lost on a passage to the West Indies in 1916.

Two schooners were built at Belliveau Cove in 1904. The *Edde Theriault* of 170 tons net was launched by P. A. Theriault. This vessel had a long career and many owners, including F. K. Warren, R. K. Bishop, R. Arthur, and ended up owned in Barbados by Alleyne, Arthur & Co. In her last years she was employed in the West Indies and was lost on the coast of British Guiana on December 19th, 1927, while loaded with sugar. The other vessel was the *Rothesay* of 196 tons net, built by J. W. Phipps for D. W. Puddington. She had a very long life for a softwood vessel, being carried on the registers forty years later. She was in the usual trades and was owned later by Fred. S. Inness and at another period by J. H. Solery. In the latter part of the war the schooner was commanded by Captain E. Hogan of Liverpool, N.S. In 1918 she was sold to French owners and later passed to the Italian flag. Her foreign re-names were *Saint Mathieu* and *Guiseppe*.

L. D. Shafner built the *C. W. Mills* of 318 tons net at Granville, N.S., in 1904. After working for years in the export and shipping business of Pickels & Mills she was sold in 1914 to the Native Lumber Co. of Gulfport, Miss.

The last vessel noted for 1904 is the *Unity* of 248 tons net, built at Tatamagouche, N.S., by A. Weatherbie for his own account. Employed in the West Indies trade, she was abandoned at sea on February 19th, 1914, while on a voyage from New York to Halifax with a coal cargo.

It should be noted that the peak years of building were passing. The number of vessels launched diminished steadily until World War One became responsible for the shortage of ocean-going bottoms and induced the great boom in shipbuilding.

Not much Activity in 1905

Launchings were resumed at Port Greville in 1905. G. E. Bentley built the *Ida Bentley* of 430 tons net and in the following year her name was altered to *Hugh S*. While on a passage from New Brunswick to Boston on November 22nd, 1908, she was sunk in a collision at the mouth of Boston Harbour. The second vessel was the *Sakata* of 395 tons net, built by the Fox River Lumber Co. This unfortunate vessel must have been on her first voyage when lost. She sailed from Nova Scotia with lumber for Havana, then proceeded in ballast toward Pensacola, Florida, and was caught in a squall and capsized on December 19th, 1905. After many days one of her crew was picked up. He was in a desperate condition and dying of thirst and hunger. In his delirium he ate his oilskins, but made a recovery and survived.

The Fox River Lumber Co. produced the third tern at Port Greville in 1905. She was the *G. M. Cochrane* of 220 tons net and early in her career she was driven ashore on Cape Cod in a storm. In a very unusual manner she escaped damage but was driven far up on the beach, where she remained in the sand for more than a year. Frank Davis of Yarmouth went to Cape Cod, bought her at auction and got her off. Her name was changed to *Albani* and Captain Fred Inness took command. She was managed by the Helen Shipping Co. of Yarmouth and was sold to Spanish owners in 1918.

At Canning, N.S., the *W. H. Baxter* of 331 tons net was launched for her namesake, who operated her until November, 1913, when she was sold to U.S. owners.

The *Edna V. Pickels* of 388 tons net was built by A. Perry at Salmon River, N.S., for the Pickels Lumber interests at Annapolis in 1905. Like several other vessels under this management, she was operated in the hard-pine trade out of southern ports by a ship's husband at Mobile, Ala., and was later owned there.

Robie McLeod built the *Mersey* of 190 tons net in 1905 at Liverpool for the Hendry fleet. While engaged in the Central American trades she was lost on the Panama coast on the Isle of Pines prior to September 5th, 1913, while on a voyage from San Andreas to New York with coconuts. A second schooner built at Liverpool in this year was the *Jean* of 190 tons net. She was launched by J. S. Gardiner for J. C. Crosbie of Newfoundland. The enemy raider *Moewe* sank this vessel in January, 1915, and carried off her crew as prisoners to Germany. At some time during her career the *Jean* had extensive damage, presumably during a storm. One of the pictures shows her at Bridgetown, Bdos., under a jury-rig, having lost all her spars and headgear except the foremast. Although it was a feat to sail a ship back to port under such conditions, I have no information as to when this happened or who her owners were at the time.

The same year J. N. Rafuse built the *A. K. Mclean* of 176 tons net for Captain Fred Remby and others of La Have. She was abandoned off the Cape Breton coast in 1911.

The last vessel for 1905 was the *Winnifred*, a small tern of 99 tons net, built by Isiah Wagner at Mahone Bay for Abraham Ernst. She was transferred to St. John's in February, 1916, and later owned by E. Lindsay. She was abandoned in December, 1922.

The 1906 Schooners

Two terns were launched at Parrsboro in 1906. The *Lucille* of 164 tons net was built by D. A. Huntley and was owned later by G. O. Hankinson and still later by A. Moulton. she joined the long list of unreported ships after leaving New York on November 29th, 1919, bound for Halifax with coal. G. M. Cochrane built the other vessel, the *Earl Grey* of 379 tons net, named after Canada's then Governor-General, and later renamed the *Louise M. Richard* and sold to United States owners in 1914.

Liverpool produced two terns in 1906. The *Water Witch* of 190 tons net was launched by J. S. Gardiner. She was owned by the J. C. Crosbie interests in Newfoundland and was wrecked at Tarifa, near the Straits of Gibraltar, on May 19th, 1918. Robie McLeod built the *Freedom* of 197 tons net for Captain Dave Ritcey of La Have, N.S. The A. S. Rendell Co. of St. John's, Nfld., bought this vessel for the export fish trade and she foundered while in ballast between St. John's and Sydney, N.S., on November 28th, 1924.

The *Emily Anderson* of 218 tons net was built by W. Anthony at Lower Selma, N.S., for F. K. Warren, Halifax, in 1908. She was put under Barbados registry in 1913 and was abandoned at sea in February, 1918. T. W. McKinley launched the *Dorothy M. Porter*, renamed the *Dorothy Duff*, of 152 tons net, at Falmouth, N.S. She was taken over by the Duff interests in Newfoundland the same year and entered the salt-fish trade. On May 17th, 1917, she encountered an enemy submarine and was destroyed about ten miles from Valencia, Spain.

Pickels & Mills of Annapolis had the *Georgina Roop* of 398 tons net built at Granville for the southern trade in 1906. Norman Roop was a part owner and master for a time. In 1918 she was rebuilt and renamed *Pineland* and soon after was sold to Estonians, who renamed her *Argo*.

Three tern schooners were built at Shelburne in 1906. The *Addie and Beatrice* of 197 tons net was launched from the yard of Joseph McGill for Captain Z. Nickerson and others of Port Clyde, N.S. This vessel was sold soon after to the Porter interests at St. Vincent, B.W.I. She was lost on one of her first voyages on a passage from the southern states to Cape Verde with a cargo of hard pine. Captain Walters was master and she was wrecked on the end of Mariquan Island in the Bahamas on April 7th, 1907. J. G. Porter of St. Vincent, B.W.I., bought another tern launched that year at Shelburne.

The *Montrose* of 198 tons net was built for a Newfoundland owner, but changed hands soon after launching. The vessel was lost through being stranded in St. Mary's Bay, N.S., on January 8th, 1910. G. A. Cox built the third tern, the *Reliance* of 191 tons net, for his own account. She was lost on the Hen and Chickens Reef off Yarmouth, N.S., on November 13th, 1911.

The McManus Model for Terns

The Shelburne builders were experimenting with the McManus design schooner about this time. This Boston naval architect's model was widely used for fishing vessels and its characteristic was a round bow, a sharper entry and a greater deadrise. Adapted to the freighting schooners, the supporters of the model claimed the rounded forefoot made the schooners quicker in stays, simplified the headgear, and the finer lines gave them better speed. The model did not suit itself to the schooners which were loaded while aground, as in the Bay of Fundy, but was suitable to the vessels which loaded in deep-water ports only. The detractors of the model claimed they were not much faster, the carrying capacity was cut down and the draft was excessive for many of the ports. Nevertheless, many of the smaller tern schooners from the yards of the south coast of Nova Scotia and Newfoundland designed on the finer lines were successful vessels.

Many of the Schooners built in 1907 came from the South Shore

There were nine vessels built in Nova Scotia during 1907. The *Annie* of 193 tons net was built at Liverpool, N.S., for A. W. Hendry and was lost at Honduras on November 16th, 1908. She was caught in a squall and capsized. The master, Mitchell Decker, frantically hauled his wife through one of the small cabin ports to save her life. It was a difficult task, as Mrs. Decker was in the cabin with her baby at the time when the squall struck. When the vessel heeled over on her beam ends, Mrs. Decker found herself on the low side with no footing, as the deck was vertical. With the added burden of her baby in her arms the situation was desperate, but with a great effort she clambered upward and thrust the baby through the port. The men then grasped the mother's arms and eased her through. The second vessel that year at Liverpool was built by J. S. Gardiner. She was the *Emma E. Whidden* of 199 tons net and was sold later to James Baird Ltd., of St. John's, Nfld., where she was renamed *Dorothy Baird* and put in the salt-fish trade. Just after World War One she was in dry-dock at Bahia, Brazil; John Churchill was master when the props let go and the vessel fell over. She was declared a total loss and the owners abandoned her. James Baird later had another *Dorothy Baird* often confused with the one noted above. This latter vessel was bought later from the Portuguese, who had used her as a Banks fisherman, and she was commanded by Captain Jack Willis when lost in the Brazil trade some years later.

Shelburne produced two terns in 1907. The *Gay Gordon* of 119 tons net was built by Joseph McGill for Newfoundland owners and she was well known during her time as a smart schooner. A report says she was lost in the ice about March, 1923. The *Roseway* of 291 tons net was built by G. A. Cox and became a constructive total loss on Anticosti in the Gulf of St. Lawrence on October 6th, 1910, but was later salvaged and sold to United States parties. About 1922, at Wolfville, N.S., while lying alongside the dock with a cargo of coal aboard, she filled with water after having been badly strained and was abandoned by her owners. She was purchased by Captain John McKenzie and Harry G. Kennedy of Sheet Harbour, and renamed *Kay and Em*, and put to carrying pulpwood along the coast. Mr. Kennedy told me they were never able to keep her tight, although they had several caulking jobs done. After some years her gear was removed and she was used as a barge until about 1932, when she was abandoned on the shore at Sheet Harbour. At this date, 1957, this old vessel is still nearly intact but is slowly falling to pieces.

Smith and Rhuland of Lunenburg launched two terns in 1907. The *H. R. Silver* of 199 tons net was built for W. C. Smith and employed in the fish-export trade. Captain D. Lundahl was master of this vessel and on one occasion she was dismasted while on a voyage to St. John's, Nfld. Eber Gerhardt was another master and the vessel was abandoned in the Atlantic in January, 1916. The other schooner was the *Mildred* of 166 tons net and owned by G. M. Barr of St. John's and later by Job & Co. She is reported as being lost on a passage from Portugal to Newfoundland in 1918.

W. A. Naugler built the small 99 ton net *Adriatic* at Bridgewater, N.S., in 1907, for George Cuner and others. She was transferred to St. John's, Nfld., and purchased by A. E. Hickman in 1917. While under the command of Captain Frank Pine she was lost at St. Lawrence, Nfld., in September, 1918.

The *Evelyn* of 287 tons net was built by A. D. Mills & Sons at Granville, N.S., in 1907. Captain E. C. Berry was her master for the first few years. She later had various Newfoundland owners, including Job Bros. and A. S. Rendell & Co. On February 25th, 1924, under Captain Nilson, she left St. John's, Nfld., for Pernambuco with a cargo of fish and disappeared with all hands and including Mrs. Nilson, who was making the voyage with her husband.

The *Kenneth C*, a large tern of 475 tons net, will be the last-mentioned vessel for 1907. She was launched at Port Greville by G. M. Cochrane for his own account. She had various masters, including A. Potter and L. Tower. The *Kenneth C* came to a violent end and it was a lucky thing for her crew that events turned out as they did. During World War One, in November, 1915, she towed out of Liverpool, England, having delivered a timber cargo there and taken in a small amount of ballast for her return voyage. Soon after casting off the tow-boat, a strong southeast wind freshened and in a short time it was blowing a gale. The light sails had not been set on the *Kenneth C* and soon it was necessary to snug her down under the reefed mainsail and forestaysail to heave-to. The wind became heavier until it was blowing hurricane force and the shortened canvas was blown away. Her head swung off and they attempted to run to leeward, although they knew that the coast of Ireland lay in that direction. The seas boarded the vessel and subjected her to severe strains. The steering gear was disabled and the schooner wallowed into the trough and her seams began to open up. By early evening the *Kenneth C* was a wreck. Her boats, bulwarks and houses were smashed by giant seas. By eight bells in the evening it was apparent that the schooner was doomed, and the master ordered all hands to stand by, as he knew the ship would drive ashore on the Irish coast during the night.

About midnight she fetched up with a bone-shattering jar on a sunken reef. The gale was howling with undiminished fury and the crew gave themselves up for lost. But the next great sea lifted the vessel and carried her over the reef and closer inshore. Succeeding seas hove the schooner in toward the land until she was jammed among some great rocks. While then in a very exposed position among the rocks, she appeared safe for the time being and the mate ventured to sound with the lead around the ship. Her bow was toward the shore and the mate found shallow water forward. He lowered himself into the water and discovered it only came to his armpits and he waded ashore, to be followed by the others. They saw the *Kenneth C* break in two as they clambered up the cliff, where they found shelter with some friendly people. None of them suffered any injury except the boy, who became hysterical after the ordeal. When they returned at daybreak the schooner had been reduced to driftwood and they went along the beach and salvaged some of their belongings.

The velocity of the gale can be realized from the fact that the *Kenneth C* cast off from the tow-boat at about eleven-thirty in the morning and fetched up at Clogher Head across the Irish Sea at about midnight, a distance of 106 miles. The storm drove her this distance in about thirteen hours and to call it anything less than remarkable would be an understatement.

Sixteen Schooners built in Nova Scotia in 1908

In the year 1908 there was a temporary revival of shipbuilding. Sixteen terns were built in Nova Scotia in various places. At the head of the Bay of Fundy the *Willena Gertrude* of 271 tons net was built at Parrsboro by T. Trahey & Sons for H. E. Mosher. Johnson Spicer owned her later and she was sunk by an enemy submarine on a passage from the Azores to the United Kingdom in October, 1917.

G. E. Bentley built the *Irma Bentley* of 414 tons net at Port Greville. This vessel was commanded for some years by Captain George Robert Otterson, who had a long career in square-rigged ships and must have been in his seventies when in charge of her. In the course of his life at sea he made one hundred voyages to Europe, three around Cape Horn, twenty-seven to Brazil and the Argentine, all in sailing ships. This schooner was put under Barbados register at the time of her launching and her last days are somewhat obscure, but she was owned latterly by R. C. Elkin & Co. She was reported lost in September, 1915, but later was reported as being towed back to Galveston while on a voyage from Galveston to Port-au-Prince, Haiti.

The *Conrad S* of 283 tons net was launched at Port Greville in 1908 by the Fox River Lumber Co. She was later bought by the Grenfell Mission for their work on the Labrador coast and was renamed *George B. Cluett*.

The Clipper 'Exilda'

This schooner is notable on account of a series of fast voyages and as a money earner. The *Exilda* of 349 tons net was built by G. M. Cochrane at Port Greville in 1908. She was owned by the Pugsley Shipping Co. but like many of the schooners had other investors. Captain A. O. Seaman of Parrsboro, N.S., a well-known builder and owner of large schooners, wrote some years ago regarding this vessel, in which he had an interest. The *Exilda* had thirteen cargoes in her and delivered them in the first year of her career. She had seven cargoes of piling from Eatonville, N.S., to New York, four cargoes of coal back to eastern ports, one cargo of lumber from Saint John and a similar one from the south coast of Nova Scotia. Captain Bedford Tower joined her after launching and remained in the vessel until after the first voyage to the United Kingdom, this starting her off to a successful career. Her great achievement was in making four consecutive fast voyages to Europe with spruce deals. Between March 22nd, 1915, and January 9th, 1916, she sailed from Parrsboro, delivered three cargoes at Preston, England and arrived at a French port with the fourth. A truly remarkable achievement for a vessel of this class, or any other class of small sailing vessel, for that matter.

On the first voyage to England the local Parrsboro men, unused to such voyages, were not keen on shipping aboard the schooner and some difficulty was experienced in obtaining a crew. The cook's berth was the most difficult to fill and after engaging several, only to have them disappear with their cash advance, the local policeman was offered a bonus of five dollars if he could produce a cook who could be depended on. In a short time he showed up with a man in tow and was promised the money if the man sailed with the vessel. When the schooner returned from England, Captain Tower was asked how the cook had made out. He replied disgustedly that the man had never cooked in his life and during the voyage they had lived on biscuits, and when he himself really got hungry he had to cook an egg in his cabin. Besides, he asked, did they not know that the policeman and the bogus cook were brothers? Captain Tower was later reprimanded by the mother of the policeman and the so-called cook for taking her boy away to sea to be killed. The Captain told her she had plenty left, as she was the mother of fourteen.

The *Exilda* was later sold to J. G. P. Murphy and was wrecked in the Roads at St. Pierre et Miquelon on December 11th, 1919.

The South Coast Schooners of 1908

In general, the schooners built along the south coast of Nova Scotia were smaller than those produced up the Bay of Fundy. This can be explained by the types of cargo they were built to carry. The big schooners were designed for the export of lumber and gypsum, while the south shore terns mostly entered the cured-fish and bulk-salt business.

Building was active along the La Have River in 1908. Melbourne Leary built the *A. V. Conrad* of 147 tons net and later she was owned by A. E. Hickman of St. John's Nfld. While on a voyage from Cadiz to Newfoundland with a salt cargo and under the command of Captain Chesley Anderson, the vessel was abandoned in a derelict condition. Captain Anderson told me that after leaving Cadiz they experienced heavy weather for seven or eight days and while lying-to, a big comber struck the rudder and broke the stock. The vessel's head fell off and she rolled very heavily in the trough of the sea. After several days the heavy weather developed into a storm from the northwest and the ship rolled so heavily that the three masts went over the side. These were cut adrift and left to drag ahead. When the weather moderated the spars were cut free of the vessel and the old schooner remained still good, and not leaking excessively. Twelve days after losing the spars they were picked up by the Italian passenger ship, S.S. *Caserta*, and were taken to Naples. The crew returned to Newfoundland as D.B.S.'s *via* London and Liverpool. The schooner was abandoned in February, 1921.

M. Leary launched another vessel at his yard on the La Have River at Dayspring the same year. She was the *Minnie F. Crosby* of 119 tons net. This vessel was stranded at the entrance of the Miramichi River in New Brunswick and a survey was held on her damaged cargo of sugar and molasses in June, 1911. The schooner was repaired and sold to French owners in 1912 and renamed *Marie Amelie*.

J. N. Rafuse built the *Inga* of 161 tons net for Captain Ollie Parks in 1908. This vessel changed hands several times and was owned by Watling & Conners of Bermuda at one period. Grace Bros. owned her later still and at that time she was registered at Jamaica. In December, 1917, she was abandoned at sea. Another builder, Robar Bros., launched the *Annie M. Banks* of 135 tons net at La Have for A. M. Banks. She was in the salt-fish trade until January 21st, 1914, when she was abandoned in the North Atlantic while on a passage from Newfoundland to Spain. W. A. Naugler built the *Fleetly* of 174 tons net up the River at Bridgewater for S. Creaser and others. This schooner foundered while on a voyage from Louisburg, N.S., to Newfoundland with coal under Captain Archibald Lohnes on February 4th, 1914. The crew were picked up.

The terns built along the La Have River in this year were all of small size.

A. W. Hendry had two terns built at Liverpool in 1908. The *Tobeatic* of 99 tons net, a small schooner, was abandoned in the North Atlantic on January 22nd, 1914, and the *Rossignol* of 199 tons net. The latter vessel must have been lost on her first or second voyage, as she went ashore and was abandoned on the San Blas coast, Panama, on March 5th, 1909.

The *Archie Crowell* of 175 tons net was built by Winslow McKay at Shelburne in 1908 for Captain Zephaniah Nickerson. Mr. McKay, now retired and living in Shelburne, told me this vessel cost $10,000 complete except for the sails and rigging, and the master of the new vessel brought these with him. Captain Everett Nickerson, son of the owner, took charge of this vessel in 1909. She was in the coconut trade on a time charter and Captain Nickerson told me this was very good business. She would load general cargo in New York or Philadelphia for the islands off Central America and on return would pick up coconuts at the various islands. Corn Island, off the San Blas coast, was usually the terminal port and they would start their voyage home from there. She carried the coconut cargo, usually about 400,000 nuts, back to New York. In 1912 the schooner was sold for $8000 to C. W. Anderson of Sherbrooke, N.S., and he in turn sold her to Newfoundland owners. Some years later, while on a voyage from Santa Paula, Brazil, to St. John's, Nfld., she lost her rudder and was abandoned in the Atlantic on February 9th, 1918.

The *General Laurie* of 198 tons net was built by H. M. Allen at Allendale. While under the command of Captain William Matthews of Dartmouth, N.S., this schooner

EXILDA. 349 tons.
Built 1908 at Port Greville, N.S.
Courtesy of Mr. F. W. Wallace

WAEGWOLTIC. 174 tons.
Built 1909 at Bridgewater, N.S.
Courtesy of the Mariners Museum

HILDA R. 99 tons.
Built 1910 at Conquerall Bank,
N.S. (A superior vessel and
the only Canadian tern built for
Southern Ocean fur-sealing.)
Courtesy of Mr. Dave Ryan

CARRIE M. WAMBACK. 109 tons. Built 1912 at Liverpool, N.S. *Courtesy of the Mariners Museum*

ANNIE L. WARREN. 223 tons. Built 1913 at Meteghan, N.S. *Courtesy of Mr. H. L. Warren*

encountered the wrecked Norwegian barque *Forth* on the 27th of September, 1915, in the Straits of Yucatan and rescued the crew. For this feat Captain Matthews was honoured with a silver cup presented by the King of Norway. The schooner passed to G. M. Barr of St. John's, Nfld., and was destroyed by a German submarine in June, 1917, while in the salt-fish trade.

L. D. Shafner built the *C. D. Pickels* of 400 tons net at Bridgetown, N.S., in 1908, for the F. W. Pickels Co. She was mostly in the southern trade and was sold to W. J. Pender of Nassau and while under the command of Captain C. M. Wilkie of La Have, on March 18th, 1916, was so badly damaged by fire at Guantanamo, Cuba, she had to be abandoned. She was bought up by Cuban owners, repaired and renamed *Viuda de Orive*.

The *Katherine V. Mills* of 216 tons net was the last tern schooner built at Granville Ferry. A. D. Mills & Co. were her owners and later she was sold to F. K. Warren of Halifax, and later still to Philip Templeton of Newfoundland. Captain John S. Smith commanded this vessel at one time. After World War One she was sold to French owners, who renamed her *Fiette* and later, *Daisy*.

The only Canadian-built Steel Sailing Ship

The last vessel mentioned for 1908 will be the *James William*, a tern of 440 tons net. This vessel is noteworthy as being the only steel sailing ship built in Canada. She was constructed by the I. Matheson Co. at New Glasgow, N.S., for the Carmichael Ship Co. and was an attempt to bring shipbuilding in Nova Scotia in line with modern practice. In performance she behaved very well and made some good passages. In December, 1930, she made the run from City Island, N.Y., to Yarmouth, coal-laden, in fifty hours, Captain Martin Pentz in command. But her original cost was too great and prohibited other attempts. In the United States seven large steel schooners were produced, including the great *Thomas W. Lawson* with her seven masts. These big schooners, built on a different principle, did not have the heavy keelsons and floors of a wooden vessel and double bottom tanks had to be installed to provide stability. The tanks, of course, were filled with water on passages when there was no cargo.

The wooden vessels had a tendency to hog after a few years. Most of the larger ones were built with a roll to the keel in the hope that after hogging moderately the vessel would still be straight. The fine ends with a long overhang plus the weight of the anchors, cables and gear forward and the weight of the cabin aft tended to produce a hog even without the addition of cargo.

The *James William* was operated until October 8th, 1934, when owned by John C. Campbell of Summerside, P.E.I., and under the command of Captain F. O. Rangdale, she went aground near Clarke City, Quebec, while loaded with pulpwood and was a total loss after twenty-seven years in service—a fact which testifies to her handling and construcion.

Decline in Shipbuilding in 1909

Only twelve terns were launched in 1909, all completed in Nova Scotia. The first three-master built on the south side of Minas Basin for some years was the *A. B. Bar-*

teaux of 380 tons net launched by W. H. Baxter at Canning. This vessel later passed to A. S. Rendell & Co. and others of St. John's, Nfld., and she was well known around the coast for many years. J. Wiltshire was master for part of the time and she was under the command of Captain T. Janes when she was lost in the ice seventy-five miles southwest from Cape Race on February 20th, 1930.

The *Eva C* of 250 tons net was built in 1909 by G. M. Cochrane at Port Greville for W. C. Smith. Captain F. Godfrey was master for a time. Like so many of the other schooners in existence at this period she passed to Newfoundland owners for the salt-fish trade. The *Eva C* was lost in this business when she was abandoned in the North Atlantic on December 9th, 1918. Also at Port Greville, J. W. Cochrane launched the *Lawson* of 274 tons net. In 1915 she was bought by Baine, Johnson & Co. of St. John's, Nfld., and put into the Brazil salt-fish trade. Afterward, she was sold to Walter B. Grieve of St. John's and was abandoned in the Atlantic on February 28th, 1919.

At Parrsboro, the *P. J. McLaughlin* of 147 tons net was fitted out for the well-known shipowner. Later she was sold to C. H. Russel and C. K. Kelly and transferred to Nassau registry. She foundered in 1926, but I do not have the place or date.

The four-masted schooner *A. F. Davison* of 503 tons net was launched at the yard of F. W. Pickels & Co. at Annapolis in 1909. She was the largest ship built there since the days of the square-riggers and was designed and built by George Wagstaff. The schooner was named for A. F. Davison of Bridgewater, a prominent man in Maritime shipping, and Captain Angus Richards was her first owner and master. In 1926 she was damaged in heavy weather off the United States coast and was towed in for repairs. She was then taken to Saint John, N.B., for a refit, but was lost soon after at Grand Manan, N.B.

The *Jeanne A. Pickels* of 299 tons net was built in 1909 by L. D. Shafner in the yard of the Pickels Co. at Annapolis. She had a short life as she was wrecked at Chance Harbour, N.B., on July 18th, 1914.

C. C. LeBlanc built the *Rosalie Belliveau* of 197 tons net at Belliveau Cove in 1909. She was transferred to Barbados registry and later to St John's, Nfld. This vessel had many owners during her career. After some years of trading to the West Indies she was bought by Newfoundland owners and passed from them to J. S. Webster & Sons of Jamaica. Malcolm Bros. also owned this schooner. She went missing since November 15th, 1926, when she left Kingston, Ja., for Turks Island with a general cargo, and after being reported off Jacmel on December 7th was never seen again.

At Liverpool A. W. Hendry added the *Ponhook* of 199 tons net to his fleet. Captain D. Geldert was master for a time and he was followed by Archibald Lohnes. She went into the salt-fish trade and was abandoned on a voyage from St. John's, Nfld., to Gibraltar on October 26th, 1917. The *Lavengro* of 269 tons net was launched by G. A. Cox of Shelburne for his own account and under Captain H. Hilton was lost at Fogo, Nfld., while loaded with fish for Naples.

The *Waegwoltic* (first of name) of 174 tons net was built by W. A. Naugler at Bridgewater for A. H. Zwicker & Co. Captain W. Creaser was the first master. This vessel was used in the export fish business. On April 24th, 1922, she was lost on Hog

Sty Reef in the Bahamas while on a passage from Mobile, Ala., to Barbados. Down the La Have River from Bridgewater at Dayspring, M. Leary built the *Burnett C* of 99 tons net. This little tern was owned first by W. Davis and later by R. C. Smith, but her last days are obscure. She was reported on March 1st, 1919, as returning damaged to Fayal, in the Azores. Even the small terns went far afield.

The last vessel noted for the year 1909 is the *Wilfred M* of 198 tons net. She was launched at the yard of Smith & Rhuland at Lunenburg and was owned by the Wilfred M Co. While on a voyage from St. John's to Brazil, laden with 4500 quintals of salt fish valued at $45,000, she encountered the German armed cruiser *Kron Prinz Wilhelm* about April, 1915, and was destroyed.

Thirteen Terns built in 1910

Port Greville was very active in 1910, producing five terns. The largest was the *W. S. M. Bentley* of 364 tons net and launched by G. E. Bentley. She was transferred to Nassau in 1912 and was operated by Brice & Granger. Later she was sold to the Dantzler interests at Gulfport, Miss., and registered there. Another medium-sized tern, the *W. M. Richard* of 323 tons net, was built for A. D. Mills. She was registered at Annapolis Royal at the time of her building and was abandoned at sea north of the Bahamas on November 4th, 1920. The *Novelty* of 266 tons net was built for Dave Ritcey of La Have. Transferred to Barbados in 1911, she was sold to A. S. Rendell and G. M. Barr of St. John's, Nfld. The last days of this vessel are obscure. E. Elderkin launched the *Jost* of 299 tons net for R. C. Elkin & Co. and later she was taken over by Job Bros. of St. John's. This vessel was lost on the coast of Brazil on July 31st, 1918. The last vessel built at Port Greville in 1910 was the *Crescendo* of 196 tons net by G. M. Cochrane for his own account. Captain S. Hilton was master for a time and she was sold to F. Buckworth & Co. and transferred to Cork, Ireland, in 1917. She was lost in February, 1918.

At Parrsboro the *Hazel Trahey* of 125 tons net was built as a two-master by J. H. Trahey. She had many owners, including W. N. Reinhardt and, later, Baine, Johnson & Co. Late in her career she was altered to tern rig and while on a passage from Cadiz to Battle Harbour, Labrador, was abandoned in the Atlantic on September 4th, 1926, the men being taken off by the s.s. *Andalusia*. During the whole trip the pumps were worked, the last week without intermission, a terrible thing aboard these old schooners with no motor-driven pumps and with a crew of only six or seven men all told.

On the south shore the *Annie Hendry* of 219 tons net was built by A. W. Hendry at Liverpool. She had a short life and joined the list of missing ships and has not been heard of since December 16th, 1911, when she left Turks Island with a cargo of salt for the Nova Scotia fisheries. Also at Liverpool, the *Seth Jr.* of 199 tons net was launched by J. S. Gardiner. She was sold to foreigners at Panama but had a Canadian crew. John S. Smith was master during this time. In December, 1917, she encountered an enemy submarine and was sunk.

The *Grand Falls* of 113 tons net was launched from the McGill yards in Shelburne in 1910 for Newfoundland owners. This small vessel sailed from Harbour Breton, Nfld., for Europe on January 7th, 1914, and was never heard from. Another small vessel built nearby the same year suffered the same fate. The *Dorothy Louise* of 125 tons net was launched by Howard M. Allen at Allendale for George C. Harris and others of Grand Bank, Nfld. In 1912 this little vessel sailed from Leixos, the small port down the river from Oporto, bound for Grand Bank, and has never been reported.

Hunting Pelagic Seals: The 'Hilda R'

For many years a small fleet of our two-masted schooners had been engaged in hunting the fur seals that inhabited the areas in the vicinity of Cape Horn and in the Bering Sea. Concentrated hunting of these seals led to their numbers being decimated and international agreements were made from time to time to conserve the herds, particularly those in the North Pacific and Bering Sea between the continents of North America and Asia. This seal hunting should not be confused with the pursuit of the hair seal which inhabits the northern seas in the vicinity of Newfoundland and which is still carried on.

The saga of the pelagic seals is an involved story of huge profits, gun fights on the high seas between the hunters of different nations, the reduction of the herds from indiscriminate slaughter and the final rules of conservation which protected the animals and which are still in existence. However, the hunting of fur seals in the southern oceans was still very profitable, as the price of a good pelt in London ranged from $25 to $40 each. These furs were classed as the finest obtainable and were much in demand.

In 1910 the Canada Sealing Co. of Halifax, N.S., decided to build a tern for this business. The *Hilda R* of 99 tons net was built at Conquerall Bank by J. N. Rafuse for the Hon. A. W. Redden and others of Halifax. The master, Captain Matthew Ryan of North Sydney, N.S., was also a shareholder. This shipmaster had formerly gained fame for his record of success in this business in which he had engaged from his early years. In 1902 he had first shipped in a sealing vessel bound for British Columbia and rose rapidly to command one of these vessels out of Victoria, B.C.

The *Hilda R* was built to a very high class, being copper fastened throughout (indeed it was said there was not a pound of black iron in her), which was very unusual in our tern schooners. There was a large amount of hardwood used in her hull and she was copper sheathed. She had excellent accommodation for her crew of twenty, which included officers, hunters, boatsteerers and crew.

The Nova Scotia interests pursued the hunting in the Antarctic regions and visited isolated islands far to the south of Australia and New Zealand. In 1911-12 the *Hilda R* made two sealing voyages to the Antarctic and sailed completely around the world on each by way of the Cape of Good Hope and Cape Horn. As the seals became scarcer and the expenses of the expeditions mounted the business was finally dropped.

The *Hilda R* was sold to John T. McRea of Harbour Grace, Nfld., to be put into the salt-fish trade, for which she was well suited. On one passage she sailed from Harbour Grace to Gibraltar in sixteen days, a creditable performance. While in this trade she was destroyed by a German submarine on November 3rd, 1917, twenty-two miles S.E. from Cape St. Mary, Spain, while under the command of Captain Yetman.

The *Arkona* of 143 tons net was launched in 1910 by A. Ernst at Mahone Bay for J. W. Smith and others. This schooner was lost on the coast of Jamaica at Savanna-la-

Mar on November 22nd, 1912, while under the command of Captain Newton Spon-
agle. She was loaded with logwood and bound for Stamford, Conn.

The last vessel mentioned in 1910 is the *F. C. Lockhart* of 268 tons net and named after
a well-known owner and shipper of the time. She was built at the F. W. Pickels yard
at Annapolis Royal. Captain A. M. King and his brother, J. T. King, who sailed as mate,
had an interest in this vessel. The King brothers had returned home after the *Florence
R. Hewson* had been condemned at Matanzas on account of great damage sustained in
a hurricane in the Florida Straits in October, 1909. J. T. King is now a retired old
gentleman at Osborne, N.S., and he told me of his days in sail. With his brother, he
joined the *F. C. Lockhart* at Annapolis Royal. She cost $22,000 ready for sea and in
those days it was a lot of money for a schooner of her size. She was built of the best
of materials and her gear included a gasolene donkey-engine, now beginning to appear
in the schooners. The great advantage of having power aboard the vessel was considered
wonderful. Up to this time all the hard work aboard had been done by hand. The ships
were pumped by wooden pumps of rough construction, the cargo was hand-cranked
out by winch. Anchors and sails were hand hauled. One can imagine these men in the
simple days of 1910 starting and watching the temperamental primitive gas engine
chugging away as the anchor cable came in. Or seeing the gush of water put out by the
attached pump. In those days a sailor rose early in port and spent the day working on
the hand winch hoisting out puncheons of molasses or bags of sugar. It would be very
difficult to get men to do that sort of work today, no matter what you paid them. It
was all in a day's work then.

The brothers did well in the *F. C. Lockhart*. During the time they were in her, about
seven years, she paid $50,000 in dividends and was sold in 1918 to W. R. Grace & Co.
for $50,000. This was an excellent return on $22,000 over eight years. All this time she
was in the hard-pine trade to Cuba and the West Indies with two trips home to Canada.

Shipbuilding declines during 1911

For some reason schooner construction almost came to a stop during 1911. In this year
there was only one small tern schooner launched in Nova Scotia and one very small
three-masted coaster built in Newfoundland. The *Ainslie* of 148 tons net was built by
A. W. Hendry at Liverpool, N.S. She was later owned by W. N. Reinhardt and R. H.
Burgess. Later she was under the command of Captain E. Wilkie and in 1927 was sold
to foreigners in Cuba. The little Newfoundland tern, the *Dorothy Lake*, of 23.8 tons net,
was built at Fortune, Nfld., and was mentioned earlier in this part.

All Schooners built in 1912 were small

As in the previous year the shipyards were not busy. For the second year in succession
there was no new construction at the head of the Bay of Fundy. At Lunenburg the
W. Cortada of 108 tons net was launched from the yard of Smith & Rhuland for Captain
E. Backman and others. This vessel joined the list of missing ships while under the com-
mand of her principal owner. She has not been heard of since sailing from Nova
Scotia on January 8th, 1915, while on a passage to Puerto Rico. Another vessel built

in Lunenburg in this year was the *Mary D. Young* of 99 tons net. This tern was one of the very few outfitted for fishing. In 1917 she was fishing out of Nova Scotia under Captain Ronald Knickle. She was sold soon after to S. Piercy of Newfoundland and was lost in the Roads at St. Pierre et Miquelon in September, 1918.

D. C. Mulhall built two small terns at Liverpool in 1912. The *Carrie M. Wamback* of 109 tons net was owned by W. Duff and others and was abandoned at sea on a voyage south on January 19th, 1914. The other was the *Ida M. Zinck* of 113 tons net owned by Captain Eleazer Zinck, who also sailed her. This was a very successful schooner. At first Captain Zinck had the idea that terns would be successful at fishing and had the vessel built with that in mind. She was launched in October, 1912, and went to Newfoundland to load fish for Brazil and brought home a cargo of salt to Lunenburg. In the spring she fitted out for salt fishing, but after one season Captain Zinck kept her in the coasting trade. In the period 1912-25 she paid back $81,760 to her owners, a handsome return on her outlay cost of $10,000. She was sold in 1925 to Captain LeBlanc of Sydney, N.S., and in 1929 passed to owners at St. Pierre et Miquelon and was renamed *Azelma*.

The only other vessel built in Nova Scotia in 1912 was the *Alvina Theriault* of 199 tons net, launched and sailed by the Theriault interests at Belliveau Cove, N.S. In the 1920's she was sold to French owners and renamed *Alvena*.

Eight Tern Schooners launched in 1913

In 1913 the yards at the head of the Bay of Fundy resumed building and launched two terns. The *Doane* of 291 tons net was built by G. M. Cochrane at Port Greville. R. S. Kerr of Fox River, N.S., and T. Rice of Tampico, Mexico, were owners of this vessel. She was lost on a passage to Tampico, on November 20th, 1920, off the mouth of the Panuca River, having just arrived at her destination. This schooner was equipped with motor auxiliary power. The *Percy B* of 281 tons net was built by T. K. Bentley at Port Greville. She was owned by the builder and J. N. Pugsley and was torpedoed near the coast of France in October, 1917.

Another war casualty was the *Bessie A. Crooks* of 199 tons net, built by D. C. Mulhall at Liverpool for Captain Arthur Crooks. It is believed this vessel was destroyed by a German raider just prior to 1917 somewhere down south. On this voyage Captain Crooks stayed home and the fate of the vessel and her crew remains unknown. Captain Crooks was later appointed to command one of the "Q" ships which operated out of Sydney, N.S., as an anti-submarine measure during the latter part of World War One. The second schooner built by D. C. Mulhall during this year was the *David C. Ritcey* of 284 tons net. This vessel was engaged in the usual trades until April 22nd, 1924, when she was abandoned at sea on a passage from New York to Placentia Bay, Nfld., with coal.

The *J. N. Rafuse* of 218 tons net was built at La Have by her namesake; Captain A. Parks, master. In August, 1918, she was purchased by J. T. Moulton of Burgeo, Nfld., and was employed in the salt-fish trade to Oporto. On a passage from Oporto to St. John's she was abandoned at sea in February, 1922. Captain Harvey and two of his crew were drowned during rescue operations. The other three were saved. It was the old story of a heavy salt cargo and long Atlantic gales.

G. A. Cox built the *Prydwen* of 295 tons net at Shelburne for his own account in 1913. After passing to Job Bros. of Newfoundland she was sold to Spanish owners and renamed *Ciudad de Tarragone*. The firm of J. Ernst & Son launched the small *Viola May* of 100 tons net at Mahone Bay. She later passed to J. Petite of Newfoundland and was lost on St. Pierre et Miquelon about 1922; P. Dicks, master.

The *Annie L. Warren* (named after the wife of the owner) of 223 tons net was built by T. German at Meteghan in 1913 for F. K. Warren, Halifax, and later was sold to A. S. Rendell & Co. of St. John's. Under the command of Captain E. G. Vallis, while on a passage from Turks Island to Lunenburg, on November 22nd, 1924, the mate, John Yarn, was lost overboard. The vessel was broken up at St. John's Nfld., in 1925.

Six Schooners built in 1914

This was another year when no large schooners were built at the head of the Bay of Fundy. At Belliveau Cove the *M. A. Belliveau* of 199 tons net was launched by C. C. LeBlanc for the Belliveau interests. They operated this vessel until after the war, then sold her to Kirkconnell Bros., of Tampa, Florida.

At Liverpool D. C. Mulhall built two terns in 1914. The *Robert J. Dale* of 197 tons net was owned by D. C. Ritcey and later by G. M. Barr of St. John's. She was named after R. J. Dale of the well-known marine insurance firm of Dale & Co., Montreal, who doubtless had a few shares in her. She was wrecked at River Head, St. Mary's, Nfld., on January 23rd, 1924, while on a voyage from Philadelphia to Placentia Bay with coal. The *Blandford* of 375 tons net, one of the largest terns built at Liverpool, was constructed by Robie McLeod. In 1917 this vessel was condemned at St. Thomas in the Danish West Indies and sold to Danish subjects.

The *Beryl M. Corkum* of 248 tons net was launched by J. N. Rafuse at La Have in 1914 for Captain S. Parks. This vessel was lost with all her crew. It is believed the schooner was a victim of the terrible hurricane which swept the North Atlantic during the latter part of August, 1924. The *Corkum* had cleared from Halifax in June with a cargo of liquor for the United States coast and was supposed to have left there before the August 26th hurricane. She was sighted floating bottom-up by the American fishing vessels *Ingomar* and the *Natalie Hammond*. At that time she was owned in Lunenburg but chartered to American parties; Captain William Zwicker and his crew of six were lost.

W. A. Naugler built the *Annie Marria* of 271 tons net for D. Getson and others of Bridgewater, N.S., in 1914. While under the command of Russel Conrad this schooner was lost on the French coast in 1919. Captain Conrad is reported to have been drowned in this casualty.

The last vessel built before the war was the *Wilfred Marcus* of 123 tons net. She was owned by G. & A. Buffett and S. Grandy, all of Grand Bank, Nfld. While under the command of Robert Anderson in the Portuguese salt-fish trade the schooner was abandoned on December 15th, 1918, during a west-bound passage with a cargo of salt.

As the war went on and the fishing industry flourished, great quantities of salt fish were exported to Europe and the Mediterranean countries, to Brazil and the West Indies. The number of tern schooners in this trade kept on increasing yearly until the early 1920's. At many places in the Maritime provinces a large number of tern and four-masted schooners were built to offset the war sinkings of Allied shipping and to engage in the generally stimulated trade conditions.

PART FIVE

World War One

For one hundred years the merchant ships of the world had been free to move across the oceans without interference. There were incidents in the Civil War in the United States, the Barbary pirates in the Mediterranean, and cases of piracy in the Far East. But in general, after the defeat of Napoleon, there were no commerce raiders in existence.

Soon after the start of World War One in 1914 the German High Command suddenly realized that they had stumbled on a way to reduce the efficiency of the Allied Merchant Marine. Their High Seas Fleet was bottled up and they dared not engage in a large-scale battle action with the British to assume command of the seas. Their surface commerce raiders were tracked down and destroyed one by one and this enemy method of sinking Allied shipping became too difficult. But the daring exploits of their submarine commanders came to their notice and as the number of ships sunk by these underseas craft mounted it was realized that here was the way to cut the lifeline to England and so reduce it that victory would be inevitable. From 1915 onward great efforts were made in Germany to increase their submarine fleet and to wage a relentless war on Allied shipping of all kinds.

The old textbooks and regulations regarding the formation and conduct of convoys dating back to Lord Nelson's time were dug out and studied. The British Admiralty soon set up a system of control ports where shipping was directed to be formed into convoys and their hazardous passage across the Atlantic was made under the escort of men-of-war.

But the shipping losses became very great and as the number of available ships declined and the number of urgent cargoes mounted, the price of ships and the value of ocean freights increased tremendously. Ships that were in established trades which had no direct connexion with the conduct of the war were withdrawn and put to carrying food, ammunition and all the impedimenta of war across the oceans to England and France. A great shortage of ocean-going bottoms soon became apparent.

The sailing vessels of that time, however, were too few in number and were too scattered to be placed in convoys of their own class and speed and it was not practical to attach them to any of the steamship convoys.

During 1914 and 1915 the war scarcely affected shipbuilding in Atlantic Canada. It was still "business as usual". Six tern schooners were completed in 1914, and in 1915 only two terns and one four-master were launched. But by 1916 far-seeing individuals realized the state of affairs and the boom got under way with nineteen schooners launched. In 1917 forty-nine were completed, in 1918 ninety-six. The year following one hundred and fourteen were built, and then the bubble burst. The national ship-building programs of the world began to pour out large new steamers and the schooners were left far astern, as they could not hope to compete on the regular ocean trades as peacetime routines were established.

Only Three Schooners launched in 1915

Two of the schooners launched in 1915 were built at Liverpool, N.S. The smallest was the *Marjorie McGlashen* of 109 tons net from the yard of D. C. Mulhall for William Duff, Lunenburg, N.S. This owner, to be noted often from this time on, was a Newfound-lander from Harbour Grace, who, during a successful fish exporting career, moved to Lunenburg, N.S., and resumed business there. He became a Federal Member of Parliament and later was appointed a Senator. The *Marjorie McGlashen* was employed in the Newfoundland-Oporto fish trade. W. W. Nutting in his book, *Track of the Typhoon*, reported speaking to this tern near the Azores while on an Atlantic passage in a yacht. The vessel was sold to A. E. Hickman & Co. of St. John's, Nfld., and was lost at Malaga, Spain, on February 11th, 1921; Captain Lodge, master.

The other vessel was one of the first of the larger schooners to be equipped with an auxiliary. The *Gilbert Islands* of 245 tons net was built by Robie McLeod for A. W. Hendry, Halifax, N.S. This vessel was designed and constructed for interests in the Pacific. After completion at Liverpool she went to New York under the charge of Captain E. J. Inness, where she had an auxiliary installed and was loaded. After waiting there for some weeks while an obstruction in the Panama Canal was being cleared, Captain Inness became impatient and proceeded toward Sydney, Australia, via the Cape of Good Hope. This passage was completed in 116 days and after delivering the vessel to her new owners Captain Inness returned home.

Captain E. J. Inness and his brother Fred S. Inness were the sons and grandsons of shipmasters out of Liverpool, N.S. Both went to sea as lads, learned their trade and after spending years in command returned ashore and engaged in business.

Captain L. C. Tower of Parrsboro

At Port Greville the *L. C. Tower* of 518 tons net, a fine four-master, was completed by G. M. Cochrane and L. C. Tower. Captain Tower took command for the first voyage, which was a cargo of spruce deals from Port Greville to the United Kingdom. This fine schooner was overtaken by an enemy submarine and destroyed. She left Port Greville on June 1st, 1915, met with bad weather on June 12th and lost her foretopmast and the end of the jib-boom. On July 1st they were off Fastnet, Ireland, when the sub-marine came up and signalled them to abandon ship. Captain Tower and his crew put their boat over and rowed to the submarine. They were taken aboard and the ship's papers were examined. When told the schooner would have to be destroyed the Captain argued, "I have no contraband aboard and the schooner is all I have in the world". It was no use. They placed two bombs and some tins of gasolene aboard the vessel and in twenty minutes she was afire. The Captain and crew then rowed ashore.

Captain Tower sailed as master for forty-three years. He was born about 1858 and went to sea in his father's schooner, *Star of the Sea*, at the age of five. At sixteen he was an ordinary seaman and four months before he was twenty-one he went master of his father's schooner *Adelaide*. In 1907 he branched out as a builder and had the *Kenneth C* built at Port Greville and spent eight years in her as master. His next venture was the *L. C. Tower*. He returned home after her loss and was active in shipping for many years and will be mentioned again in this work.

The Building Boom gets under way

The increased trade and the losses suffered by Allied shipping began to be felt by 1916. The tern schooners in operation were returning handsome dividends to their owners and the market for bottoms was excellent, so the building began.

Captain L. C. Tower, who had lost his new four-masted schooner in 1915, had another four-master of the same size, the *Ada Tower* of 528 tons net, built at Port Greville, again associated with G. M. Cochrane. In 1918 this schooner passed to other hands and was owned at one time by Freeman Hatfield. Jeanette E. Rattray in her book *Ship Ashore* notes that the *Ada Tower* was wrecked at Sayville, L.I., in 1926, and her crew of eight were saved. Apparently she was not badly damaged and was afloat soon after. On October 28th, 1929, this vessel went ashore at Jacksonville Beach, Florida, and became a total loss.

G. M. Cochrane was the builder of another fine vessel that year. The *Lillian H*, a large tern of 424 tons net, had a very short life, being torpedoed off the coast of Ireland on January 19th, 1917. It is noted that the register of the vessel was retained by the commander of the submarine.

Several fine large schooners were built at Port Greville during this period by George Wagstaff. He had earlier been associated with his father at Granville, N.S., where they had built the *A. F. Davison* and the *F. C. Lockhart*. About 1910 he went to the West Coast of Canada, but returned to Nova Scotia in 1916 to resume his work in the shipyards. In 1916 the first of the schooners was launched. The *F.A.J.E.* of 357 tons net was named after the initials of the Elderkin daughters. Mr. Elderkin sold this vessel to French fishing interests, who renamed her the *M.F.C.* Mr. Wagstaff is still actively employed in building vessels and with his associate, Mr. Hatfield, had a fine new dragger on the ways when I visited Port Greville in the summer of 1955. The dragger was built to the highest standard, being planked in oak and birch, and presenting a fine appearance.

W. R. & C. A. Huntley launched the *Minas Queen* of 456 tons net at Parrsboro in 1916. On her maiden voyage she was sunk off the coast of France after encountering a German submarine, with the loss of all her crew but one. Captain W. L. Loomer was master and he and all his crew appear to have been U.S. citizens. The vessel was owned by Job & Co., of St. John's, Nfld.

Near Parrsboro, at Advocate Harbour, T. K. Bentley built the *Cumberland County* of 425 tons net for J. N. Pugsley and others. Captain B. Tower was master and this vessel was soon in difficulties by being stranded on Southwest Reef, Tortugas, Florida, on March 27th, 1917. She was abandoned to the underwriters and sold to A. D. Cummings & Co. of Philadelphia. They repaired the vessel and renamed her *Pauline C. Cummings* under U.S. registry.

Across Minas Basin at Cheverie an old shipyard was put in commission and the *Minnie G. Parsons* of 321 tons net was built by G. M. Parsons. The Parsons interests built seven of these schooners at Cheverie during this period and they all had the Parsons family names. The *Minnie G* was wrecked at Cadiz, Spain, on February 14th, 1919.

The French Shore in 1916

Along the French shore of southwest Nova Scotia, schooner building was resumed in 1916. At Belliveau Cove the *Emma Belliveau* of 223 tons net was launched by C. L. LeBlanc for B. Belliveau & Co. This schooner was under the command of Captain A. Nicholls when she stranded at Cap Rond on the Cape Breton coast in 1917. She was salvaged and went on until November 24th, 1920, when she foundered twenty miles west of the Isle of Flores in the Azores.

At Meteghan, a shipyard was purchased in 1915 by Dr. T. H. MacDonald, a local practitioner, and one of the men who anticipated the demand for cargo vessels. He built four vessels there before selling the yard in 1918. Two of these vessels were four-masted schooners, one was a barquentine and the last one a tern. The first three were sold at a solid profit before they left the ways, but the fourth was too late for the market and was not a financial success. Dr. MacDonald told me she was a very fine vessel and possibly the best of the four. Like many other fine schooners built during the inflated times at great expense there was little chance of returning her building cost to her owners once the war was over and the shipping decline set in. The first of these vessels built by Dr. MacDonald, for Adam B. McKay of Hamilton, Ont., was the *Letitia L. McKay* of 544 tons net. She cost about $70,000 to complete and was quickly sold to French interests and renamed *Cape Boulhaut*.

At Shelburne in 1916

Shelburne was a busy place in 1916. G. A. Cox launched the largest tern there up to that time. The *Admiral Drake* of 309 tons net was owned by A. S. Rendell & Co. and others of St. John's and was employed as a general trader until November 17th, 1927, when she was lost at Scatarie, Cape Breton. The *Sunset Glow* of 240 tons net had a lengthy career after launching from the yard of the Estate of Jos. McGill. Captain G. B. Dean was a longtime master in this vessel. She was owned by Harvey & Co. of St. John's and for some years she was in the fish trade to Spain, Portugal and Brazil. It is noted that in February, 1927, when homeward bound from Bahia, Brazil, she was caught in the ice off Newfoundland and was extricated from a very dangerous position by the s.s. *Nerissa.* In later years refrigeration machinery and an auxiliary were installed in her for the carriage of frozen fish. In October, 1949, William Dicks, master, she was lost at

Fogo, Nfld., while laden with a coal cargo. This vessel lived out her full life of hard work for thirty-three years, showing the good workmanship and materials that had gone into her.

Winslow McKay launched two terns in 1916. The *Emily H. Patten* of 152 tons net was owned by John B. Patten and William Forsey of Grand Bank, Nfld. After many voyages across the Atlantic this vessel was abandoned in mid-ocean on February 1st, 1929. She was first commanded by Captain Abe Thornhill and later by Cyril Squires. Captain Squires told me she performed very well and on one occasion went from Marystown, Nfld., to Barbados in twelve days. On another voyage from Pernambuco to Barbados she made little headway on account of calms but picked up the wind in 1° south latitude and went on to Barbados in twelve days. Both this vessel and the one following had very good averages in their passages in the salt-fish trade. The second vessel, the *Edith M. Cavell* of 134 tons net, named after the heroic British nurse of World War One, was built for the Penny interests in Newfoundland and was very successful. Her first master was E. G. Vallis and he was succeeded by J. J. Whalen. Captain Whalen later became well known in shipping circles as Marine Superintendent for the Newfoundland Government. He told me the *Edith* was a very fine vessel and on one occasion in 1922 made a passage from Ramea, Nfld., to Lisbon in nine days. This round-bow, spike-bowsprit schooner was built from an excellent model. She cost $16,000 and Captain Whalen reported that she paid for herself about four times over before being sold to the Portuguese fishing interests about 1926. She was renamed *Rosita* at that time, and later *Finaldie*. The Portuguese were so impressed with her sailing and sea qualities that they took off her lines and used them in the construction of several larger schooners for their own use.

In the severe winter of 1922-23, when many of our small vessels were lost, Captain Whalen had a long hard passage from Oporto toward Ramea with salt. The voyage took ninety days and he arrived at Lunenburg with part of the cargo jettisoned and the schooner badly damaged by ice and heavy weather. To give a complete picture of this passage and the difficulties encountered a summary of Captain Whalen's Protest follows:

The Hard Passage of the 'Edith M. Cavell'

Here is the text of the Protest noted by Captain J. J. Whalen, Master of the British schooner *Edith M. Cavell* of the burthen of 134 tons net of St. John's, Nfld., together with Aloysius Cheffay, mate, and Harold Crew, one of the crew of the said schooner, who solemnly declared that the said schooner left Oporto, Portugal, on the 19th day of January, 1923, at 1.30 o'clock p.m. bound for Ramea, Newfoundland, with a cargo of salt, with hatches well secured and battened, and the said schooner in good and seaworthy condition, tight, staunch and strong, and properly and sufficiently manned and equipped in every respect for the said intended voyage.

"All went well until Tuesday the thirtieth day of January, 1923, when the schooner was in latitude 41° 34′ N., longitude 37° 41′ W. and was hove-to under a two-reefed mainsail in a west-north-west gale, when a heavy sea was shipped, breaking the mizzen boom in four places, and the mizzen gaff in two places, and breaking in the companion-way doors, and partly filling the cabin. The weather continued boisterous, but the vessel was kept on her course until the seventh day of February when the vessel was hove-to under the single reefed mainsail in a northwest gale, with a heavy sea, and a huge sea was shipped breaking the lifeboat, carrying away poop deck ladders, tearing away the dory from its lashings, and carrying away the cabin skylight. The wind moderated at eleven a.m. and the vessel proceeded, with boisterous weather, and heavy seas, and shipping large quantities of water daily, until the fourteenth day of March, 1923, at eight o'clock a.m. when drift ice was encountered in Lat. 43° 55′ N., Long. 54° W., through which the vessel proceeded all day, and hove up in the ice for the night. On the following day, vessel proceeded through the ice with north-north-west wind under reefed mainsail, stormsail, jib and forestaysail, and at ten o'clock the whole mainsail was hoisted and the vessel proceeded. At two o'clock hoisted the foresail and at two thirty p.m. the ice tore off the iron stem plate and damaged the stem. At five o'clock p.m. the steamer *Rosalind* was sighted, and a supply of food was obtained, and we asked to be reported. On the morning of the sixteenth of March about 35 tons more or less of the cargo of salt was hoisted to the deck from the forward hold, and stowed on the poop, and the vessel's chains were hauled aft in order to put the vessel down aft and lift her damaged stem out of the water. The vessel was then in field ice, and it was possible to work on the ice, when iron clamps were placed over the damaged parts of the stem with sheet iron over all, and secured with spikes. The vessel was then so much out of trim that she could not proceed, or be steered, when an opportunity came to proceed, and it was necessary in order to make the vessel navigable to jettison the salt which was stowed on the poop (which was done) and which could not be replaced in the hold as it would cause the damaged portion of the stem to come in contact with the ice when the vessel proceeded, and such would result in further damage and leaking. The vessel was then leaking forty strokes an hour, and remained jammed in the ice until the eighteenth of March when the ice slacked at one p.m. and the foresail was set and vessel proceeded south-south-east toward open water which was reached at six o'clock p.m., and vessel proceeded on a southwest course, continuing to make water as before. On the following morning the wind veered to the south-west, and the vessel proceeded west-north-west until eleven o'clock a.m. when heavy field ice was again sighted, and the course was shifted to south-east, and the vessel proceeded until seven o'clock p.m. when sail was taken in and vessel hove-to under two-reefed mainsail in order to await daylight. On the morning of March twentieth the wind blew a gale from the south-south-west, veering to the south-west at nine o'clock a.m., the vessel was kept hove-to all of that day, and at two o'clock on that day the wind shifted to west and north-west with terrific sea and snow squalls, and very frosty weather during which time the vessel got badly iced up. At eight o'clock a.m. on the morning of the twenty-first the wind moderated and stormsail and forestaysail were hoisted and vessel proceeded in a north-north-east direction until two o'clock p.m. when some ice was sighted, but vessel was kept on her course until seven o'clock p.m. when very heavy ice was sighted, and at eight p.m. the ice was found to be packed tight, and we kept her off to the open water.

"On the morning of March twenty-second, some loose ice was in sight and vessel proceeded and cleared the ice at three o'clock a.m. At eight o'clock a.m. on the twenty-second of March the vessel's stem was found to be badly cut into, about four inches under the waterline, with stem bolts projecting, and the vessel continued to leak as before, and as it was impossible to proceed on the voyage it was decided to head for Halifax, which was done, and the vessel proceeded toward Halifax until Thursday, April the fifth, when land was made off Lunenburg, and as the wind was unfavourable it was decided to make Lunenburg, where the vessel arrived the same day and anchored in the stream.

"And these appearers do further say that before and during and after all of the occasions hereinbefore referred to, the said John J. Whalen and the rest of the crew of the said schooner used their every endeavour to navigate the said schooner in a safe and proper manner, and used all possible skill, seamanship and ability to prevent loss to the said schooner, or to her apparel and cargo, and to save the said schooner."

From the foregoing it is seen that navigating these small terns across the Atlantic in winter was a hard task, one requiring constant vigilance, the exercise of ingenuity in the face of disaster, a constant fight against fatigue and the determination to bring the ship home safely.

The Liverpool Schooners of 1916

At Liverpool, N.S., D. C. Mulhall launched the *Gwendolen Warren* of 274 tons net for F. K. Warren, Halifax, N.S., and named after his daughter. She was sold shortly after to Bowring Bros. of Newfoundland. Her master in this company was Captain George Elford, but while he was being relieved for a voyage by Captain John Kendrick, the vessel was lost in the ice off St. John's on March 25th, 1920, after the rudder had become unshipped.

One of the companies organized to carry out schooner construction in those days of 1916 was the Southern Salvage Co. at Liverpool, N.S. They built the *Marion J. Smith* of 332 tons net for W. C. Smith, fish merchant of Lunenburg; Captain A. Geldert, master. The schooner foundered at sea about December 7th, 1920, while on a voyage from the United Kingdom toward Halifax in ballast. Captain Cyrus Parks and his crew arrived home safely.

Capture of the 'Percé'

J. S. Gardner of Liverpool, N.S., launched a fine tern in 1916. The *Percé* of 308 tons net was new when her owners, Robin, Jones & Whitman, fish merchants of Halifax, loaded her with dried salt fish for Pernambuco, Brazil. Captain Carl Kohler was master and he had his newly-wed bride aboard for the voyage. Captain B. G. Hooper of the Dominion Coal Co. told me of this voyage as he was an A.B. in the schooner at the time. After a good passage south, while just north of the Equator, she encountered a large full-rigged sailing ship showing Norwegian colours. The big ship altered course to pass close to the schooner. As the distance closed, the Norwegian dipped his flag. Having been informed about raiders, Captain Kohler decided not to hoist his ensign but pose as a neutral as long as possible. But his bride thought this very impolite and pleaded with Captain Kohler to return the courtesy, which he proceeded to do, hoisting the "Red Duster" to the peak of the spanker gaff. As soon as the ensign broke out the big ship hauled down the Norwegian flag, ran up the German ensign, dropped a section of her bulwarks and fired a shot across the bows of the schooner before the eyes of the astounded Captain Kohler. This ship was Count Von Luckner's *Seeadler*, which had recently escaped through the Allied blockade and was engaged in sinking Allied shipping at a great rate. Captain Kohler, his bride and crew had to leave the ship in a hurry and go aboard the German raider and see their fine schooner destroyed. The prisoners received the best of care aboard the *Seeadler* until the large number of them made it necessary for their host to drop them off. This took place when the French barque *Cambronne* was captured off Rio. The raiders reduced the French ship's sail area by cutting away her upper masts to slow her down and thus delay her reaching port in a hurry to spread the news. The crews of the eleven ships destroyed by Von Luckner were put aboard the barque and they took twenty days to sail to Rio. As a daring enemy at the time, Count Von Luckner had a very good record and was most considerate to all the Allied seamen he took off the victims of his privateering. In after-war years, the Count was hospitably received in both the United States and Canada as a seaman and chivalrous foe.

The La Have Schooners of 1916

J. N. Rafuse launched two schooners along the river in this year. The *Agnes P. Duff* of 178 tons net was built at Conquerall Bank for William Duff. She was sold to Campbell and McKay of Newfoundland soon after; Captain J. J. Whalen, master. This was one of the very successful schooners and it is reported by Captain Whalen that just after World War One he made a very successful round trip, taking eight months to carry out the following: Loaded 5000 drums of salt fish at St. John's to Pernambuco for orders and discharged at Maceio, Brazil, then loaded raw sugar for Rio, discharged there and took in ballast for Santos. At Santos, Brazil, loaded leaf tobacco in bales for Madrid, the freight on which was $35,000 paid in advance. This cargo was discharged at Cadiz, Spain, and salt was loaded for home. He was away for eight months and grossed $60,000. Captain Whalen stated she was no great shakes as a sailer, but she was consistent. On one occasion he loaded deals at Pictou, N.S. for the United Kingdom and ten days after passing Cape Race, with booms swung out in a fair wind, arrived at Queenstown, Ireland, for orders. She was lost in the early 1920's by driving ashore at Renews Island, Nfld., after being hove-to in a gale while under the command of Captain J. Snow.

The other La Have schooner was the *W. N. Reinhardt* of 271 tons net, built for her namesake and others of La Have. Her later owner is given as Burnham Tower and she was lost on Race Point, Cape Cod, Mass., but I do not have the date.

At Bridgewater, W. A. Naugler launched the *Asquith* of 271 tons net for Nova Scotia owners. Her first master was E. B. Sarty and she was soon sold to A. E. Hickman & Co. of St. John's, for the salt-fish trade. She was abandoned at sea on January 22nd, 1922, while on a passage from Seville, Spain, to Newfoundland.

L. C. TOWER. 518 tons. Built 1915 at Port Greville, N.S. *Courtesy of Mr. F. W. Wallace*

EDITH M. CAVELL. 134 tons. Built 1916 at Shelburne, N.S. *Courtesy of Captain J. J. Whalen*
(Jammed in the ice off Newfoundland. Spanker boom broken.)

ADAM B. MACKAY.   441 tons.   Built 1917 at Port Greville, N.S.   *Courtesy of Mr. G. Wagstaff*

ANNIE B. ANDERSON.   466 tons.   Built 1917 at Parrsboro, N.S.   *Courtesy of the Mariners Museum*

MARION G. DOUGLAS.   449 tons.
Built 1917 at Fox River, N.S.
Courtesy of the Abbass Studios, Sydney, N.S.

BIANCA (Second of name).   313 tons.   Built 1917 at Liverpool, N.S.   *Courtesy of Mr. F. W. Wallace*

CAPE D'OR. 373 tons.
Built 1918 at Cape D'Or, N.S.
Courtesy of Captain Malcolm Wilkie

REBECCA L. MACDONALD.
762 tons. Built 1918 at Meteghan, N.S.
Courtesy of the Mariners Museum

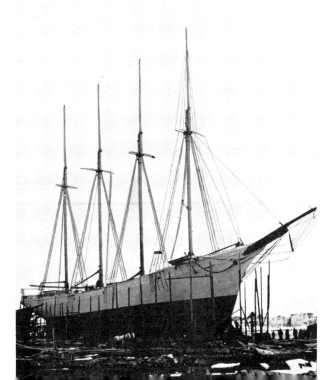

Lunenburg, 1916

Smith & Rhuland launched the *Hillcrest* of 299 tons net for Dawson Geldert and others of Lunenburg in 1916. She was employed in the usual trades until March 3rd, 1926, when she ran ashore while on a voyage to Newfoundland. Captain Geldert and his crew were taken off.

The Building Boom gets under way

It has been mentioned before, but notice should be taken of the large number of vessels registered outside of Canada. Applications for registry at St. John's, Nfld., and Bridgetown, Barbados, these ports being in British colonies and outside of Canada, were made while the ships were still on the building stocks. By registering the ships outside of Canada, owners were able to engage uncertificated officers to man the schooners. In the Nova Scotian newspapers of the time are frequent references to the difficulties of obtaining certificated masters and mates to take charge of the new ships. It was alleged that the standards required under the Canada Shipping Act were too high and it was impossible, on account of the educational requirements, for the great majority of capable and efficient seamen who manned these ships to obtain the necessary certificates. The Government was requested to relax the regulations in order to keep the vessels under Canadian registry, but nothing was done. In the United States vessels up to 700 tons were permitted to sail without certificated men in command. Taking into consideration the value of the ships, it is reasonable to conclude that the owners put only capable men in charge of their property. By its failure to take any constructive steps the Canadian Government drove a large fleet of vessels out of the country's Registry.

In the meantime the economic aspect of the shipping business had altered greatly. Sailors' wages went from $30.00 to $45.00, cooks' from $40.00 to $65.00, mates' from $45.00 to $70.00 and masters' from $75.00 to $125.00 per month. The great change was in ocean freights, as the existing steamships were either requisitioned for the war effort or destroyed by enemy action. The demands of the Allied war effort caused a great increase in ocean transportation. By 1916 the freight on deals from Nova Scotia to the United Kingdom had gone from 40 to 400 shillings a standard. Coal freights from United States ports to Nova Scotia went from 85 cents to $3.30 per ton. Lumber freights from Nova Scotia to Boston went from $3.50 to $6.50 a thousand board feet.

Carpenters, caulkers and riggers who had left the shipyards after the decline in shipbuilding and had gone on to other occupations streamed back to their old jobs at greatly increased wages.

In all existing yards the orders for new vessels piled up. Some new firms were organized to buy up timber rights and set up equipment to build. It was a great period for the shipbuilders.

Many of the owners of the yards looked to the new era of shipbuilding as a return to the great days of Maritime shipping when our large square-rigged wooden sailing ships were to be found in all the ports of the world. They claimed that with the comparative low capital cost and the small operating expenses, the large schooners would be able to carry some classes of cargo cheaper than the steamers, even in peacetime.

In Newfoundland, where the fish trade had increased enormously, there was a shortage of carriers. Bottoms were not to be had at any economic price, so they expanded their resources to build their own terns.

The Nova Scotia French Shore Schooners of 1917

After a lapse of many years, construction was resumed at Little Brook. Two large terns, the *Speedway* of 544 tons net, and the *Socony* of 314 tons net, were launched. The *Speedway* was built by S. St. Clair Jones for foreign owners. After a short time she went to Australia and was owned there. Some years later she returned to Canada and was owned by J. H. Bonner and registered at Vancouver, B.C. She was destroyed by fire and sank off Cape Flattery on the west coast on January 24th, 1925. The *Socony* was built to the order of an American oil company and was lost soon after on the Isle of Pines, Cuba, but I do not have the date.

At Grosse Cocques, Captain Omer Blinn launched the *Herbert Warren* of 272 tons net for F. K. Warren, Halifax, and also acted as master for the time before she was sold to James Baird, Ltd., of St. John's. It is reported that this vessel disappeared with her crew on a passage from Portugal with salt early in 1923. Mr. F. K. Warren had extensive holdings in many of the schooners. The *Herbert Warren* was named for his son, who succeeded his father in the shipping firm of that name, which is still actively engaged in the shipping business.

B. N. Melanson of Gilbert's Cove launched the *Edith M. Green* of 189 tons net, an auxiliary tern fitted with a gasolene engine. She was sold to the French fisheries and renamed *Suzaky*.

The *Esther Hankinson* of 292 tons net was built by A. A. Theriault at Belliveau Cove and after being operated by her builders for a short period was sold to a syndicate from St. John's, Nfld., and was abandoned in mid-Atlantic on November 1st., 1924. The A. H. Comeau Co. produced two terns this year. The *G. Blanche* of 280 tons net was short-lived. She was sold after launching to John O., & Arthur Williams of St. John's, and was lost on the Brazilian coast on June 3rd, 1919. The *Racewell* of 337 tons net was operated by the Close Shipping Co. until she was sold to French owners. She was renamed, first *Johan* and later *Fleur de France*, and under her French owners was refitted as a barquentine.

The *Charles A. Ritcey* of 360 tons net was built by E. L. Comeau at Meteghan for Captain C. Dave Ritcey of Riverport, N.S. Captain Ritcey had owned several previous terns, including the *Freedom* and the *Novelty*. He took charge of the *Charles A. Ritcey* after her launching and made fast passages in her until he handed over to Captain Otis Acker. On the following voyage the schooner was lost at Rose Head, Lunenburg County, on September 15th, 1920. Later Captain Ritcey took command of the *Holmes, A. Frank*, a four-masted New Brunswick schooner, until she was lost in 1922. He then went to the barquentine *Maid of England* for a short time, then returned home to buy an interest in the tern *Chautauqua*. In 1924, at the age of forty, he retired from the sea and bought a furniture business in Lunenburg.

Annapolis interests had a tern built at Meteghan in 1917. The *Motherland* of 384 tons net passed quickly to St. John's, Nfld., interests. The schooner was lost far afield when she burned off Mauritius on March 6th, 1922, while on a passage from Port Natal to Mauritius with coal.

One Tern launched at Annapolis in 1917

The Annapolis Shipping Co. launched the *Beechland* of 419 tons net. F. W. Pickels was the principal owner and the vessel was sold to Thos. Harling of Montreal for foreign interests in Spain. She was renamed first *Klosofi* and later *Club Nautico*. This latter name rather implies that she was employed as a floating club of some sort. The schooner was carried in the registers until 1947.

The Tragedy of the 'E. E. Armstrong'

This fine vessel of 371 tons net was launched at Hantsport by Henry Boudreau for local owners. After a short time in commission, Captain Herbert Saunders, master, she sailed from Kingston, Jamaica, for Martinique, on August 17th, 1918. She was loaded below decks with flour and mangrove bark but had no deck cargo. The schooner disappeared on the passage and was never again heard of. The insurance on the hull of this vessel amounted to $70,000 and the freight was covered for $10,000.

The Head of the Bay of Fundy in 1917

At Cheverie, the G. M. Parsons interests built the large tern *Ralph S. Parsons* of 394 tons net. This vessel was sold soon after completion to United States firms, being owned successively by W. R. Grace & Co., E. M. Baird and finally by the Neches Transportation Co. of Port Arthur, Texas. At one time she had the re-name *Lena Ford*.

J. Willard Smith, associated with Ira S. Crowe, had the *Kathleen Crowe*, 431 tons net, built at Hillsburn, N.S. The first master in this vessel was Captain Ezra Forsyth, who sailed the J. W. Smith vessels for many years. In 1891 he received his master's certificate in sail and acted as master in many of the three- and four-masted schooners. In 1938 he passed his examination for master of a steamship after a period of forty-seven years as master in sail. A short time later, while on a leave of absence from a ship, he died at the age of seventy-nine. The *Kathleen Crowe* was sold to Portuguese owners and renamed *Sarah* and later *Augusto*.

W. R. Huntley of Parrsboro, N.S.

This well-known shipbuilder was the son of Daniel Huntley, who built big square-rigged ships for the Churchills and others of Hantsport. W. R. Huntley was born at Hantsport in 1848 and later moved to Parrsboro, where he opened a yard of his own. He built many of the best-known three- and four-masted schooners, including the *Florence R. Hewson, Earl of Aberdeen* and *H. J. Logan*. In association with his son, C. A. Huntley, some of the largest and finest schooners were constructed in their yard. They built the *Annie B. Anderson*, a large tern of 466 tons net, in 1917. The schooner was operated by the builders and others. She was lost through stranding at Anegada in the Virgin Islands on December 8th, 1920, while under the command of Captain E. H.

(Belayin Pin) Kirby. Jack Willis was mate at the time and he often told me what a strict disciplinarian Captain Kirby was—hence the nickname.

At Port Greville, L. E. Graham built the *Stella II* of 356 tons net for Andrew King. This schooner was first called *Khaki Lad*. The vessel was soon sold to James Baird, Ltd., of St. John's, Nfld., and was lost at the Straits of Gibraltar on January 1st, 1920. George Wagstaff and H. Elderkin launched the *Adam B. McKay* of 394 tons net for A. B. McKay of Hamilton, Ont., who became interested in Maritime schooners at this time. The schooner was first chartered and later sold to the Niger Company of London for their African nut trade at a price of $110,000. When she was taken over by the Niger Co. at Jacksonville, Fla., she was only a year old, but already the teredos, or marine borers, had attacked her to the extent that fifty strakes of planking had to be renewed. The *McKay* was sold to French interests in 1922 and renamed *Chevalier Bayard*.

One large schooner, the *William Melbourne* of 435 tons net, was launched at Spencer's Island in 1917 from the yards of J. E. Pettis for the C. T. White interests in New Brunswick. After a few years she was sold to Captain Sidney Richards and A. S. Publicover. Later she was bought by K. Cochrane of Port Greville and while commanded by Sidney Richards was lost at Cape Chignecto in 1928 while undergoing repairs.

At Advocate Harbour, the *E. H. Wharton Davies* of 463 tons net was built by T. K. Bentley and P. N. Pugsley. She was sold to the Niger Co. of London and later to French interests, who renamed her *Solidor* and later *Maia*. This schooner was carried on the registers until after World War Two. While owned by the Niger Co., who acquired several of these schooners to carry on their African business until they could replace their steamer war losses, the vessel was commanded first by Captain A. Crooks and later by Captain E. Hogan of Liverpool, N.S. The Niger Co. owned large concessions in Nigeria and had well-established trades between the colony and the United Kingdom and also with the United States. Palm oil, ivory and other articles from the colony were sold in New Orleans and usually the vessels carried back barrel staves, shooks and general cargo. The *E. H. Wharton Davies* had a long passage in 1919, taking ninety-six days for the voyage from New Orleans to Beruta on the Niger River. The schooner encountered long periods of calms and eventually completed the voyage. She loaded a cargo of palm kernels for the United Kingdom and on the tropical part of the voyage was again delayed by calms. Several of the crew died from beri-beri and malaria and Captain Hogan put his vessel into Madeira. At that time there were some American sailors waiting to be repatriated and they were taken as workaways to get the ship to England. The Americans were glad to get the chance to go to England, as from there they were speedily sent home.

Fox River, 1917

Two schooners were launched at Fox River in 1917 by G. M. Cochrane. The *Esther Adelaide* of 425 tons net was first owned by M. D. Gavin and H. C. Gillespie. G. M. Cochrane and J. N. Pugsley were the builders. She had many owners and masters through the years. Some of the men who commanded this schooner are reported to be L. Merriam, S. Swain, Wm. H. Knox and R. C. Merriam. She was engaged in the usual

Bay of Fundy trades until 1934, when she was abandoned on the beach at Parrsboro. In 1936 she was bought, reconditioned, renamed *Citnalta* and put back in the old trades. Her last owners were the Caravel Coastal Service, Ltd., of Saint John, N.B., While on a voyage from Boston to Bermuda she was carried by the tide in calm weather through Plum Gut, Long Island Sound, struck a submerged object, leaked heavily and sank on May 3rd, 1942.

The other schooner was the *Marion G. Douglas* of 449 tons net. This vessel cost $90,000 to build and was continually in trouble for one reason or another all her life. W. N. Reinhardt and others of La Have, N.S., were her first owners and Sydney Corkum the first master. She loaded a timber cargo in the Bay of Fundy for the United Kingdom and when off the north coast of Ireland, while in a strong wind, some trouble developed with the steering gear. Another ship being near, the vessel was abandoned, the crew taken off and returned immediately to Canada. In the meantime the derelict vessel, with sails set and in good order except for her broken-down steering gear, was picked up and towed to an Irish port. When the owners were notified, they sent Captain U. E. Woemer to Ireland in a hurry to pay the schooner's bills and get her back. It can be imagined that this was a costly business. Once back in Canada, she engaged in the usual trades until 1921, when she was seized by the crew for back wages in Norfolk, Va. She was bought by U.S. interests, renamed *Cynthia J. Griffin* and registered at Boston. Some years later she was bought by R. S. Kerr of Parrsboro and returned to her original register and name. She was sold to a U.S. citizen again in 1927 and is reported to be the last non-auxiliary sailing vessel to make the westbound passage of the Panama Canal. In 1927 she was picked up abandoned at sea for the second time. Off San Diego a Japanese steamer found her drifting and towed her in. She was sold for expenses and bought by Louis D. Barrere of Los Angeles, renamed *Mary Lou* and so passed from Canadian registry.

The Shipbuilder's Interest

Many of the vessels built in these yards were constructed on speculation with no definite buyer in sight. It was usual for the builder to bring in capital from interested people to build a new vessel when his yard would otherwise be idle. If no prospective buyer was found by the time the schooner was completed it was customary to put her to work as soon as possible, managed by the builder and the syndicate who put up the money. In other cases the shipbuilder often took a large share in a vessel built to order for an individual or firm.

Liverpool launched Seven Terns in 1917

Robie McLeod launched the *Maid of Harlech* of 270 tons net for F. K. Warren of Halifax. Her first master was Captain C. P. Moore and it appears she had a short life. The *Shipping Illustrated* of September 14th, 1918, states that she was towed into Oran, Algeria, after having been torpedoed or shelled by a German submarine and deserted by her crew. The authorities corresponded with the owners at Liverpool, N.S., about repairing, but it seems the work was not completed. The *Ariceen* of 358 tons net was built for Ashbournes, Ltd., of Twillingate, Nfld. After a short life in the salt-fish trade she was a total loss by stranding at Twillingate Harbour on October 29th, 1921.

The Nova Scotia Shipbuilding and Transportation Co. was set up at Liverpool to construct sailing vessels, and the first one they built was the *Ruby W* of 296 tons net. She was fitted with auxiliary oil engines of 100 h.p. and was owned by Walter B. Grieve of St. John's, Nfld. This vessel was abandoned 400 miles south of Cape Race on December 7th, 1921, when returning from Pernambuco in ballast, the crew being taken off by the Danish s.s. *Gudron Maersk*.

The *Bianca* of 313 tons net, the second schooner of the name, was built by J. S. Gardiner and like the previous vessel was fitted with an auxiliary. She was owned by Bowring Bros., of St. John's, Nfld. Memories and records are vague regarding this schooner, but she was torpedoed or shelled by a German submarine during the summer of 1918, and was towed into an Atlantic port by the American fishing vessel *Commonwealth*. She was repaired, and on October 1st, 1919, was abandoned in mid-ocean while on a voyage from Labrador toward Gibraltar with fish.

The Southern Salvage Co. built three terns at Liverpool in 1917. The *Frances Inness* of 299 tons net was commanded and part owned by Captain F. S. Inness and was later sold to a freighting firm in British Guiana, where she was used in the coastal trade until the end of her days. The other two vessels were smaller. The *Frank R. Forsey* of 158 tons net was owned by S. W. Forsey of Newfoundland. She was sold later to S. Harris of Grand Bank and some years later passed to French owners at St. Pierre et Miquelon. The third schooner, the *Winthewar* of 149 tons net (a breakdown of her name exemplifies the spirit of the times), was owned by Reinhardt Bros. and was lost on Bon Portage Island, Shelburne County, N.S., on July 3rd, 1922. When the *Winthewar* ran aground she was commanded by Captain William J. Rider. In the crew were mate Hubert Lyda, cook Edward Herman and seaman Archie Kendall. The ship struck at midnight and the crew got ashore without delay and made their way to Bon Portage Lighthouse, where they were looked after by the keeper.

In subsequent storms parts of the hull of the *Winthewar* were thrust up on the beach. Hurricane Edna, in September, 1954, brought a very high tide to the area and the great seas lifted the remains of the smart little tern and drove the old weathered remnant a hundred yards inshore against the trees, where it still remains. Captain Leander Publicover told me he salvaged the spars from this schooner for his *Village Queen*, which he was having built at the time.

Robie McLeod of Liverpool, N.S.

One of the most prominent shipbuilders in Nova Scotia over a long period of time was Robie McLeod. His career started as an apprentice while working with his father, John McLeod. Prior to 1850 the elder McLeod had started building small schooners, mostly for the Newfoundland trade, and the size of the vessels had gradually increased, so that by 1854 he produced the barque *Invincible* of 444 tons which was credited with many fast passages, including one from Miramichi to Liverpool, England, in under eleven days. Between the years 1850 and 1873, when he was lost while delivering a vessel to Newfoundland, he built upwards of thirty-five vessels. At that time his son, Robie McLeod, then a very young man, took over his father's position as master shipbuilder. His first vessel was the *Flash*, which had been started by his father and which he finished.

From 1873 until the year 1919, when he retired from shipbuilding, he built and designed upwards of 178 vessels of various tonnages and types from 80 to 500 tons. He built from his own models only, models of practically every type of vessel in use during the period, including barques, barquentines, brigs, brigantines, topsail schooners, tern schooners, fishing schooners, tug boats and small steamers.

His models were also used in many shipyards in Nova Scotia. In the year 1893, in competition with thirty other designers and builders throughout Canada, he won the Dominion First Prize of $400.00 for the finest model, including specifications and working details, of a freighting and fishing schooner. In 1896 he also designed and built the famous Saint John pilot schooner *Howard D. Troop*, credited with being one of the finest and fastest vessels of this class on the Atlantic coast.

The many types of sailing craft built by Robie McLeod were noted for their beauty of design, fast passages and the large financial returns which they brought to their owners. Although many of the vessels he produced were built to the order of individuals or firms, he nevertheless was a part owner in a number of them. Others he built on speculation and operated until a suitable buyer came along.

Hector McLeod, the son of Robie McLeod, wrote me that his father had received offers to take charge of leading yards in the United States and even Germany at several periods of his career, but declined them all. He preferred to work and spend his life in his native town of Liverpool. In this respect his career differed from another famous shipwright and builder who had been born earlier at nearby Jordan River, Shelburne County, N.S. Donald McKay left his native land and emigrated to the United States after learning his trade in the local shipyards. His subsequent career as a designer and builder of clipper ships is too well known to be retold here.

Shelburne Building in 1917

The Newfoundland shippers were now experiencing a great boom in exporting their cured-fish products and to move them to markets were ordering schooners from all the established yards. The *Little Stephano* of 125 tons net was the first of these schooners launched by the McGill Estate at Shelburne in 1917. W. B. Kean was her first master and she was owned by the Little Stephano Co. In April, 1926, she was abandoned in mid-Atlantic while in the Portuguese trade after having drifted about for more than a fortnight with her sails blown away, rudder post broken and leaking badly. Their second vessel was the *General Maude* of 140 tons net, first owned by G. C. Harris of Grand Bank, Nfld. She was later sold to J. B. Foote & Sons of Newfoundland and was abandoned on March 23rd, 1926, while westbound from Cadiz with a cargo of salt, her crew being taken off by the s.s. *Aztec*. The *Sparkling Glance* of 217 tons net was the third schooner. She was owned by John Harvey of St. John's and was abandoned in mid-Atlantic on February 9th, 1921.

The G. A. Cox yard launched two terns in 1917. The *Jean Campbell* of 277 tons net was a very unlucky vessel and made no money for her owners. On her delivery voyage from Shelburne to St. John's she took thirty-five days and was given up for lost. She was owned variously by W. S. Munroe, W. Campbell and also Davis & Benson. She finally loaded a coal cargo in Cape Breton, but it went afire and she burned her side out before delivery. The other vessel was the *Vogue* of 196 tons net.

The 'Vogue' was a Money-maker

W. N. Reinhardt and others of La Have owned her first and C. M. Wilkie was her master and part owner. She cost $33,500 ready for sea. Soon after, Captain Wilkie bought out the other interests and in one year carried out the following voyages: loaded lumber at Bridgewater, N.S., for New York, from there with coal to Santo Domingo City, in ballast to Belize and loaded coconuts for New York, coal to Halifax, flour to St. John's, Nfld., dry fish to Brazil, coco beans to New York and back to Halifax, with coal. Captain Wilkie told me she was a very smart schooner and her profit for the twelve months was $28,000. He then sold her to A. E. Hickman & Co. for $48,000 where Captain Frank Pine was her first master. He was succeeded by George Yarn, who told me she loaded a cargo of slop fish in northern Newfoundland. On this voyage the vessel was abandoned on November 17th, 1921, on account of her leaky condition. Her bottom had become eaten away by the attacks of marine teredos picked up during her previous voyages to the West Indies. Captain Yarn and his crew were taken off by the Norwegian s.s. *Elite Clausen*.

Other Schooners at Shelburne, 1917

Winslow McKay launched the *Gladys M. Hollett* of 150 tons net for W. H. & T. V. Hollett of Burin, Nfld.; Captain A. T. Cluett, master. When quite new she was overtaken by a German submarine off Halifax. The crew were ordered off and the schooner was shelled. Owing to the fact the mate, Mike Brown, had battened down the 'tween deck hatch the schooner retained buoyancy. As she filled she fell over on her side but did not sink. The crew rowed in to the Sambro Lightvessel at the entrance to Halifax Harbour and later a towboat was sent out to bring the *Gladys* in. There is a story in connexion with this episode. It is reported that a man by the name of Burgess, of not very good character, had been released from prison in Newfoundland on account of the man-power shortage and had been shipped as master aboard a Burin vessel. The ship and her crew disappeared and were presumed lost. But when the *Gladys* was boarded by a party from the German submarine, three of the Burin men swore that Burgess was one of the boarders. The schooner was repaired and went on until March 30th, 1923, when she was lost in the ice off Cape Race.

The last vessel produced in Shelburne in 1917 was the *Misty Star* of 270 tons net. She was launched from the yard of Shelburne Shipbuilders, Ltd., for John Harvey of St. John's, Nfld. This schooner was built especially for the fish trade between Newfoundland, Europe and Brazil. She was coppered from the waterline down and all over the keel. The sails required 2644 yards of canvas. Iron knees were used to stiffen the deck

CECIL JR.   204 tons.   Built 1918 at Shelburne, N.S.   *Courtesy of Mr. F. W. Wallace*

AVON QUEEN, ex JESSIE LOUISE FARQUIER.   939 tons.   Built 1918 at Hantsport, N.S.
Courtesy of Mr. Melville Bell Grosvenor

J. E. BACKMAN. 399 tons. Built 1918 at Meteghan, N.S.
Courtesy of Mr. Smith, Bridgewater

CHAUTAUQUA. 354 tons. Built 1918 at Liverpool, N.S.
Courtesy of Zwicker & Co.

E. L. COMEAU. 539 tons. Built 1918 at Meteghan, N.S.
Courtesy of the Mariners Museum

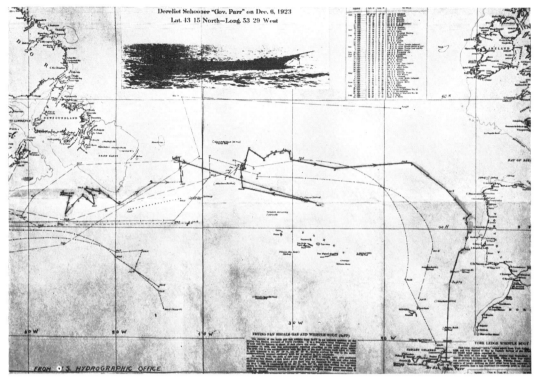

Chart of the drift of the GOVERNOR PARR.

Courtesy of the U.S. Hydrographic Office

GOVERNOR PARR.   912 tons.   Built 1918 at Parrsboro, N.S.

Courtesy of the Mariners Museum

beams and the total weight of these amounted to 10,580 lb. She took five months and fifteen days to build and was completely fitted to comply with the standards of her class. The schooner was lost on the coast of France on December 13th, 1919.

The La Have Schooners of 1917

The yard of M. Leary at Dayspring sent out the *Reginald R. Moulton* of 112 tons net in 1917. This round-bow schooner was built for the fleet of J. T. Moulton of Newfoundland, who was one of the most active shippers of the time. This vessel arrived at Burgeo in ballast and loaded export fish for the Portugal and Brazil trade until January 1919, when she was wrecked at Leixoes, near Oporto. She was condemned and her master, Captain Daniel MacDonald, and his crew returned home on another Moulton schooner. She was bought by Portuguese interests, raised and repaired, then handed over to Burgeo & La Poile Export Co. and was employed as a fish carrier to the usual ports. In 1925 she was refitted as a two-masted Bank fisherman and in 1928 was sold to Notre Dame, Nfld., parties who lost her by running ashore near her home port the same year.

J. N. Rafuse & Sons produced two medium-sized terns at Conquerall Bank on the La Have River in 1917. The *Inspiration* of 283 tons net was launched for M. J. Parks but soon passed to James Baird, Ltd., of St. John's. She was abandoned in mid-Atlantic in the winter of 1924-25 and her crew was taken off by the R.M.S.P. *Cardiganshire*. The *Integral* of 343 tons net, a much larger vessel, was owned by the builder and others. Later she was operated by Zwicker & Co. of Lunenburg and was laid up in the La Have River about 1936 and never went to sea again.

At Bridgewater, N.S., W. A. Naugler built the *Daniel Getson* of 295 tons net for her namesake. This schooner was active during her long life in the coasting trade and had many good passages to her credit. In 1938 she was sold to United States owners and was renamed *Wanderthirst*.

Schooners built in Various Places in 1917

Smith & Rhuland of Lunenburg built the *Frances Louise* of 147 tons net for H. W. Adams of that port. This schooner was engaged in the fish and salt trade until 1927, when she was sold to owners in the Dutch West Indies and renamed *Three Sisters*. The *Jean Dundonald Duff* of 345 tons net was built by J. Ernst & Son of Mahone Bay for Wm. Duff and others of Lunenburg. She was soon sold to Newfoundland and first owned by W. B. Grieve and later by Baine, Johnson & Co. She was abandoned in the North Atlantic on October 15th, 1923.

The *Lewis Brothers* of 675 tons net, a four-master, was built by the Lewis Hardwood Co. at Sheet Harbour, N.S. F. A. Kaiser, now a master in the Mersey Paper Co. ships of Liverpool, N.S., told me he joined this schooner as a young sailor when she was new and stayed in her a year. On the first voyage to New York to load general cargo she was found to be very weak and before loading she was dry-docked and had her fastenings doubled up. They sailed for Port Elizabeth, South Africa, under Captain J. W. (Bully) Larkin and after a voyage of 150 days arrived at their destination. Captain Kaiser told me the food ran short but they were not hungry. Some items like sugar and tea ran out and they were heartily sick of their monotonous diet of salt fish, salt meat and potatoes. They discharged the cargo, loaded wool for New York and made the passage back in sixty days. Captain Kaiser and most of the crew signed off there.

Soon after, the schooner came under the command of Captain J. B. Chute, who had formerly commanded the steel barque *Belmont*, built in Scotland but operated later by U.S. owners. This man was known as a hard case and hardly the type to commit suicide as was reported. He had quarreled with the mate, Vernon Bracklehurst, and others of the crew. The master was found shot in his cabin and the ensuing trial was held at Nassau. The crew had to be extradited from Key West, Fla., at the request of the British authorities, and the accused were acquitted of the crime. The schooner was in the hard-pine trade at the time and was kept at that work until September, 1925, when she burned at Pascagoula, Miss., one of the main southern lumber ports.

The Start of the Building Boom in Newfoundland

In this year of 1917 six tern schooners were built in Newfoundland at various places. The great shortage of shipping extended to Newfoundland, and with the big demand for salt fish abroad local shipbuilding was undertaken to get the product to market. The price of salt fish on the foreign market increased enormously as the disruption of the peacetime routines was extended.

As a rule the Newfoundland-built schooners were not a success. They were constructed by men who were expert only at building smaller craft. In the haste of producing the schooners it was general that the wood was not of good quality.

The largest of these schooners was the *Arnish* of 467 tons net built at St. George's, Nfld., and owned by J. Flett. She was abandoned in a sinking condition 120 miles east of Fogo on November 2nd, 1919. J. Manuel built the *Pauline Martin* of 298 tons net for M. E. Martin at Norris Arm. This schooner was abandoned in mid-Atlantic on December 9th, 1918. A. E. Hickman & Co. associated with the Swyers interests had A. Chaulk build the *Joan Hickman* of 295 tons net at Charlottetown, Nfld. This vessel was wrecked on the Spanish coast between Bonanza and Huelva, while on a passage from St. John's to Gibraltar with codfish on February 18th, 1920. Samuel Harris had the *Roberta Ray* of 164 tons net built at Grand Bank and this vessel was abandoned in the North Atlantic on March 12th, 1921. At Placentia, T. Kemp launched the *Elizabeth Fearn* of 246 tons net for G. C. Fearn & Son. Captain J. Kemp was her first master. She was sold to William Campbell and others of St. John's and was stranded and lost at Quidi Vidi, near St. John's, on February 12th, 1921; P. McLellan, master.

The final vessel noted for the year is the *Imprimus* of 177 tons net built by D. Pelley at Port Blandford, Nfld. This vessel was owned by A. E. Hickman & Co. and was abandoned about 300 miles south of Bermuda with a cargo of salt aboard from Grand Turk to St. John's, Nfld., on October 7th, 1921.

War Building in New Brunswick, 1918

By 1918 it was generally understood that the war had brought on a tremendous demand for shipping. Investors flocked to the shipyards to put their money into building new ships. Those schooners in existence at this time were paying back their cost in a year or less and still freight was offering at a higher rate every month.

In New Brunswick, where for many years no large sailing vessels had been built, the old yards were started again. At Saint John the *Dornfontein*, a four-master of 666 tons net, was launched by the Marine Construction Co. This fine new schooner was lost almost within sight of her home port. When on her maiden voyage, outbound, she encountered a German submarine off Brier Island in the Bay of Fundy. Her crew were ordered off and the vessel was set afire. This took place on August 2nd, 1918.

To set up the shipyards and get the ships completed as quickly as possible the Marine Construction Co. used all the short cuts they could devise. The routine of the old days was not considered good enough, so, instead of producing a full-sized ship from a hand-carved half-model, these vessels were built from blueprints drawn up by a naval architect in line with the most modern practice. Many of the old methods for shaping the timbers and boring the holes for fastenings were scrapped and power saws and electric augers were used. That some of the old-timers did not agree with the new methods is seen from an interview with an elderly shipwright for *Macleans Magazine* in 1927 written by L. A. Cunningham.

"In the old days we developed our own systems of building, of bevelling and fastening. When the trade fell off our methods were unused for a period of about thirty years. Then during the war came what they called the revival of shipbuilding—the raising of a ghost, I thought it. A few of us old men were called on once more to take up adze and mallet. I was summoned to the Back Shore and there I met a marine architect that they had brought up from the States. He told me his system, modern you might expect. But I give my word, it was inferior, and in many ways far behind the methods we used in the old days at Courtney Bay.

"I helped with the building of that schooner and another. It was hard going; most of the labour was unskilled. All the old ship carpenters, caulkers and blacksmiths who could hobble that far came and went to work. Something pathetic about them—picking up tools they had never thought to use again. The raw hands took to the work very well and by the time we had finished two ships we had a fine crew at work. But then the revival ended.

"One day I was waiting for a car to take me and other men to the Straight Shore, where we were working on the *Dornfontein*, a four-masted schooner. While we waited we talked about the difficulty we had in getting skilled men for a delicate bit of work. There was to my knowledge only one man in Saint John capable of doing it. Him I had last seen as a youth in his father's shipyard. 'Tom Braithwaite,' I said, 'is the only man in Saint John who could fill the bill.'

" 'Yes, and that's me,' cut in a voice that sounded more like a croak. I looked around. Right at my elbow was an old man leaning on a cane. When I had seen him last, he was a boy——"

At the old yards at St. Martin's a local company built the *Celina K. Goldman* of 477 tons net. This vessel was manned by a Nova Scotian crew including Captain C. Trefrey of Chebogue and mates John Lewellan and A. B. Taylor of Parrsboro. The vessel was stranded on the coast of Uruguay on September 24th, 1919, and abandoned. She was sold to Uruguay owners, repaired and renamed *Chivo*.

At the head of the Bay of Fundy on the New Brunswick side at Alma the firm of C. T. White & Son, lumber merchants, built two large terns. The *Merideth A. White* of 453 tons net was used as a lumber carrier for a few years, then was sold to the African Oil Nut Co. of London and so passed out of the Canadian Register. The other, the *Vincent A. White* of 452 tons net, had various owners, including J. H. Solery, H. F. Dunn and E. C. Adams. About 1926 she was renamed *Estonia* and passed to G. E. Hartling and his brother. In turn they sold her to the Arklie Lumber Co. of Halifax. She was kept busy on the West Indies trade, lumber down and salt or molasses back. On October 25th, 1935, she sailed from Turks Island and encountered a heavy storm, losing her sails and rudder, and was abandoned in a sinking condition. Her crew of ten were rescued by the Norwegian tanker s.s. *South America*.

At another old yard, Moss Glen, where in the great old days many large wooden ships and barques had been built, the *Ada A. McIntyre* of 423 tons net was launched by P. McIntyre for his own account. The schooner was a total loss on Schoodic Island, Maine, on October 20th, 1923.

These five large schooners were the only ones to be completed in New Brunswick during 1918.

The Nova Scotia Schooners of 1918

The coast between Yarmouth and Digby on the Bay of Fundy has long been known as the "French Shore". In this area live many of the descendants of the original French settlers of Nova Scotia. These people had small farms, but all through their history they have fished in the sea, built ships and sailed them. The revival of shipbuilding along this coast was very active in 1918-19.

The men of this area were very practical, being handy with tools, and many were skilled shipwrights. Back from the coast the timberlands had an ample supply of lumber, so the work was soon under way.

To start at Yarmouth and work up the Bay seems to be the most logical course. Two schooners were launched at Yarmouth in 1918. The *Montclair* of 419 tons net, built by the Yarmouth Shipbuilding Co., had a chequered career. She was owned by Job & Co. at first and later by the Hazelwood Co. of Montreal. In 1924 she was sold to United States citizens, but C. B. Merriam brought her back to Canadian registry. She spent a considerable time under charter to rum-runners and was lost on a sand bar off Orleans, Mass., on March 4th, 1927, and became a total loss. The wreck of this schooner has been aptly described by Henry Beston. Caught off Cape Cod in bitter weather, her gear useless under a heavy coating of ice, her crew half frozen and exhausted, the *Montclair* struck far out from shore. In the wild tumultuous swell the vessel pounded while her foremast and mainmast worked free and swung about wildly until they split the forward part of the vessel apart. Only one of the crew made the shore and survived.

The other tern, the *Cape La Have*, of 316 tons net was launched by E. B. Ergott for W. N. Reinhardt and others of La Have. The cost of this schooner was $80,000, which was a great increase over the cost of a comparative vessel a year or so before. The *Cape La Have* was active until 1929. In February of that year she is noted as having had a hard passage from Turks Island to Lunenburg. After sixteen days out she met repeated gales which blew her off the coast. After a passage of twenty-nine days the schooner made a landfall at Sandy Point, Shelburne County, and was towed by the C.G.S. *Arras* to Lunenburg. Captain Eber Sarty reported an exceedingly rough and stormy passage with the sails and gear badly damaged. Later that year the schooner was a total loss at the Caicos Islands in the Bahamas.

Large Schooners were launched at Meteghan in 1918

Five large schooners were commissioned at Meteghan in 1918. They included a four-master, the *Rebecca L. MacDonald* of 762 tons net, built by Dr. T. H. MacDonald at a cost of $90,000. She was sold immediately at a good profit to J. T. Knight & Co. and resold the same year to the Bank of British West Africa. On account of being in difficulties she was sold at Barbados in July, 1921, by order of the Colonial Court of Admiralty to John Blackwood Ltd. and S. P. Musson & Son, Ltd., of Barbados. While operated by these owners she returned to Barbados on April 5th, 1922, in a badly strained and leaky condition. She was laid up and later dismantled.

E. L. Comeau launched two large schooners at Meteghan. The *E. L. Comeau* of 539 tons net was built and managed by the Clan Shipping Co. Several years later, while under charter to U.S. rum-runners, she was seized by a U.S. Court and sold on June 4th, 1924, to foreigners at Tampa, Florida, and renamed *Rosa Ferlita*. The other schooner was the *J. E. Backman* of 399 tons net, owned by her namesake. This vessel burned at sea twelve miles southwest of Watlings Island in the Bahamas on September 4th, 1921.

There were two schooners called *Richard B. Silver* launched in Nova Scotia during this period. The first of the name was built at Meteghan in 1918 by the R. H. Hawes Construction Co. for Lunenburg interests; A. H. Zinck, master. This schooner was abandoned at sea very shortly after launching. In April, 1919, while on a passage from Santos to Havre, the crew left her in a sinking condition and were landed at Cayenne, French Guiana. It appears that the owners used the same name for a vessel they had built at Mahone Bay, N.S., in 1919. The second vessel will be dealt with later.

J. E. Gaskill built the last noted tern for this year at Meteghan. The *Scotia Belle* of 345 tons net was owned by A. A. Colter and was transferred to St. John's the same year. She soon passed to French owners and was renamed *Capitaine Huet*.

Along the Shore between Meteghan and Weymouth

A short distance away at Meteghan River the *Alma R* of 413 tons net was launched by the R. H. Howes Construction Co. She was transferred to Nassau and sold to the Bahamas Products Co. and refitted as a twin-screw auxiliary. The schooner was wrecked on Conception Island on March 10th, 1932, while on a voyage from Miami, Fla., to Baracoa, Cuba, in ballast.

Between Meteghan River and Weymouth more vessels were being built at the smaller places. All that the builders required was a level place for the keel blocks and an open field to set up the saws, planers, forge and steam box. And the labour—they came from all the farms nearby and flocked to the yards for the good wages. At White's Cove the *Donald and Keith* of 285 tons net was launched by the Westport Shipbuilding Co. under the supervision of Captain L. F. Barkhouse, the schooner being named after his two sons. She was commanded by his son, Captain R. McD. Barkhouse, when on her maiden voyage from Saint John, N.B., to Barbados. This schooner proved to be speedy and it is reported that she once logged ninety-four and a half miles in eight hours. At Barbados the vessel closed a cargo through New York brokers on deadweight capacity, $40.00 per ton with option Bordeaux or Havre, calling at Cherbourg for orders. In Bordeaux the vessel was sold to Potet-Lemere & Co. So well had the vessel been kept that an agent wanted to know whether she was a yacht or a merchant carrier. The French renamed her *Rouzic* and she was in the news many years later. On April 6th, 1932, she foundered in the Bay of Biscay and carried down twenty-five of her crew, four others being saved. At that time she was fitted out as a fisherman.

M. Belliveau built the *Frances J. Elkin* of 555 tons net at Church Point for the R. C. Elkin Co. of Saint John. She was employed in the West Indies trades until the early thirties, when she was laid up at Saint John. In December, 1934, the vessel was sold at auction and brought $80.00 for her fittings.

At Saulnierville the *Miriam H* of 359 tons net was launched by F. P. Comeau for A. S. Rendell & Co. of St. John's, Nfld. In 1924 she became a total loss after striking against the West Pier at Wabana, Nfld. J. E. Gaskill built the *Mollie and Melba*, 388 tons net, at Grosse Cocques. This schooner was sold to Portuguese owners and was renamed *Basselour, Joansenho* and finally *Areosa*. At the same place the Warren Shipbuilding Co. built the *Maid of Brazil* of 387 tons net. This vessel had a very long life. In 1921 she was sold to French owners and later to Finland and had the following re-names: *Notre Dame de Bizeux* and *Oma*. As *Oma* an auxiliary engine was installed and she continued in service until badly damaged by fire at Helsinki in November, 1957, and was declared a total loss. This was probably the last tern in service, with the exception of the *Bessie Marie*, which was still working as a motor coaster in the Newfoundland trade in 1960. C. H. Collins built the *Blanche H. Collins* of 503 tons net for the Portuguese at Little Brook. They renamed her *Algarve* and sold her about 1926 to the French, who gave her the name *Notre Dame D'Europa*.

Three schooners were completed at Belliveau Cove in 1918. The *Louis Theriault* of 386 tons net was built by A. A. Theriault and sold on the stocks to the Socony Oil Co. She loaded an oil cargo at a U.S. port for Australia, where she worked out her life and never returned to Canada. This schooner is mentioned by Alan Villiers in his book, *The Set of the Sails*. Villiers as a young man in 1919 at Melbourne, Australia, was trying to get away to sea in sail but was unable to locate a berth. Some of his friends went in the *Louis Theriault*, but he decided to wait for a square-rigged ship. This well-known writer had no use for any sailing vessel unless she was equipped with square sails. At this time hundreds of fore-and-aft vessels were being built in Canada and the United States. The occasional new barquentines of the period in these areas were regarded as throwbacks, showing the complete surrender to fore-and-aft rig from a practical point of view.

The second schooner noted at Belliveau Cove in 1918 is the *Charles Theriault* of 282 tons net, built by P. A. Theriault. She was lost on what must have been her maiden voyage. She was attacked by a German submarine on July 10th, 1918, off the French coast and abandoned. As often happened with a lumber-laden schooner, she did not sink or break up, but was salvaged by the French, repaired and renamed *Pierre Tristan*. The third vessel, the *Maplefield* of 411 tons net, was built by the Hankinson interests. She was later sold to United States parties.

Weymouth Schooners of 1918

The *Maid of Canada* of 330 tons net was built at Weymouth in 1918 for W. N. Reinhardt and others of La Have. Captain C. M. Wilkie owned her later and she was sunk in a collision off Sambro Island on September 4th, 1922. The second vessel noted was the *Farlings* of 410 tons net. She was built by E. R. Gaudet for Beazley Bros. of Halifax. Later owned by Job Bros. of St. John's, Nfld., she drove ashore on the reefs off the east coast of Barbados on September 15th, 1921, and was a total loss. The *Westway* of 234 tons net was built by S. St. C. Jones for Captain Ezra Forsyth, but the schooner was later managed by the builder. She was a total loss on Gull Rock Bar at the entrance to St. Mary Bay, N.S., on November 8th, 1925.

One Schooner built at Annapolis in 1918

The Annapolis Shipbuilding Co. launched one tern in 1918. The *Hilda M. Stark* of 510 tons net was taken over by W. R. Grace & Co. In 1922 she was sold to the Whitney-Bodden Co. of Mobile, Ala., and renamed *Stranger*.

Farther along the shore, at Margaretsville, the *Eveline Wilkie* of 349 tons net was built by J. A. Balcom for W. N. Reinhardt and others of La Have. Captain E. A. Wilkie was her first master and stayed in her as long as she remained under Canadian registry. On December 4th, 1935, this vessel was in the news, as she rescued the crew of the tern *E. C. Adams* when she was abandoned and set afire off the North American coast. Captain Wilkie acquired ownership of the *Eveline* and sailed her out of Nova Scotia ports until the early forties, when he sold her to shipping interests in Jamaica for island trading. This schooner was one of the few that carried on without the addition of auxiliary power while living out a very long life for a vessel of her class.

A four-masted schooner, the *Huntley* of 520 tons net, was launched at Scott's Bay, N.S., by D. A. Huntley for W. W. Hebb of Halifax. She was equipped with two oil engines and was sold to parties in Newfoundland. Captain J. King was master when she was lost on Cape Spear, Nfld., early in 1920.

Two of the Largest Schooners built in Atlantic Canada

At Hantsport the firm of Farquier and Porter launched two fine large four-masters. The largest of these, although her tonnage worked out smaller, was the *Jessie Louise Fauquier* of 939 tons net, better known by her re-name, *Avon Queen*. She was first operated by the Avon Transportation Co., but soon passed to Captain R. A. McLean of Chatham, N.B., who commanded the big schooner until she was lost. This vessel was equipped with two small auxiliary engines, but was dependent mainly on her sails for propulsion. At one time, while under repair at Meteghan along with several other large vessels, she broke away from the dock during a gale and stranded on the track of the marine railway, but was subsequently repaired. Captain McLean had many harrowing voyages in this vessel and she was finally lost on a voyage from Turks Island with salt toward Saint John, N.B., when she was abandoned in a sinking condition off Watlings Island in March, 1937, the crew being taken off by the s.s. *Fairfax*. After this experience, Captain McLean, in partnership with Lawrence Sweeney of Yarmouth, N.S., bought a large barquentine which had been built in Maine for the New England coal trade and had been laid up for many years. This vessel, the *Reine Marie Stewart*, had been one of the last large vessels built in New England and had been used very little before being laid up. She had been maintained in New England in excellent condition. After being towed to Yarmouth, she was completely reconditioned as a four-masted schooner. Unfortunately she was not lucky and was continually in trouble until she stranded at the entrance to Yarmouth, N.S. Her cargo was removed and she was refloated, but her damage was so extensive that repairs were never undertaken.

The other large four-masted schooner was the *Margaret F. Dick* of 989 tons net. She was owned by the British Colonies Transportation Co. and was commanded by Captain Marshall O'Hara. She loaded her first cargo at Saint John, N.B., for Durban and Port Natal, South Africa. She was then put to carrying coal from United States ports to France and Italy. On her return voyages she often brought salt from the Spanish Islands. On one of these voyages with salt for Halifax and Lunenburg the big schooner encountered heavy head winds and very bad weather conditions. After seventy days of battling the *Dick* was a wreck, sails torn away and pumps that were not broken down were plugged with salt. In November, 1920, Captain O'Hara was forced to abandon the schooner at 41° 40′ N. and 55° 45′ W., being taken off by the Dutch s.s. *Learsum* and taken to Amsterdam. Captain O'Hara told me the hardships of this voyage so sickened him of the sea that he left and became the instructor of the Navigation School at Halifax. However, many years later after he had retired from teaching, he often relieved masters in the small freighters along the coast. He died in 1956.

Other Schooners built along the South Coast on Minas Basin

Harvey MacAloney built the *General George H. Hogg* of 407 tons net at Canning in 1918. Mrs. L. L. McKay is noted as the first owner, but later the schooner passed to R. C. Elkin & Co. She was lost by running ashore at Cranberry Island, Me., on January 12th, 1923.

The Parsons interests at Cheverie launched two large terns in 1918. The larger was the *Martha Parsons* of 455 tons net. She was bought by F. K. Warren of Halifax and was destroyed by fire at Spencer's Island on December 14th, 1923. The smaller of the vessels was the *Don Parsons* of 427 tons net. This vessel was operated by the Parsons interests until she was sold to United States owners in 1922. Soon after she was bought back and was lost almost immediately by running ashore on Cranberry Island, Me., during a heavy snowstorm. Captain Donald Card, the master, had his wife with him

MAX HORTON. 139 tons. Built 1918 at Conquerall Bank, N.S.

WESTWAY.   234 tons.
Built 1918 at Weymouth, N.S.
Courtesy of the Canadian Pacific Railways

JOHN W. MILLER.   266 tons.
Built 1918 at Mahone Bay, N.S.
Courtesy of Mr. W. D. Maclean

on this voyage and all were saved from the wreck. Captain Card had earlier been in command of the large square-rigged ships owned in the vicinity and had gone into the barges of the gypsum fleet until World War One brought on a demand for deep-sea masters.

Across the Basin at Noel, G. M. Barr of St. John's, Nfld., had the *Samuel Courtney* of 441 tons net built. This vessel had twin auxiliaries installed at the time of her building and was destroyed by fire in Gibraltar Bay on May 8th, 1920. Also at Noel, Osmond O'Brien launched the *J. Miller* of 357 tons net. She was owned by J. Petite of Newfoundland and was lost on Cape Papas, in the Mediterranean, on June 27th, 1921. This vessel later appeared as *Aghios Andreas*, so must have been salvaged by Greek interests.

The 'Governor Parr'

It has been said that the *Governor Parr* of 912 tons net was the most handsome schooner built in Atlantic Canada. This four-master, in her gleaming white paint, was the masterpiece of her builder, W. R. Huntley of Parrsboro.* She was built for A. F. Davison of Bridgewater, N.S., and her master, Captain A. D. Richards of La Have. On September 27th, 1923, she sailed from Ingramport, N.S., toward Buenos Ayres with a cargo of lumber. Shortly after sailing she encountered a storm and heavy weather and lost her mizzen and spanker masts and had other extensive damage. The crew were taken off by the American s.s. *Schodack* on October 3rd, 1923. Packed with over a million board feet of lumber, the abandoned vessel became a derelict which attained fame for the extent of her drift across the Atlantic Ocean. Remaining afloat and a menace to navigation for a year, several attempts were made to destroy her, and even to tow her in. All of these efforts failed. She was last sighted still afloat on October 14th, 1924, off the Canary Islands, some two thousand miles east of the spot where she was abandoned, but the distance covered by her wandering greatly exceeded that figure. A chart of her drift was made by the U.S. Hydrographic Office and is reproduced in this work. Captain Angus Richards and one of the seamen lost their lives in this casualty. It has been said that the *Governor Parr* had a very large cargo with an excessive deck load and this factor may have brought about her loss.

Another fine four-master built nearby was the *Frieda E* of 669 tons net, named after a daughter of H. W. Elderkin. George E. Wagstaff was her designer and builder and she was launched at Port Greville. Captain Leonard Berry commanded this fine schooner during her short career, as she burned at sea on March 10th, 1921, while on a voyage from Gulfport, Miss., to Bahia Blanca, Brazil.

J. T. Moulton ordered a new tern from L. E. & Austin Graham at Port Greville in 1918. The *Milnorine* of 366 tons net also had a short career. She was delivered in November, 1918, and after some delays completed loading her cargo at St. John's, Nfld., for Brazil. At a Brazilian port she loaded for the West Indies and there took a cargo for France. From France she went to Cadiz and there loaded 700 tons of salt for Burgeo, Nfld. She was lost in the Atlantic on this voyage in December, 1919. Captain Joseph Vatcher and his crew were rescued by a passing ship.

* The schooner was named after one of the early governors of Nova Scotia.

Other Schooners in the Parrsboro Vicinity, 1918

G. M. Cochrane of Port Greville was the builder of many large schooners. He was succeeded by K. J. Cochrane, his son, who served a long apprenticeship in shipbuilding. When the business declined he became an engineer for the Nova Scotia Department of Highways and for a time held the Federal Liberal Parliamentary seat for Cumberland County, N.S. At Fox River in this year they launched the *Alfred Ock Hedley* of 461 tons net for the A. B. McKay Shipping Co. The schooner was chartered to the Niger Co. of London for their African-United States trade. In this trade, Niger River to New Orleans, they carried tobacco, staves and puncheons out and palm kernels back to New Orleans. Captain A. M. King was master in the ship while in this trade and his brother, J. T. King, was mate. There was a profitable sideline in this trade. Monkeys could be purchased very reasonably in Africa and usually they brought back several, for which a ready market existed in New Orleans at $35.00 a head. The *Hedley* passed to Nassau registry in 1923 and joined the missing ships, having left Bermuda on September 5th, 1926, and has not been heard of since.

A tern built by S. J. Soley at Fox River at this time was the *Northcliffe* of 291 tons net. Fulton Williams, now a master in the Dominion Coal Co., told me he shipped in this vessel when she was new and he was only seventeen years old. Captain H. Hilton was master and C. G. Williams, now Superintendent of Lights for the Department of Transport in Nova Scotia, was mate. They sailed on a series of voyages which took about eighteen months and included lumber from Nova Scotia to the West Indies, oil from Port Arthur to Pernambuco and other cargoes to the United Kingdom and France. On returning to Canada, they paid off at Paspebiac, Que. On May 16th, 1923, this vessel, while on a voyage from Turks Island to Bucksport, Me., ran ashore near East Hampton, N.Y., and became a total loss.

At Economy, H. C. McKay launched the *Truro Queen* of 386 tons net for himself and H. D. McLean, with Captain Jonathan Borden Marsh in charge. It is reported that she made fast and profitable voyages until he relinquished command in July, 1920, and retired ashore at the age of eighty-one. She was lost on a voyage from Norwalk, Conn., to St. George, N.B., when she ran ashore in a dense fog at Egg Rock off Jonesport, Me., on July 10th, 1924, and became a total loss.

The four-masted *Eugenie Owen McKay* of 560 tons net was built by Pugsley & Robinson at Diligent River. She was operated by W. N. Reinhardt in the usual trades until she was caught in a gale 260 miles northwest of Bermuda on January 4th, 1926, and was abandoned in a sinking condition. At Advocate, T. K. Bentley launched the four-master *Adamac* of 527 tons net. This vessel was sold immediately to Italian owners and had the following re-names, *Citta de Genova* and later *Alma*. J. E. Backman had the *Ella L. Winters* of 374 tons net built at Eatonville by J. W. Kirkpatrick. This vessel was burned at sea seventy miles north of Puerto Rico on November 7th, 1920.

The last vessel to be mentioned as being built in this area in 1918 is the *Cape D'Or* of 373 tons net. Launched by S. M. Field for W. N. Reinhardt and others of La Have, N.S., she came to a tragic end. This schooner cost $75,000 ready for sea and Captain C. M. Wilkie was her master and part owner. This Captain had just completed a successful year in the *Vogue*. The schooner was in the usual trades until on a voyage from Turks Island to La Have with a salt cargo, on April 30th, 1925, while hove-to off Cape La Have almost within sight of home, the vessel was run down by the s.s. *Clackamus*, Norfolk to Halifax with coal and owned by W. N. MacDonald of Sydney. The schooner sank quickly, taking down all with her except a man on deck who ran aft to clear the lifeboat. The Captain's wife, his brother St. Pierre Wilkie, Peter Tobin and Justin Warren of Newfoundland were drowned. The Captain, his mate Gerald Kent and Roy Dunsworth fought their way out of the cabin and forecastle and were subsequently rescued. Captain Wilkie told me he took the *Cape D'Or* when new and loaded a general cargo at Saint John for Cape Town, South Africa, the freight on which was $30,000, and made the passage in fifty-six days. After that she loaded coal for the west coast of Africa, then to Lisbon with coffee and home with salt. A very satisfactory round and very profitable.

These were the great days for the large schooners of Atlantic Canada with many cargoes offering, rising freight rates and prosperity ahead. The stimulus of the success of these vessels in being at the end of the war led the investors on to the point where too many expensive schooners were completed.

The South Coast of Nova Scotia in 1918

This was the busiest year to date in the shipyards along the south shore. To start at Shelburne, where five terns were launched in this year, the *Cecil Jr.* of 204 tons net was built by the Shelburne Shipbuilding Co. for A. Kean of St. John's, Nfld. A picture of this vessel on the stocks shows her to have the lines of a fine yacht, but I have been told she was nothing wonderful as a sailer. Her loss, like many others reported in this work, took place in the Atlantic while returning from Spain, salt-laden. The winter gales caused excessive leaking and the crew had been at the pumps incessantly for weeks. As there were only five men and the Captain, they were almost completely played out when the rudder carried away. When they attempted to leave in their own boat it was smashed in the heavy seas. After that it was a case of keeping the pump going to the last, but fortunately, on March 22nd, 1926, the British s.s. *War Diwan* came up. A boat was launched and the rescue was effected most gallantly. The rescuers were later presented awards for their bravery.

The second vessel completed by the same firm in this year was the *Flowerdew* of 306 tons net for Patten and Forsey of Newfoundland. She was abandoned 300 miles off Florida on October 15th, 1927; Captain J. Belben, master. To go into some detail on this schooner, it is noted that she required 2681 yards of canvas duck for her sails, eleven shots of $1\frac{5}{16}$-inch stud link chain (165 fms.). She had two bower anchors, one 2122 lb., one 1420 lb., a stream anchor of 419 lb. and a kedge. Not all of these vessels were built to the highest standard at this time. Their equipment was not uniform and in many cases was put aboard at the discretion of the owners.

James Harding, a master shipbuilder for many years with the firm who built the above noted vessels, retired in 1956. He is one of the few men left in the province with the knowledge and skill to design and build a large sailing vessel.

The McGill interests in Shelburne produced two terns in this year. The first one was small, the *General Smuts* of 159 tons net, was built for G. C. Harris of Grand Bank, Nfld., and later owned by S. Piercy. It has been reported that this vessel was lost on the way out from Portugal about 1926. In all, the Harris interests accumulated a considerable fleet of the *General* schooners. In this year the McGill yard also built the *Normandie* of 217 tons net for the French fisheries.

Winslow McKay's yard launched the *Jean McKay* of 194 tons net for J. B. Patten of Grand Bank. She worked out her life in the salt-fish trade and was abandoned in the North Atlantic on October 21st, 1930, while under the command of Captain Cyril Squires. Winslow McKay was well known for the fine workmanship that went into the schooners he built. In recent years he retired from active work.

Seven Terns launched at Liverpool in 1918

The Nova Scotia Shipbuilding and Transportation Co. were active in this year, launching four terns. The careers of these four vessels took them all over the world. The most prosaic of them, the *Gordon T. Tibbo* of 154 tons net, was delivered for J. C. Bellman of Grand Bank, Nfld. George Tibbo was master of this vessel when she was abandoned in the North Atlantic in January, 1926. The *E. Hogan* of 175 tons net was built for Hendry, Ltd. She was sold immediately to owners in Cape Town, South Africa, and given the re-name *Protea*. A news report on this schooner describes her as being a good sailer, but a Jonah. She cost her South African owners twelve thousand pounds sterling to purchase, was copper sheathed and fitted out in the best manner. In 1924 she was sold in execution in South Africa after failing in the coastal trade. Her new owners did no better and she became involved in a lawsuit which kept the *Protea* moored to a railroad dock in Cape Town for eight years while her cargo of salt still lay in her hold. During this lay-up, her dock dues amounted to such a sum, she was bought in by the railway for thirty shillings for the reason that any other bidder would have had to pay her back dock dues at the rate of seven pounds ten a month from the time of her seizure.

The third schooner, the *Abemama* of 337 tons net, also went far afield. After taking a cargo out to Australia or New Zealand, she was bought by parties in Auckland, New Zealand, and worked out her life far from her native land. The last vessel launched by the same company was the *James J. Joy* of 391 tons net. She was first owned by Job Bros. of Newfoundland, and was fitted with two auxiliary oil engines. She was sold to Greek owners and had the following re-names, *Zetta* and later *Elias*.

A newcomer to the shipbuilding business, T. M. Rawding, built the *Cape Race* of 332 tons net for F. H. Ellis & Co. The vessel later passed to Mark Burke of Newfoundland and finally to R. G. Benson of St. John's. She was lost near St. Shott's, Nfld., on July 29th, 1932.

Near Liverpool, at Brooklyn, the *Drallim* of 379 tons net was built for the Spier Shipping Co. by the Southern Salvage Co. This schooner was soon in difficulties and was seized for debt in Barbados. She was bought in by John Blackwood of Barbados on August 2nd, 1920.

T. M. Rawding in association with McKean launched another vessel, the *Chautauqua* of 354 tons net, for Zwicker & Co. of Lunenburg. Her first master was Henry Burke, a well-reputed veteran seaman who had sailed out of Lunenburg in many of the sailing ships. He left a notebook, to which I have referred many times, and he notes that he made some smart passages in this schooner during the five years he commanded her. On June 1st, 1920, he left Halifax lumber-laden to the Fastnet Rock, Ireland, to receive orders. At six o'clock in the evening of the eleventh day from Halifax he hove-to about one half-mile from Fastnet Rock and ran up signals asking for orders. Orders were received to proceed to Preston, England, and the vessel arrived there on the thirteenth day from Halifax. On another passage in this vessel, he left Lunenburg on October 12th, 1920, bound for Havana. On the eighth day they sighted Watlings Island and on the tenth day they anchored in Havana. The vessel was sold to J. Petite about 1926 and was lost on the Silver Banks in the West Indies while on a passage from Barbados to Turks Island. Martin Frampton, the master at this time, wrote that it was the hurricane season and after a run through the islands and north through Mona Passage it became calm, the sky looked low enough to be on deck and things did not look good with the Silver Banks to leeward and the strong westerly currents. The ship struck late that night and was abandoned at daylight. She was full of water and the crew got into the boat and sailed to Turks Island. The Captain was sent home by steamer and the crew, under mate Jack Willis were returned home by the tern *E. P. Theriault* as distressed British seamen.

J. N. Rafuse and Sons a Busy Firm in 1918

This firm completed no less than five terns during the year. The *Industrial* of 287 tons net was launched at Salmon River for J. E. Backman and others of La Have and had a very short life. On October 4th, 1918, she encountered a German submarine northwest of Bermuda and was destroyed. Also at Salmon River they built the *Bernice R* of 324 tons net for M. J. Parks of La Have. This schooner also had a short life and burned off Gaspé, Que., with a coal cargo from New Campbellton, C.B., to Campbellton, N.B., and was a total loss on August 22nd, 1921.

J. T. Moulton had the *Ronald B. Moulton* of 138 tons net, a round-bow schooner, built by the Rafuse interests. She was in the fish and salt trades until March, 1921, when on a voyage from Cadiz to Burgeo, Nfld., she was abandoned in the Atlantic. Captain James Guy and his crew were taken off by a passing steamer.

The *B. L. Rafuse*, a large tern of 481 tons net, was launched by the company at Conquerall Bank. She was considered a very fine schooner and was delivered to Captain Z. H. Richards, master and part owner. She was abandoned at sea while on fire on September 12th, 1919, thirty miles off Sombrero Island in the West Indies.

The final vessel was the *Max Horton* of 139 tons net. She was owned by Wm. Forsey of Newfoundland and was abandoned in the North Atlantic while in the salt-fish trade on March 20th, 1926.

Other La Have Schooners of 1918

Two schooners were completed at Bridgewater, N.S., in 1918. The *Edith Dawson* of 397 tons net was built and operated by the Bridgewater Shipbuilding Co., but in her last years she was sold to Newfoundland owners. She was burned at sea while on a voyage from Turks Island in December, 1932. The *William A. Naugler* of 295 tons net, W. A. Naugler, builder, was owned by Daniel Getson and was lost on Grand Turk on September 14th, 1928.

J. T. Moulton had the *Margaret Moulton* of 174 tons net built at Dayspring, N.S., by M. Leary. She was delivered new in August, 1918, and loaded at Rose Blanche and Burgeo, Nfld., for Oporto, but was driven ashore at Leixoes, Portugal, and became a total loss with 6200 quintals of fish aboard. Captain Thomas Rose and his crew were brought home by the tern *Ronald B. Moulton*, then at Oporto. The wreck was sold to the Portuguese, who had her refitted for service and gave her the following re-names, *Boa Sorte*, and later *Maria Carlota*.

The little *Russell S. Zinck* of 121 tons net was built by F. A. Robar at Dayspring. She had many owners, including W. R. Zinck, Ritcey Bros. & A. Ryan. This last owner sold her to Barbados parties.

Only one Lunenburg Tern in 1918

J. B. Young built the only tern in Lunenburg in this year. The *E. D. Bailey* of 162 tons net is reported to have been first rigged as a two-master, but later was refitted as a tern. She was first owned and sailed by Captain R. Knickle, but soon passed to Newfoundland owners. The final owners were W. & J. Moores of Bay de Verte, Nfld., and the schooner was abandoned at sea off the Brazil coast on November 3rd, 1924.

The Mahone Bay Vessels, 1918

The Ernst Shipbuilding Co. launched the *William Duff* of 365 tons net for her namesake. Captain Howard Corkum was master and she was lost at sea while on a voyage from Turks Island on January 25th, 1919, the crew being taken off by a passing ship.

The McLean Construction Co. built two terns at Mahone Bay in 1918. The original company was founded by John McLean, who came to Mahone Bay from Shelburne about a century ago. When John McLean died in 1910 the business was carried on by his sons, one of whom, William D., is President at this date, 1959. The firm known as John McLean & Sons still build wooden vessels of various types as required by modern shipping. They built the *Margery Mahaffy* of 143 tons net in 1918 for Adams & Knickle of Lunenburg; St. Clair Geldert, master. The schooner was soon sold to Rendell & Co. of St. John's, Nfld. She was lost in that province at West Mistaken Point on October 9th, 1921. The other vessel was the *John W. Miller* of 266 tons net. This schooner passed to J. C. Crosbie, Ltd. of St. John's and was in the Brazil trade. On November 28th, 1930, she sailed from Newfoundland with 4625 drums of salt fish for Bahia and Pernambuco. On the passage she encountered heavy weather and commenced leaking. On December 25th the *Miller* signalled a passing ship to take the crew off, but the signals were mistaken for "Christmas Season's Greetings", and the steamer passed them by. Five days later the vessel was abandoned and the crew were taken off by the German s.s. *Wido*.

A schooner built at Mahone Bay was the *Alice M. Moulton*. She was one of several which did not appear in any of the classification registers of the time because they were lost so soon after being commissioned. The *Alice* was delivered to J. T. Moulton in October, 1918. She proceeded to Labrador and loaded salt fish for Greece. This voyage completed, she engaged in the coastal trade for a few months, then loaded salt fish at Burgeo for Oporto. She was lost on this voyage in October, 1919. Captain Charles Dicks and his crew were rescued by a passing ship.

The Chester Basin Shipyard

In this boom year of building a company was organized to build a large vessel at Chester Basin. The *Arthur H. Zwicker*, a four-master of 507 tons net, was owned in Lunenburg. Captain W. Creaser was the first master and he was succeeded by Dawson Geldert. After a career in the usual trades, this schooner sprang a leak after leaving Turks Island with a cargo of salt. Sam Farrell of North Sydney told me he was a crew member when they abandoned the vessel on June 2nd, 1928, and rowed 160 miles to Abaco in the Bahamas.

Other Yards on the South Coast, 1918

J. Lewis & Sons, who had launched the four-masted *Lewis Brothers* at Sheet Harbour the previous year, built another four-master, the *Cashier* of 663 tons net. Freeman Hatfield was master and part owner of this vessel. F. A. Kaiser, previously noted as a seaman aboard the *Lewis Brothers*, had returned home and joined the *Cashier* when she left on her first voyage. She carried a lumber cargo to Montevideo, sailing on Armistice Day, 1918. From Montevideo she went to Buenos Ayres to pick up a cargo of maize for Havana. Then to Mobile for a cargo of hard pine for Genoa. Back light to Mobile, she towed to Gulfport and loaded case oil for the west coast of Africa. She returned home with mahogany—664 large timbers. By this time the shipping slump was in effect and the *Cashier* joined the other schooners in competing for the scarce cargoes. She was in various trouble and was sold in 1927 by the Marshal of a U.S. Court in Alabama. She returned to her birthplace shortly after and was laid up. Her bones lie at the head of Ship Harbour, N.S.

The Eastern Shipbuilding Co. built the *Impressive* of 341 tons net at Ship Harbour, N.S., for C. H. Ritcey of Lunenburg. She was commanded by George Corkum and was wrecked on Bahama Bank on December 17th, 1920.

Building at Other Old Yards in 1918

The *Riseover II* of 139 tons net was the salvaged wreck of the *Limelight*, built in 1908 at Souris, P.E.I. She had been stranded at Wine Harbour, N.S., in 1914, and when the demand for schooners became acute, the wreck was brought to Point Tupper, C.B., and rebuilt under the direction of A. V. Forbes. She was bought by J. T. Moulton for the salt-fish trade. After one very lengthy voyage to Oporto and return, she was sold to Venezuelan owners in May, 1921.

At nearby Port Hawkesbury, H. W. Embree built the *Marion Grace*, a little tern of 81.5 tons net. She was owned by the Dominion Fisheries Ltd. and was fitted with an auxiliary. This little vessel became a total loss near St. Pierre et Miquelon on February 12th, 1921.

After a lapse of many years shipbuilding was revived along Northumberland Strait. The *Clarence A. Moulton* of 248 tons net was launched by D. S. McLaren at New Glasgow for J. T. Moulton of Burgeo. She was the first wooden ship to be launched in Pictou County in twenty-five years and the first on the East River since 1822. The vessel was launched sideways from the yard of the McNeil Shipbuilding Co., and it was said to be the first attempt of this sort in the province. This was in August, 1918. The schooner was delivered in September, 1918, at Burgeo and her only fish cargo was loaded at Catalina, Nfld., for Greece. The cargo was landed in good condition, although her master, Captain John Andrews, reported the schooner to be very leaky. She proceeded to Cadiz and went on dry-dock to be surveyed. It was found that the bottom was literally eaten out by teredos (marine borers), which meant practically a new bottom and caulking all over. This is what she got at a cost of $32,000 and many months delay. She eventually arrived at Burgeo in April, 1920, with a salt cargo, taking about nineteen months on the round voyage, which pretty well established a record. No fish cargo being available, she was sent to Sydney, N.S., to load coal for France, but when close to her discharging port caught fire and the vessel burned to the water's edge. Her crew, including Captain Max Vatcher, were landed by a fishing boat.

The shipyards at River John came to life again when two schooners, one large and one small, were completed. The *Cambrai* of 529 tons net was launched by the MacKenzie Shipping Co. for Job Bros. of St. John's. This vessel was not a success and was always in trouble. Early in 1921 she was seized in the United States and sold to a U.S. citizen. She was burned at Galveston in 1921. The small schooner was the *Cyril T* of 117 tons net built by C. H. McLennan and W. W. Hebb. This vessel was sold before completion and was taken to Newfoundland by her new owner to be finished. She was owned by William Davis of St. John's and was lost seven miles south of Cape Broyle on June 8th, 1925.

Prince Edward Island, 1918

The first large vessel built in this island for many years was the *Victory Chimes* of 294 tons net. J. A. MacDonald was the builder at the old yards at Cardigan. After some years she was sold to B. E. Merriam of Parrsboro and she worked out her life in the Bay of Fundy trades. About 1936 she was abandoned on the beach at Parrsboro and slowly disintegrated.

A Large Schooner built on the St. Lawrence in 1918

While Quebec once had very extensive shipyards and sent out thousands of wooden ships, the art had died out except for building small bateaus. In 1918 the Quebec Shipbuilding Co. launched the *Edgewood*, a four-master of 699 tons net. She appears not to have been a success, running into the usual debt troubles, and was sold under order of the U.S. Court at St. Thomas in the Virgin Islands on November 23rd, 1920, and was bought in by C. H. Kinch of Barbados.

The fate of the above ship was repeated many times during this period. The schooners were built as a speculation, and when the market was flooded with large new vessels which could not be employed profitably the owners often decided not to send good money after bad and let the schooners go for their debts.

Newfoundland in 1918

As has been mentioned before, the Newfoundland salt-fish export trade boomed during World War One. The overseas market expanded enormously and the fish producers had difficulty in finding ships to carry their products abroad. In the end they had vessels built in the other provinces, mostly in Nova Scotia, and they built some themselves. The profits were high in this trade and a lucky schooner could soon pay for herself if she made a few quick trips. Fourteen tern schooners were completed in Newfoundland during 1918. As the building sites were scattered, there will be no attempt to classify them by districts.

The *Carl R. Tibbo* of 173 tons net had D. Power as her builder and she was owned by the Tibbos of Grand Bank. She was lost at Seldom-Come-By on the coast of Newfoundland on December 19th, 1919. The *Mintie* of 100 tons net was launched at Trinity Bay for W. F. Coaker. Later owned by E. Collishaw, she was abandoned in mid-Atlantic on January 10th, 1921, while under the command of Captain Norman Sheppard.

Also at Grand Bank, the *General Currie* of 162 tons net was launched for Samuel Harris, Ltd. In April, 1922, this vessel drove ashore at St. Pierre et Miquelon and was a total loss.

Two moderate-sized terns were built by F. H. Forsey at Marystown. The *General Byng* of 196 tons net was first owned by the Marystown Trading Co., but later passed to Percy L. Carr. After ten years in the trade she was lost in the Atlantic on March 9th, 1928. The other vessel was the *Jean and Mary* of 194 tons net, built for A. F. Buffett of Grand Bank.

Loss of the 'Jean and Mary'

In December, 1921, this schooner was waiting for weather in St. John's loaded with coal for Twillingate; A. T. Cluett, master, and five others in crew. There was a fish cargo at Twillingate collected for shipment to Europe and already time had been lost. It was decided to tow the *Jean and Mary* and speed the job of getting the ship away across the Atlantic. The tow boat *Ingraham*, Captain C. P. Moore, was engaged for the job. So at four in the afternoon of December 4th, 1921, they set off with the wind in the west and had a fine time north. The subsequent disaster can best be described by a long extract from Captain Moore's letter to one of the owners.

"... the next morning at 7 a.m. we passed by Cape Bonavista, the wind on the same point. A delightful time. At noon on that day we passed Cabot Island. The wind then started to veer a little to the south. At about 2.45 p.m. we passed Cat Island Harbour, the wind being then southeast. The barometer started to fall and when about three miles farther on the first snow came. Penguin Island was then about five miles ahead. We put on all possible speed to make Penguin before it got too thick, but just before we got there the storm burst on us like a thunderstorm, a pure hurricane with blinding snow, and there was nothing left for me to do only try to keep off the land. The wind then being east, as you know it was present death to continue my course without making Penguin Island, as you will see by looking at the chart. Well, we kept her off the land until 1 a.m., when we grounded in the breakers. The first sea that swept over us broke in the engine-room windows and put out the fires. She was then pounding on the bottom. I then cut the towline to give the vessel a fighting chance, as the schooner was then afloat sixty-five or seventy fathoms astern. We were lost then and that was all we could do for her. I did not see the vessel only on certain times we could see her light. The wind and snow were so blinding it was impossible to see or do anything. About 2.30 a.m. the snow cleared a little and the light came out. I saw then I was on the northwest point of North Penguin Island. The vessel dragged us there, the wind then being north by east. We remained on the head of the wreck until daylight. We fired guns and drew the attention of the lighthouse. They came down and after a long while we got a line ashore and rigged it to our foremast head and we rigged a bosun's chair and were pulled on shore, about half the distance being through the sea. The *Ingraham* was then broken off at the mainmast. The next morning, the sea being smooth, we got off the island. I went down to the South Island and on the northwest point I found the schooner beat to pieces. Her masts and rigging being on one side of a rock, and her hull broken up and gone to the floor heads. Her bottom was split in two pieces and one side about fifty feet from the other. I do not think you would find a piece of decking or frame much longer than ten feet, as it was all broken up in small pieces. Her rudder case was up against the grass on the beach about three hundred yards from the rest. I think there was every part of her strewn around, so you will see by the position the vessel is in that we were lost before the schooner.

"Captain Grandy, I could not have done more for that schooner if all my family had been aboard her. I made up my mind that evening and said to my mate that the schooner would be lost that night and if we did not cut her clear we would die with them, as I knew it was an impossibility to keep her off the land with the force of wind that was blowing. And one cannot do more than lay down his life for another . . ."

The letter went on to state that none of the bodies were found. Subsequently, the following spring, two of these bodies were recovered and taken to Musgrave Harbour for burial.

Other Newfoundland Schooners

The Fisherman's Union Trading Co. at Port Union had a schooner called the *Nina L. C.* of 355 tons net built there. My information on this schooner is brief, but it is believed she was lost on her maiden voyage returning from Brazil through springing a leak. This fate overcame several of the schooners built during this era in Newfoundland.

J. Wiseman built the *Norma B. Strong* of 157 tons net at Little Bay Island for W. S. Munroe and she was abandoned in the North Atlantic on February 8th, 1922. One of the largest schooners launched was the *Armorel* of 379 tons net built by the Newfoundland Shipbuilding Co. at Harbour Grace for Tessier & Co. She was sold to French owners.

The *Mabel Davis* of 188 tons net was also a vessel with a short life. Built at Boyd's Arm by R. White for William Davis, this vessel was abandoned in the North Atlantic on May 10th, 1919. J. T. Currie built the *Barbara Barr* of 229 tons net at Britannia Cove for G. M. Barr and others of St. John's. Captain J. Snelgrove was master and she was lost in St. Mary's Bay, Nfld., on March 19th, 1921.

An auxiliary three-masted schooner, the *Dobbie* of 274 tons net, was launched by D. Pelley at Port Blandford for J. O. & A. Williams. She was sold to the Miquelon fishing fleet and renamed *Miquelon*. The *Katheen*, a large three-masted auxiliary of 356 tons net, was sold to Greek owners after having been built at Norris Arm by J. Manuel.

The *Union Jack* of 242 tons net was completed in this year of 1918 by E. Stone at Trinity Bay for W. S. Munroe of St. John's. Jack Willis was sometime master in this vessel, but at the time of her loss he was mate and Martin Frampton was in command. I do not have the date, but she was lost in about the same place as the *Jean and Mary* while enroute from Seldom-Come-By to Bay Roberts with a cargo of lumber. The schooner was running through the narrow channel with the wind fresh and fair aft. She jibed and carried away her masts, went ashore and was a total loss. This vessel was reported to have been a good sailer. Captain Frampton wrote that on one occasion he towed out of St. John's loaded with fish for Pernambuco just behind the *Jean Wakley*, a Newfoundland-owned Essex-built tern, commanded by Jerry Petite, also bound for Pernambuco. About twenty days later, when one of the crew of the *Union Jack* was aloft, he sighted a tern schooner going in the same direction and which was assumed to be the *Wakley*. On the morning of arrival at the Fairway Buoy off Pernambuco the *Jean Wakley* was also approaching, both twenty-eight and a half days out of St. John's. This was considered a good passage for vessels of this class.

The last vessels noted as being built in Newfoundland in 1918 were both launched by A. Chaulk at Charlottetown. The smaller one, the *Florence Swyers* of 157 tons net, was owned jointly by J. T. Swyers and A. E. Hickman and is reported to have cost upward of $75,000. As mentioned before, when the capital cost of these schooners reached a high figure it was almost impossible for them to earn enough to pay off their investment. Edward Swyers, son of one of the owners, told me this vessel never paid off her building cost. She foundered forty-five miles south-south-east of Cadiz on May 30th, 1925; Captain George Anstey, master. The other schooner was much larger and also was owned jointly by A. E. Hickman and J. T. Swyers. The *Ruth Hickman* of 386 tons net had a short existence and was lost at Dingle Bay, on the coast of Ireland on February 1st, 1920.

PART SIX

The End of the War

The surrender of the warring Central Powers in November, 1918, actually brought to an end the urgent need of the Allies to produce new shipping, but the building of ships went on. In the United States a government company, the U.S. Emergency Fleet Corporation, had been set up after the entry of that country into the war for the purpose of bringing into being a fleet of propeller-driven cargo vessels of many classes. The object was not to build fine ships of good workmanship and materials but to produce without delay ships of simple design that could carry cargo across the seas. Although the work was rushed, the ships did not come into effective use before the end of the war. As contracts had been let, and the work was in hand when the war finished, the government accepted the ships on completion and employed a large number of them. This tonnage helped to flood the ocean freight markets and brought on the shipping decline in 1920 and had a deflationary effect on the large cargo-schooner fleet of Atlantic Canada.

In our provinces the schooners in being in 1918 had done very well and this led their optimistic owners and others to expand still further and more schooners were built. The coming of peace did not at first affect the ocean freights, as in many cases goods and materials had been ordered long in advance and transactions had to be completed. There was much money in circulation and from a commercial viewpoint business continued to boom.

During the latter part of 1918 and the early part of 1919 many large schooners were ordered in Atlantic Canada. In all during 1919 the number of these vessels launched reached the imposing figure of one hundred and fourteen terns and four-masted schooners for the cargo trades. Some of these schooners did well and kept on in the business for which they were built and lasted for many years. Some were sold or chartered before or after launching at rates which ensured a profit after the building cost had been paid. Others were unlucky and did not strike good charters, fell into disrepair and never made any money. Many were lost needlessly because, as their value depreciated, many precautions in the general practice of seamen were not adhered to, and they were lost through burning or stranding. Others went into rum-running and this enterprise brought many to a dull ending through seizure by revenue cutters and subsequent sale abroad. In any case, the rum business was hard on the vessels, as they tended to become run-down and after a certain stage of depreciation had been reached it was too expensive to put them back into first-class shape.

The Postwar Schooners of New Brunswick, 1919

The great forests of New Brunswick were called on again for ships' timbers. Seven large schooners, six of them four-masters, and a large tern, were launched in 1919.

After the *Dornfontein* had been launched at Saint John by the Marine Construction Co., they laid down the *Randfontein*, a four-masted steam auxiliary schooner of 799 tons net. I do not know the first use this vessel was put to, but she was soon sold to German owners and renamed *Cobo*. She was later owned in Guernsey and later still in Norway, and had the additional re-names, *Foldin I* and *Melolie*.

Also at Saint John, the New Brunswick Shipbuilding Co. launched the *Cutty Sark* of 609 tons net, a four-masted schooner. This vessel should not be confused with the still-existing famous tea clipper of the same name which was built at Dumbarton in 1869. This oldtime clipper ship has recently been placed in a permanent dock as a memorial to the great days of British sail. The Canadian schooner *Cutty Sark* was owned by her builders and managed by R. C. Elkin & Co. of Saint John. She was abandoned midway between Bermuda and Nova Scotia and set afire on June 12th, 1929.

The *Quaco Queen* of 479 tons net, the only tern of the year, was the last vessel ever built at the once important yards at St. Martins, N.B. She was owned by the Hon. Walter Foster and S. E. Elkin, but was later sold to Nova Scotians. She was equipped with two 100-h.p. Fairbanks-Morse oil engines as auxiliary power and had a carrying capacity of 600,000 board feet of lumber. On January 30th, 1929, she was abandoned in a waterlogged condition 300 miles east of Bermuda. The crew were taken off.

At Alma, N.B., the C. T. White Co., long interested in lumbering and shipping, launched the *Bessie A. White* of 594 tons net, and four-masted. This schooner, like the previous one, was equipped with oil engines. At about this time some of the schooners equipped with auxiliary power were listed as "steamships" in the registers. This alteration in classification seems to have been a gradual procedure, but many schooners subsequently fitted with power were recorded in the register as "sailing" vessels. The *Bessie A. White* remained in the lumber trade of the Bay of Fundy. Captain L. L. Merriam was her first master and she was wrecked at Smith's Point, on the south side of Long Island, N.Y., and became a total loss on February 6th, 1922.

The north shore of New Brunswick produced three large four-masted schooners in 1919. Two of the schooners lasted only a short time and the survivor was lost in an unusual casualty. The *Edward A. Cohan* of 597 tons net was launched at Rexton, near Richibucto, N.B., by her sole owner, J. H. Solery. She was a total loss by fire at Moss Point, Miss., on July 2nd, 1921, while awaiting a lumber cargo. The *Holmes, A. Frank* of 637 tons net, built by the Miramichi Construction Co. at Nordin, N.B., was owned by James Robinson of Millerton, N.B. This schooner was reported as being lost on the Newfoundland coast, having drifted ashore in fog; Captain F. S. Inness, master. This was in 1922.

The third schooner, the *Harry A. McLellan* of 643 tons net, was also a four master, and was built by the McLellan Foundry and Machine Works at Campbellton, N.B. Her first master was J. P. Salter and he was followed by Captain R. A. McLean, who was first master, then owner. Captain McLean has been mentioned before as owner-master of the *Avon Queen*. The *Harry A. McLellan* was badly damaged in the early 1930's at Meteghan, where she was moored to the wharf along with the *Avon Queen* and the *Peter McIntyre*. These vessels broke away from their moorings during a gale and the *McLellan* stranded across the rails of the marine railway and broke her back on the falling tide. As the range of tide is great at this place, being over twenty feet, the damage to the vessel was so great she was never repaired and was hauled over to the beach and abandoned.

The Nova Scotia Boom Year of 1919

The great success of the schooners in being during the latter part of the war prompted owners to put their profits into new shipping. All around Nova Scotia, in old and recently established yards, men were busy on new vessels and during all this year and well into 1920 ships kept going down the ways. The capital value of these schooners had increased with the cost of materials and labour to the point where possibly about $7,000,000 was spent in construction in 1919. This was a very large sum in those days and represented the profits from many operated schooners and the savings of many individuals.

In the last part I started by describing the activity along the "French Shore" of Nova Scotia, and will do so again.

The *Breakers* of 517 tons net was one of the few four-masters built in Nova Scotia during 1919. It had become too costly to build the larger schooners, for several reasons. The easy-to-get timber was gone and it required additional money to go far back in the wood-lots for the big stuff. The *Breakers* was launched at Yarmouth, N.S., by E. B. Ehrgott, E. G. Baker and others of that place. She was sold on completion to United States owners late in 1919 and renamed *Balsa*. Later she passed to other owners and was renamed *Edith C. Tilden*.

At Meteghan, Dr. T. H. MacDonald completed his fourth vessel, the tern *W. S. MacDonald* of 382 tons net. This vessel has been described as being very well built, as her material was cut out for a much larger schooner. The builder was cautious of the situation in shipping at the time and at the last moment decided to construct a much smaller schooner than originally planned. The completed tern was a very strong vessel, but was the only one of the four completed by Dr. MacDonald that was not a financial success. Her building cost was about $55,000 and she was sold to United States owners, who renamed her *Louis B. Beauchamp*. It is reported she was later engaged in rum-running. Still later she was owned by R. B. Kirkconnel of Tampa, Fla., and was broken up in 1934.

Also at Meteghan, A. A. Theriault built the *Leo LeBlanc* of 393 tons net. She is reported to have cost $62,000 and was operated by the builder and later by the Hankinson Shipping Co. of Weymouth, N.S. She had various well-known masters, including

O. Comeau, B. Bonnenfant and Henry Burke. The schooner went aground and became a total loss at Turks Island on February 12th, 1931.

Two large terns were launched at Meteghan River in 1919. The *Celeste D* of 595 tons net was very large for a three-masted schooner of this era. She was built by E. N. Doucet and was operated by the Doucet Shipbuilding Co. until she was destroyed by fire at a United States port in 1921. The other was the *Maria A. Howes* of 425 tons net and was built and operated by the Howes Construction Co. until about 1926, when she was bought by C. B. Merriam of Parrsboro, N.S., and sold soon after to R. B. Colwell of Halifax, who in turn disposed of her to F. K. Warren of that city. On August 24th, 1927, she was burned at sea off the island of St. Vincent in the British West Indies, and became a total loss.

One large tern was built at Saulnierville in 1919. At that place Frank P. Comeau built the *Nettie C* of 387 tons net for the Acadian Shipping Co. In later years she was owned by Christopher Splane and Captain Newton A. Wilkie. In 1927 her name was changed to *Dawn Wilkie,* and she was abandoned as a total loss off the Nova Scotia coast on January 22nd, 1933.

On the next site at Comeauville, two large terns took to the water. The *J. W. Comeau,* 343 tons net, was launched by R. J. LeBlanc for his own account. Martin Penz was master in this vessel and Eber Sarty the mate when she was abandoned with a lumber cargo on the way from Nova Scotia to the West Indies on January 8th, 1924. At the same time and place the *G. H. Murray* of 354 tons net was launched by S. F. Comeau for J. W. Comeau. This schooner was named after a long-time Premier of Nova Scotia and had a short life under the British flag, as she became a total loss on the reefs off the northwest coast of Cuba on February 3rd, 1920. The wreck was sold and salvaged by Cuban interests, who operated her under the same name for some years after.

J. E. Gaskill, well-known builder, merchant and shipowner of Grand Manan, N.B., launched the *C. Maud Gaskill* of 397 tons net for his own interest at Little Brook, N.S. This vessel was active in the local shipping until she was lost at Salt Cay in the Turks Island group on December 14th, 1928.

Notice should be taken of the large size of the schooners enumerated for this period. Many were capable of lifting cargoes of 800 tons and over. The next vessel noted is the *Charlotte Comeau* of 728 tons net, a four-master built by I. Comeau at Little Brook for his own account. This schooner was a total loss very soon after, as on September 16th, 1921, she burned to the water's edge at Spencer's Island, N.S.

One of the schooners I have little data on is the *Canadian Maid.* This vessel of 294 tons net was built by M. D. Belliveau at Church Point, for Ritcey Bros. of Riverport, N.S. She disappeared with her crew while on a voyage and has not been heard of since April 4th, 1921.

Also at Church Point, N.S., J. E. Gaskill, above mentioned, built the *Scotia Maiden* of 519 tons net for his own account. This schooner had auxiliaries and it is presumed she was chartered to French interests. Captain Carl Kohler, previously recorded as master of the tern schooner *Percé,* was in charge. The Declaration of Protest in regard to her loss states she left Marseilles, France, with a general cargo bound on a lengthy passage for Tahiti in the Pacific, on February 6th, 1923. After leaving port, light winds were encountered and the vessel used her sails and engines as required. On February 10th, while under all sail in light airs and the starboard auxiliary operating, the hot exhaust pipe started a fire in the ship near the fuel tank. The fire got out of control and the crew had to leave in a hurry. When they were about 500 yards from the ship the fuel tank exploded and the ship was utterly destroyed. The crew were picked up by the s.s. *Fenchurch* and taken to Valencia, Spain.

Many of these schooners came to a violent end. The *Maid of Scotland* of 439 tons net, built at Church Point, N.S., in 1919 by F. K. Warren of Halifax for his own interest, was one of these. She was sunk in a collision on February 11th, 1924, off Partridge Island at the entrance to Saint John, N.B. Her master, Wallace Haughn, and his son Grover were drowned in the accident.

Belliveau Cove in 1919

Two Belliveau and two Theriault schooners were launched here in 1919. B. Belliveau & Co. launched the *Rose Anne Belliveau* of 382 tons net and the *Edith Belliveau* of 238 tons net for their own account. These schooners were in the West Indies and the United States trades as long as they lived. The *Rose Anne* was wrecked on the coast of Digby County, N.S., on January 19th, 1929, and the *Edith* ran ashore and was a total loss at Cockburn Harbour in the Caicos Islands, Bahamas, on August 14th, 1933. In a Boston paper, although I have not the date, a news item states that the *Rose Anne*, under Captain R. V. Comeau, made a very fast run from Belliveau Cove to the Boston light-vessel and completed the run of 240 miles in twenty-four hours. On another occasion she left Boston for Belliveau Cove, loaded 250,000 board feet of rough spruce lumber and arrived back in Boston in seventeen days. This was as good as a steamer could do.

The Theriault interests, composed of several brothers and brothers-in-law, built two sturdy schooners that lasted out the expectations of softwood schooners. Both of them did it "the hard way". The *St. Clair Theriault*, named after one of the firm, is fully covered in another part of this account. The *E. P. Theriault* of 310 tons net was the last of the large schooners launched at Belliveau Cove. She was built of the best selected timber available and that she was a sturdy craft is well borne out by her story. She cost $62,000 ready for sea, but returned only part of the cost to her owners. Mr. E. P. Theriault, now retired and living at Weymouth, N.S., for whom the vessel was named, told me her first two years in service were quite good. She earned about $19,000 and then ran into expense and trouble when she stranded at Race Rock in Long Island Sound. Her first master was Captain Joseph Oliver and later Captain D. Doucet took over. Later still Captain Bernard Bonnenfant was master. Captain Jack Willis reported that when he was sent home from Turks Island in the *E. P. Theriault* as a D.B.S. after the wreck of the *Chautauqua*, Captain Bonnenfant was master, but died a few days out from Turks Island. The schooner was tried in all the trades, including the U.S. hard-pine ports, but could hardly pay her way. In the late 1920's she passed to Captain Archie Publicover of La Have, N.S., who had a long career in sailing vessels of different sorts.

At one time he acquired United States citizenship and when he took over the *E. P. Theriault* he registered her in the name of his ward, Miss Ivy Wamboldt. This young lady acquired a master's certificate in the West Indies and sailed the *Theriault* as owner-master with Captain Archie acting as mate.

The schooner was often in the news during the thirties. In the papers of the time are many references to Captain Ivy as the vessel made her passages to and from the West Indies. During these times the large schooners were becoming fewer and the arrival of a sailing vessel usually meant a newspaper story of some sort. In January, 1937, the schooner sailed from Turks Island for Lunenburg under Captain George Corkum. The weather was bad and after proceeding about 300 miles north under stormy conditions the rudder was unshipped by a savage sea and lost. The undaunted Captain Corkum proceeded on his voyage without a rudder and steered the vessel with her sails—heaving-to when the wind came ahead and trimming them to get the best effect when the wind hauled aft and there was a chance to shorten the distance to Nova Scotia. This procedure was slow and when about 300 miles off Cape Hatteras on February 15th, the stores were running low so Captain Corkum hailed the passing steamer *Amazone* and obtained further supplies from her. On March 13th the schooner eventually arrived off Cape La Have, N.S., and was towed in. It was a remarkable performance to navigate a sailing vessel, of a class called awkward by their detractors, a distance of about 1500 miles without a rudder in the worst of the winter season when heavy head winds were to be expected to a much greater degree than anything of a favourable nature.

On several occasions during these years she had severe long passages and on one voyage took thirty-eight days from Turks Island to Nova Scotia and arrived with sails torn away and leaking. But she always made it.

Captain Corkum had another chance in this schooner to show what kind of a man he was. In October, 1938, while loading at Turks Island, he experienced crew trouble. According to the master and owner, the crew sold their heavy clothes and oilskins for rum, then at sailing time attempted to leave the vessel in the ship's boat. On being stopped by the Captain, they jumped over the side and swam ashore. As there were no other men available, Captain Corkum, the mate William Snow and a lad, William Burns, making his first voyage to sea, were left alone. Captain Corkum decided to sail with his remaining two men and made the voyage to Lunenburg, N.S., in fifteen days. While tern schooners have made the 1500-mile voyage in much better time, the circumstances of the case made the passage extraordinary and Captain Corkum received the praise and acclaim of his fellow-mariners in the salty old port of Lunenburg.

Shortly after this the *Theriault* was sold to owners in Jamaica and was put into the island trade. In 1942, while on a passage from one of the lumber ports in Florida to Jamaica, she was intercepted and shelled by a German submarine raider in the vicinity of the Dry Tortugas. The tough old schooner was abandoned, filled with water, but remained intact. She drifted in the Gulf Stream and stranded on the north coast of Cuba. The wreck and her cargo were bought by Cuban interests, who repaired the schooner and installed an auxiliary. She continued on for some years after under the name *Ofelia Ganedo*.

Weymouth Schooners of 1919

The *Marine* of 453 tons net was a fine schooner built by Beazley Bros., Weymouth, N.S., at a cost of about $125,000 for owners including A. Moulton, Neil Hall and I. H. Mathers, all of Halifax. She was one of the vessels built at a high cost that soon became a drug on the market. After running into debt she was sold at auction in Halifax in 1922 for about $5500 to W. Trenholm of Louisburg, N.S. Some years later she was sold to the Willegar interests of Parrsboro, N.S., and worked out her life in the usual trades and was finally abandoned on the beach at Parrsboro about 1936.

The only other vessel built in Weymouth in 1919 had a long and varied career. The *Charles F. Gordon* of 369 tons net was also built by Beazley Bros. and was operated by them until March, 1923, when she was stranded at Cay Sal in the Bahamas. The wreck was bought by United States citizens and renamed *J. O. Webster*. She was active in rum-running and in the coastal trade until 1935, when she was taken up into the Great Lakes by Grant H. Piggott of J. T. Wing & Co. and renamed *J. T. Wing*. At this time she was the only sailing vessel operating on the Great Inland Waters and was employed carrying cedar posts and pulpwood until she was laid up in 1939. But she had another chance and in the same year was bought as a training ship for U.S. Sea Cadets and renamed *Oliver H. Perry*. Later Mr. Piggott repurchased the old schooner and established her at Belle Isle Park, Detroit, as a Marine Museum under Curator Joseph E. Johnson.

But she could not last for ever and dry rot set in. Repairs of this sort are very expensive and late in 1956 it was decided to dismantle the museum and break up the schooner.

Sturdy Vessels built in 1919

The last-mentioned schooners had long lives. Several of those to follow had the same characteristic. The *Jean F. Anderson* of 396 tons net was a handsome schooner built at Port Wade, across from Digby, N.S. She was acquired by Captain Leander Publicover from her first owners and later passed to his brother, Captain Archie Publicover. While her career was not spectacular like some of the others, she made consistently good passages in the West Indies and United States trades under masters like George Corkum, Eber Sarty and Leo Bell. This schooner differed from most of the others in that she had a very long poop deck which extended forward to the mainmast. She was sold in 1941 for island trading to Jamaica parties for a reputed $15,000. On her last voyage, while still owned by Captain Publicover, she made a fast passage from Nova Scotia to Barbados with lumber, across to Grand Turk to load salt and back home in fifty-three days. In 1942, while on a passage from Jacksonville, Fla., to Bermuda, she sprang a leak and foundered.

Three Schooners launched at Annapolis in 1919

The *Mapleland* of 566 tons net was a landmark for many years at Annapolis, N.S. She was built by the Annapolis Shipping Co. under the direction of L. D. Shafner. This schooner had a few successful voyages at the beginning of her career, including a fast passage from Nova Scotia to Garston, England, with lumber and return to Shelburne, N.S., for orders in fifty-nine days. When freight rates fell the schooner was laid up at

Annapolis and maintained in good order to await better freight rates or a good sale. Neither of these things came to pass and by 1935 she was a decayed old wreck and was ultimately towed down the Basin to Port Wade and left on the beach to disintegrate.

The *Peaceland* of 262 tons net was the last tern operating out of the Bay of Fundy. She was built by the same concern as the *Mapleland* and was completed in the short time of 146 days. She was the last schooner ever built at Annapolis. The *Peaceland* was operated by her builders under Captain Vernon Hirtle of Mahone Bay until a sale could be arranged. W. S. Wasson of Parrsboro was an early owner and he was followed by R. M. Ogilvie, who worked her in the Bay of Fundy trade for many years. On February 2nd, 1943, she was sold to United States citizens and was lost off Cape Hatteras the same year. There is a story in this connexion.

Disappearance of the 'Peaceland'

The survivor of this schooner was George Noble, the cook. The vessel loaded cement and machinery at Norfolk, Va., for her first voyage under the U.S. flag. It was winter and soon after leaving land she began to leak badly, so Captain Walsh, the master, put back to shelter behind a point of land on the Virginia Capes and anchored not far from shore to await better weather. A Coast Guard cutter came along to investigate but found everything under control. The cook requested that he be put ashore in the cutter to get some new lenses for his glasses and was granted permission to go, provided he took along and mailed some letters for the others. He reported that when he last saw the schooner she was wallowing deep "like a pig in a mudhole". The crew of six were lined up along the rail to give him a wave as the cutter drew away.

When the cook came back twenty-four hours later the *Peaceland* was gone. Nobody knows what happened to her. After a month or so three bodies drifted ashore. Possibly she just loosened up and came apart in the heavy rolling—she was a softwood vessel and twenty-four years old.

The final vessel for the Annapolis area in 1919 is the *Ononette* of 483 tons net. She was built at Hillsburn, Annapolis County, on the Bay of Fundy shore, by J. W. Smith for his own account. This vessel had the misfortune to break through the ways as she was being launched and stuck fast. Tugs had to be obtained to drag her afloat. Apart from this poor start she appears to have completed her life in an unspectacular way in the Bay of Fundy–U.S. trade until she was wrecked at Advocate Harbour, N.S., on November 7th, 1930, while loaded with piling.

Margaretsville and Hall's Harbour, 1919

J. A. Balcom launched the *Fundy King* of 376 tons net at Margaretsville, N.S., in 1919. This vessel soon had a new name and owner. She was operated for many years as the *Maid of France*, owned by F. K. Warren, and had many masters, including O. Comeau, D. Morrisey, A. Berringer and Johnny S. Smith. In the thirties she was abandoned on the flats in Lunenburg Harbour and had become a derelict when the war came on. The hulk was bought by Captain Archie Publicover of La Have, N.S., and taken to nearby Dayspring. Drawing on his long experience in West Indies trading, Captain Publicover had the old vessel rebuilt as an auxiliary after his own ideas. She had passenger accommodation and means to handle deck passengers in the islands. The vessel was re-named *A. S. Publicover* and sailed south in 1942. Her luck was out, as on this passage she leaked heavily and foundered near Bermuda.

The *Bona H* of 454 tons net had a short life. She was built at Hall's Harbour, N.S., by G. B. Hatfield for his own account and others and was a total loss by fire off the coast of Cuba on April 27th, 1921.

South Side of Minas Basin, 1919

The *Cape Blomidon* of 408 tons net was built at Canning, N.S., by H. MacAloney for his own account. She was commanded for many years by Captain Barkhouse and appears to have had an uneventful career. In 1933 she was in service and commanded by Captain Ray Merriam. The schooner was abandoned on the beach at Parrsboro and was partly broken up in 1937.

A Race in 1928

The *Cape Blomidon*, the *Fieldwood* and the American tern *Lincoln* had loaded lumber and laths at Halifax for New York. The three schooners prepared for sea at the same time and sailed on March 2nd, 1928. This was a perfect set-up for a race. After the first day out the weather turned very bad and the vessels sought shelter, the *Cape Blomidon* putting into Liverpool and the other two made Shelburne. When it moderated on the morning of the 5th the *Lincoln* and *Fieldwood* resumed the voyage, but that night it breezed up from the southward and the schooners lost track of one another. The next morning the wind jumped out of the north, a heavy gale with snow, and the *Fieldwood* made the best of it, running before the storm and got in over Nantucket Shoals and thence to City Island, the entry port to New York City on Long Island Sound, where she arrived on March 11th. In that storm the *Lincoln* hove-to on the starboard tack and made Bar Harbour, Maine, having suffered some damage. The *Cape Blomidon* did it the easy way, and after waiting until the norther had died down, set sail and proceeded, arriving with the *Lincoln* at City Island on the 19th.

To resume, at Hantsport, N.S., the Falmouth Shipbuilding Co. launched the *Favonian* of 428 tons net for Halifax owners. This vessel cost $125,000 ready for sea and, being in debt, was sold at auction in 1922 for the small sum of $4500, showing the serious drop in value of these schooners just three years later. For all purposes the *Favonian* was sound and as good as new. Her new owners were G. E. Hartling and his brother, both of Halifax. After about four years' operation they sold her to John Campbell of Prince Edward Island. While under the command of Captain Rangdale, on a voyage from Barbados with a cargo of molasses, she ran ashore near Seaforth, N.S, and became a total loss on November 5th, 1926.

The G. M. Parsons interests at Cheverie built two terns in 1919. The *Gertrude Parsons* of 341 tons net was operated by them until she was pronounced a total loss by stranding at Tennycape, N.S, in December, 1929. The wreck was purchased by Kenneth Cochrane and towed to Port Greville, N.S, for repairs. While in operation again, she was later a total loss by fire at Port Greville in September, 1934. The second tern, the *Frances Parsons* of 237 tons net, had a long life. After the builders had operated her for a few years she was sold to the Willigar interests and engaged in the usual Bay of Fundy trades until she was sold to Captain Van Sande of Kingston, Ja., in January, 1943. The schooner loaded a general cargo in Halifax for Puerto Rico and foundered 200 miles northwest of Bermuda on April 22nd, 1943. The crew took to their boat and after drifting around for three days were picked up.

The North Side of Minas Basin, 1919

In this year schooners were not built as actively along this shore as in 1918. It would seem the market for the larger vessels normally built in this district was slower and the demand moved toward the south shore, where the small handy schooners were built. At Parrsboro only two terns were sent out. The *Stewart T. Salter* of 226 tons net was built by B. G. Dyas for S. T. Salter. This vessel was owned for many years by the Salter interests and in the thirties was sold to Captain A. B. Taylor of Parrsboro. She had small auxiliaries installed and was employed in the Bay of Fundy trades. As a consequence of heavy weather, Captain Taylor was compelled to abandon the vessel off the United States coast on May 15th, 1938, but owing to the lumber cargo she remained afloat and was towed in by the Coast Guard. She was sold in Gloucester and repaired.

The *Whiteway* of 418 tons net was launched from the yard of W. R. Huntley & Son at Parrsboro for C. T. White & Son, who operated her for some years, then sold her to W. E. Wasson. While on a voyage from New York to Yarmouth, N.S., with coal, she ran ashore near the entrance to the latter port on August 30th, 1928, and was considered a total loss. She was salvaged by her owners and had auxiliaries installed, but her luck did not change and on August 28th, 1934, she struck on Seal Island in the Bay of Fundy and became a total loss.

Three schooners were launched at Port Greville in 1919. The largest of these was the four-master *George Melville Cochrane* of 820 tons net, built by her namesake for W. N. Reinhardt and others of La Have, N.S. This was the last of the big fore-and-aft sailing vessels built in Canada. She was taken to Saint John to be rigged and later loaded timber for Buenos Ayres. Her life was extremely brief. The fine new schooner was towed out of Saint John on the afternoon of February 24th, 1919, and set her sails in fine winter weather for her long passage. Her master was Arthur Conrad, and as the darkness set in the wind freshened. Later, the watch on deck suddenly noticed the lee rigging was very slack, but before anything could be done a heavier squall struck the ship and she was dismasted and became a derelict in the strong tidal currents and high swell off Brier Island, N.S. The only explanation for this mishap is that the screw turnbuckles must have been defective and stripped under the strain of the freshening wind. In any case, the schooner drifted ashore and was a total loss on her first day out.

Geo. M. Wagstaff launched two terns at Port Greville in 1919. The *Barbara W* of 286 tons net was named after his daughter and owned by Wagstaff and H. Elderkin & Co. She was wrecked on a voyage from Boston to Wolfville, N.S., at the entrance to Boothbay Harbour, Maine, on November 28th, 1922. The other schooner, the *Jennie*

V. Merriam of 454 tons net, was owned by R. A. McInnis and was lost by fire off Hope-well Cape, N.B., on November 16th, 1921.

At Advocate, N.S., the *Nova Queen* of 432 tons net was launched for T. K. Bentley and J. N. Pugsley. This vessel was prominent in coastal shipping during her life and had some very good passages to her credit. In 1934 the schooner sailed from Weymouth, N.S., on June 15th, with lumber for Havana, Cuba. She sailed from there to Charleston, S.C., where she arrived on July 23rd, under charter to load and complete a passage to St. George's, Bermuda, on or before August 1st. This left her only a short time to load and reach her port of discharge. At Charleston, on July 23rd, at 11 a.m., they received orders from New York to place the vessel at the loading pier to take cargo at 1 p.m. and sail at 7 that evening.

A large number of negro stevedores, highly efficient workers, completed loading the cargo of 8000 creosote railway ties in six hours, and this is a record that cannot easily be forgotten. At 7 p.m. the *Nova Queen* towed to sea and made the run of approximately 650 miles to anchorage in the outer roads at St. George's—arriving just about one hour before a new duty on the cargo came into effect. After discharging the cargo she came north in ballast and arrived at Meteghan on August 11th. This was considered a very good round trip for a sailing vessel.

The *Nova Queen* did not have long to live after her fine performance. On December 4th, 1934, she sailed from Turks Island with a cargo of salt for Yarmouth, N.S., and was never reported again.

The Old Work Horse

S. M. Field built the *Seaman, A. O.* of 435 tons net for Captain A. O. Seaman in 1919 at Cape D'Or, N.S. This vessel was notable in several ways. First, it was unusual to name a vessel with the initials following the surname. Captain Seaman was a man with a strong will and always did things his own way. The schooner was sold after a few years to R. C. Elkin & Co. of Saint John, who renamed the schooner *Frederick P. Elkin*. Year after year they kept her busy on the West Indies run. Wood products down and molasses or salt back to Nova Scotia or New Brunswick. She became familiar in the West Indies ports and in the harbours of Atlantic Canada. As time went on, motor pumps were installed in place of the hand pumps, and as she leaked more copiously additional pumps were fitted. The schooner flattened out under the weight of heavy cargoes over the years and her hog was seen as the hump in the spring stay became more pronounced. She spent World War Two on the same run and was unmolested by raiders, although other surviving sailing vessels were not so lucky. About 1946 she was purchased by H. O. Emtage & Co. of Bridgetown, Barbados. After this the schooner was kept in the West Indies inter-island trade and in the early 1950's was dismantled at Barbados. It was a long life for a hard-worked softwood ship.

Three large terns with the prefix *Minas* were launched in 1919. Two of the three came from Spencer's Island. The *Minas Princess* of 465 tons net was built by the Fowler-head S. B. Co. for Bentley, Pugsley and others. After many years in the usual trades she was sold foreign and removed from Canadian registry in 1937. The *Minas Prince* of 457 tons net was built by D. E. Pettis for B. L. Tucker and others. She had various other owners through the years, including Hugh Gillespie & Co. and later Captain Wallace H. Smith, who had charge of the vessel for a long period. The *Prince* made a very good passage from Parrsboro to England, and it is reported she was only fourteen days shore to shore. On another occasion she made a passage to England, discharged a lumber cargo and returned to her home port in sixty days. After many years in the Bay of Fundy trades she sustained a bad damage at Parrsboro in 1932 due to stranding, but was repaired. In 1937 Captain Wallace Smith died. His son, Captain Douglas Smith, took the ship over later. Captain Murray Willegar had charge of the schooner on a passage from Cheverie, N.S., to New Haven, Conn., loaded with gypsum, when a storm was encountered and the old schooner sank on September 18th, 1940.

The third vessel was the *Minas King* of 470 tons net built at Bass River, N.S., by J. S. Creelman for his own interest and that of B. L. Tucker. She had various masters in her long career, including H. Randall and C. F. Merriam. She was laid up in the late thirties, but soon after World War Two started she was purchased by the Dominion Coal Co. for use as a coal bunker barge at Saint John, N.B. Several years later she broke away from her moorings in a gale and stranded across a bar in the harbour. She had to be broken up for removal as a menace to navigation.

Other schooners built in the locality were the *J. L. Ralston* of 462 tons net launched by J. W. Kirkpatrick at Eatonville, N.S., and named after the well-known citizen of Amherst, N.S., who later became a Federal M.P. and was Canadian Defense Minister throughout most of World War Two. The schooner was lost through burning in Santo Domingo Harbour on April 5th, 1921.

Another of the last of the four-masters was the *Cumberland Queen* of 634 tons net built at Diligent River, N.S., by C. Robinson for J. N. Pugsley and others. During a voyage to England in 1921 this schooner drew favourable comment in shipping circles in regard to her handsome appearance and a fine photograph appeared in the current Liverpool magazine *Seabreezes*. In May of 1922, while on a voyage from Turks Island to New York with salt, she struck on Cape Hatteras, opened up and sank. She was salvaged and towed into Norfolk Va., on March 5th, 1923, and was sold as a wreck for $600.00 to A. P. Vane of Philadelphia. The schooner was repaired and resumed work under the name *Emerett*.

Barnhill Bros. built a tern of 244 tons net named after their firm at Two Rivers, N.S. The *Barnhill Bros.* had a very short life, being wrecked on Hogsty Reef in the Bahamas on November 10th, 1919.

The *Hiram D. MacLean* of 447 tons net was built by MacLean & McKay at Economy, N.S. After a short period of management by the builders she was sold to French interests at St. Pierre et Miquelon and renamed *St. Pierraise*. Also at Economy the same firm built the *Acadian Queen* of 440 tons net. This vessel had the same fate as many others and was burned off Turks Island on August 22nd, 1921.

The South Shore of Nova Scotia in 1919

While a few moderately sized schooners were built along the south coast in 1919, the majority were the small handy terns required for the fish export trade out of Newfoundland and from the fishing ports of Nova Scotia. The fish merchants collected their small shipments in the minor ports and coves around the coast. They found it more economical to ship these cargoes in one of the small terns rather than send a large schooner or steamer to spend valuable time collecting a large cargo from various places.

Most of the little schooners launched in Nova Scotia in 1919 were under 200 tons, and were ordered by Newfoundland owners. In addition many schooners of this size were being built in Newfoundland for the same purpose, that of moving their large salt-fish export in small loads to the Latin countries in Europe and South America.

Shelburne, N.S., 1919

The G. C. Harris interests in Newfoundland had two *Generals* built in Shelburne in 1919 by the J. B. McGill Shipbuilding and Transportation Co. The *General Horne* of 179 tons net, with Captain B. Roger in charge, was believed to have struck on the Virgin Rocks off the southeast coast of Newfoundland. She was later sighted drifting bottom-up and all her crew were lost. The *General Jacobs* of 167 tons net was built for G. C. Harris and J. W. King, but later the Harris interest was bought by H. B. Clyde Lake and Harry Lake of Fortune, Nfld. Some years later she was badly damaged by fire at Burin, but was repaired and renamed *John Millet*. On July 17th, 1933, George Walters, master, she was abandoned in the Atlantic when returning from Portugal with a load of salt. The crew were taken off safely.

The Shelburne Shipbuilding Co. also produced two terns in 1919 and both were well known in their own way. The larger tern, *Helen Mathers* of 363 tons net, was owned by I. H. Mathers of Halifax. Her stormy career started with a voyage to Europe, during which she lost all her sails. Soon after returning she was driven ashore on the coast of Texas in June, 1921, and remained on the beach for a year until she was sold to new owners in the Cayman Islands and renamed *Ellice B*. The schooner was then chartered to rum-runners and in February, 1925, arrived at Lunenburg, N.S., with a cargo of liquor in her hold. Four of the crew were jailed soon after arrival for alleged assault on other crew members. The schooner was libelled by the crew for back wages and she soon became prominent on account of the unusual aspect of the case. The supercargo, who was reported to be in charge, disappeared immediately the ship entered port and no responsible person appeared on behalf of the owners of the cargo, which consisted of 40,000 cases of liquor and which represented a very large investment. Shortly after, another claim was made on the vessel and her cargo by the owners of the schooner *Veronica*, from which it was alleged the liquor had been high-jacked on the high seas during the previous October or November. It was claimed that the owners were New York gangsters, but the facts remain obscure. The matter was cleared up by the auction of the vessel at a sheriff's sale on April 25th, 1925, for the sum of $10,200 to Captain S. Shaw of Dartmouth, N.S. The liquor cargo, valued at $150,000, was attached by a German Marine Insurance Company for $20,000 damage done to the *Veronica* for piracy on the high seas. The schooner was renamed *South Head* and some time later missed stays at the entrance to Halifax Harbour, went ashore at Herring Cove and became a total loss.

MAPLEFIELD.   566 tons.
Built 1919 at Annapolis Royal, N.S.
Courtesy of the Canadian Pacific Railway

E. P. THERIAULT. 310 tons. Built 1919 at Belliveau Cove, N.S.
Courtesy of the Mariners Museum

FRANCES PARSONS and MARINE
(Laid up at Parrsboro, N.S.) *Courtesy of Mr. Giles M. S. To*

CAPE BLOMIDON. 408 tons. Built 1919 at Canning, N.S.
Courtesy of the Mariners Museum

JEAN F. ANDERSON.   396 tons.   Built 1919 at Port Wade, N.S.
Courtesy of Captain Leander Publicover

The smaller vessel had a better record and was more durable. The *Donald II* of 200 tons net was built to the order of W. & T. Hollett of Burin, Nfld. She had various owners, including C. Iverson and W. Trenholm, and in May, 1937, was sold to American parties after a lengthy career in the coasting trade. They used her for a scientific expedition but I do not know the details.

At Allendale, N.S., T. M. Rawding launched two terns in 1919. The *General Plumer* of 149 tons net was one of the small fish carriers for G. C. Harris of Grand Bank, Nfld. It is reported that this vessel was lost with all hands coming out from Portugal with a cargo of salt; Captain L. Hickman, master. The other tern was the *Cape Pine* of 311 tons net and was also for Newfoundland owners. She was sold to French interests at St. Pierre et Miquelon and renamed *Burin*.

Five Terns launched at Liverpool, N.S., and Vicinity, 1919

The Nova Scotia Shipbuilding and Transportation Co. built three of these schooners. The *Faustina*, a small tern of 146 tons net, was first owned by J. F. Creaser but soon passed to Newfoundland owners. It is reported that this schooner capsized near the Newfoundland coast on the way home from Portugal, Captain J. Sibley, master; all the crew being lost. She remained afloat and was towed to St. John's, repaired and resumed her career. While owned by George Penny of Rameau, Nfld., and John Penny of Halifax, she was abandoned in the North Atlantic on October 15th, 1930. Captain Steve White and the crew were taken off by a passing ship.

The *Audrey P. Brown* of 218 tons net was the second of these schooners and she was built for C. H. Ritcey. Captain R. Brown was master and this schooner joined the list of missing ships, and has not been reported since leaving Shelburne on August 23rd, 1928. The third was the *W. H. Eastwood* of 357 tons net, a small four-master owned by a group from La Have, N.S., led by Fraser Gray. Her first master was M. H. Randall and she had several owners until bought by J. W. Cruikshank of Sydney, N.S. It is reported that the schooner was wrecked on the coast of Labrador while loaded with salt just prior to World War Two. She was fitted with auxiliary power and was managed by the son of the owner, J. T. Cruikshank of Halifax.

Samuel Piercy of Newfoundland had the *Myrtle Piercy* of 149 tons net built by McKean & Rawding at Liverpool, N.S. She was in the Portuguese fish trade until January 1st, 1926, when she was abandoned in the Atlantic. She was reported as a derelict and had a short drift as reported on the U.S. Hydrographic Pilot Chart for February, 1926.

The last vessel noted will be the *General Pau* of 329 tons net. This schooner had no Newfoundland connexions like the other *General* vessels. J. E. Backman was a principal owner of this schooner and Captain Ralph Wilkie had command for a long period. About 1929, while on a voyage from St. John's, Nfld., to Brazil, the schooner encountered head wind and calms in the neighbourhood of the Equator and after ninety-two days of trying to reach their destination, being set back by the equatorial current and the variable weather, they put into Barbados for cleaning, overhaul and fresh stores. Soon after completing this voyage the schooner caught fire while at anchor at Riverport, N.S., and became a total loss on May 25th, 1930.

The La Have, N.S., Schooners of 1919

The La Have River was very busy in this year, with thirteen schooners being launched along its banks up to Bridgewater. As noted previously, many of these schooners were built to the order of Newfoundland owners. The *Con Rein* of 299 tons net was launched at East La Have for Conrad & Reinhardt, hence the name. C. W. Parks was her first master and, while I do not have the details on the casualty, she was run down by a United States submarine on August 29th, 1921, off Block Island and became a total loss. These builders also launched a smaller tern about the same time for Captain M. J. Parks. The *Douglas E. Parks* of 136 tons net continued in service for Captain Parks until she foundered off Cape Fourchu, Cape Breton, on February 20th, 1932.

F. A. Robar launched the *Maid of La Have* of 222 tons net at Dayspring for Captain J. L. Publicover and others of La Have. This vessel was lost, when new, while on a voyage to Brazil. She encountered a storm and had her jib-boom carried away. It has been reported that this was the only damage the vessel received, but she was abandoned and left when a steamer came along on March 10th, 1920. Captain Publicover told me this was a heartbreaking loss, as there was no insurance and the master and crew should have done better and made temporary repairs to enable the schooner to make port.

M. Leary launched three of the fish-carrying terns in 1919. The *Little Princess* of 199 tons net was built for Abraham Kean of St. John's, Nfld. This vessel should not be confused with the smaller vessel of the same name that belonged to the "Company of little ships", owned in England and operated for many years in the same fish trade. The *Little Princess* was abandoned in the Atlantic on November 24th, 1923, while in the Portuguese trade. The *Innovation* of 190 tons net was built for Captain M. Randall and foundered off Cape Canso, N.S., on July 26th, 1921. The third, the *Gordon E. Moulton* of 195 tons net, was laid down for Fraser Gray but was sold to J. T. Moulton before launching. From August, 1919, to March, 1921, she was continuously employed as a fish carrier to Portuguese ports, returning with salt. Then she was chartered to an American concern to ply between the West Indies ports and off the United States coast with liquor cargoes. She left there in March, 1924, in a very run-down condition and was abandoned twenty miles off Burgeo, Nfld. Captain Stephen Collier and his crew rowed to Burgeo in their boat.

Conquerall Bank, N.S., in 1919

J. N. Rafuse & Sons were active at Conquerall Bank on the La Have River and in this year launched five terns. One was of a moderate size and the other four were small fish carriers for Newfoundland owners. The largest, the *St. Clair Ritcey* of 332 tons net, was sold to the French fisheries and renamed *Mousquetaire*.

The other four vessels were very similar and could have been built from the same model. The *Ricketts, V.C.* of 155 tons net (named after a Newfoundland winner of the Victoria Cross) was launched for William Forsey of Grand Bank, Nfld. The fate of this little vessel is uncertain, but my best information is that she was lost at Petit Bois Island, Miss., on August 26th, 1921.

Team Sixteen of 154 tons net was built for A. Moulton, and while I do not have the details of her loss, she did not live long and was struck off the Register on September 15th, 1920. The *Ruby and Dorothy* of 160 tons net was first owned by the Burin Export and Import Co. and later by the R and D Shipping Co. In July, 1926, she was sold and went under the French flag.

The *Catherine M. Moulton* of 155 tons net was built for J. T. Moulton of Burgeo, Nfld. She was delivered in July, 1919, and was engaged in the European salt-fish trade until March, 1922, when she was chartered to the Americans for the off-shore liquor trade. In 1925 she returned to Burgeo and loaded fish for Oporto. She was abandoned at sea on that voyage in October, 1925. Captain George Douglas and his crew were rescued by a passing ship.

Bridgewater, N.S., 1919

Daniel Getson had the *Charles and Vernon* of 296 tons net built for his own interest at Bridgewater by W. A. Naugler. This schooner was active in the trades for many years under the command of Captain Byron Getson and she was well known as a handsome schooner. She was lost through springing a leak while on a voyage from Port Reading, N.J., for Bermuda with coal off Cape May on April 24th, 1937. Captain Sylvester Dunphy and his crew were taken off by a passing ship. The other schooner built at Bridgewater this year was the *E. C. Adams* of 330 tons net, launched by the Bridgewater Shipbuilding Co. for Captain H. G. Corkum. This schooner also had a fairly long life and, like the previously described vessel, came apart in heavy weather at sea. She was kept busy in the usual trades in an uneventful way until the Fall of 1933. While proceeding through Northumberland Strait in September of that year she anchored to await a better chance, but the wind freshened and she dragged ashore near River John, N.S. It was three months before she was refloated. In December, 1934, while on a passage from Turks Island with salt, the schooner encountered a succession of heavy gales and sustained damage to her gear and hull. She leaked very badly and was only kept afloat through the great exertions of her crew of five men under Captain Howard Corkum. They were weak and exhausted after many days of bitter cold off the Nova Scotia coast when the Canadian tern *Evelyn Wilkie*, Captain E. A. Wilkie, showed up and with much hazard courageously took the crew off the stricken vessel. The hands of two of the seamen were in such bad condition from the long hours at the pumps and the intense cold that they had to be hospitalized on arrival ashore.

Other Ports on the South Coast of Nova Scotia in 1919

The *Marshal Foch* of 351 tons net was built by L. S. Canning at Wards Brook, N.S., for W. C. Smith and Captain Archibald Geldert, both of Lunenburg. This was an especially fine vessel and after a few years in the coasting trade she was selected and purchased by the famous American author, Zane Grey, to pursue his favourite sport of deep-sea fishing. The schooner was taken to the Smith & Rhuland yard at Lunenburg, renamed *Fisherman*, and refitted as a fine home afloat. She was coppered, had two diesels, electric lighting and refrigeration installed. Sixteen staterooms, five bathrooms and a four-room suite for the owner were fitted. The accommodation was completed with dining-room and lounge. The crew quarters were enlarged to accommodate sixteen officers and men. She sailed on December 1st, 1924, for Panama, where the owner and his party boarded and proceeded to the Galapagos Islands and later to Los Angeles. Captain King of Annapolis was the first master but later he was relieved by Alex Heisler. The schooner was later sold to a missionary society in the Pacific and was lost by drifting ashore on the New Zealand coast.

Only one tern was launched at Lunenburg in 1919. J. B. Young built the *Lila E. D. Young* of 155 tons net for his own account, but sold her to J. T. Moulton. There is some confusion regarding this schooner, as in 1899 the *Lila D. Young*, a two-master, was built in the same yard and was eventually sold to Newfoundland owners. The *Lila E. D. Young*, the tern, was bought by J. T. Moulton in December, 1919, and was constantly employed in the salt-fish trade to Portugal and the Mediterranean until April 8th, 1930, when she was abandoned in a sinking condition off the Spanish coast. Captain Stanley Collier and his men were taken off by the s.s. *Frieval*.

Mahone Bay, 1919

The two firms of shipbuilders at Mahone Bay, N.S., the Ernst Shipbuilding Co. and the McLean Construction Co., each launched three terns in 1919. The former company built the *Sir Donald* of 350 tons net for their own account and after a short time sold her to United States owners. This schooner had the name *Golden Rod* at one period and was owned by the Whitney-Bodden Co. and registered at Mobile. Her title was never properly cleared and as a Canadian-registered ship she foundered in the Bahamas on September 27th, 1927. The *Enid E. Legge* of 233 tons net was built for J. T. Moulton of Burgeo, Nfld. She was kept in the fish trade until business became slack in 1923 and early in 1924 was chartered to United States operators as a rum-runner until September, 1925, when she returned to the Oporto fish and salt trade. This schooner had some very good passages to her credit. In *Western Ocean Schooners* is recorded a passage of thirteen days, Newfoundland to Oporto, the best noted for this class of vessel. She was abandoned on March 11th, 1929, while returning from Brazil. Captain James Buckland and his crew were taken off and landed at an American port. The third vessel was also for J. T. Moulton, and she was the *Frances E. Moulton* of 208 tons net. Captain Daniel Mac-Donald was master in this vessel during her life. She was chartered to rum-runners for a period, but soon returned to the fish trade. Late in 1925 she was lost near Cape Ray, Nfld., while on a passage from Burgeo to Channel, Nfld., with a part cargo of salt. Captain MacDonald and his crew got back to Burgeo safely.

The McLean Construction Co. also built three terns at Mahone Bay in 1919. They were all launched for the H. W. Adams Co. of Lunenburg. The *John M. Wood* of 273 tons net, under the command of Captain St. Clair Geldert, was sunk in a collision with the s.s. *Lake Eloat* on May 22nd, 1920, and was a total loss. The *Ethlyn* of 169 tons net continued in the trades for which she was built for many years. Captain J. P. Strum was master in this ship for a long period. In January, 1935, she was sold to United States owners and put under Puerto Rican registry. Later she was sold to Dominican owners

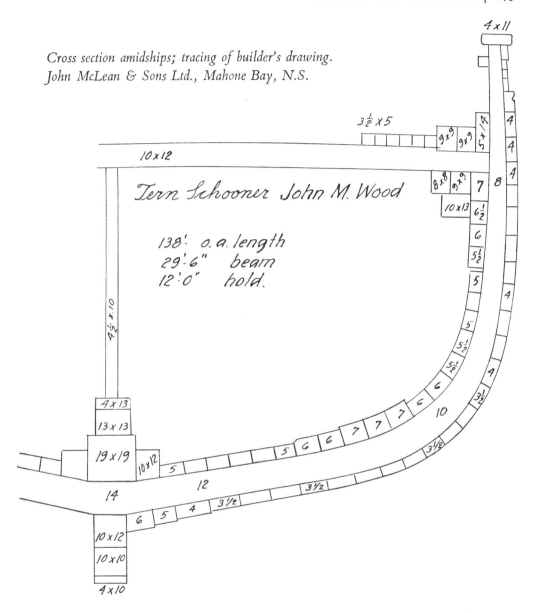

Cross section amidships; tracing of builder's drawing.
John McLean & Sons Ltd., Mahone Bay, N.S.

Tern Schooner John M. Wood

138' o.a. length
29'-6" beam
12'0" hold.

and renamed *Palma de Ozama*, and was carried on the registers up to 1955, although I do not know if she remained in service that long. The third vessel was the *Richard B. Silver*, the second tern bearing the name, of 224 tons net; A Zinck, master. In 1925 her name was changed to *Abundance* and in 1931 she was bought by Louis Kenedy.

Louis Kenedy

This unusual man, born into a well-to-do New York family, had left college after the first year to take a job on a small coasting schooner. His ambition was to be master of a cargo sailing vessel and make his living that way. The idea that the age of steam had long since taken over shipping meant nothing to him. After knocking about the United States coast in small vessels and with other odd jobs, he saved a small amount of cash, went to Lunenburg and bought the fine tern schooner *Abundance*, then lying at Lunenburg, caught in the squeeze of the depression. The *Abundance* had originally cost $56,000 and was twelve years old, but was in excellent condition and had new rigging and sails. He was able to buy her for the small sum of $2000. Freights at that time were very low and little money could be made with a cargo schooner except by cutting all corners possible, having the crew do all the work, including maintenance, repair and cargo handling. As Louis Kenedy was both master and owner, he had complete charge of the enterprise and was learning the business fast when the *Abundance*, while on a passage from Barbados to Turks Island, had the misfortune to break off her rudder head in rough weather. Captain Kenedy let the schooner run before the wind intending to make Kingston, Ja., for repairs. Unfortunately, the freshening wind was advance notice of a hurricane, the presence of which he had no way of ascertaining until it was too late. He attempted to heave-to in the vicinity of Morant Point at the east end of Jamaica, but the sails blew away. The vessel was worked inshore, where he hoped to anchor until the big storm passed, but it was not to be and the schooner dragged her anchors and was dashed ashore. This was in November, 1933. Although he continued in this business, the *Abundance* was the only Canadian schooner he owned.

Louis Kenedy's enterprises interested me and I could understand his feeling for sailing ships, especially at this time when they were on the way out. By the 1930's none had been built for more than a decade and the only trades left to them were the lumber exports to the United States and the West Indies. Available return cargoes were coal from the United States to Maritime ports, or molasses and salt back from the Southern Islands. The only reason that this small specialized trade was left to them was because the capital investment in the schooners was small and they could be run very cheaply.

Captain Kenedy could see it only one way. He wanted a cargo sailing vessel and to make his living "the hard way".

He subsequently had other schooners, but we are not interested in them here. One of them foundered in the Gulf Stream, another was intercepted in mid-ocean by a German submarine and sunk, Kenedy and his crew being picked up after sailing a considerable distance toward shore in their dories. Another large sailing vessel he owned was the *City of New York*, a veteran of Antarctic exploration. He currently has a large ketch for charter in the West Indies. His rugged determination to sail windships has made him the envy of many men who saw him do the things they would like to have done.

Other Building Sites in Nova Scotia, 1919

William Duff of Lunenburg had the *Mary G. Duff* of 349 tons net launched at Chester Basin by a building company there. Captain R. Lohnes was her first master and after a short time in the coasting trade she was sold to French owners and renamed *La Parisienne*.

At Dartmouth, N.S., W. K. McKean built the *Amy G. McKean* of 465 tons net for his own interest. This schooner was christened by her namesake, Mrs. F. H. M. Jones of Chester Basin, N.S. Mrs. Jones, then a schoolgirl, was told they would "launch on board" and she thought this meant "lunch on board". She remembers she was very disappointed on discovering the error. The vessel was operated continuously by Mr. McKean and had many very good trans-Atlantic passages to her credit until she was abandoned at sea on January 5th, 1931, when returning from the United Kingdom. The *M. O. Crowell* of 416 tons net was built by J. N. Rafuse & Sons at Ship Harbour, N.S., for their own interest and that of M. J. Parks. She was abandoned in the Atlantic on November 8th, 1927.

The firm of Freeman & Griffin at Issac's Harbour sent out two terns for J. T. Moulton of Burgeo in 1919. The *Gladys Street* of 123 tons net was the repaired old *Madeira*, which had been built at Lunenburg in 1898. George E. Hartling of Halifax told me this vessel was owned by himself and his brother and they sold her to Newfoundland parties, who had her rebuilt. This job was not too successful. She was loaded in Newfoundland after delivery and sailed for Oporto, but her master, Captain Gunnery, decided she was leaking too much and put back to St. John's. The schooner was surveyed and it was decided to discharge the cargo and send it on by another vessel. When the repairs were completed, Mr. Moulton chartered the vessel to Philip Templeton with the provision that Mr. Templeton put his own crew aboard. She loaded a fish cargo for Greece and my information is not clear as to whether she was abandoned on the east-bound or west-bound voyage, but Captain Edgecombe and his crew were forced to abandon the schooner in mid-ocean in March, 1920. This firm launched the *Ena A. Moulton* of 180 tons net for the same owner and she went into the export fish trade to Portugal, the Mediterranean ports and Brazil. As this business became slack about 1923 and American adventurers were paying good charter rates to carry liquor from the legal ports of export to the off-territory limits of the American coast, the *Ena* was chartered and did not re-enter the fish-carrying trade for two years. She was lost on a voyage, Oporto to Burgeo, in December, 1927; Captain Max Vatcher and his crew, forced to abandon the vessel, were taken off by a passing steamer.

The Scotia Lumber Co. built a tern at Sherbrooke, N.S., in 1919. The *Mabel E. Gunn* of 367 tons net was launched for the local lumber company and was owned by C. W. Anderson and A. A. Gunn. John McKinley was master for most of her career. J. R. Dingle reported that she was in collision with the s.s. *Lake Silver* in 1921 and sustained bad damage forward. The schooner spent most of her life in the New York lumber trade, but in 1925 loaded laths for the building boom in Miami. She was one of the first Canadian schooners to be attracted to this business and many followed to carry lumber, laths and shingles for the tremendous expansion that took place in Florida. The *Mabel E. Gunn* was at this time commanded by Captain Almon Parks and after discharging her cargo proceeded to Turks Island for salt. Early in the morning after her arrival, while still in quarantine, she caught fire forward and was a total loss on November 20th, 1925.

The first large sailing vessel built in Cape Breton for many years was the *County of Richmond*, a tern of 245 tons net. John J. Johnston, a merchant of Johnstown, C.B., organized a company with Alex Finlayson as manager and others of Sydney and North

Sydney as shareholders. John Condon of Newfoundland was engaged as master-ship-wright. Mr. Johnston supplied all the required timber from wood lots in the vicinity. This vessel was a long time building, due to the inexperience of the labour in this class of work and the scarcity of some of the materials. In addition, when ready to be launched, the piles supporting the launching ways spread, and the vessel had to be raised up and the ways secured before she went down to the water. She was towed to North Sydney to have her masts stepped and completed. Due to delays, she is reported to have cost about $90,000, which is high for a vessel of her size. At North Sydney, in August, 1919, she was taken over by J. T. Moulton for his Portugal and Brazil trade. In February, 1921, she was en route from St. John's, Nfld., to Burgeo, and on this voyage she capsized and was lost with all hands off Ramea, Nfld. It has been reported that this vessel was a good carrier but very full in her lines and was not a good sailer.

The McNeil Shipbuilding Co. of New Glasgow launched two large schooners in 1919 for their own interest. The *Susan Cameron* of 558 tons net was a four-master. Captain R. A. Lohnes was one of the early masters in this vessel, which was engaged in the usual trades. She was transferred to Jamaican registry in 1929 and is reported as being dismasted in 1934. The *Annabel Cameron* of 458 tons net was a tern and was commanded by Captain E. H. Kirby. While engaged in the usual trades she was abandoned at sea on December 6th, 1926, forty-eight miles north of Georges Shoal. She became a derelict and drifted to a position about 150 miles due south of Halifax, where she was last reported on January 29th, 1927.

Shipbuilding had been carried out from earliest times at Pugwash and many large ships had been sent out to sail the trade lanes of the world. The last large sailing vessel built there was the tern *William McL. Borden* of 336 tons net. The vessel was delivered to Newfoundland owners immediately and was destroyed by fire on what must have been her first voyage. This occurred on October 30th, 1919, and it is said the casualty took place off the Spanish coast.

Only One Schooner launched in Prince Edward Island, 1919

The *Barbara MacDonald* of 162 tons net was built at the old shipyard at Cardigan, P.E.I., by J. A. MacDonald. This vessel was lost on her first voyage from Cardigan toward St. John's, Nfld., when she struck on Black Head, Cape Pine, Nfld., on December 14th, 1919, while under the command of Captain Tom Whittle.

St. Lawrence River, Quebec, 1919

The *Germain L* of 145 tons net, later renamed *Quebec Trader*, was not a deep-sea sailing vessel, but is mentioned here because she was rigged as a three-masted schooner. She was built at St. Anne de Monts and after completion was altered to an auxiliary and operated along the river as a freighter.

The Newfoundland Schooners, 1919

The Newfoundland fish exporters were having vessels built in Nova Scotia to fill the great demand for shipping, while at home all resources were employed to build their

MARIE LOUISE H.   383 tons.
Built 1919 at Charlottetown, Nfld.
Courtesy of Mr. A. V. Forbes

PEACELAND.   262 tons.
Built 1919 at Annapolis Royal, N.S.
Courtesy of Canning's Studio, Parrsboro, N.S.

AMY G. McKEAN.
465 tons. Built 1919 at
Dartmouth, N.S.
Courtesy of Mr. F. W. Wallace

HERBERT FEARN. 325 tons.
Re-names JEAN F. McCRAE
and MILDRED PAULINE.
Built 1919 at Placentia, Nfld.
*Courtesy of the North Sydney
Marine Railway*

own vessels. As the Nova Scotia yards were at full employment, with consequent high wages resulting in a costly schooner, the Newfoundland yards were able to pay much lower rates and thus produce a cheaper vessel.

The schooners constructed during this period in Newfoundland were not of good quality and with a few exceptions did not last long. To repeat a few of the faults—they were built of unseasoned timber of poor grade, were too light in design and were insecurely fastened. On the other hand, quite a few were lost as a result of stranding, but this was the fault of the navigators and not the construction of the vessel.

The G. C. Harris interests launched two *Generals* at the Marystown yard in 1919. The *General Knox* of 154 tons net was built by J. Forsey. This vessel was abandoned in the North Atlantic on October 14th, 1919. It is reported that while hove-to in a storm on her maiden voyage, she was boarded by a great sea which so damaged her that it was impossible to work the ship and Captain James Harris and his crew were later taken off by a passing steamer. The *General Allenby* of 145 tons net was built at Grand Bank, Nfld., by E. Harris. This schooner was in the fish trade until June, 1922, when she was lost at Ville de Conde, near Oporto.

A second schooner built at Marystown by J. Forsey was the *Violet Buffett* of 174 tons net for G. & A. Buffett. This vessel was lost near Burin, Nfld., when returning from Portugal on her maiden voyage. Captain Thomas Pierce of Fortune, Nfld., was master and the date was March 20th, 1920.

The *John E. Lake* of 202 tons net was another schooner that did not complete her maiden voyage. She was built by J. Miles at Fortune, Nfld., and became a total loss on a sandbank south of Bahia, Brazil, while bound there in 1920 with a cargo of fish; Captain E. Hiller, master.

J. Lake built two terns at Fortune in 1919 for the Lake interests. The *Eileen Lake* of 200 tons net was abandoned in the winter of 1920 on St. Pierre Bank, between Cape Breton and Newfoundland. Captain H. Noseworthy and his crew took to the lifeboat and in the bitter winter weather the cook died the first night. After three days and nights of rowing, the survivors got to St. Pierre et Miquelon. The *Russell Lake* of 132 tons net lived longer than most. This schooner was in the foreign fish trade until March, 1929, when she was wrecked at the entrance to Burgeo and all the crew under Captain Frank Stoodley were lost except the cook, George Day, who made it to shore safely.

The A. E. Hickman Co. of St. John's had three terns built in Newfoundland in 1919. The details of only one of these is clear. The *Optimist* of 110 tons net, a very small vessel, was built at Glovertown by B. Barry. She was a fish trader until January 28th, 1922, when she was abandoned in the Atlantic. The details of the *Marie Louise H* of 383 tons net, large for this type, are not clear and she may have been built in Nova Scotia. She lasted only a short time and was abandoned in the Atlantic on February 20th, 1920. Memories are also vague on the *Louise Hickman*. It is reported that she was built in Nova Scotia and lost in 1921 on her first voyage out from Portugal. Some of these vessels were not in commission long enough for the facts of their ownership and details to be completed before they were lost, and the official records left are confusing,

T. Wells built the *Pierce Wells* of 119 tons net at Hare Bay, Nfld., for Rueben F.

Horwood. This schooner lasted only a short time and her final entry cannot be deciphered. The *Pelleen* of 389 tons net was built at Port Blandford, Nfld., by D. Pelley for J. O. & A. Williams and was a fish trader. She had various owners, the final one being Arthur House, and she was wrecked at Cape Piercly, St. Pierre et Miquelon, on December 9th, 1924.

The Port Union Shipbuilding Co. at Port Union, Nfld., built the *President Coaker* or 260 tons net for the Fisherman's Trading Union. She was named after Sir William Coaker, the founder of the Union. Captain Edgar Quinton told me he made two salt-fish cargo-carrying voyages in this schooner as a seaman and that she was commanded at first by Captain A. Butler. Later, under Captain Sheppard, while on the way home from Brazil, she was lost with all hands just north of Cape Race in January, 1924. It is presumed she ran ashore in thick weather and broke up, as her anchors and chains were found afterward in Shoal Cove, near Cape Ballard.

Two small schooners were built at Norris Arm. The details on the *Rose M* of 148 tons net are vague. She was owned by the Norris Arm Shipbuilding Co. and was lost on a voyage from Fogo, Nfld., toward Gibraltar about January 14th, 1919. The *Neerod* of 129 tons net was built by the same company and owned by George G. Glenny. She was lost on Carbonear Island, Nfld., on December 11th, 1919.

A company formed at Placentia, Nfld., launched the *Herbert Fearn* of 325 tons net. This round-bow schooner had a long career and was one of the last of this large fleet to survive. Early in her career, while under the command of one of her owners, Captain J. Kemp, this vessel was run down in the English Channel and badly damaged. The schooner was hastily abandoned by her crew excepting one man, Bonnia by name, who was forgotten in the excitement and left aboard asleep in his bunk. The schooner remained afloat, was picked up and towed into Plymouth for repairs. After being operated for a time by her builders she was bought by J. T. McCrae and renamed *Jean F. McCrae*. In time she had auxiliaries installed and her topmasts were taken down. Captain Abel Thornhill was in this schooner when she was owned later by R. T. Sainthill & Co. of North Sydney, N.S. Her name was changed for the third time to *Mildred Pauline*. She disappeared in 1942 while returning from Barbados toward Nova Scotia. It is presumed she was the victim of a German submarine raider.

W. G. French built the *Over the Top* (a familiar expression in those late First World War days) of 166 tons net at Notre Dame Bay. Bishop, Sons & Co. were the first owners. Later owners were J. H. McKinnon, T. H. McPeak and lastly J. C. Penny of Halifax. About 1926 her name was changed to *Sunner* and she was abandoned off the Nova Scotia coast on March 9th, 1928.

The A. E. Hickman Co. owned the *Armistice* (another war name) of 198 tons net built by J. Norris at Englee, Nfld. This vessel was abandoned off the Spanish coast on December 23rd, 1922, while in the fish trade.

The Newfoundland Ships and their Crews

To many readers it may seem that practically all these little ships came to a violent end. The phrases "abandoned in the Atlantic" and "the crew taken off by a passing steamer" occur with monotonous frequency in the registers. Others were lost through navigation hazards while proceeding along the coast in fog, snowstorms or gales. Very few of this great fleet ended their days by rotting away on a beach.

In the older European countries the shipwrights took more time and used better materials to build their vessels. English oak, selected planking and solid fastenings were their answer to the ravages of time and the strains set up in a seaway. It must be remembered that our vessels were built of softwoods, with the exception of certain key parts as outlined in Part II. In addition they were built hurriedly, and most of them without great capital investment. There is no doubt that in service the majority were overloaded, especially in the bulk salt trade, and were badly strained soon after launching. To have a new vessel in those days meant she could be loaded until the sheerstrake was in the water amidships, the load-line requirements not affecting vessels of this class.

The pumping was primitive. In the later vessels there was a wrecking pump run off the donkey-engine, but the main pumps, usually two in number, were fitted at the mizzenmast and in many of the Newfoundland tern schooners of this time were made of wood. Better vessels had pumps of cast iron with wooden pipes running to the bilge. They were worked with a hand brake, just a simple up-and-down action that at best produced only a feeble stream. The wooden pumps were difficult to keep tight and if air seeped into the wooden pipes the suction was cut down, with consequent decrease in efficiency.

The problem of keeping a wooden ship afloat is resolved by pumping out water faster than it leaks in. The addition of good efficient pumps meant extra dollars in a comparatively small investment, so was avoided, if possible. On the other hand, manpower was cheap, so the seamen in these vessels spent many hours daily pumping away on a hand brake. In bad weather, with the vessel's seams and butts working, opening and closing, a steady stream of water entered the ship and it had to be got rid of. The situation became desperate when the men broke down with fatigue or the pumps became inoperative. This latter defect happened often. As the water rose in the wells, it dissolved some of the homeward salt cargo and turned it into a heavy brine. In addition to being very much heavier than sea-water to lift in the pump, the fluid had the ability to deposit a crust inside the pump and suction pipe and thus cut down on the efficiency and capacity of the equipment.

The Newfoundland seamen were brought up to a hard life afloat. The seas bounding Newfoundland are cruel. There are periods of ice, others of fog, and always the threat of a storm blowing up on the steep rocky shore. They built all their small craft themselves, so they well knew what they had to work with. The men were tough and had absolutely no fear of the sea. Unlike the seamen of many other countries, they were born and brought up at the edge of the ocean and from early youth were afloat, first in dories and punts, then in the small fishing vessels and coasters. They shipped aboard a schooner for a voyage to Portugal with open eyes, knowing well the perils, discomforts, hard work and possible loss of their vessel. The fish product of their villages had to be taken to market in the cheapest and most efficient way. The small tern and two-masted schooner was the answer and they made the passage back and forth across the ocean for many years with very small crews.

The masters of most of the vessels were not certificated, and their knowledge of celestial navigation was very rudimentary. Many of them could do no more than obtain a latitude from a noon sight on the sun, "eighty-nine forty-eight" method. It was their custom on departure to go on dead reckoning as long as possible toward their destination, then, by determining when they were in the correct latitude by means of a meridian altitude, they sailed along the parallel to their port of discharge.

From deck boy to master they were able, hard-working and courageous. They sailed their lengthy ocean traverses in a fashion that had changed but little from those of Columbus and Cabot four centuries before.

P A R T   S E V E N

He thought he heard the old mate say,
'Just one more drag and then belay.'

Many of the people who had invested their money in schooners after World War One found themselves in difficulties. The vessels which had operated during the war and the early postwar period had returned large profits. In early 1919 it appeared to many that the day of the sailing vessel had returned. The freight rates were still very high and far out of proportion to reality. It has been reported that the freight on lumber from Nova Scotia to the West Indies rose as high as $65.00 a thousand board feet, paid in advance. This was many times the normal rate. For a larger-sized tern a cargo of 500,000 board feet was about average, so her freight to the West Indies would have been about $32,000 and with the additional freight of her cargo home, even the most expensively built schooner could soon pay herself off. So the building went on.

Some of these later schooners were a long time building on account of the scarcity of materials and labour. A few of them listed as being built in 1920 were started early in 1919. When it was seen that their cost was going to be high, their owners pressed on their completion to get them into the good freight market. But many were too late and the shareholders found themselves with expensive schooners on their hands for which no profitable cargoes offered. It was a very unfortunate situation.

The French Shore, Nova Scotia, 1920

W. R. Longmire of Bridgetown, N.S., had the *Ronald C. Longmire* of 149 tons net built at Meteghan. This little tern had a long life and a series of owners. She was engaged in the United States and West Indian trades and was finally owned by Captain L. F. Barkhouse of Westport, N.S. Captain Barkhouse had a long career at sea which he started at the age of seventeen by stowing away on a coastal ship. Before the ship sailed he was discovered and put ashore. His father, an industrious farmer, was very strongly opposed, but soon the young Barkhouse had convinced his father that a seafaring career was the life for him. In 1938 the schooner was sold to Captain Van Sande of

Jamaica, and Captain Barkhouse, at that time seventy-four, attended to the refitting of the schooner for her voyage south. He found a crew and sailed away to Jamaica and delivered the vessel. The *Ronald C. Longmire* stayed in the island trade until September, 1943, when, on a voyage from Abaco in the Bahamas to Jamaica, loaded with lumber, she was caught in a hurricane and lost with all hands.

A schooner with a short life was the *Roxana Burton* of 130 tons net. She was built to the order of Captain John Burton and others of North Sydney, N.S., at Grosse Cocques. This vessel is reported to have cost $90,000 (surely a very large sum for such a small vessel), and her loss by fire in the Mediterranean on July 11th, 1921, dealt her owners a hard blow.

B. N. Melanson built the *Melanson Bros.* of 288 tons net at Gilberts Cove. Her life was also very short. Mr. Melanson wrote that this vessel was completed in 1920, but the date of her loss on the coast of Barbados is given as January 1st, 1920. She must have been completed late in 1919 and on her maiden voyage when stranded.

At Church Point, Belliveau Bros. launched the *Lucy R* of 104 tons net. This little schooner soon passed to United States owners at Rockland, Me. Nearby, at Comeauville, S. F. Comeau launched the *A. H. Comeau* of 144 tons net. This vessel was sold to Zwicker & Co. of Lunenburg and renamed *Sceptre* after a brigantine launched in 1890 which the firm operated for many years. The new *Sceptre* was not fated to last long, as she stranded at East Caicos Island in the Bahamas on June 22nd, 1922, and became a total loss.

The *Acadian* was the last large sailing vessel built at Weymouth and the second last one along the French shore. She had a stormy career. She was built by Beazley Bros. and owned by the Hankinson interests. The schooner was chartered to rum-runners and was one of the first vessels to appear on rum row. One August night in 1923 she turned back the pages of history to the days of the buccaneers. When at sea about twenty miles off Rockport, Mass., a band of armed men came alongside in search of the money which had been collected in payment for the cargo of liquor that had been discharged. The story of the battle never came out, but when she put into Gloucester next day, her Captain and cook were dying of wounds. When prohibition was repealed the schooner became legitimate again and returned to the trade for which she had been built and loaded lumber at a Bay of Fundy port. On December 30th, 1933, she was abandoned off the United States coast in a sinking condition. The United States cutter *Mojave* boarded her a few days later and destroyed the schooner with some charges of dynamite as a menace to navigation. During her career she had the re-names *Utilla* and *J. Scott Hankinson*.

Minas Basin in 1920

The large schooners were nearly finished. Only two came out of the Basin in 1920. The big *Fieldwood* of 435 tons net was built at Canning, N.S., by Lockwood & Fielding (hence the name) and her first owner was given as H. J. Steck. This schooner was in all the regular trades and had a succession of owners, including Gillespie & Co., C. W. Anderson and finally E. L. Croft. In 1938 the freight on deals to the United Kingdom was good and she was chartered for a voyage. The lumber was loaded at Halifax and the schooner sailed under Captain Johnny S. Smith. After a few days out the vessel was found to be leaking excessively and she put back to Halifax. The deck cargo was removed and she was dry-docked and given a complete caulking. Reloaded, she started out again, but foundered south of Sable Island on December 19th, 1938, her crew being taken off.

Although this schooner was a trader for many years and was one of the survivors of the fleet, she had a fault in design that was never completely cured. She was very hard on rudder stocks, and J. R. Dingle, who sailed a long time as mate in her, told me that during his service in the vessel the stock had to be renewed twice—and on other occasions there had been trouble. Several of the well-known masters had charge of this vessel at different times, including Ezra Forsyth, Hants Cole and Harris Oxner.

The 'Fieldwood' struck by Lightning

On a passage north in 1926 the *Fieldwood* was in the Gulf Stream during a storm. The night following the storm the sea fell flat and nature put on a fireworks display with vivid bolts of lightning and echoing volleys of thunder. Suddenly a great streak of lightning struck the foretopmast at the lower truck, cut it off completely and ran down the backstay to the serving, which it sliced off as with a very sharp knife, then jumped into the water, leaving a sorry mess of gear aloft. Captain Hants Cole was master at this time.

The other schooner also had a long life but a more tragic demise. The *Ena F. Parsons* of 221 tons net was the last schooner built by the Parsons interests at Cheverie. She was active in the Bay of Fundy trades until, under Captain Daniel Desmond, the managing owner, the vessel was involved in her sad ending. She was towed out of Weymouth, N.S., on October 9th, 1933, loaded with lumber for Boston. With Captain Desmond was his son Richard, who was mate, and Richard's wife, who was cook, and two sailors. The wind was freshening as the vessel set sail and cast off the towline. What happened remains a mystery, but two days later a coaster, the *Connoisseur*, Captain Moyle Crouse, came into Yarmouth, N.S., and reported a derelict floating bottom-up about forty miles off that port. It is presumed that in the approaching storm Captain Desmond tried to bring the vessel to the wind to reduce sail and she was dismasted and capsized. A few days later the wreck was towed into Westport, N.S., but the bodies were never recovered.

The North Side of Minas Basin, 1920

The last four-master to go down the ways was the *Whitebelle* of 572 tons net. W. R. Huntley & Son built her for C. T. White & Son of Sussex, N.B., and she was in the trades out of the Bay of Fundy until December 1st, 1928, when on a voyage from Saint John to New York she stranded at Beaver Harbour, N.B., and was a constructive total loss. The wreck was recovered and repaired and the schooner resumed her regular trades. Under Captain Flowers she foundered off West Quoddy Head on May 22nd, 1931.

Two large terns were launched at Port Greville in 1920. J. K. Cochrane launched the *Frederick H* of 390 tons net for his own interest and others. This tern was in the usual trades until July 2nd, 1933, when she was wrecked on the Silver Banks in the Bahamas. The crew took to their boat and sailed to Grand Turk, ninety miles to the northwest. The *Burpee L. Tucker* of 465 tons net was built by Geo. E. Wagstaff for S. T. Salter and B. L. Tucker. This fine schooner ended her days on one of the great hazards of the east coast. Seal Island, surrounded by rocky reefs, situated a few miles west of the southern end of Nova Scotia, stands astride the route in or out of the Bay of Fundy. From early days it was used as a summer fishing station and the shores of the island were strewn with wreckage from the unfortunate ships which struck there, usually in fog, snow or howling storms. Reckoning of a ship's position in this vicinity is difficult to keep, owing to the great tides sweeping in and out of the Bay of Fundy. This is especially so in the case of sailing vessels making their way along the coast in thick weather and an unknown number of ships were cast on these rocks and never heard of again.

In the early 1800's a kind-hearted young woman of Barrington, N.S., named Mary Crowell, saw the ragged and weary crew of a ship which had been wrecked at nearby Cape Sable a day or so previously. Later on she married the Captain of these men, but the memory of their plight stuck in her mind until one day she began to think of the fate of the sailors cast on Seal Island a few miles away with steep shores and no aid or shelter whatever if they survived to drag themselves above the high-water mark. On a spring trip to the island some visitors found the body of a man kneeling over a pile of sticks with his tinder box in his hands. Mary Hichens, as she was then called, was so touched by this story that she prevailed upon her sailor husband to set up a strong cabin on the island, and along with another couple they spent their winters in this lonely spot for twenty-seven years. During this period about twelve wrecks a year occurred, but they always provided assistance for the unfortunate sailors. Due to the efforts of these kind people and to their everlasting memory, a lighthouse was established and Richard Hichens and Edward Crowell looked after the light turnabout, six months each, and a yearly salary was provided by the Government. To a recent date the light has been tended by descendants of Mary Hichens.

It was here the *Burpee L. Tucker* ended her career. On January 12th, 1927, the schooner was proceeding in ballast and in a blinding snowstorm struck the rocks and was pounded to pieces. The crew were rescued with the greatest difficulty.

Captain A. O. Seaman was the sole owner of the *Rupert K* of 378 tons net, built by J. W. Kirkpatrick at Spencer's Island and named after Rupert Kirkpatrick. This vessel was soon destroyed as a result of two casualties. She loaded coal at New Campbellton, Cape Breton, and near her port of discharge at Campbellton, N.B.—a short passage—the coal cargo caught fire. The schooner sprang a leak after stranding on the river bank while fire-fighting operations were in progress and became a total loss on July 29th, 1921.

The *T. K. Bentley* of 466 tons net was built by her namesake at Advocate Harbour. She had several owners, but was finally owned and operated by Captain J. J. Taylor. After working out her life in the Bay of Fundy and West Indian trades she was abandoned on the beach at Parrsboro in 1942. In a news report in the Fall of 1938 it is related that Captain Taylor of this vessel and Captain Ralph Ogilvie of the American-built

ENA F. PARSONS. 221 tons. Built 1920 at Cheverie, N.S. *Courtesy of the Peabody Museum*

B. R. TOWER.   343 tons.   Built 1920 at Diligent River, N.S.

Courtesy of Captain J. Cutten

COTE NORD.   147 tons.

Built 1920 at Mahone Bay, N.S.

Courtesy of Mr. W. D. McLean

McLEAN CLAN.   239 tons.
Re-names IRENE MYRTLE, IRENE FORSYTHE,
SANTA CLARA. (Photo shows vessel as a U.S.
naval "Q" ship.)   *Courtesy of the U.S. Navy*

NELLIE T. WALTERS. 139 tons. Built 1920 at Shelburne, N.S.
Courtesy of the North Sydney Marine Railway

tern *Albert H. Willis,* while at Portland awaiting a change in the weather for a passage to New York, became involved in an argument. This was a dispute as to which schooner had the most speed and seaworthiness—surely a basis of argument as long as there have been ships and men. Both Captains were Parrsboro men and the stakes were fixed as a case of whiskey and a case of beer for the winner of a race from Portland to City Island, N.Y. It is reported that the *Bentley* won the race with the *Willis* nowhere in sight.

The last large tern noted for this area and one of the last sailing vessels to be launched at the head of the Bay of Fundy was the *B. R. Tower* of 343 tons net. She was built by Pugsley and Robinson at Diligent River and J. N. Pugsley owned her. She was not fated to last long and was wrecked on the Northeast Reef of Turks Island on May 4th, 1922.

The South Shore of Nova Scotia in 1920

T. M. Rawding was active in schooner building at Allendale in 1920. One of the schooners he launched was the *Tahitian Maiden* of 138 tons net, built to the order of Hendry Bros. of Halifax for French owners in the Pacific. In later years this vessel was renamed *Tahiti.* Another schooner, the *Maxwell C* of 170 tons net, was later renamed *Albert Revillon* and was built for the Revillon Freres Trading Co. for their Quebec, Labrador and Hudson Bay service. This was one of the first of the larger schooners to be fitted with the shaft of the auxiliary projecting through the quarter. Detractors of the scheme claimed that with this type of installation the vessel would be difficult to steer and the off-set propeller would be liable to damage from ice. In service it was found that this arrangement did not materially affect steering, or prove more vulnerable than the conventional type of propeller, and many later vessels were thus equipped. The schooner was later taken over by the Hudson Bay Co. and renamed *Fort Garry.*

At Allendale the third vessel was the *Spencer Lake* of 148 tons net built for H. B. Clyde Lake of Newfoundland. She was designed for the Portuguese fish trade and is notable for a very good passage of fifteen days from Oporto to St. John's. On January 15th, 1926, she was dismasted while on a passage and abandoned. The crew were taken off by a steamer.

The 'General Trenchard'

The fourth vessel built by T. M. Rawding in 1920 was the *General Trenchard* of 149 tons net, launched at Allendale for G. C. Harris of Grand Bank, Nfld. She was abandoned in the Atlantic on March 10th, 1929, under the command of Captain Clarence Williams. Robert S. Munn related the story of her loss in an issue of *Sea Breezes* in 1929.

The schooner left Grand Bank on February 16th, 1929, for Oporto laden with salt codfish in bulk, well manned and victualled, fit to carry out her intended voyage.

For the first week the usual stormy weather was encountered with strong variable winds. On the 23rd in a northwest gale the vessel was under foresail and forestaysail, with the deck full of water and hove-to. That night the foresail blew out and the vessel was run before the sea with the decks continually awash. In the late afternoon of the 24th she shipped a sea over the stern which smashed in the cabin doors and flooded the cabin. The vessel was then brought head to sea under a stormsail and forestaysail while the crew bailed out the cabin and made repairs. Shortly after, another sea boarded the vessel forward and carried away the bowsprit and cathead, smashed the dory and opened the vessel so that the water poured through the fo'c'sle deck. The schooner was then swung away from the sea to allow the crew to cut away the bowsprit, which was smashing against the planking in the high swell. The difficult task of sawing the wire stays proved impossible in the rough sea with the vessel driving her head under every few seconds. The vessel was kept off before the wind with the man at the wheel lashed in place while the rest of the crew worked to get the bowsprit clear and fit extra stays from the masthead to keep the foremast steady. The gammon strap had been wrenched out of place and no longer provided secure support for the forestay. There was considerable water in the vessel and it was necessary to keep a man constantly at the pump.

The next day the bowsprit was finally cleared and examination showed that the stem was started and oakum was spewing out along the seams. The following day, still running off before the westerly storm, with the vessel leaking badly and a man at the pump continuously, the crew spent the day jettisoning part of the cargo. By the next day, the tenth out from port, the gale moderated and in a strong breeze from the south the vessel was again brought head to sea under the stormsail and forestaysail, but the sea continued so high the men were unable to work at repairs about the deck. With some of the strain gone, due to the lightened cargo, the schooner rode easier and did not leak as much.

On the eleventh day the weather continued the same and a steamer was sighted. The master thought that if the crew held up, and conditions did not get any worse, he might get the vessel to land, so he did not pass a signal.

On March 1st the wind came from the south-south-east and freshened. The crew were engaged steadily at the pumps and that day the cook fell ill. In the afternoon a ship was sighted in the gathering darkness but did not see the signal which they now were showing. That night the cook was too sick for any work and thus the crew had to perform the extra tasks. The next day, the twelfth, the foremast was found to be working loose and in the evening the schooner shipped another big sea and the water poured into her. At this time, March 2nd, it was evident that the schooner was doomed. The next day one of the sailors collapsed from exhaustion. A good lookout was kept for passing ships and the pump was kept going steadily.

Strong winds and high seas prevailed. By March 6th, no ship having showed up, the crew repaired the lifeboat, which had been badly damaged, and kept pumping. On the afternoon of the eighth, with the sea still high and the ship hove-to, a plank sprung in the stern and they heard the water running in—and still no ship in sight. Happily the wind dropped out that night and the sea flattened and they were able to hold their own with the pumps. At 7 a.m. on March 10th, the s.s. *Merchant* came up and took them off after sixteen days of winter storm and eventually they all got home safely. So ended another gallant little ship.

Liverpool, N.S., Schooners in 1920

The Nova Scotia Shipbuilding and Transportation Co. launched the *Isobel Moore* of 157 tons net and the *Olive Moore* of 158 tons net in 1920. The *Isobel* was first owned by

F. Moore and managed by the A. E. Hickman Co. of St. John's. She was later owned by Captain F. J. Pine and was lost in Fortune Bay, Nfld., on May 16th, 1930. The *Olive* was owned by the A. E. Hickman Co. and like the *Isobel* was later owned by F. J. Pine. She was abandoned in the North Atlantic on November 8th, 1930.

Ownership of the Schooners

In most of the schooners there were usually several owners. All ships are divided into sixty-four even shares and it was the exception for one man or firm to take on the full responsibility for a vessel. Very often the owner of a building yard took some shares and also persons connected with the shipping business in some form or another. Then there were people who invested as a straight speculation. Where I have given the owner as one person he may have held many shares, or only one or two, but was designated as managing owner by the common consent of the other shareholders. In many cases a master mariner would go to an established shipping concern or to a shipbuilding yard and propose that a ship be built for a certain trade and that he would put up part of the money and command the vessel. Other men made a specialty of promoting the building of one or more schooners with a small amount of capital in each and acted as managing owner, broker and general agent.

In this way "risk capital" was spread out and a man did not have "all his eggs in one basket". A marine casualty was absorbed among several and if the schooner was successful all interested parties would receive a dividend.

Shelburne, N.S., in 1920

Shelburne Shipbuilders Ltd. launched three of the fish-trading terns in 1920. The *Roy Bruce* of 150 tons net was built for R. T. Hollett of Great Burin, Nfld. This was a staunch schooner classed by Bureau Veritas for twelve years and was lost by being run down at sea in February, 1924, just southeast of Cape Race, when returning from Spain with a cargo of salt. It is reported that all the crew were lost in the mishap. The derelict was reported on February 27th, 1924, by the s.s. *Huronian* and after a considerable drift to the east, by the s.s. *Jeserie* on March 8th, 1924. It is presumed she broke up after this date, as she was not observed again. The latter ship reported that the schooner had evidently been in a collision and at that time presented a three-foot freeboard to the wind. The same builders also launched the *Marguerite Ryan* of 147 tons net for D. A. Ryan of Newfoundland. Soon after, under the ownership of W. R. Howley and J. T. McCarthy, both of Newfoundland, she was abandoned in the North Atlantic on February 2nd, 1923.

The *Nellie T. Walters* of 139 tons net was the third of the schooners built by Shelburne Shipbuilders Ltd. in 1920. R. T. Sainthill & Co. of North Sydney, N.S., were the managing owners and Captain T. Walters had an interest and command of the vessel. She was one of the schooners designed with a round bow and on her trial trip at Shelburne amazed the local sailors by her handiness and her speed in stays. Some thought her a yacht as she tacked up the harbour against a head wind. The lines of this vessel, as drawn by H. I. Chapelle from her block model, are reproduced in the illustration following page 218. The sail plan is also drawn.

Passages of the 'Nellie T. Walters'

While there is much talk among the old sailors of fast passages, it is difficult at this date to verify many of them. I have heard that a tern left Burgeo, Nfld., for Oporto, loaded with fish and returned with a cargo of salt in twenty-eight days. The crew had to be put at odd jobs to finish out their month. To return to hard facts, it is recorded that the two-topmast schooner *Devil* sailed from Punch Bowl, Labrador, on August 26th, 1872, and six days and eighteen hours later was reported on the other side. This schooner had a figurehead of his Satanic majesty and it was claimed by many superstitious sailors that she owed this speedy passage to that gentleman.

In 1836 the small Newfoundland-built brig *Charles* made an eastbound passage from St. John's to Bristol in under ten days.

The best recorded Atlantic passage in these small terns in modern times was thirteen days, made by the *Enid E. Legge*. But the best average made over a number of years was by the *Nellie T. Walters*. In 1926 she made the run from Marystown, Nfld., to Oporto in fourteen days. Over the years 1922 to 1927, taking passages both ways and including one slow one in 1926 which took thirty-one days, her average was twenty-two days, which she performed with remarkable consistency.

The *Nellie T* came to grief in 1939 while on a passage with coal from Sydney, N.S., to Trinity, Nfld., when she struck on St. Mary's Shoal and was a total loss, but her crew escaped.

Along the La Have River in 1920

Fred Robar built two small terns at Dayspring, N.S., in 1920. The *Donald T* of 162 tons net, William Duff, Lunenburg, owner, did not last long and was abandoned at sea on January 15th, 1921. The other, the *A. W. Chisholm* of 146 tons net, was owned by the Chisholm Shipping Co. and had numerous masters in her life, including J. Tanner, P. D. Rafuse, E. Ernst and finally George Corkum. This schooner was one of the last engaged in the old trades and made her final voyage from Shelburne heavily laden with lumber toward the West Indies. Southeast of Bermuda she ran into a storm and filled with water. Her crew clung to the half-submerged wreck for several days before they were rescued by a Swedish freighter on February 28th, 1940.

The third vessel launched at Dayspring in 1920 was the *William S. MacDonald* of 252 tons net, built by M. Leary for W. H. Eastwood and Fraser Gray and others of La Have, N.S. Captain C. W. Parks was master for part of her brief life before she was abandoned at sea off Long Island on October 24th, 1923, after filling with water. She became a total loss.

J. N. Rafuse & Sons, at Conquerall Bank, launched three terns in this year. The *Suzanne* of 264 tons net was built to the order of the French Fishing Fleet. The *Retraction* of 148 tons net was built for Philip Templeton of Bonavista, Nfld., and was engaged in the salt-fish trade until she was abandoned in mid-Atlantic on February 5th, 1926.

The third schooner had a long and varied career. The *A. Moulton* of 150 tons net was built for the Moulton interests in the salt-fish trade. Captain P. D. Rafuse told me he had this schooner for a voyage in the early 1920's with fish to Brazil, loaded coconuts at Jamaica for New York, then home with coal. Captain C. L. Anderson took over the vessel in 1922 and was a general trader until the schooner was sold to Boston interests for rum-running. Later, she was taken to Lunenburg to have auxiliaries installed; her rig was cut down to a two-master and she was renamed *Waegwoltic*. She was again engaged in rum-running and was detained at Key West for infractions, following which she was sold by a Sheriff's Court and put to porgy fishing. Later she was bought by Newfoundland parties, Frank Pine, master, renamed *Mount Pearl* and put into the coasting trade. Some years later she was given her final re-name *Cape Bonavista* and had to be abandoned off the Newfoundland coast on January 31st, 1946, when she developed a bad leak.

Conrad and Reinhardt built the *Marion L. Conrad* of 155 tons net for their own interest at La Have in this year. Captain H. G. Corkum was the first master in this vessel and she was in the usual trades until about 1930, when she was sold to owners in Boston. The last vessel built along the river in 1920 was the *Hazel P. Myra* of 191 tons net built for owners in Lunenburg, including P. L. Myra, by the Bridgewater Shipbuilding Co. Captain P. D. Rafuse was master in this schooner for a while and she was later owned by J. E. Backman and was abandoned at sea in a sinking condition on February 28th, 1938.

Fraser Gray

Mr. Fraser Gray of La Have, N.S., had a long association with the fishing and tern schooners of that district. He first went to sea as a cook, but came ashore in 1901 to become associated with the firms that later became known as the La Have Outfitting Co. In a reorganization in 1908 he was made managing director and has continued in that capacity ever since.

Mr Gray had an interest in several of the tern schooners built along the south coast during the period of their popularity. In 1957 he passed his eighty-fourth birthday. Hale and hearty, he still drove his own car. He wrote that his later investments in the schooners did not turn out well, as he was one of those left with large expensive vessels launched after the war when the freight rates became so depreciated that they could not earn back the money that had gone into them.

Chester and Mahone Bay in 1920

The *Mary L. Oxner* of 169 tons net was an unlucky schooner and was lost on what must have been her maiden voyage. She was built by the Chester Shipbuilding Co. for William Duff and E. C. Adams of Lunenburg, N.S., and was wrecked on the Silver Banks in the Bahamas on September 13th, 1920. The same company also launched the *D. D. McKenzie* of 148 tons net for the McKenzie Shipping Co. She had various owners in the locality and Captain F. Ernst was master for some years. In 1932 she was sold to United States owners, who altered the schooner to a yacht, the hold being converted into staterooms and living quarters. She was renamed *Sachem*.

At Mahone Bay the Ernst Shipbuilding Co. launched two terns in 1920 and both were for foreign interests. The *Raymonde* of 252 tons net was destined for the French fisheries, and the other, the *F. S. Burgoyne* of 143 tons net, was sold soon after completion to owners in the Dutch West Indies and renamed *Ave Maria*.

The McLean Construction Co. of Mahone Bay built two three-masted schooners in 1920 and both were notable in their own way. The *Cote Nord* of 147 tons net was a new type with a round bow, spike bowsprit, no topmasts and fitted with oil auxiliaries. She was thus the first of these vessels built with sails as a secondary propelling power. Her sails were to help out when the wind suited and, of course, in the event of her engines failing. She was built for the St. Lawrence River and Gulf north shore service, but did not prove suitable, and was bought by Lunenburg interests. She had various owners and went under the French flag for a short period during which she had the re-name *Amphitrite*. Her final owner, again under her original name, was Angus Genge of Flowers Cove, Nfld., and she was wrecked at South Petty Harbour, Nfld., on June 23rd, 1932, and became a total loss.

The Tern that joined the U.S. Navy in World War Two

The other vessel launched by this company was the *McLean Clan* of 239 tons net for H. W. Adams of Lunenburg with Captain St. Clair Geldert as master. The schooner was in the coastal trades for many years. In the 1930's she was bought by Captain Thomas Antle, who had her renamed *Irene Myrtle* and under his command she continued in the usual trades. By 1939 she was neglected and in poor condition. Small auxiliaries had been installed and her topmasts were down, but the war stimulated freight business and she was given a new lease on life. Captain Antle died aboard the vessel while she was loading coal at New London, Conn., for Yarmouth, N.S., in the summer of 1942.

About this time the United States Navy began looking for a sailing ship to outfit as a "Q" or decoy ship to be used in anti-submarine warfare, and among the several vessels of her class available, the *Irene Myrtle* was chosen. They renamed her *Irene Forsyth*, designation IX-93. She was taken to the New London Navy Base and under the orders of Commander Gerald Thompson was fitted with new engines, a 4-inch quick-firing gun, three automatic weapons, a mousetrap anti-submarine rocket weapon, radar and sonar. Sailing from port to the Great Bight off Nantucket Island in September, 1943, under Commander R. Parmenter, U.S.N.R., the crew altered the profile and rigging and concealed her armament so she looked like a Portuguese Bank fisherman. Temporary houses covered the guns, the bulwarks were hinged so they could quickly be dropped out of the way and the rigging was fitted with pelican hooks so that it could be moved from the line of fire.

Shortly after putting out to sea to cruise around waiting for an enemy submarine to put in an appearance, she was caught in a hurricane east of Bermuda and suffered considerable damage. She managed to reach Hamilton Sound, Bermuda, and was reconditioned, but prior to sailing again the project was cancelled, due to the success of the baby flat-tops that had driven the submarines from the area. She was ordered back to the United States, where the Maritime Commission used her as a training ship until the end of the war, when she was sold.

The old vessel was then purchased by Cuban interests and renamed *Santa Clara*.

They used her in the Caribbean trades, lugging heavy cargoes, and she was so sturdy she could still earn a dollar for her owners. But six years in the island trade was all she could take. Late in 1951, after thirty-one years of hard service, the old schooner met some bad weather. Heavily laden, she was unable to meet the challenge of the seas and on December 21st, 1951, not far off La Ceiba, she filled and sank.

Sherbrooke, N.S., 1920

C. W. Anderson, lumberman and timber merchant of Sherbrooke, N.S., associated with A. A. Gunn, built the *Gunn and Anderson Brothers* of 362 tons net. This was the last large sailing vessel built along this part of the coast. The schooner had a short career and foundered in the Gulf of Mexico in September, 1921, while under the command of Captain George Schmisser, through having struck some submerged object.

The Last Vessel built in Cape Breton

The *Jessy and Alice* of 110 tons net was built at Young's Cove, Dingwall, Cape Breton, by H. O'Brien. This round-bow schooner was constructed of local materials, which included considerable oak from the vicinity. When the hull was completed there was some difficulty getting her over a shoal bar, but this was accomplished by giving the vessel a heavy list, thus reducing her draft. She was taken to North Sydney, had her masts stepped, and was completed there. The *Jessy and Alice* was prominent in the coasting trade for many years. Her owners were H. W. Taylor and later S. F. Fletcher. In 1926 she was jointly owned by G. O. Hankinson and Arthur Moore. In 1931 she was sold to French owners at St. Pierre et Miquelon and renamed *Galiano*. It is reported that she was later lost through burning near St. Pierre.

Only one other schooner was built in Nova Scotia in 1920 and she was the last to go down the ways of the old shipyard at River John. The *Mary F. Anderson* of 418 tons net was well known for her lofty spars and fine lines. She came from the yard of C. H. McLellan and was built for Anderson and McLellan. She remained under their management until run into by the s.s. *Fanad Head* in 1926 off the Nova Scotia coast. Captain Harris Oxner was master at the time and the wreck was towed into Halifax and condemned.

Prince Edward Island, 1920

The last large sailing vessel launched on the Island was the *Anna MacDonald* of 192 tons net. She was built for J. A. MacDonald by D. S. McLaren at Cardigan. This vessel was stranded and became a total loss at Kittywitz Shoal near Prospect, N.S., on August 27th, 1924.

New Brunswick, 1920

The story of the big sailing ships of New Brunswick was completed by the launching of the *Peter McIntyre* of 487 tons net by her namesake at Saint John. After a short time engaged in the Bay of Fundy trades she left Saint John, N.B., on November 9th, 1923, and was run into by the oil tanker *Herbert L. Pratt* at the Delaware Breakwater while lying at anchor. The vessel became a constructive total loss and was sold at auction the following spring. The details after this accident are not complete, but she was repaired and in the early 1930's was laid up at Meteghan with two other large schooners. During a gale the schooners parted the moorings that held them to the breakwater. All the schooners were damaged and the *Peter McIntyre* was abandoned on the beach there and slowly disintegrated.

Quebec, 1920

C. H. Nadeau built the *Mina Nadeau* of 316 tons net at Port Daniel, Que., and brought another great industry to a finish. She was the last of thousands of large sailing ships built along the shores of the St. Lawrence. She was built for the lumber trades from the river ports, but was soon sold to W. Ogilvie of Parrsboro, who operated the schooner in the usual trades out of the Bay of Fundy until she was a total loss by fire off Spencer's Island on January 30th, 1931.

Newfoundland, 1920–21

Eight schooners were launched in various parts of Newfoundland in 1920 and three in 1921, which nearly completed the construction of terns in Newfoundland. With one exception these vessels were built for the purpose of exporting salt fish.

The *Newton Lake* of 151 tons net was built at Belloram for Freeman Lake and had a brief career. Under Captain George Elford she was abandoned in the Atlantic on a passage from Cadiz on January 6th, 1921, the crew being taken off by the s.s. *Campbella*. A short time later George Elford had another experience of this kind. The *Helen Jean* of 117 tons net, built at Milltown, Nfld., in 1920, by J. Miles for the A. E. Hickman interests, was returning in 1922 from a voyage to Brazil under Captain Elford and stopped at Turks Island for a cargo of salt. A few days out the vessel began to leak heavily, but fortunately H.M.S. *Capetown*, the flagship of the North Atlantic Squadron cruising in the vicinity, encountered the schooner and towed her back to Turks Island. The vessel was condemned and sold. Her new owners were D. T. Malcolm and others and she was lost with all hands the following year in a Caribbean hurricane.

J. Forsey built two terns at Marystown, Nfld., and both fared better than most of the Newfoundland vessels. The *Ria* of 154 tons net was launched for G. & A. Buffett and was in the fish export trade until she was abandoned at sea. It is reported that thirty-seven days after leaving Cadiz with salt for Grand Bank, Nfld., she lost her sails in a storm and after drifting at the mercy of the rough sea was abandoned on November 17th, 1931, fifty-four days out and short of food and water. Captain George Douglas and his crew were rescued by the s.s. *Aztec*. The second vessel was the *General Rawlinson* of 149 tons net, delivered to the Harris interests for their export trade. Captain James Harris told me he was in charge of this vessel on a voyage to Oporto with fish. The passage was nearly completed and they had towed in to go alongside with the pilot still on board. It was blowing hard and it was decided to anchor the schooner off the dock and await more moderate weather. Both anchors were let go, but in the freshening breeze she dragged, struck against the dock, filled with water and sank. This event

MARY B. BROOKS. 214 tons. Built 1926 at Plympton, N.S.
Courtesy of the Peabody Museum

RUPERT K. 378 tons. Built 1920 at Spencer's Island, N.S.

Courtesy of Mr. F. W. Wallace

BESSIE MARIE. 152 tons. Built 1929 at Burlington, Nfld.
Hove down at dock in winter for work on bottom.

Courtesy of Ashburnes Ltd

happened on January 7th, 1922, and in July of that year the crew, having stood by for that period, raised the vessel and she was surveyed, condemned and sold. The schooner was renamed *Pacos de Brando* and used by the Portuguese as a Bank fisherman. Captain Harris told me he visited aboard the vessel on the Grand Banks in 1949 and she appeared to be in good condition.

The *General Ironsides* of 157 tons net was the last of the *General* vessels built for the Harris interests. She was launched at Grand Bank, Nfld., and shortly after was sold to S. Shaw. In 1927 the schooner was towed into St. Pierre et Miquelon in a damaged condition and abandoned there, but it appears the wreck was bought by Portuguese interests, repaired and renamed *Nossa Senora dos Anjos*.

The *Nancy Lee* of 114 tons net, a small vessel, was built at Campbellton, Nfld., by Horwood & Co. for their own business. This little schooner was active in the Portuguese trade until October 24th, 1925, when she was abandoned in the Atlantic.

There are few details about the *Monchey*, built at Harbour Grace for Tessier Bros. Captain Martin Frampton wrote that he joined this vessel in the building yard in January, 1921. One of the carpenters who had worked on the vessel took him to one side and said: "You will never get her across the Atlantic", but would not elaborate on the reason. The schooner was towed to Port Union and loaded with bulk salt fish for Oporto. They were three days in the ice before getting clear of the coast and then encountered the usual winter gales. He writes that one week after sailing he had to abandon the vessel, as it was impossible to keep the water out of her. The reason he gives is that the ice pulled much of the oakum from the seams and she filled to the beams. They were living on the deck of the cabin, surely an uncomfortable place in January off the coast of Newfoundland, when an oil tanker bound for Norfolk, Va., took them off.

The *Mollie Fearn* of 118 tons net was one of the best of the small Newfoundland schooners. She was built at Placentia for W. Campbell and others, but later was owned by James Baird, Ltd., and renamed *Tishy*. At some time she had auxiliaries installed and a later owner was J. Quinton. Her final owner was W. B. Blackmore and she was lost in Bonavista Bay, Nfld., on December 6th, 1950.

There are only a few further terns to consider for Newfoundland and three of these were launched in 1921.

The *Ronald M. Douglas* of 189 tons net was built in 1921 at Bay D'Espoir by Morgan Roberts for T. Douglas and W. Garland. This schooner had good average passages on her voyages in the export fish trade. But the usual fate overcame her in the North Atlantic on the way from Oporto and she was abandoned on November 12th, 1930, while under the command of T. Douglas.

The *C. Bryant* of 141 tons net was built for the Fisherman's Trading Union at Port Union in 1921. Soon after she passed to Ellison Collishaw of St. John's. She was abandoned 360 miles northeast of Bermuda on March 26th, 1928.

Captain Martin Frampton joined the *Humorist* of 141 tons net in the yard of E. Stone at Trinity Bay, Nfld., for the Munroe Export Co. The vessel was named after the Derby winner of that year. Captain Frampton took charge of rigging the vessel and sailed her for two years in the European trade. The vessel was one of the better ones built in Newfoundland and lasted until she ran ashore at the entrance to Argentia, Nfld., on December 20th, 1933; Captain John Dominy, master.

Another Note on Ship Losses

The proportion of schooners which foundered at sea appears to be very high. This is especially noticeable in certain of the trades, and in particular the two main salt routes. The fisheries demanded a great deal of salt for preservation purposes and it was brought in bulk from Spain and Portugal and from Turks Island in the West Indies. It was carried mostly in the sailing vessels, for several reasons. When carried in an iron or steel ship a proportion of the salt became rust-stained and so lost some of its value. The freight rate in the sailing vessels was cheaper and on account of the small amount carried, one consignee usually took an entire cargo. Another reason was because the vessels were returning home in any case after delivering a cargo of export fish or lumber and a salt cargo completed their round.

In the case of both these routes there is a marked similarity in that each involved a long passage across the open stormy ocean. Once started, these voyages had to be completed, no matter what weather conditions were encountered. Another noteworthy fact is that the great majority of the casualties occurred in the bad-weather months of winter-time.

The schooners which were kept in strictly coastal trade did not encounter prolonged rough water so often. On a voyage between Nova Scotia and the United States it was usual to skirt the coast and on the approach of threatening weather to take refuge in a selected harbour. These stopping places were well defined and often many vessels of different types would collect to await a favourable chance to get on with the voyage. On the approach of a fair wind the blocks creaked as the sails went up slowly, the wind-lasses clanked as the anchor cables rumbled in and away they went. By cautious short runs the strict coaster was able to avoid encounters with the great Atlantic storms and all the strains and damage they were able to inflict.

The Last Three-master in Newfoundland

The *Bessie Marie* of 152 tons net was the last three-masted schooner built in Newfoundland. She was designed as an auxiliary coaster and sealer and was never fitted with topmasts, so was not a true sailing vessel. She was built to the order of Ashburne's Ltd. by E. K. Mills at Burlington, Nfld., in 1929. In 1941 she was altered to a two-master, and in 1956 she was fitted with a new auxiliary at North Sydney, N.S. Captain E. W. Roberts stayed in this ship as master for fourteen years and then was succeeded by Captain Sydney Gosse. This sole survivor of the schooner fleet was still in operation in the Fall of 1959.

Shipbuilding dwindles to a Finish

In the early 1920's, although there was a surplus of fine new schooners afloat, a few more were launched. The good times had passed the period when these sailing vessels were built, but the schooners in existence were to go on for many years. Some of the people who believed most strongly in the economic use of sailing ships, and who did not admit their day was gone, still remained active. At Chester Basin, N.S., the *W. C. Kennedy* of 112 tons net was launched in 1922 for William Duff, Lunenburg, N.S. Captain P. D. Rafuse was master, followed by George Corkum, and the little schooner was engaged in the usual trades. Early in 1926 she delivered a cargo of salt fish in the West Indies, then proceeded toward Turks Island for a cargo of salt. She ran ashore there on March 5th, 1926, and became a total loss.

Captain J. Leander Publicover of La Have, N.S., ordered the *Village Queen* of 123 tons net from F. A. Robar at Dayspring, N.S. The little schooner was in the coastal trades, usually under the command of one of Captain Publicover's sons until she ran ashore near Cape St. Mary, Digby County, on September 28th, 1938. Captain Publicover also operated two large American-built schooners in the baled-pulp trade from the La Have River to United States ports, with coal back if any was offering. Both vessels were lost in casualties—the *Laurie Annie Barnes* was a total loss on Nantucket Shoals about 1937 and the *Lillian Kerr* was run down by an Allied convoy south of Nova Scotia with the loss of all hands, including Captain Publicover's son, who was master, and John Richards, his son-in-law, who was mate.

The last of this class of fore-and-after built in Canada was the *Mary B. Brooks* of 214 tons net. Construction was started in 1920 by W. D. Foley at Plympton, N.S., near the head of St. Mary Bay. After the vessel was framed, work was stopped, owing to the decline in demand for these cargo schooners. In 1925 work was resumed by a company formed by Captain E. J. Kinney and Asa Davidson of Yarmouth, N.S., but was stopped once more in the Fall, as the schooner changed hands again. The two former owners retained an interest when the half-built vessel was taken over by S. St. Clair Jones, Captain George Brooks and others to replace their tern schooner *Westway*, which was lost in 1925 in St. Mary Bay. Construction was completed in April, 1926, and she was employed carrying lumber and pulp between provincial and New England ports until April, 1938, when she was sold to Captain A. Reid of Kingston, Jamaica. After some years in the island trades she was abandoned on the beach at Turks Island.

In 1937 the Royal Canadian Navy decided to build a three-masted schooner for training purposes. A hull model similar to that of the *Bluenose* was selected and she was fitted with a spike bowsprit, lofty masts and topmasts and an auxiliary. I saw this schooner being built at Meteghan and although she had a finely shaped hull, she never looked right. It has been said that she was an indifferent sailer and was poorly balanced. The war came on soon after she was completed and the schooner was used as a store vessel until hostilities ended and she was sold to become a motor coaster. She is only mentioned here as being a Canadian-built three-masted schooner and has no real connexion with the cargo-carrying terns.

Thus ends the record of Atlantic Canada's cargo sailers, for no more were built. Many remained in service for years after all construction ceased, but with the exception of the previously mentioned altered *Bessie Marie*, all are gone by now.

The fore-and-afters succeeded the great fleet of square-riggers built in eastern Canada and in special trades made use of wind and canvas for ship propulsion into an era when the Canadian square-rigged craft had vanished from the seas.

The sail-driven cargo-carrying vessel has quietly disappeared from Atlantic Canada and from all the waters of North America. Sail has also been discarded by the fishing fleets of both Canada and the United States. The internal-combustion engine has superseded canvas and wind in every phase of commercial seafaring endeavour and the windships are but a memory today. Their centuries of heroic and romantic tradition exists but vicariously in the yachtsman's craft, or in government training vessels.

While one may harbour nostalgic regrets at the passing of a colourful seafaring age, it would obviously be impractical to yearn for a revival of something that is definitely gone forever. And though the spirit of adventure still abounds in the hearts of our youth, and the glamour of the sailing ship still has its appeal, there is no gainsaying the fact that life aboard them was harsh and hazardous and ill-paid for the work demanded of the crews. If the old-time sailing fleets were in existence today, it is extremely doubtful if sufficient men could be mustered to man them. Our present-day seamen are under no illusions.

And so another sailing-ship era passes on to live only in the memories of middle-aged and older men and in historical record such as I have set forth in this work. It has been a task which has its compensations in recounting for posterity the story of Canadain seafaring endeavour in the ships themselves, their builders and owners and the gallant men who sailed them.

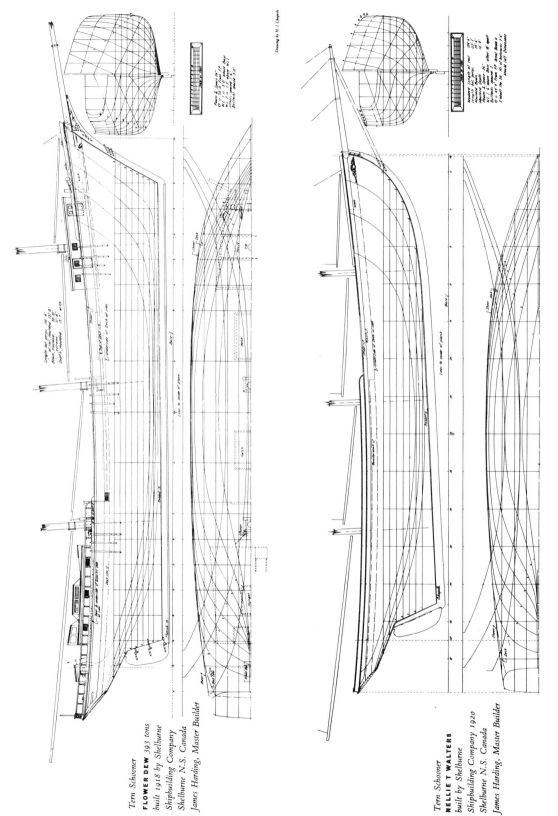

Tern Schooner
FLOWER DEW *393 tons*
built 1918 by Shelburne
Shipbuilding Company
Shelburne N.S. Canada
James Harding, Master Builder

Tern Schooner
NELLIE T WALTERS
built by Shelburne
Shipbuilding Company 1920
Shelburne N.S. Canada
James Harding, Master Builder

Drawing by H. I. Chapelle

Drawing by H. I. Chapelle

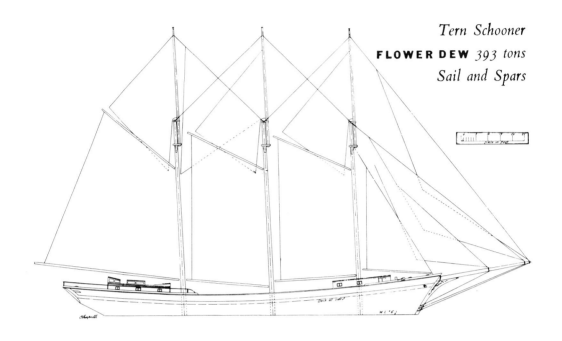

Tern Schooner
FLOWER DEW *393 tons*
Sail and Spars

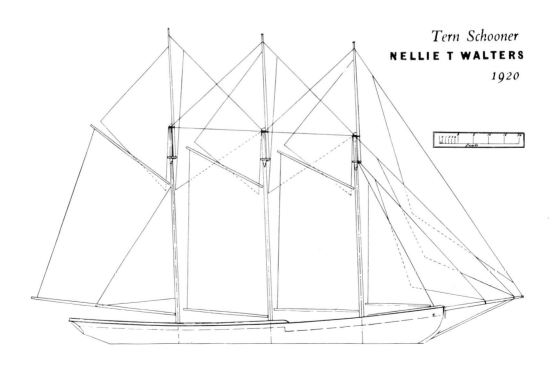

Tern Schooner
NELLIE T WALTERS
1920

ALPHABETICAL LIST

of the Three- and Four-masted Canadian-built Schooners

Four-masters marked with an asterisk★

Name Registered	Dimensions	Net Tonnage	Year Built	Place Built
A. B. Barteaux	153 × 35 × 12.5	380	1909	Canning, N.S.
A. B. Crosby	93 × 28 × 9.9	174	1884	Parrsboro, N.S.
A. Elida *ex* Alberta				
A. F. Davison★	171.9 × 36 × 12.9	503	1909	Annapolis Royal, N.S.
A. F. Randolph	94 × 27.3 × 9.7	155	1866	Canning, N.B.
A. H. Comeau	105.5 × 26.6 × 10.2	144	1920	Comeauville, N.S.
Renamed **Sceptre**				
A. J. McKean	73.1 × 21.9 × 8.3	58	1896	La Have, N.S.
Renamed **Kildare**				
A. K. MacLean	105.5 × 26.8 × 11	176	1905	La Have, N.S.
A. Moulton	116.6 × 26 × 10.6	150	1920	Conquerall Bank, N.S.
Renamed **Waegwoltic, Mount Pearl, Cape Bonavista**				
A. S. Publicover *ex* Fundy King, *ex* Maid of France				
A. T. Davison	122.5 × 30 × 15	361	1892	Parrsboro, N.S.
A. V. Conrad	101.6 × 27.2 × 10	147	1908	La Have, N.S.
A. W. Chisholm	116.4 × 26.3 × 11.4	146	1920	Dayspring, N.S.
Abemama	133.6 × 32.6 × 12.2	337	1918	Liverpool, N.S.
Abundance *ex* Richard B. Silver				
Acadian	111.6 × 27.8 × 12.7	212	1920	Weymouth, N.S.
Renamed **Utilla, J. Scott Hankinson**				
Acadian Queen	150 × 35.5 × 12.8	440	1919	Economy, N.S.
Ada A. McIntyre	147.9 × 35.1 × 12.7	423	1918	Moss Glen, N.B.
Ada Tower★	175.5 × 36.4 × 12.9	528	1916	Port Greville, N.S
Adamac★	165.2 × 36 × 12.9	527	1918	Advocate, N.S.
Renamed **Citta de Genova, Alma**				
Adam B. MacKay	147.4 × 35.8 × 12.1	394	1917	Port Greville, N.S.
Renamed **Chevalier Bayard**				
Addie and Beatrice	113 × 29 × 11	197	1906	Shelburne, N.S.
Adelene	102 × 28.6 × 9.9	193	1885	Rothesay, N.B.
Admiral Drake	130.8 × 32.3 × 12.5	309	1916	Shelburne, N.S.
Adonis	140 × 32 × 11.3	316	1903	Bridgetown, N.S.
Adriatic	96 × 26.8 × 10	99	1907	Bridgewater, N.S.
Advance	126 × 31.8 × 10.7	294	1902	Canning, N.S.
Advent	127.3 × 32.4 × 10.3	256	1902	Parrsboro, N.S.
Aghios Andreas *ex* J. Miller				

Name Registered	Dimensions	Net Tonnage	Year Built	Place Built
Agnes P. Duff	106.2 × 27.6 × 10.2	178	1916	Conquerall Bank, N.S.
Ainslie	112.4 × 26.9 × 10	148	1911	Liverpool, N.S.
Albani	126 × 29.9 × 11	249	1902	Liverpool, N.S.
Renamed **Santa Maria**				
Albania ex **G. M. Cochrane**				
Albert D. Mills	139.5 × 32 × 11.7	326	1903	Meteghan River, N.S.
Albert Revillon ex **Maxwell C**, renamed **Fort Garry**				
Albert T. Young	124.9 × 26.9 × 14.8	271	1874	Prince Edward Island
Renamed **Heistad**				
Alberta	157.1 × 36.1 × 15.7	610	1888	Avondale, N.S.
Renamed **A. Elida**				
Aldytha	109 × 28.3 × 10.8	231	1873	Kingston, N.B.
Alert	108 × 26.8 × 12	248	1889	Port Gilbert, N.S.
Alexandra	105 × 27.8 × 9.8	178	1901	Weymouth, N.S.
Alfhild ex **Bothnia**, ex **McPherson**				
Alfred Ock Hedley	152.6 × 36 × 12.6	461	1918	Fox River, N.S.
Algarve ex **Blanche H. Collins**				
Alice M. Moulton	not known	197	1918	Mahone Bay, N.S.
Allen A. McIntyre	121.9 × 28.6 × 9.2	199	1891	Perry's Point, N.B.
Alma ex **Adamac**				
Alma R	142 × 34.4 × 12.9	413	1918	Meteghan River, N.S.
Alvena ex **Alvina Theriault**				
Alvina Theriault	112.5 × 31 × 10	199	1912	Belliveau Cove, N.S.
Renamed **Alvena**				
Amphitrite ex **Cote Nord**				
Amy G. McKean	141.4 × 33.3 × 12.4	465	1919	Dartmouth, N.S.
Anna MacDonald	105.5 × 25.3 × 10	192	1920	Cardigan, P.E.I.
Annabel Cameron	156.7 × 34.5 × 13	458	1919	New Glasgow, N.S.
Annettina ex **J. L. Nelson**				
Annie	115 × 28 × 10.9	193	1907	Liverpool, N.S.
Annie B. Anderson	154.4 × 35.4 × 13	466	1917	Parrsboro, N.S.
Annie Bayard	111 × 26.5 × 11.2	205	1870	Indiantown, N.B.
Annie Hendry	125.1 × 29.3 × 11	219	1910	Liverpool, N.S.
Annie L. Warren	117 × 30.6 × 10.8	223	1913	Meteghan, N.S.
Annie M. Banks	92.2 × 27 × 10.6	135	1908	La Have, N.S.
Annie M. Parker	138.9 × 32.8 × 12.2	398	1902	Tynemouth, N.B.
Annie Marcia	129.4 × 31.4 × 11.5	271	1914	Bridgewater, N.S.
Archie Crowell	106 × 27 × 10	175	1908	Shelburne, N.S.
Arclight	91 × 27.6 × 8.8	103	1898	Souris, P.E.I.
Areosa ex **Mollie and Melba**				
Argo ex **Georgina Roop**, ex **Pineland**				
Ariceen	135.8 × 33 × 12.5	358	1917	Liverpool, N.S.
Ariel ex **J. K. Dawson**				
Arkona	97.8 × 27.6 × 10.9	143	1910	Mahone Bay, N.S.
Armistice	118.8 × 28.6 × 10.7	198	1919	Englee, Nfld.
Armorel	117 × 30.8 × 14.8	379	1918	Harbour Grace, Nfld.
Arnish	140.5 × 31.2 × 14.6	467	1917	St. George's, Nfld.
Arona	159.7 × 35 × 12.9	532	1891	Avonport, N.S.
Arrow	112.2 × 27.4 × 11.3	183	1902	Liverpool, N.S.

Name Registered	Dimensions	Net Tonnage	Year Built	Place Built
Arthur H. Wight	103 × 25.5 × 8.9	99	1904	Liverpool, N.S.
Arthur H. Zwicker★	158.8 × 36 × 12.9	507	1918	Chester Basin, N.S.
Arthur M. Gibson	131 × 31.5 × 11	296	1890	Gibson, N.B.
Asquith	126.4 × 31.4 × 11.5	271	1916	Bridgewater, N.S.
Athlete	114 × 29.2 × 12.4	197	1893	Advocate, N.S.
Renamed **Cousins Reunis**				
Audrey P. Brown	123.4 × 28.9 × 10.8	218	1919	Liverpool, N.S.
Augusto *ex* **Kathleen Crowe**				
Austin	126.3 × 31.3 × 17.2	320	1873	Tusket, N.S.
Ave Maria *ex* **F. S. Burgoyne**				
Avon Queen★ *ex* **Jessie Louise Fauquier**				
B. C. Borden	149.8 × 34.6 × 12.3	385	1894	Port Greville, N.S.
B. L. Rafuse	157.8 × 32.2 × 12.8	481	1918	Conquerall Bank, N.S.
B. P. King	96 × 24.5 × 9.7	133	1870	Shelburne, N.S.
B. R. Tower	140 × 33 × 10.9	343	1920	Diligent River, N.S.
Bahama	123 × 32.8 × 11.9	321	1892	Canning, N.S.
Renamed **Rescue**				
Balsa★ *ex* **Breakers**				
Barbara Barr	126.1 × 29.6 × 11.1	229	1918	Britannia Cove, Nfld.
Barbara MacDonald	96.1 × 25.5 × 9.8	162	1919	Cardigan, P.E.I.
Barbara W	127 × 31.5 × 11.7	286	1919	Port Greville, N.S.
Barnhill Bros.	144.4 × 34 × 12	374	1919	Two Rivers, N.S.
Bartholdi	126 × 30 × 12.2	298	1891	Black Point, N.S.
Bassilour *ex* **Mollie and Melba**				
Beatrice McLean	117.7 × 31 × 9.7	249	1889	Salmon River, N.B.
Beaver	117.8 × 28 × 9.2	192	1890	Perry's Point, N.B.
Beechland	170.5 × 35 × 12.9	419	1917	Annapolis, N.S.
Renamed **Klosofi, Club Nautico**				
Benefit	116.8 × 28.9 × 10.2	229	1900	Port Greville, N.S.
Bernice R	134 × 30.5 × 11.6	324	1918	Salmon River, N.S.
Beryl M. Corkum	121.5 × 30 × 11	248	1914	La Have, N.S.
Bessie A. Crooks	110.6 × 28.6 × 10.4	199	1913	Liverpool, N.S.
Bessie A. White★	182.6 × 37 × 12.9	594	1919	Alma, N.B.
Bessie Marie	108.6 × 26.4 × 10.5	152	1929	Burlington, Nfld.
Bessie Parker	117 × 29.6 × 10.4	227	1889	Tynemouth, N.B.
Bianca	not known	180	1888	Windsor, N.S.
First of name				
Bianca	129.1 × 33.2 × 11.7	313	1917	Liverpool, N.S.
Second of name				
Blanche H. Collins	163.6 × 35.7 × 13	503	1918	Little Brook, N.S.
Renamed **Algarve, Notre Dame D'Europa**				
Blandford	133.3 × 31.7 × 13.1	375	1914	Liverpool, N.S.
Blomidon	123 × 31.1 × 11.5	271	1891	Canning, N.S.
Bluenose	104 × 27 × 10.4	166	1903	Falmouth, N.S.
Boa Esperanca *ex* **King of Avon**				
Boa Sorte *ex* **Margaret Moulton**				
Bona H	147.6 × 35.5 × 12.2	415	1919	Hall's Harbour, N.S.
Bothnia *ex* **McPherson**				
Bravo	99.7 × 25.5 × 10	147	1895	Lunenburg, N.S.

Name Registered	Dimensions	Net Tonnage	Year Built	Place Built
Breakers★	161.1 × 35.6 × 13	517	1919	Yarmouth, N.S.
Renamed **Balsa, Edith C. Tilden**				
Bride	148.3 × 28.5 × 17.1	443	1873	Bideford, P.E.I.
Bridegroom	151.1 × 29.9 × 17.9	498	1874	Bideford, P.E.I.
Bridesmaid	157 × 29.7 × 17.3	487	1875	Bideford, P.E.I.
Renamed **Flora**				
Britannia	124.8 × 31.6 × 11.5	264	1900	Noel, N.S.
Brooklyn	116.4 × 30.4 × 11.8	247	1901	Liverpool, N.S.
Burin ex **Cape Pine**				
Burleigh	101 × 25.6 × 10.7	121	1904	Shelburne, N.S.
Burnett C	94.6 × 25.3 × 10.4	99	1909	La Have, N.S.
Burpee L. Tucker	156.5 × 35.5 × 13	465	1920	Port Greville, N.S.
C. Bryant	94 × 26.8 × 11	141	1921	Port Union, Nfld.
C. D. Pickels	172 × 33.4 × 12.5	400	1908	Bridgetown, N.S.
Renamed **Viuda de Orive**				
C. E. White	111.4 × 27.9 × 10.5	227	1886	Saint John, N.B.
C. Maud Gaskill	143.5 × 33.2 × 12.4	397	1919	Little Brook, N.S.
C. W. Mills	141 × 31.8 × 11.4	318	1904	Granville, N.S.
Calabria	151.8 × 35.4 × 16.2	530	1881	Parrsboro, N.S.
Caledonia	113 × 28.6 × 11	188	1903	Liverpool, N.S.
Cambrai★	165.7 × 35.8 × 13	529	1918	River John, N.S.
Camp Boulhaut ex **Letitia T. McKay**				
Canada	116.9 × 27.5 × 10.6	199	1900	Lunenburg, N.S.
Canadian Maid	128 × 28.8 × 11.8	294	1919	Church Point, N.S.
Canaria	128 × 30.6 × 10.4	242	1893	Salmon River, N.B.
Cape Blomidon	144.9 × 34.1 × 13	408	1919	Canning, N.S.
Cape Bonavista ex **A. Moulton**				
Cape D'Or	133.5 × 34.5 × 12.8	373	1918	Cape D'Or, N.S.
Cape La Have	137.8 × 32.2 × 12.3	316	1918	Yarmouth, N.S.
Cape Pine	126.7 × 32.2 × 11.8	311	1919	Allendale, N.S.
Renamed **Burin**				
Cape Race	126.7 × 32.2 × 11.7	332	1918	Liverpool, N.S.
Capitaine Huet ex **Scotia Belle**				
Carib II	112 × 28 × 11.2	195	1901	Shelburne, N.S.
Carlotta	104.9 × 27.7 × 11.3	244	1882	Hopewell Cape, N.B.
Carl R. Tibbo	103.1 × 28.4 × 11.6	173	1918	Grand Bank, Nfld.
Carrie M. Wamback	113.7 × 26.1 × 10.6	109	1912	Liverpool, N.S.
Cashier★	170 × 37 × 13.7	663	1918	Sheet Harbour, N.S.
Castano	118 × 29 × 10.6	215	1901	Bear River, N.S.
Catherine	109.4 × 28.5 × 10.3	196	1903	Meteghan River, N.S.
Catherine M. Moulton	119.2 × 26 × 11.4	155	1919	Conquerall Bank, N.S.
Cavalier	109 × 28 × 10.5	234	1893	Pugwash, N.S.
Cecil Jr.	115.2 × 28.2 × 11.3	204	1918	Shelburne, N.S.
Celeste D	164 × 37.4 × 15.6	595	1919	Meteghan River, N.S.
Celina K. Goldman	158.8 × 35 × 12.4	477	1918	St. Martin's, N.B.
Renamed **Chivo**				
Charles A. Ritcey	138 × 32.6 × 12	360	1917	Meteghan, N.S.
Charles and Vernon	136.2 × 32 × 11.8	296	1919	Bridgewater, N.S.
Charles E. Scammel	126 × 28 × 10	254	1872	Saint John, N.B.

Name Registered	Dimensions	Net Tonnage	Year Built	Place Built
Charles F. Gordon	139 × 33.7 × 12.7	369	1919	Weymouth, N.S.
Renamed **J. O. Webster, J. T. Wing, Oliver H. Perry**				
Charles Theriault	130 × 31.6 × 12	282	1918	Belliveau Cove, N.S.
Renamed **Pierre Tristan**				
Charlevoix	154 × 34.3 × 12.8	427	1899	Port Greville, N.S.
Charlotte Comeau★	172 × 37.4 × 15.5	728	1919	Little Brook, N.S.
Chautauqua	137.1 × 32.8 × 12.2	354	1918	Liverpool, N.S.
Cheslie	129.2 × 33 × 12	330	1896	Port Greville, N.S.
Chevalier Bayard *ex* **Adam B. McKay**				
Chivo *ex* **Celina K. Goldman**				
Chrissie C. Thomey	102 × 26.9 × 10	123	1908	Burgeo, Nfld.
Christina	135 × 31.6 × 12	365	1874	St. Andrew's, N.B.
Citnalta *ex* **Esther Adelaide**				
Citta de Genova *ex* **Adamac**				
Ciudad de Tarragona *ex* **Prydwen**				
Clara J. Wilbur	107 × 28.1 × 10.5	197	1883	Dorchester, N.B.
Clarence A. Moulton	115 × 30 × 10.7	248	1918	New Glasgow, N.S.
Clifton	135.4 × 32.4 × 16	473	1883	Windsor, N.S.
Club Nautico *ex* **Beechland**				
Cobo *ex* **Randfontein**				
Coniston	143.1 × 32.7 × 11	360	1891	Saint John, N.B.
Conrad S	137.3 × 32.1 × 11.2	283	1908	Fox River, N.S.
Renamed **George B. Cluett**				
Con Rein	129.5 × 30.6 × 11.6	299	1919	La Have, N.S.
Coral Leaf	150.5 × 33.6 × 12.7	374	1902	Spencer's Id., N.S.
Corona	98.6 × 25.8 × 10.4	179	1904	Cardigan, P.E.I.
Cote Nord	125.2 × 26.6 × 10.6	147	1920	Mahone Bay, N.S.
Renamed **Amphitrite**				
Cousins Reunis *ex* **Athlete**				
County of Richmond	107.3 × 31 × 12.4	245	1919	Johnstown, C.B., N.S.
Crescendo	114.9 × 30 × 9.9	196	1910	Port Greville, N.S.
Cristina *ex* **J. E. Pettis**				
Cumberland County	149.4 × 35.8 × 12.6	425	1916	Advocate Harbour, N.S.
Renamed **Pauline C. Cummings**				
Cumberland Queen★	179 × 38 × 13.2	634	1919	Diligent River, N.S.
Renamed **Emerett**				
Cutty Sark★	181.6 × 36 × 16	609	1919	Saint John, N.B.
Cynthia J. Griffin				
ex **Marion G. Douglas**				
Cyril	93.2 × 25 × 9.6	74	1901	Mahone Bay, N.S.
Cyril T	92 × 27 × 9	117	1918	River John, N.S.
D. D. McKenzie	119.9 × 25 × 11	148	1920	Chester Basin, N.S.
Renamed **Sachem**				
Daisy *ex* **Katherine V. Mills**				
Damaraland	113 × 30.4 × 10.8	198	1902	Liverpool, N.S.
Daniel Getson	132.6 × 32 × 11.6	295	1917	Bridgewater, N.S.
Renamed **Wanderthirst**				
Dara C	146 × 35 × 12.8	380	1901	Port Greville, N.S.
Davida	126.9 × 25.6 × 16.4	377	1881	Parrsboro, N.S.

Name Registered	Dimensions	Net Tonnage	Year Built	Place Built
David C. Ritcey	124.6 × 32 × 11.4	284	1913	Liverpool, N.S.
Dawn Wilkie ex Nettie C.				
Deerhill	136.6 × 33.2 × 11	332	1891	Moss Glen, N.B.
Delight	85 × 23.9 × 9.2	109	1894	Souris, P.E.I.
Delta	118.8 × 30.5 × 11.9	286	1892	Cheverie, N.S.
Devonport	119 × 27.8 × 12.5	291	1878	Georgetown, P.E.I.
Dilia ex Leah A. Whidden				
Doane	129.6 × 33.9 × 11.8	291	1913	Port Greville, N.S.
Dobbie	118 × 30 × 12	274	1918	Port Blandford, Nfld.
Renamed Miquelon				
Don Parsons	154.1 × 34.2 × 12.4	427	1918	Cheverie, N.S.
Donald and Keith	120 × 29.7 × 11	285	1918	White's Cove, N.S.
Renamed Rouzic				
Donald II	109.6 × 27 × 11.2	200	1918	Shelburne, N.S.
Donald T	116.4 × 26.3 × 11.4	162	1920	Dayspring, N.S.
Doris M. Pickup	141 × 33 × 12.3	372	1901	Annapolis, N.S.
Dornfontein*	171.1 × 40.1 × 13.2	666	1918	Saint John, N.B.
Dorothy Baird ex Emma E. Whidden				
Dorothy Duff ex Dorothy M. Porter				
Dorothy Lake	63.2 × 13.8 × 6.4	23.8	1911	Fortune, Nfld.
Dorothy Louise	106.9 × 27 × 10	125	1910	Allendale, N.S.
Dorothy M. Porter	98 × 26.7 × 10.6	152	1906	Falmouth, N.S.
Renamed Dorothy Duff				
Douaumont ex Harry Miller				
Douglas E. Parks	122.5 × 27.3 × 10.6	136	1919	La Have, N.S.
Drallim	126.9 × 32.9 × 12.8	379	1918	Brooklyn, N.S.
Duchess of Cornwall	105 × 25.6 × 10.4	129	1901	Burgeo, Nfld.
E. A. Post	107 × 25.5 × 17	198	1903	Shelburne, N.S.
E. A. Sabean	121.8 × 30.2 × 11.1	267	1901	Liverpool, N.S.
E. C. Adams	126.2 × 30.9 × 11.2	330	1919	Bridgewater, N.S.
E. D. Bailey	118.6 × 27.3 × 10	162	1918	Lunenburg, N.S.
E. E. Armstrong	139.5 × 33.6 × 12.1	371	1917	Hantsport, N.S.
E. Hogan	117.3 × 26.4 × 11.8	175	1918	Liverpool, N.S.
Renamed Protea				
E. H. Wharton Davies	152 × 35.9 × 12.9	463	1917	Advocate Harbour, N.S.
Renamed Maia, Solidor				
E. L. Comeau	169 × 37.3 × 13	539	1918	Meteghan, N.S.
Renamed Rosa Ferlita				
E. M. Roberts	133.2 × 32.9 × 12	296	1903	Port Greville, N.S.
E. Merriam	120 × 27.8 × 13	331	1882	Port Greville, N.S.
E. P. Theriault	140 × 32.3 × 13.3	254	1919	Belliveau Cove, N.S.
Renamed Ofelia Gancedo				
Earl Grey	144.3 × 34 × 12.1	379	1906	Port Greville, N.S.
Renamed Louise M. Richard				
Earl of Aberdeen	154.7 × 35.2 × 12.6	416	1894	Parrsboro, N.S.
Renamed Maria Helena, Maria Ferreira, Minho				
Edde Theriault	104 × 27.3 × 10	170	1904	Belliveau Cove, N.S.
Edgewood*	191 × 36.8 × 15.5	699	1918	Quebec
Edith Belliveau	122 × 30.2 × 10.2	238	1919	Belliveau Cove, N.S.

Name Registered	Dimensions	Net Tonnage	Year Built	Place Built
Edith C. Tilden *ex* **Breakers**				
Edith Dawson	144.6 × 33 × 12.7	397	1918	Bridgewater, N.S.
Edith M. Cavell	107.2 × 26.2 × 10.4	134	1916	Shelburne, N.S.
Renamed **Rosita, Finaldie**				
Edith M. Green	110 × 28.7 × 11.7	189	1917	Gilbert's Cove, N.S.
Renamed **Suzaky**				
Edna V. Pickels	154.5 × 35 × 12	388	1905	Salmon River, N.S.
Edward A. Cohan★	171.2 × 37.4 × 13	597	1919	Rexton, N.B.
Edyth	120.4 × 27.2 × 11.2	197	1901	Mahone Bay, N.S.
Efeu *ex* **Gordon**				
Effie Howard	58 × 14.6 × 6	23.6	1902	Sheet Harbour, N.S.
Eileen Lake	not known	200	1919	Fortune, Nfld.
Elias *ex* **James J. Joy**				
Elizabeth Fearn	137.9 × 27.6 × 11.6	246	1917	Placentia, Nfld.
Ella L. Winters	147.2 × 33.2 × 12	374	1918	Eatonville, N.S.
Ellice B *ex* **Helen Mathers**				
Elma	130.1 × 31 × 11.4	299	1892	Margaretsville, N.S.
Elsie	112 × 27 × 9.3	149	1903	Shelburne, N.S.
Emerett★ *ex* **Cumberland Queen**				
Emily Anderson	118.4 × 30.6 × 10	218	1906	Lower Selma, N.S.
Emily H. Patten	108.4 × 26 × 10.8	152	1916	Shelburne, N.S.
Emma Belliveau	125 × 30 × 10.5	223	1916	Belliveau Cove, N.S.
Emma E. Whidden	118.4 × 31.3 × 10.9	199	1907	Liverpool, N.S.
Renamed **Dorothy Baird**				
Emma R. Smith	130.8 × 29.8 × 15.6	387	1883	Hantsport, N.S.
Empress	118 × 30.8 × 12.6	335	1901	Montague, P.E.I.
Ena A. Moulton	116 × 27.8 × 11.5	180	1919	Issac's Harbour, N.S.
Ena F. Parsons	112.4 × 28.6 × 10.1	221	1920	Cheverie, N.S.
Enid E. Legge	118.1 × 27.6 × 10.9	233	1919	Mahone Bay, N.S.
Esther Adelaide	148 × 36 × 12.4	425	1917	Fox River, N.S.
Renamed **Citnalta**				
Esther Hankinson	138 × 32.4 × 9	292	1917	Belliveau Cove, N.S.
Estonia *ex* **Vincent A. White**				
Ethlyn	128.6 × 28.6 × 11	169	1919	Mahone Bay, N.S.
Renamed **Palma de Ozama**				
Ethyl B. Sumner	136.9 × 33 × 12.1	353	1901	Harvey, N.B.
Eugenie Owen McKay★	167 × 36 × 13	560	1918	Diligent River, N.S.
Eva C	126.5 × 31 × 10.6	250	1909	Port Greville, N.S.
Eva Maud	114 × 27.7 × 13	267	1880	Maitland, N.S.
Evadne	129.2 × 34 × 12.1	361	1900	River John, N.S.
Eveline Wilkie	138.5 × 32.6 × 12.1	349	1918	Margaretsville, N.S.
Evelyn	107 × 26.5 × 10.6	167	1899	Shelburne, N.S.
Evelyn	142.6 × 30.9 × 11.5	287	1907	Granville, N.S.
Exception	143.5 × 33.5 × 12.6	380	1892	Spencer's Id., N.S.
Exilda	144.9 × 34 × 11.4	349	1908	Port Greville, N.S.
Experiment	9ft. draft	228	1872	Shelburne, N.S.
F.A.J.E.	149.2 × 33.5 × 11.5	357	1916	Port Greville, N.S.
Renamed **M.F.C.**				
F. C. Lockhart	125 × 31.4 × 11.8	268	1910	Annapolis Royal, N.S.

Name Registered	Dimensions	Net Tonnage	Year Built	Place Built
F. Richard	81.5 × 23 × 8.2	94	1882	Meteghan, N.S.
F. S. Burgoyne	135 × 28 × 11.3	143	1920	Mahone Bay, N.S.
Renamed **Ave Maria**				
F. W. Pickels	146 × 33 × 12.5	385	1902	Bridgetown, N.S.
Farlings	122.6 × 34 × 12	410	1918	Weymouth, N.S.
Faustina	103.1 × 26.2 × 10.7	146	1919	Liverpool, N.S.
Favonian	142.2 × 33.7 × 12.2	428	1919	Falmouth, N.S.
Fieldwood	154.6 × 33.8 × 13	435	1920	Canning, N.S.
Fiette *ex* **Katherine V. Mills**				
Finaldie *ex* **Edith M. Cavell**				
Fisherman *ex* **Marshal Foch**				
Fleetly	108.5 × 29 × 10.8	174	1908	Bridgewater, N.S.
Fleur de France *ex* **Racewell**				
Flora *ex* **Bridesmaid**				
Florence R. Hewson	133 × 31 × 12	289	1893	Parrsboro, N.S.
Florence Swyers	101.7 × 29.4 × 11.6	157	1918	Charlottetown, Nfld.
Flowerdew	111.9 × 31.9 × 12.3	306	1918	Shelburne, N.S.
Foldin I *ex* **Randfontein**				
Fort Garry *ex* **Albert Revillon**				
Frances	120 × 29.3 × 11.2	259	1903	Weymouth, N.S.
Frances	125.2 × 31 × 11	293	1889	Saint John, N.B.
Frances E. Moulton	122.5 × 28 × 10.3	208	1919	Mahone Bay, N.S.
Frances Inness	129.9 × 32 × 11.7	299	1917	Liverpool, N.S.
Frances J. Elkin	165.3 × 36.8 × 13	555	1918	Church Point, N.S.
Frances Louise	125.6 × 28.2 × 10.2	147	1917	Lunenburg, N.S.
Renamed **Three Sisters**				
Frances Parsons	112.8 × 31 × 11.1	237	1919	Cheverie, N.S.
Frank R. Forsey	115.8 × 25.7 × 10.7	158	1917	Liverpool, N.S.
Frederick H	148 × 34.5 × 12.3	390	1920	Port Greville, N.S.
Frederick P. Elkin *ex* **Seaman, A.O.**				
Fred E. Scammell	118 × 28 × 10	234	1871	Saint John, N.B.
Fred H. Gibson	123 × 33 × 12.6	418	1894	St. Mary's, N.B.
Freddie C. Ebbett	not known	259	1873	Black River, N.B.
Freedom	112.9 × 28.6 × 10.9	197	1906	Liverpool, N.S.
Frieda E★	199 × 36.9 × 19	669	1918	Port Greville, N.S.
Fundy King	141 × 32.7 × 13.5	376	1919	Margaretsville, N.S.
Renamed **Maid of France, A. S. Publicover**				
G. Blanche	132 × 30.5 × 11.5	280	1917	Meteghan River, N.S.
G. E. Bentley	131.1 × 32.2 × 10.8	250	1892	Port Greville, N.S.
G. H. Murray	137.5 × 32.3 × 14.4	354	1919	Comeauville, N.S.
G. M. Cochrane	113.2 × 30 × 10.6	220	1905	Port Greville, N.S.
Renamed **Albania**				
G.T.D. *ex* **Tyree**				
Galena	130 × 32.6 × 12.9	381	1883	Hantsport, N.S.
Galiano *ex* **Jessy and Alice**				
Gazelle	133.7 × 30 × 10.5	263	1887	Courtney Bay, N.B.
General Allenby	109 × 26.8 × 11.1	145	1919	Grand Bank, Nfld.
General Byng	113.1 × 28.1 × 11.5	196	1918	Marystown, Nfld.
General Currie	107.4 × 26.6 × 10.6	162	1918	Grand Bank, Nfld.

Name Registered	Dimensions	Net Tonnage	Year Built	Place Built
General George H. Hogg	146.5 × 34.5 × 12.5	407	1918	Canning, N.S.
General Horne	107.6 × 26.1 × 10.2	179	1919	Shelburne, N.S.
General Ironsides	110.2 × 27.3 × 11.4	157	1920	Grand Bank, Nfld.
Renamed **Nossa Senora dos Anjos**				
General Jacobs	108.6 × 25.7 × 10.3	167	1919	Shelburne, N.S.
Renamed **John Millet**				
General Knox	106.4 × 27 × 11	155	1919	Marystown, Nfld.
General Laurie	112.6 × 29.2 × 10.5	198	1908	Allendale, N.S.
General Maude	104.6 × 25.7 × 10.4	140	1917	Shelburne, N.S.
General Pau	122.1 × 32 × 12.7	329	1919	Brooklyn, N.S.
General Plumer	102.4 × 26.6 × 10.3	149	1919	Allendale, N.S.
General Rawlinson	106.9 × 26.9 × 11.1	149	1920	Marystown, Nfld.
Renamed **Pacos de Brando**				
General Smuts	107.1 × 30.2 × 10.2	159	1918	Shelburne, N.S.
General Trenchard	106.5 × 26.2 × 10.4	149	1920	Allendale, N.S.
George B. Cluett *ex* **Conrad S.**				
George Ewart	99.6 × 26.2 × 11	148	1913	Fortune, Nfld.
George Melville Cochrane★	183.5 × 37 × 18.9	820	1919	Port Greville, N.S.
Georgina Roop	162 × 35.3 × 12	398	1906	Granville Ferry, N.S.
Renamed **Pineland, Argo**				
Germain L	96.3 × 26.7 × 9.3	145	1919	Ste. Anne des Monts, Que.
Renamed **Quebec Trader**				
Gertie	63.6 × 20 × 6.6	45	1893	Windsor, N.S.
Gertrude Parsons	132.5 × 31.1 × 12.3	341	1919	Cheverie, N.S.
Gilbert Islands	119.8 × 30.9 × 11.6	245	1915	Liverpool, N.S.
Gladys M. Hollett	113.2 × 26.7 × 10.6	150	1917	Shelburne, N.S.
Gladys McLaughlin	141.7 × 32.7 × 12.7	420	1892	Hopewell Cape, N.B.
Gladys Street *ex* **Madeira**	101.9 × 25 × 10.2	Remeasured and rebuilt 1919, Sheet Hbr., N.S.		
Glenrosa	142.7 × 31.2 × 13	504	1890	Cheverie, N.S.
Golden Rod *ex* **Sir Donald**				
Golden Rule	104 × 25.5 × 9	163	1902	Shelburne, N.S.
Gorden	138.5 × 26.5 × 16.3	350	1878	Bideford, P.E.I.
Renamed **Push, Efeu, Potengy**				
Gordon E. Moulton	122.6 × 27.6 × 10.7	195	1919	Dayspring, N.S.
Gordon T. Tibbo	121 × 26.4 × 11.6	154	1918	Liverpool, N.S.
Governor Parr★	200 × 39.8 × 18.5	912	1918	Parrsboro, N.S.
Grace Rice	87 × 25.4 × 9.9	145	1883	Weymouth, N.S.
Grand Falls	113 × 26.3 × 10	113	1910	Shelburne, N.S.
Granville	123.9 × 30 × 11.3	300	1889	Parker's Cove, N.S.
Grenada	161 × 34.6 × 15.1	635	1888	Horton, N.S.
Guiseppe *ex* **Rothesay**				
Gunn and Anderson Brothers	140.4 × 33.4 × 12.1	362	1920	Sherbrooke, N.S.
Gwendolen Warren	125 × 30.8 × 10.7	274	1916	Liverpool, N.S.
Gwenmarena *ex* **Souvenir**				
Gypsum Emperor★	166 × 36 × 16	695	1892	Parrsboro, N.S.
Gypsum Empress★	174 × 36.4 × 16.5	723	1892	Horton, N.S.
Gypsum King	161 × 37.4 × 17.6	640	1890	Parrsboro, N.S.
Renamed **Millie**				

Name Registered	Dimensions	Net Tonnage	Year Built	Place Built
Gypsum Prince★	174 × 35.7 × 16.7	723	1892	Hantsport, N.S.
Gypsum Princess	169 × 36 × 18.8	664	1892	Parrsboro, N.S.
Gypsum Queen	155.5 × 37.8 × 16	609	1891	Parrsboro, N.S.
H. B. Homan	131.5 × 31.1 × 10.5	299	1888	Courtney Bay, N.B.
H. J. Logan★	175.3 × 37.3 × 18.9	772	1902	Parrsboro, N.S.
H. P. Kirkham	101 × 27 × 11	186	1891	Liverpool, N.S.
H. R. Silver	114 × 29 × 10.7	199	1907	Lunenburg, N.S.
Harry	153.8 × 35 × 12.5	421	1892	Parrsboro, N.S.
Harry	165.5 × 28.1 × 17.4	525	1881	Prince Edward Island
Harry A. McLellan★	178.4 × 35.5 × 14.4	643	1919	Campbellton, N.B.
Harry Miller	114.1 × 30 × 10.3	243	1904	Waterborough, N.B.
Renamed **Douaumont**				
Harry Troop	116.6 × 28 × 10.6	199	1901	Liverpool, N.S.
Harry W. Lewis	121.6 × 31.5 × 11	297	1889	Hopewell Cape, N.B.
Hartney W	123.3 × 32.2 × 11.2	271	1903	Port Greville, N.S.
Hattie May	94.6 × 25.1 × 10	149	1890	Clifton, N.S.
Havelock	112 × 30.3 × 11.2	212	1901	Bridgetown, N.S.
Renamed **San Jose, Jose Luis Orive, Tres Amigos**				
Hazel L. Myra	109.6 × 27.6 × 11.4	191	1920	Bridgewater, N.S.
Hazel Trahey	93.4 × 28.6 × 9	125	1910	Parrsboro, N.S.
Helen	115.6 × 31 × 11	198	1904	Liverpool, N.S.
Helen E. Kenny	126.8 × 30.2 × 11.5	294	1891	Black River, N.B.
Helen Jean	99.4 × 27.6 × 10.7	117	1920	Milltown, Nfld.
Helen Mathers	140.8 × 32.9 × 13.4	363	1919	Shelburne, N.S.
Renamed **South Head, Ellice B.**				
Helen Stewart	102.2 × 28 × 10.8	180	1903	Lunenburg, N.S.
Helene *ex* **Moss Rose**				
Herbert Fearn	131.6 × 30.9 × 11.3	325	1919	Placentia, Nfld.
Renamed **Jean F. McCrae, Mildred Pauline**				
Herbert J. Olive	12ft draft	315	1873	Carleton, N.B.
Herbert Warren	129 × 31.5 × 11.4	272	1917	Grosse Cocques, N.S.
Hibernia	132.5 × 31.8 × 11.7	298	1902	Noel, N.S.
Hieronymous *ex* **King of Avon**				
Hilda M. Stark	171.5 × 35 × 13.2	510	1918	Annapolis, N.S.
Renamed **Stranger**				
Hilda R	120 × 26 × 11	99	1910	La Have, N.S.
Hillcrest	132.6 × 32.5 × 11.8	299	1916	Lunenburg, N.S.
Hiram D. MacLean	152 × 35.5 × 12.8	447	1919	Economy, N.S.
Renamed **St. Pierraise**				
Holmes, A. Frank★	174 × 38.5 × 13	637	1919	Nordin, N.B.
Hugh S *ex* **Ida Bentley**				
Humorist	111.6 × 26.6 × 12.6	141	1921	Trinity Bay, Nfld.
Huntley★	175.8 × 37 × 12.7	520	1918	Scott's Bay, N.S.
Ida Bentley	154.2 × 34.2 × 12.8	430	1905	Port Greville, N.S.
Renamed **Hugh S**				
Ida M. Shafner	101 × 29.7 × 10.3	184	1888	Bridgetown, N.S.
Ida M. Zinck	117.2 × 27.4 × 10.6	113	1912	Liverpool, N.S.
Renamed **Marie Azelma**				
Impressive	129.7 × 32.1 × 12	341	1918	Ship Harbour, N.S.

Name Registered	Dimensions	Net Tonnage	Year Built	Place Built
Imprimus	123.9 × 29.7 × 13.3	177	1917	Port Blandford, Nfld.
Industrial	112.5 × 30 × 11.6	287	1918	Salmon River, N.S.
Inga	100.2 × 27 × 10.3	161	1908	La Have, N.S.
Innovation	120.6 × 28.4 × 10.8	190	1919	Dayspring, N.S.
Inspiration	129 × 30.2 × 11.6	283	1917	Conquerall Bank, N.S.
Integral	135.6 × 32 × 12	343	1917	Conquerall Bank, N.S.
Invictus	150 × 32 × 11.5	327	1904	Salmon River, N.S.
Iolanthe	128 × 32.5 × 13	393	1883	Avondale, N.S.
Irene Forsyth ex Maclean Clan				
Irene Myrtle ex Maclean Clan				
Irma Bentley	151.5 × 35.5 × 12.4	414	1908	Port Greville, N.S.
Isabel ex Leah A. Whidden				
Isis ex Emma R. Smith				
Isobel Moore	122 × 26 × 10.6	157	1920	Liverpool, N.S.
Ivanhoe	103 × 25.9 × 9	99	1904	Liverpool, N.S.
J. E. Backman	145.2 × 33.6 × 13	399	1918	Meteghan, N.S.
J. E. Pettis	119.9 × 29.4 × 12.4	292	1879	Parrsboro, N.S.
Renamed **Cristina**				
J. K. Dawson	124.4 × 30.5 × 10.7	249	1900	Liverpool, N.S.
Renamed **Ariel**				
J. L. Nelson	124.4 × 29.4 × 11	249	1902	Lunenburg, N.S.
Renamed **Annettina**				
J. L. Ralston	156.5 × 35.6 × 13	462	1919	Eatonville, N.S.
J. Miller	140.3 × 34.4 × 11.8	357	1918	Noel, N.S.
Renamed **Aghios Andreas**				
J. N. Rafuse	113.4 × 28.3 × 11.6	212	1913	La Have, N.S.
J. O. Webster ex Charles F. Gordon				
J. Scott Hankinson ex Acadian				
J. S. Sterry ex P. J. Palmer				
J. T. Wing ex Charles F. Gordon				
J. W. Comeau	134 × 32 × 13.1	343	1919	Comeauville, N.S.
J. W. Durant	91.8 × 26.9 × 9.3	124	1890	Parrsboro, N.S.
J. W. Hutt	140.5 × 32 × 12.3	349	1901	Liverpool, N.S.
James J. Joy	136.3 × 33 × 12.4	391	1918	Liverpool, N.S.
Renamed **Elias, Zetta**				
James William	146.4 × 33.5 × 12.7	440	1908	New Glasgow, N.S.
James Wotherspoon	129.7 × 31.4 × 9.8	268	1889	Port Greville, N.S.
Jean	118 × 28.9 × 11	190	1905	Liverpool, N.S.
Jean and Mary	114.5 × 28.4 × 11.4	194	1918	Marystown, Nfld.
Jean Campbell	129.2 × 30.7 × 12.5	277	1917	Shelburne, N.S.
Jean Dundonald Duff	123.6 × 31.8 × 12.8	345	1917	Mahone Bay, N.S.
Jean F. Anderson	140 × 33.3 × 12.6	396	1919	Port Wade, N.S.
Jean F. McCrae ex Herbert Fearn				
Jean McKay	119.3 × 27.1 × 11.3	194	1918	Shelburne, N.S.
Jeanne A. Pickels	139 × 33 × 12	299	1909	Bridgetown, N.S.
Jennie Parker	112 × 29.2 × 10.2	211	1887	Tynemouth, N.B.
Jennie V. Merriam	156.4 × 35 × 12.8	454	1919	Port Greville, N.S.
Jessie Louise Fauquier★	201.8 × 39.2 × 18.5	939	1918	Hantsport, N.S.
Renamed **Avon Queen**				

Name Registered	Dimensions	Net Tonnage	Year Built	Place Built
Jessy and Alice	91.4 × 24.3 × 9.6	110	1920	Dingwall, C.B., N.S.
Renamed **Galiano**				
Joan Hickman	129.1 × 28.4 × 12	295	1917	Charlottetown, Nfld.
Joao Sinho *ex* Mollie and Melba				
Johan *ex* Racewell				
John E. Lake	not known	202	1919	Fortune, Nfld.
John E. Shatford	100 × 25.6 × 10.6	154	1890	Shelburne, N.S.
Renamed **Vera Cruz II**				
John G. Walter	114.5 × 31.3 × 10.2	209	1903	Parrsboro, N.S.
John Harvey	not known		1912	Belleoram, Nfld.
John M. Wood	115 × 29.5 × 12	273	1919	Mahone Bay, N.S.
John Millet *ex* General Jacobs				
John S. Parker	123 × 29.9 × 10.5	239	1891	Tynemouth, N.B.
John W. Miller	122.5 × 30.5 × 11.5	266	1918	Mahone Bay, N.S.
Jose Luis Orive *ex* Havelock				
Jost	134.1 × 32.2 × 11.2	299	1910	Port Greville, N.S.
Juanita	102.9 × 23.1 × 9.1	147	1897	Liverpool, N.S.
Katheen	140 × 32.9 × 10.6	356	1918	Norris Arm, Nfld.
Katherine V. Mills	118 × 29.8 × 10.2	216	1908	Granville Ferry, N.S.
Renamed **Fiette, Daisy**				
Kathleen Crowe	146.5 × 35.6 × 12.8	431	1917	Hillsburn, N.S.
Renamed **Sarah, Augusto**				
Kay and Em *ex* Roseway				
Keewadon	108 × 28.4 × 10.1	189	1889	Port Greville, N.S.
Renamed **Myrtle V. Hopkins**				
Kenneth C	162.2 × 35.4 × 12.9	475	1907	Port Greville, N.S.
Kildare *ex* A. J. McKean				
King of Avon	156 × 35.2 × 12.8	417	1904	Hantsport, N.S.
Renamed **Hieronymous, Boa Esperanca**				
Klosofi *ex* Beechland				
L. C. Tower★	175.5 × 36.4 × 12.9	518	1915	Port Greville, N.S.
L. W. Norton	139 × 33 × 15.4	510 (gr.)	1890	Hantsport, N.S.
La Parisienne *ex* Mary G. Duff				
La Plata	141.9 × 29.9 × 10.2	350	1889	Saint John, N.B.
Laconia	149.3 × 37.2 × 12.8	485	1890	Port Greville, N.S.
Lady Mulgrave	87 × 20.3 × 10.1	108	1858	Arichat, N.S.
Lady of Avon	142 × 32.6 × 11	417	1902	Hantsport, N.S.
Ladysmith	176.2 × 35.9 × 17.9	596	1902	Lower Economy, N.S.
Laura	129.6 × 31 × 12.4	299	1901	Liverpool, N.S.
Laura C	122.6 × 30.5 × 11	249	1902	La Have, N.S.
Lavengro	127 × 30.4 × 12.9	269	1909	Shelburne, N.S.
Lavonia	129.2 × 32 × 10.7	266	1903	Port Greville, N.S.
Lawson	128.8 × 31 × 10.8	274	1909	Port Greville, N.S.
Le Mousquetaire *ex* St. Clair Ritcey				
Leah A. Whidden	117 × 31 × 10.8	199	1903	Liverpool, N.S.
Renamed **Isabel, Dilia**				
Lena Ford *ex* Ralph S. Parsons				
Lena Pickup	130 × 30.3 × 12	292	1890	Granville Ferry, N.S.
Leo	97.2 × 24.6 × 10.8	120	1882	Mahone Bay, N.S.

Name Registered	Dimensions	Net Tonnage	Year Built	Place Built
Leo LeBlanc	143.5 × 33.1 × 14.3	393	1919	Meteghan, N.S.
Leonard Parker	127.9 × 29.8 × 10.4	246	1897	Tynemouth, N.B.
Letitia L. McKay★	165 × 36 × 13	544	1916	Meteghan, N.S.
Renamed **Camp Boulhaut**				
Lewanika	128 × 32.3 × 11.2	298	1894	Port Greville, N.S.
Lewis Brothers★	178.5 × 37.4 × 14	675	1917	Sheet Harbour, N.S.
Lila E. D. Young	122.3 × 27.3 × 10.6	155	1919	Lunenburg, N.S.
Lillian Blauvelt	106 × 28 × 10.1	174	1902	Meteghan River, N.S.
Renamed **Marylucy**				
Lillian H	152.6 × 36 × 12.8	424	1916	Fox River, N.S.
Lillie	130.9 × 31.5 × 11.7	311	1894	Maitland, N.S.
Lily	136.5 × 28.5 × 12.5	368	1871	Hantsport, N.S.
Limelight	98.6 × 26.5 × 9	139	1908	Souris, P.E.I.
Rebuilt and renamed **Riseover II**				
Little Princess	122.4 × 28 × 10.9	199	1919	Dayspring, N.S.
Little Stepano	99.2 × 25.7 × 10	125	1917	Shelburne, N.S.
Lizzie R	112 × 26.6 × 11.1	210	1872	Hopewell, N.B.
Lolita A	100.6 × 29 × 10.8	176	1903	Liverpool, N.S.
Lord of Avon	132 × 32.5 × 11.9	325	1901	Hantsport, N.S.
Lothair	106.4 × 27 × 9.1	195	1871	Portland, N.B.
Louis B. Beauchamp *ex* **W. S. MacDonald**				
Louis Theriault	146.5 × 32.6 × 12	386	1918	Belliveau Cove, N.S.
Louise M. Richard *ex* **Earl Grey**				
Lucille	102.5 × 28.8 × 10	164	1906	Parrsboro, N.S.
Lucy R	96.5 × 23.3 × 8.9	104	1920	Church Point, N.S.
Maclean Clan	125.2 × 27.6 × 11.4	239	1920	Mahone Bay, N.S.
Renamed **Irene Myrtle, Irene Forsyth, Santa Clara**				
McClure	104.4 × 27.1 × 10.8	191	1900	Tatamagouche, N.S.
McPherson	122.3 × 28.4 × 12.6	271	1868	Halifax, N.S.
Renamed **Alfchild**				
M. A. Belliveau	115 × 30.2 × 10.2	199	1914	Belliveau Cove, N.S.
M. A. Nutter	120 × 28.2 × 11.7	291	1881	Portland, N.B.
M.F.C. *ex* **F.A.J.E.**				
M. J. Taylor	150.5 × 33.6 × 12.7	377	1901	Spencer's Island, N.S.
M. L. Bonnell	127.4 × 31 × 10.9	297	1889	Saint John, N.B.
M. O. Crowell	135.6 × 32.2 × 12	416	1919	Ship Harbour, N.S.
Mabel Davis	126 × 28.2 × 11.2	188	1918	Boyd's Arm, Nfld.
Mabel E. Gunn	142 × 33.5 × 11.5	367	1919	Sherbrooke, N.S.
Madeira	101.9 × 25 × 10.2	123	1898	Lunenburg, N.S.
Rebuilt and renamed **Gladys Street**				
Magellan	103 × 28 × 11.6	226	1882	Hopewell, N.B.
Maia *ex* **E. H. Wharton Davies**				
Maid of Brazil	141 × 32.6 × 12.8	387	1918	Grosse Coques, N.S.
Renamed **Oma, Notre Dame de Bizeux**				
Maid of Canada	128 × 31.3 × 13.5	330	1918	Weymouth, N.S.
Maid of France *ex* **Fundy King**				
Maid of Harlech	124.5 × 31.3 × 10.7	270	1917	Liverpool, N.S.
Maid of La Have	111.3 × 29.6 × 12.7	222	1919	Dayspring, N.S.
Maid of Scotland	148 × 33.2 × 12.7	439	1919	Grosse Coques, N.S.

Name Registered	Dimensions	Net Tonnage	Year Built	Place Built
Maplefield	146.5 × 32.3 × 12.1	411	1918	Belliveau Cove, N.S.
Mapleland	173 × 35 × 13.3	566	1919	Annapolis Royal, N.S.
Maple Leaf	48 × 15 × 5	21	1902	Welford, N.B.
Maple Leaf	120.1 × 30 × 11	199	1901	Chester Basin, N.S.
Margaret F. Dick★	199 × 39.1 × 18.5	989	1918	Hantsport, N.S.
Margaret G	138.9 × 32.2 × 11.1	299	1902	Port Greville, N.S.
Margaret May Riley	123.5 × 30.5 × 11.2	241	1900	Granville, N.S.
Renamed **Roclincourt**				
Margaret Moulton	120.4 × 28 × 12.5	174	1918	Dayspring, N.S.
Renamed **Boa Sorte, Maria Carlota**				
Margery Mahaffy	116.2 × 27 × 11	143	1918	Mahone Bay, N.S.
Marguerite Ryan	106.6 × 26.4 × 10.8	147	1920	Shelburne, N.S.
Maria A. Howes	143 × 34.4 × 13	425	1919	Meteghan River, N.S.
Maria Carlota *ex* **Margaret Moulton**				
Maria Ferreira *ex* **Earl of Aberdeen**				
Maria Helena *ex* **Earl of Aberdeen**				
Marian J. Smith	128.2 × 33.8 × 11.4	332	1916	Liverpool, N.S.
Marie Amelie *ex* **Minnie F. Crosby**				
Marie Azelma *ex* **Ida M. Zinck**				
Marie Louise H	140.1 × 31.6 × 13.6	383	1919	Charlottetown, Nfld.
Marine	147 × 34.8 × 13	453	1919	Weymouth, N.S.
Marion G. Douglas	166.4 × 36 × 12.8	449	1917	Fox River, N.S.
Renamed **Cynthia J. Griffin, Mary Lou**				
Marion L. Conrad	134.3 × 27.5 × 11.2	155	1920	La Have, N.S.
Marion Grace	87 × 19.6 × 9.3	81	1918	Port Hawkesbury, N.S.
Marion Louise	106.9 × 28.2 × 10.7	196	1901	Pugwash, N.S.
Maritana	156.6 × 32.2 × 13	490	1903	River John, N.S.
Marjorie J. Sumner	136 × 31 × 12.8	354	1902	Maitland, N.S.
Marjorie McGlashen	113.7 × 26.1 × 10.6	109	1915	Liverpool, N.S.
Marshal Foch	134.4 × 35 × 11.6	351	1919	Ward's Brook, N.S.
Renamed **Fisherman**				
Martha Parsons	158.9 × 34.5 × 13	455	1918	Cheverie, N.S.
Mary B. Brooks	99 × 30.1 × 10.1	214	1926	Plympton, N.S.
Mary D. Young	114.2 × 26.3 × 10.2	99	1912	Lunenburg, N.S.
Mary F. Anderson	139.3 × 34 × 11.5	418	1920	River John, N.S.
Mary G. Duff	143 × 32.5 × 11.6	349	1919	Chester Basin, N.S.
Renamed **La Parisienne**				
Mary Hendry	124.2 × 28.4 × 11.7	249	1899	Liverpool, N.S.
Mary Lou *ex* **Marion G. Douglas**				
Mary L. Oxner	120 × 28 × 11	169	1920	Chester Basin, N.S.
Marylucy *ex* **Lillian Blauvelt**				
Max Horton	118.2 × 25.8 × 11.4	139	1918	Conquerall Bank, N.S.
Maxwell C	125.7 × 27.6 × 11	170	1920	Little Brook, N.S.
Renamed **Albert Revillon, Fort Garry**				
Melanson Brothers	120 × 28 × 12	288	1920	Gilbert's Cove, N.S.
Melba	142.4 × 32.4 × 12.4	388	1899	Gardiner's Creek, N.B.
Melolie *ex* **Randfontein**				
Meridith A. White	163.4 × 35.5 × 12.8	453	1918	Alma, N.B.
Mersey	117.4 × 28.5 × 10.9	190	1905	Liverpool, N.S.

Name Registered	Dimensions	Net Tonnage	Year Built	Place Built
Mildred	107 × 27 × 10.8	166	1907	Lunenburg, N.S.
Mildred B ex W. S. M. Bentley				
Mildred Pauline ex Herbert Fearn				
Millie ex Gypsum King				
Milnorine	146.3 × 33.5 × 12	366	1918	Port Greville, N.S.
Mina Nadeau	120 × 32 × 11	316	1920	Port Daniel, Que.
Minas King	154.2 × 36 × 12.8	470	1919	Bass River, N.S.
Minas Prince	149.5 × 35.8 × 12.7	457	1919	Spencer's Id., N.S.
Minas Princess	152.5 × 35.8 × 12.7	465	1919	Spencer's Id., N.S.
Minas Queen	170 × 35.4 × 12.9	456	1916	Parrsboro, N.S.
Mineola	127.2 × 32 × 10.7	270	1902	Port Greville, N.S.
Minerva ex Mola				
Minho ex Earl of Aberdeen				
Minnie F. Crosby	100.8 × 27.2 × 10	119	1908	La Have, N.S.
Renamed Marie Amelie				
Minnie G. Parsons	138 × 33.5 × 11.3	321	1916	Cheverie, N.S.
Minnie Louise	101 × 27.5 × 11.8	223	1883	Sherbrooke, N.S.
Mintie	93 × 24 × 9.6	100	1918	Trinity Bay, Nfld.
Miquelon ex Dobbie				
Miriam H	146 × 33.3 × 12.4	359	1918	Saulnierville, N.S.
Misty Star	131 × 31 × 11.7	270	1917	Shelburne, N.S.
Moama	143.1 × 32.7 × 12	384	1892	Black River, N.B.
Mola	137.8 × 32.6 × 11.1	351	1892	Black River, N.B.
Renamed Minerva				
Molega	91.7 × 27 × 8.2	148	1888	Conquerall, N.S.
Mollie and Melba	141 × 32.6 × 12.8	388	1918	Grosse Cocques, N.S.
Renamed Bassilour, Joao Sinho				
Mollie Fearn	102 × 27.2 × 9.6	118	1920	Placentia, Nfld.
Renamed Tishy				
Mona	126.6 × 32.9 × 12	299	1903	Liverpool, N.S.
Monchey	not known		1920	Harbour Grace, Nfld.
Moneta	115 × 28.6 × 10.6	199	1891	Annapolis, N.S.
Montclair	142.4 × 33.6 × 13	419	1918	Yarmouth, N.S.
Montrose	113 × 30 × 11.3	198	1906	Shelburne, N.S.
Morales	105.1 × 26.7 × 10.6	168	1896	Lunenburg, N.S.
Morning Dew	130 × 28 × 12	279	1873	Saint John, N.B.
Moskwa	152.5 × 35 × 15.9	593	1890	Saint John, N.B.
Moss Glen	109.6 × 27.3 × 8.9	198	1873	Saint John, N.B.
Moss Rose	88.6 × 26.3 × 10.4	149	1892	Pleasantville, N.S.
Renamed Helene				
Motherland	167 × 34.8 × 12.8	384	1917	Meteghan, N.S.
Mount Pearl ex A. Moulton				
Mousquetaire ex St. Clair Ritcey				
Myrtle Leaf	135.8 × 33.3 × 12.4	336	1903	Spencer's Id., N.S.
Myrtle Piercy	104.7 × 26.7 × 10.2	149	1919	Liverpool, N.S.
Myrtle V. Hopkins ex Keewadon				
Narka	98.8 × 25.6 × 10.5	154	1896	Lunenburg, N.S.
Nancy Lee	116.1 × 28.6 × 10.6	114	1920	Campbellton, Nfld.
Neerod	92.3 × 27.2 × 7.3	129	1919	Norris Arm, Nfld.

Name Registered	Dimensions	Net Tonnage	Year Built	Place Built
Nellie Louise	115.4 × 29.3 × 11	243	1901	La Have, N.S.
Nellie M	114.9 × 29.1 × 11.4	231	1900	Burnt Bay, Nfld.
Nellie T. Walters	113.4 × 26 × 10.5	139	1920	Shelburne, N.S.
Nettie C	150 × 33.3 × 13.1	387	1919	Saulnierville, N.S.
Renamed **Dawn Wilkie**				
Nettie Shaw	117 × 30.4 × 10.5	250	1890	Advocate, N.S.
Newburgh Renamed **Nievre**	135.8 × 32.8 × 15.8	481	1888	Windsor, N.S.
Newton Lake	not known	151	1920	Belleoram, Nfld.
Nievre ex **Newburgh**				
Nina L	88.5 × 24.2 × 10.2	95	1907	Notre Dame Bay, Nfld.
Nina L. C.	137 × 31 × 12.6	355	1918	Port Union, Nfld.
Norma B. Strong	106 × 27 × 12.4	157	1918	Little Bay Island, Nfld.
Normandie	138 × 30 × 11.3	217	1918	Shelburne, N.S.
Northcliffe	146.5 × 31.8 × 10.8	291	1918	Fox River, N.S.
Nossa Senora Dos Anjos ex **General Ironsides**				
Notre Dame de Bizeux ex **Maid of Brazil**				
Notre Dame D'Europa ex **Blanche H. Collins**				
Nova Queen	150 × 35 × 13	432	1919	Advocate, N.S.
Novelty	117.7 × 30.6 × 11.1	266	1910	Port Greville, N.S.
Ocean Lily	108 × 25.2 × 9	136	1885	Boularderie, C.B., N.S.
Ofelia Gancedo ex **E. P. Theriault**				
Olive Moore	120 × 25.8 × 11.6	158	1920	Liverpool, N.S.
Oliver H. Perry ex **Charles F. Gordon**				
Oma ex **Maid of Brazil**				
Omega	112 × 30.1 × 10.4	199	1896	Cheverie, N.S.
Ononette	156 × 35.2 × 13.2	483	1919	Annapolis, N.S.
Ophelia	98.5 × 25.2 × 9.5	120	1902	Shelburne, N.S.
Ophir	123.9 × 29.8 × 11.5	249	1901	Spencer's Id., N.S.
Optimist	100.5 × 24.3 × 11	110	1919	Glovertown, Nfld.
Orinoco	123.9 × 28.5 × 12.3	298	1883	Portland, N.B.
Over the Top	107.3 × 26.9 × 10	166	1919	Notre Dame Bay, Nfld.
Renamed **Sunner**				
P. J. McLaughlin	96.9 × 28 × 8.8	147	1909	Parrsboro, N.S.
P. J. Palmer	136.8 × 32.4 × 12.9	415	1881	Dorchester, N.B.
Renamed **J. S. Sterry**				
Pacos de Brando ex **General Rawlinson**				
Palma	123.5 × 29.1 × 11	249	1901	Lunenburg, N.S.
Palma de Ozama ex **Ethlyn**				
Pauline C. Cummings ex **Cumberland County**				
Pauline Martin	138.6 × 31.5 × 12.5	298	1917	Norris Arm, Nfld.
Peaceland	114 × 30 × 10.6	262	1919	Annapolis, N.S.
Pelleen	145.3 × 30.4 × 12.4	389	1919	Port Blandford, Nfld.
Percé	124.5 × 32.9 × 11.7	308	1916	Liverpool, N.S.
Percie Wells	106 × 25.7 × 10.4	119	1919	Hare Bay, Nfld.
Percy B	128.4 × 32.9 × 10.8	281	1913	Port Greville, N.S.
Peter McIntyre	162.3 × 35 × 12.8	487	1920	Saint John, N.B.
Phileen	112.3 × 30.6 × 11.8	265	1917	Dartmouth, N.S.
Phoenix	144.3 × 34.1 × 12.5	396	1884	Parrsboro, N.S.
Pierre Tristan ex **Charles Theriault**				

Name Registered	Dimensions	Net Tonnage	Year Built	Place Built
Pineland *ex* Georgina Roop				
Ponhook	116.3 × 29.5 × 11.4	199	1909	Liverpool, N.S.
Potengy *ex* Gordon				
Preference	126 × 30 × 10.7	243	1893	Canning, N.S.
President Coaker	115.1 × 29.4 × 11.2	260	1919	Port Union, Nfld.
Prosperare	147.3 × 34.3 × 11.9	378	1901	Port Greville, N.S.
Protea *ex* E. Hogan				
Prydwen	138 × 31.3 × 12.8	295	1913	Shelburne, N.S.
Renamed **Ciudad de Tarragone**				
Push *ex* Gordon				
Quaco Queen	158.9 × 35.5 × 12.1	479	1919	St. Martin's, N.B.
Quebec Trader *ex* Germain L				
R. L. Dewis	126 × 32.6 × 11.8	324	1891	Parrsboro, N.S.
Racewell	139.5 × 32.8 × 12	337	1917	Meteghan River, N.S.
Renamed **Johan, Fleur de France**				
Ralph S. Parsons	155.2 × 33.8 × 12.1	394	1917	Cheverie, N.S.
Renamed **Lena Ford**				
Randfontein★	209.8 × 37.8 × 18.2	799	1919	Saint John, N.B.
Renamed **Cobo, Foldin, Melolie**				
Raymonde	127.5 × 30.8 × 12	252	1920	Mahone Bay, N.S.
Rebecca L. MacDonald★	187 × 36 × 16	762	1918	Meteghan, N.S.
Reginald R. Moulton	113.6 × 26 × 11.2	112	1917	Dayspring, N.S.
Reliance	107 × 28.5 × 11.6	191	1906	Shelburne, N.S.
Rescue *ex* Bahama				
Retraction	119 × 26 × 11	148	1920	Conquerall Bank, N.S.
Ria	100.7 × 27.6 × 11.4	154	1920	Marystown, Nfld.
Richard B. Silver	142.2 × 34.6 × 13	400	1918	Meteghan, N.S.
(First of name)				
Richard B. Silver	123.3 × 27.7 × 11.2	224	1919	Mahone Bay, N.S.
Renamed **Abundance**				
Ricketts, V.C.	119.2 × 26 × 11.4	155	1919	Conquerall Bank, N.S.
Rio	127.9 × 27.6 × 11.8	317	1881	Hantsport, N.S.
Riseover II *ex* Limelight				
Rita	115.1 × 28.6 × 10.4	197	1891	Bridgetown, N.S.
Robert Ewing	142.5 × 33.4 × 12	399	1892	Advocate, N.S.
Robert J. Dale	113.2 × 28.6 × 10.4	198	1914	Liverpool, N.S.
Roberta Ray	116.2 × 26.8 × 10.9	164	1917	Grand Bank, Nfld.
Roclincourt *ex* Margaret May Riley				
Ronald	131.1 × 32.2 × 10.9	268	1903	Port Greville, N.S.
Ronald B. Moulton	118.2 × 25.8 × 11.4	138	1918	La Have, N.S.
Ronald C. Longmire	102.5 × 27.1 × 10.1	149	1920	Meteghan, N.S.
Ronald M. Douglas	113 × 26.9 × 9.9	189	1921	Bay D'Espoir, Nfld.
Rosa Ferlita *ex* E. L. Comeau				
Rosalie Belliveau	114 × 29 × 10	197	1909	Belliveau Cove, N.S.
Rose Anne Belliveau	130.5 × 30.8 × 10.5	382	1919	Belliveau Cove, N.S.
Rose M	92.7 × 26.8 × 9.8	148	1919	Norris Arm, Nfld.
Roseway	120 × 28.4 × 12.4	244	1907	Shelburne, N.S.
Renamed **Kay and Em**				

Name Registered	Dimensions	Net Tonnage	Year Built	Place Built
Rosita ex Edith M. Cavell				
Rossignol	119.5 × 30.2 × 11	199	1908	Liverpool, N.S.
Rothesay	128.9 × 31.4 × 11.1	196	1904	Belliveau Cove, N.S.
Renamed Saint Mathieu, Guiseppe				
Rouzic ex Donald and Keith				
Roxana Burton	120 × 27.7 × 10	130	1920	Grosse Cocques, N.S.
Roy Bruce	108.9 × 27.3 × 10.8	150	1920	Shelburne, N.S.
Ruby and Dorothy	120.6 × 26 × 11.2	160	1919	Conquerall Bank, N.S.
Ruby W	129.7 × 33 × 11.4	286	1917	Liverpool, N.S.
Rupert K	147.6 × 33.9 × 12.1	378	1920	Spencer's Id., N.S.
Russell Lake	96.6 × 26.5 × 10.5	132	1919	Fortune, Nfld.
Russell S. Zinck	109.1 × 26.5 × 10.8	121	1918	Dayspring ,N.S.
Ruth Hickman	141 × 33.8 × 12.8	386	1918	Charlottetown, Nfld.
St. Bernard	90.8 × 26.7 × 9.1	124	1901	Parrsboro, N.S.
St. Clair Ritcey	134 × 30.5 × 11.6	332	1919	Conquerall Bank, N.S.
Renamed Le Mousquetaire				
St. Clair Theriault	135.5 × 31.6 × 11.3	284	1919	Belliveau Cove, N.S.
St. John	128 × 28.2 × 11.5	248	1881	Rothesay, N.B.
St. Olaf	130.6 × 33.1 × 11	277	1903	Parrsboro, N.S.
St. Pierraise ex Hiram D. McLean				
Sainte Marie	96 × 26 × 9.6	167	1888	Church Point, N.S.
Saint Mathieu ex Rothesay				
Saint Maurice	119.9 × 31.3 × 11.3	272	1896	Port Greville, N.S.
Sachem ex D. D. McKenzie				
Sakata	149 × 35 × 12.2	395	1905	Port Greville, N.S.
Samuel Courtney	154.5 × 35.5 × 13.6	441	1918	Noel, N.S.
San Jose ex Havelock				
Santa Clara ex McLean Clan				
Santa Maria ex Albani				
Sarah ex Kathleen Crowe				
Sceptre ex A. H. Comeau				
Scotia Belle	139 × 32.7 × 12	345	1918	Meteghan, N.S.
Renamed Capitaine Huet				
Scotia Maiden	149 × 33.4 × 12.8	519	1919	Church Point, N.S.
Seaman, A. O.	152 × 34.5 × 12.7	435	1919	Cape D'Or, N.S.
Renamed Frederick P. Elkin				
Seth Jr.	130 × 30.3 × 11.1	199	1910	Liverpool, N.S.
Severa ex Severn				
Severn	147.9 × 32.4 × 14.9	446	1884	Avondale, N.S.
Severn	143.6 × 29.3 × 15.7	398	1884	Egmont Bay, P.E.I.
Renamed Severa				
Shenandoah	109.5 × 28.3 × 11.2	198	1891	Margaretsville, N.S.
Silver Leaf	130.7 × 31.8 × 12.3	283	1903	Spencer's Id., N.S.
Sirdar	145 × 35.6 × 15.6	498	1899	River John, N.S.
Sir Donald	142.5 × 33 × 12.6	350	1919	Mahone Bay, N.S.
Renamed Golden Rod				
Sir Hibbert	120.2 × 28.4 × 10.2	246	1893	River John, N.S.
Sirocco	129.5 × 32.3 × 10.3	298	1891	St. Martin's, N.B.
Socony	136 × 31.9 × 12	314	1917	Little Brook, N.S.

Name Registered	Dimensions	Net Tonnage	Year Built	Place Built
Solidor *ex* **E. H. Wharton Davies**				
South Head *ex* **Helen Mathers**				
Souvenir	61 × 17 × 6.3	31	1903	Meteghan River, N.S.
Renamed **Gwenmarena**				
Sparkling Glance	107.7 × 28.1 × 10.8	217	1917	Shelburne, N.S.
Speedway	155 × 35.3 × 17.2	544	1917	Little Brook, N.S.
Spencer Lake	106.4 × 26.4 × 10.3	148	1920	Allendale, N.S.
Spring	10ft. draft	150	1870	Shelburne, N.S.
Stella II *ex* **Khaki Lad**	137 × 32.9 × 11.6	356	1917	Port Greville, N.S.
Stewart T. Salter	115.5 × 30.7 × 10.2	226	1919	Parrsboro, N.S.
Stranger *ex* **Hilda M. Stark**				
Strathcona	125.6 × 29.8 × 10.7	251	1902	Mount Denson, N.S.
Success	112 × 27.4 × 11	199	1900	Liverpool, N.S.
Sunner *ex* **Over the Top**				
Sunset Glow	124 × 30 × 11.1	240	1916	Shelburne, N.S.
Susan Cameron★	163.7 × 36.3 × 13.1	558	1919	New Glasgow, N.S.
Suzaky *ex* **Edith M. Green**				
Suzanne	127.3 × 30.6 × 12	264	1920	Bridgewater, N.S.
Renamed **Suzon**				
Suzon *ex* **Suzanne**				
Syanara	125 × 29.2 × 12.2	318	1884	Portland, N.B.
T. K. Bentley	160 × 35.5 × 13.1	466	1920	Advocate, N.S.
Tacoma	106.8 × 28.7 × 10.4	209	1890	Port Greville, N.S.
Tahiti *ex* **Tahitian Maiden**				
Tahitian Maiden	110.4 × 26.4 × 10.7	138	1920	Allendale, N.S.
Renamed **Tahiti**				
Team Sixteen	119.2 × 26 × 11	154	1919	Conquerall Bank, N.S.
The Gay Gordon	103 × 25.2 × 10.5	119	1907	Shelburne, N.S.
Theta	148 × 34.8 × 12.1	420	1901	Cheverie, N.S.
Three Sisters *ex* **Frances Louise**				
Tishy *ex* **Mollie Fearn**				
Tobeatic	102.5 × 25.5 × 10.6	99	1908	Liverpool, N.S.
Tres Amigos *ex* **Havelock**				
Trojan	150.5 × 36 × 15.2	557	1890	Port Greville, N.S.
Truro Queen	150.5 × 34.7 × 12	386	1918	Economy, N.S.
Tyree	126.5 × 30 × 11.9	326	1890	Bridgewater, N.S.
Renamed **G.T.D.**				
Ulrica	137.8 × 32.4 × 10.3	298	1892	Apple River, N.S.
Union Jack	121.4 × 28.8 × 12	242	1918	Trinity Bay, Nfld.
Unique	79 × 29.4 × 8.5	95	1902	River John, N.S.
Unity	117.8 × 31.7 × 11.7	248	1904	Tatamagouche, N.S.
Uruguay★	170 × 36.8 × 17.4	726	1889	Windsor, N.S.
Utilla *ex* **Acadian**				
Valkyrie	136.1 × 32.3 × 10.6	323	1889	Saint John, N.B.
Vamoose	142.4 × 32.8 × 11.3	349	1891	Saint John, N.B.
Venture	111 × 27.3 × 13.5	170	1938	Meteghan, N.S.
Vera Cruz II *ex* **John E. Shatford**				
Vera Cruz VI	92 × 24 × 8.9	110	1901	Shelburne, N.S.
Victory Chimes	129.7 × 30.2 × 11.5	294	1918	Cardigan, P.E.I.

Name Registered	Dimensions	Net Tonnage	Year Built	Place Built
Village Queen	90 × 28.5 × 11	123	1923	Dayspring, N.S.
Vincent A. White	152.4 × 35.4 × 12.8	452	1918	Alma, N.B.
Renamed **Estonia**				
Viola May	114.3 × 26.2 × 10.2	100	1913	Mahone Bay, N.S.
Violet Buffett	108.6 × 27.6 × 11.5	174	1919	Marystown, Nfld.
Virginia	92 × 26.3 × 10.3	133	1902	Lunenburg, N.S.
Viuda de Orive ex **C. D. Pickels**				
Vogue	108.2 × 28.6 × 10.7	196	1917	Shelburne, N.S.
W. C. Kennedy	118.2 × 25 × 11	112	1922	Chester Basin, N.S.
W. Cortada	117.2 × 26.3 × 10.4	108	1912	Lunenburg, N.S.
W. H. Baxter	not known	331	1905	Canning, N.S.
W. H. Eastwood★	153.8 × 27 × 12.4	357	1919	Liverpool, N.S.
W. M. Richard	138.4 × 33.6 × 11.5	323	1910	Port Greville, N.S.
W. N. Reinhardt	124.8 × 30.2 × 11.6	271	1916	La Have, N.S.
W. N. Zwicker	145.2 × 32.1 × 12.5	398	1901	Clyde River, N.S.
W. S. Bentley	141.4 × 34.1 × 11.9	364	1910	Port Greville, N.S.
Renamed **Mildred B**				
W. S. Fielding	115 × 27.9 × 11.1	199	1901	Liverpool, N.S.
W. S. MacDonald	146.5 × 32.7 × 12.3	382	1919	Meteghan, N.S.
Renamed **Louis B. Beauchamp**				
Waegwoltic	108.5 × 29 × 10.6	174	1909	Bridgewater, N.S.
Waegwoltic ex **A. Moulton**				
Walleda	124.5 × 31.4 × 11.2	249	1892	Port Greville, N.S.
Walter Holly	131.6 × 31.2 × 10.6	273	1888	Gardner's Creek, N.B.
Wanderthirst ex **Daniel Getson**				
Wandrian	135.3 × 32.3 × 12.5	311	1883	Parrsboro, N.S.
Wanola	126.3 × 31.9 × 10.5	272	1899	Port Greville, N.S.
Waterside	101 × 28.2 × 8.6	161	1889	Waterside, N.B.
Water Witch	114.3 × 28.9 × 11.4	190	1906	Liverpool, N.S.
Wentworth	not known	328	1889	Port Greville, N.S.
Westway	112.2 × 29.5 × 10.5	234	1918	Weymouth, N.S.
Whitebelle★	172 × 37.4 × 13	572	1920	Parrsboro, N.S.
Whiteway	154 × 35 × 12.4	418	1919	Parrsboro, N.S.
Wilfred M	116.9 × 30 × 9.8	198	1909	Lunenburg, N.S.
Wilfred Marcus	100 × 25.5 × 10	123	1914	Shelburne, N.S.
Willena Gertrude	132.1 × 32.4 × 11.2	271	1908	Parrsboro, N.S.
William A. Naugler	132.6 × 32 × 11.6	295	1918	Bridgewater, N.S.
William Duff	142.8 × 32.1 × 12.6	365	1918	Mahone Bay, N.S.
William McL. Borden	125.5 × 30.3 × 11.4	336	1919	Pugwash, N.S.
William Melbourne	146.4 × 35.5 × 12.7	435	1917	Spencer's Id., N.S.
William S. MacDonald	122.5 × 28 × 11.2	252	1920	Dayspring, N.S.
Windermere	118 × 30 × 12.5	299	1892	Port Medway, N.S.
Winnifred	102.3 × 25.5 × 10	99	1905	Mahone Bay, N.S.
Winthewar	117.3 × 25.7 × 11.1	149	1917	Liverpool, N.S.
Zebra	92.4 × 25.9 × 9.4	142	1859	La Have, N.S.
Zeta	132.2 × 32 × 12	335	1902	Cheverie, N.S.
Zetta ex **James J. Joy**				

BALLADS

Corbitt's Barquentine

Come all you brave Annapolis boys,
And I'll tell you what I've seen,
On a voyage to Demerara
In a fancy barquentine.
The thirtieth day of August in 1883
The Eva Johnson took our lines
And towed us out to sea.

The two mates picked their watches
And unto us did say,
"If you do not know your duty, boys,
She's the hottest out of the Bay".
"O Lord, O Lord, what have I done?"
So bitterly did I scream,
"That I should be shanghaied on board
Of Corbitt's Barquentine".

The rising sun next morning
Shone on six seamen bold,
And one big dog named "Rover",
Made seven hands all told.
The dog was the chum of the Second Mate
And when the work was done,
Instead of going forward,
He would lie aft in the sun.

I think they were connected,
If I may rightly guess,
For neither one spoke English,
And they both said "Yaw" for "Yes".
The wind is to the westward now,
She heads across the "Stream",
The angry waves are rolling over
Corbitt's Barquentine.

Our Captain on the quarter,
While thirteen days pass by,
A sail ahead and to windward,
One morning did espy.
"Now mind your helm carefully,
Don't let her swing about
And if the wind holds steady,
We soon shall make her out."

It proved to be the Myrtle,
With three long days of start
And with a fair and steady breeze
That drove her like a dart.
But now we exchange signals,
She's to leeward of our beam,
She dips her colours gracefully
To Corbitt's Barquentine.

Oh, now we're shoving lumber
And the sweat like rain does pour,
Awaiting for eight bells to strike
So we can get ashore.
We then go up to Trargard's Bay,
Upon some drunken spree,
Or else we're off a-dancing
At some nigger "Dignatee".

But if our friends could see us now,
You'd bet that we'd be shy,
For we have sweethearts by the score
Though we court them on the sly.
Down come a "yeller gal"
Dressed up like a queen,
Inquiring for the steward
Of Corbitt's Barquentine.

219

Now we're loading sugar
And for Boston we are bound,
We'll take our sand and canvas,
And we'll wash and scrub her down.
And after that is finished
To painting we will go,
We are in hopes when this is done
We'll get our watch below.

Old Neptune he has favoured us,
With a fair and lovely breeze,
And like a thing endowed with life,
She bounds across the seas.
Old "Scotty" caught a dolphin,
Turned yellow, red and green,
The blood lies spattered on the deck
Of Corbitt's Barquentine.

Now under a goose-winged tops'l,
With a double reefed mains'l,
With head towards the Nor'ad, boys,
She rides a furious gale.
If "Honest Tom" was with us now,
To hear those wild winds blow,
He'd wish to God that he was out
Of Corbitt's Gundalow.

Our course being west–north–west, my boys,
If I remember right,
With everything all sheeted home,
She heads for Boston Light.
The sun upon the State House dome
So brightly does it gleam,
It glitters forth a welcome
To Corbitt's Barquentine.

Now we sight Nova Scotia's shores,
With outstretched arms exclaim,
Like William Tell, "ye crags and peaks,
I'm with you once again".
Then up along that Granville Shore,
Majestically we sail,
We pass Goat Island on our lee
All through the rain and hail.

Aad now we lie at anchor,
Abreast this gay old town,
We'll run aloft St. George's Cross
And reef the Tory crown.
The people are remarking, here
It is their only theme,
"There lies the George E. Corbitt
She's a handsome barquentine".

The Loss of the 'John Harvey'
or
The Heroism of the Belleoram Boys

Ye landsmen who live on the shore,
How can you understand,
The perils of the ocean,
When you are on the land.
There's many a brave young sailor lad,
For adventure's sake do roam,
Gives up the struggle for his life
Far from his native home.

The wind it blew a hurricane,
The worst one of the year,
The John Harvey sailed from Gloucester,
Bound for Saint Pierre.
With a load of general cargo,
As loud the wind did roar,
When on the tenth of January
The vessel went ashore.

The skipper gave orders to his men,
The vessel to dismast her,
The boats were frozen to the deck,
And the seas swept fore-and-aft her.
Said Captain Kearly to his men,
"My boys, it is no use,
I fear that we are doomed to die
On the shores of Gabarus".

Then young John Keeping, a rope he took,
And tied it round his waist,
Said he would swim for the nearest land,
And the icy foam he faced.
Oh, bitterly cold was that winter's night,
The sea rolled mountains high,
All tossed and battered by the wave
Was that bold Belleoram boy.

The wind it blew a hurricane,
The night was bitter cold,
'Twould chill the heart of a sailor lad,
A hero young and bold.
When tossed and battered by the sea,
He at last the shore did reach,
And with his badly frozen hands
Made fast a line to the beach.

The crew of the Harvey got ashore,
There were six of them all told,
They owe their lives to God above,
And the Keeping boy so bold.
But Keeping and the brave young Foote,
By exhaustion overcome,
Died on the shores of Gabarus
Far from their native home.

The survivors walked to some fishing shacks,
That stood along the shore,
Much hampered by their heavy boots,
And the oilskins that they wore.
They had no match to light a fire,
How awful was their plight,
As they struggled for existence
On that cold winter's night.

But help soon came from Gabarus,
And to them the tale was told,
Of the loss of the John Harvey,
And the Keeping boy so bold.
God's blessing rest upon them,
They did all that they could do,
To comfort and aid the survivors
Of the Harvey's shipwrecked crew.

Captain Kearly and his hardy boys,
A sad disheartened band,
With the bodies of their comrades,
Went back to Newfoundland.
As they followed the caskets to the train,
The tears fell from their eyes,
As they thought of the noble actions
Of those brave Belleoram boys.

Good people of Belleoram,
With you we sympathize,
Don't fret or mourn for those brave boys,
For Heaven was their prize.
And all ye brave young sailor lads,
Think of those noble youths,
Who died far away from their native land
On the shores of Gabarus.

From the *Newfoundlander*, November, 1952
Courtesy of Michael Harrington.

INDEX